岸本斉史

movies, so I go see them pretty And since I watch movies I decided to spend what little I had to purchase a DVD player. ho...now I can enjoy movies with incredibly high image quality and Dolby Digital sound! Or so I thought, except that the movies I wanted to watch hardly ever came out on DVD, so I couldn't watch them anyway.

Recently, however, the popularity of DVDs has finally risen, and more and more DVDs are coming out!! Yes! Except...now I'm so busy drawing manga that I don't have time to watch them, even though I want to! Waah!

—*Masashi Kishimoto, 2000*

Author/artist Masashi Kishimoto was born in 1974 in rural Okayama Prefecture, Japan. After spending time in art college, he won the Hop Step Award for new manga artists with his manga **Karakuri** ("Mechanism"). Kishimoto decided to base his next story on traditional Japanese culture. His first version of **Naruto**, drawn in 1997, was a one-shot story about fox spirits; his final version, which debuted in **Weekly Shonen Jump** in 1999, quickly became the most popular ninja manga in Japan.

NARUTO VOL. 5
The SHONEN JUMP Graphic Novel Edition

This graphic novel contains material that was originally published
in English in **SHONEN JUMP** #19-23.

STORY AND ART BY MASASHI KISHIMOTO

English Adaptation/Jo Duffy
Translation/Mari Morimoto
Touch-up Art & Lettering/Heidi Szykowny
Design/Sean Lee
Editors/Shaenon K. Garrity and Frances E. Wall

Managing Editor/Elizabeth Kawasaki
Director of Production/Noboru Watanabe
Vice President of Publishing/Alvin Lu
Vice President & Editor-in-Chief/Yumi Hoashi
Sr. Director of Acquisitions/Rika Inouye
Vice President of Sales & Marketing/Liza Coppola
Publisher/Hyoe Narita

Printed in the U.S.A.

Published by VIZ Media, LLC
P.O. Box 77010
San Francisco, CA 94107

SHONEN JUMP Graphic Novel Edition
10 9 8 7 6 5 4 3
First printing, November 2004
Second printing, April 2005
Third printing, July 2005

viz
media

www.viz.com

PARENTAL ADVISORY
RATED **T** TEEN
NARUTO is rated T for Teen and is recom-
mended for ages 13 and up. This volume
contains realistic & fantasy violence.

THE WORLD'S
MOST POPULAR MANGA
SHONEN JUMP
GRAPHIC NOVEL
www.shonenjump.com

SHONEN JUMP GRAPHIC NOVEL

NARUTO™

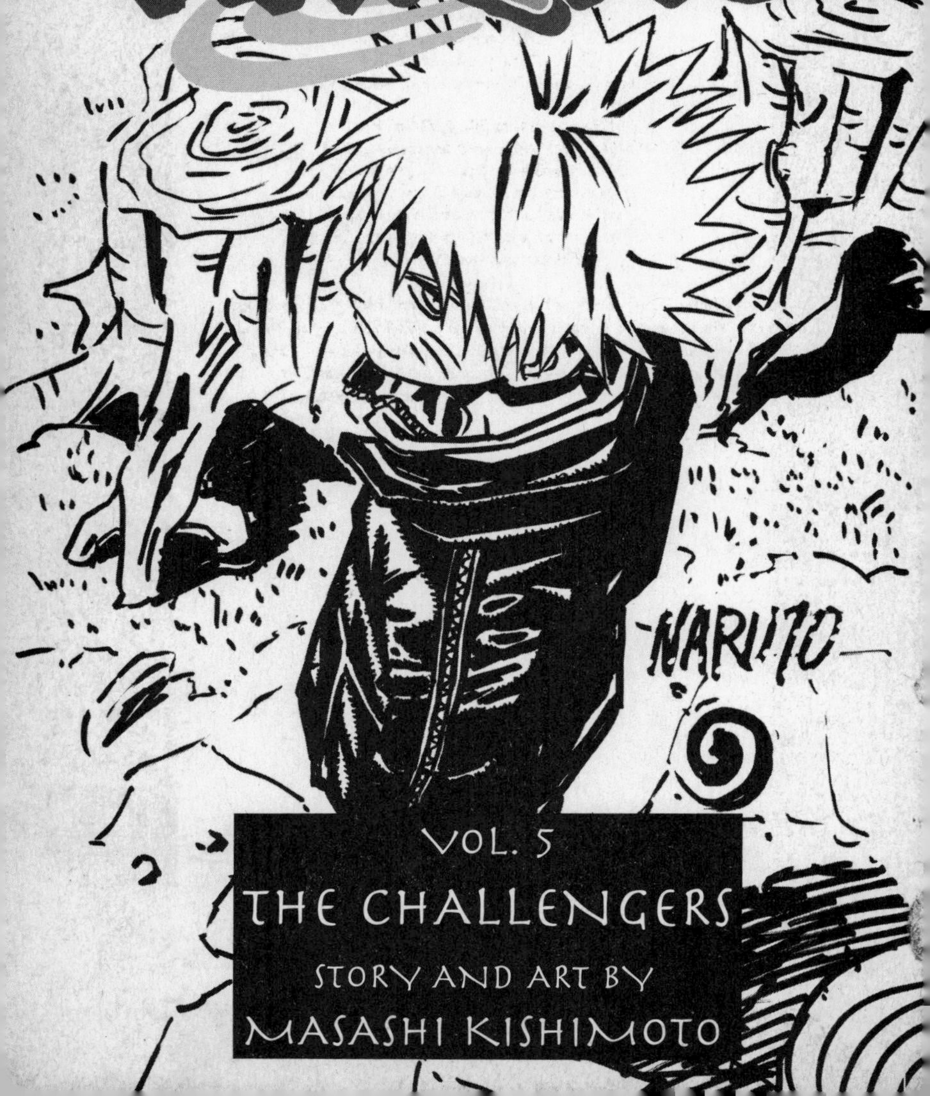
NARUTO

VOL. 5

THE CHALLENGERS

STORY AND ART BY
MASASHI KISHIMOTO

SAKURA サクラ

Smart and studious, Sakura is the brightest of Naruto's classmates, but she's constantly distracted by her crush on Sasuke. Her goal: to win Sasuke's heart!

NARUTO ナルト

When Naruto was born, a destructive fox spirit was imprisoned inside his body. Spurned by the older villagers, he's grown into an attention-seeking troublemaker. His goal: to become the village's next *Hokage*.

SASUKE サスケ

The top student in Naruto's class, Sasuke comes from the prestigious Uchiha clan. His goal: to get revenge on a mysterious person who wronged him in the past.

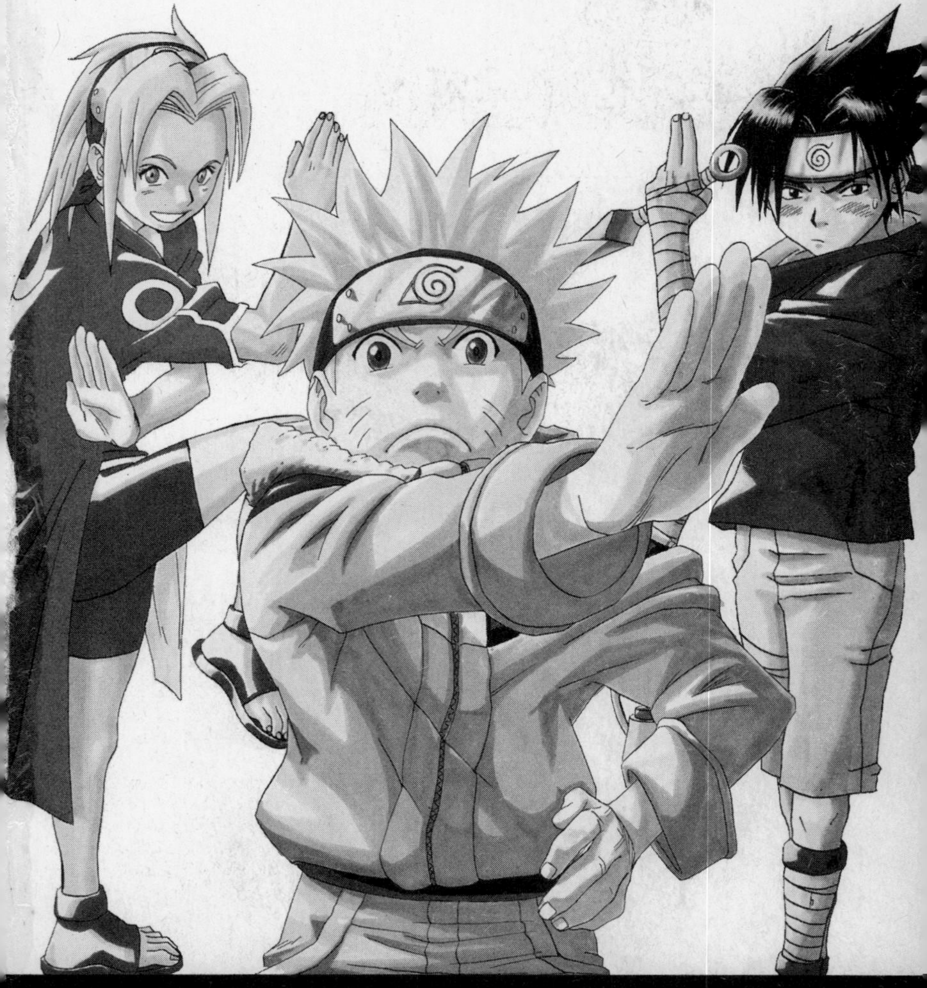

KAKASHI カカシ

The elite ninja assigned to train Naruto, Sasuke and Sakura. His *Sharingan* ("Mirror-Wheel Eye") allows him to reflect and mimic enemy *ninjutsu*.

ROCK LEE ロック・リー

One of the many student ninja from foreign villages who have traveled to Konohagakure for the Junior Ninja Selection Exams. What does this creepy kid have in mind when he challenges Sasuke to a duel? Sasuke is about to find out!

THE STORY SO FAR...

Twelve years ago, a destructive nine-tailed fox spirit attacked the ninja village of Konohagakure. The *Hokage*, or village champion, defeated the fox by sealing its soul into the body of a baby boy. Now that boy, Uzumaki Naruto, has grown up to become a ninja-in-training, learning the art of *ninjutsu* with his classmates Sakura and Sasuke.

Naruto, Sasuke and Sakura have been nominated by their instructor Kakashi to take the Junior Ninja Selection Exams, which they must pass to advance to the next level of ninja training. The village is crawling with student ninja from villages near and far, who are all determined to ace the exams. On their way to turn in the applications, they observe their fellow students' advanced skill and training, and Naruto and his classmates begin to suspect that they're in way over their heads....

NARUTO

VOL. 5
THE CHALLENGERS

CONTENTS

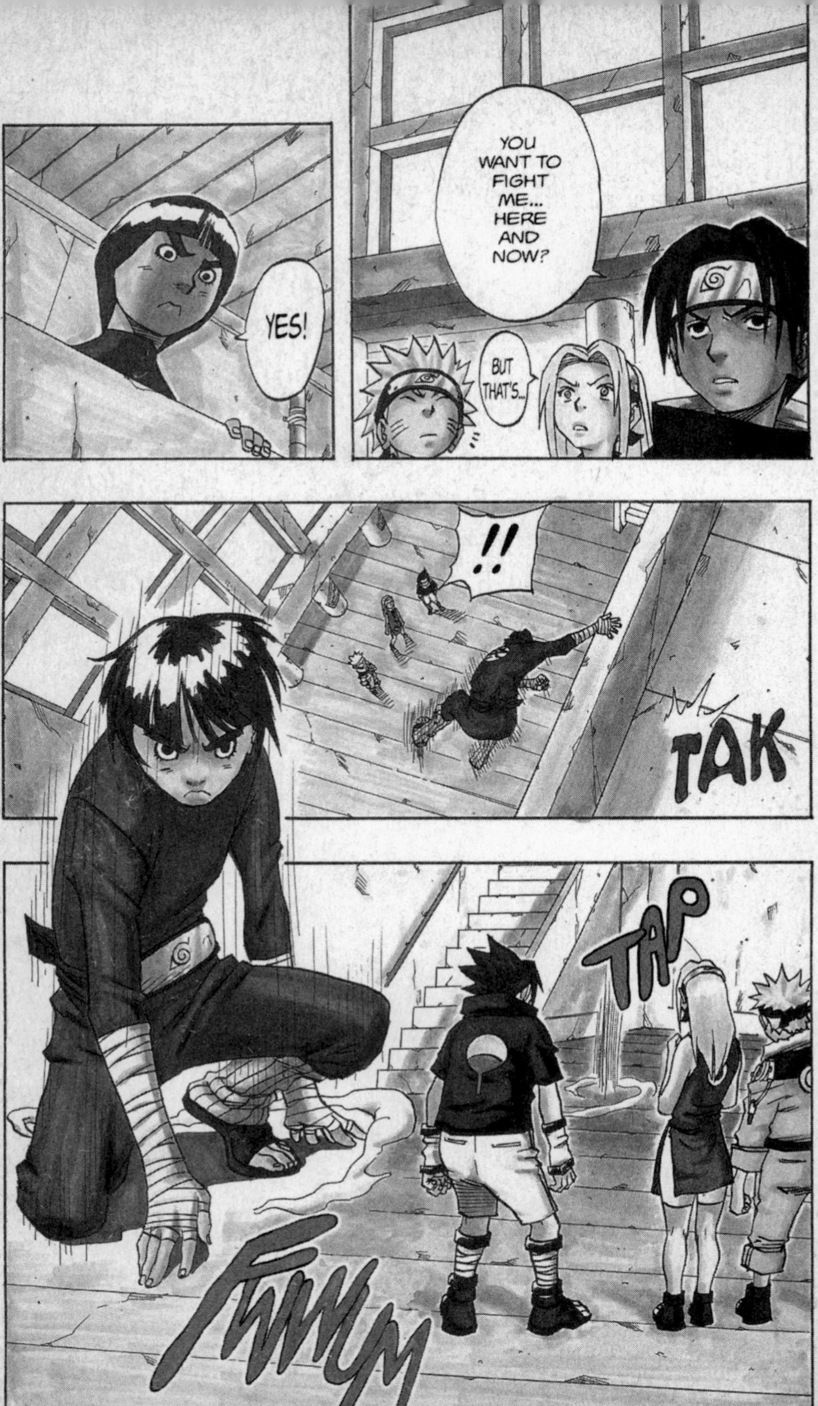
YOU WANT TO FIGHT ME... HERE AND NOW?
BUT THAT'S...
YES!
!!
TAK
TAP

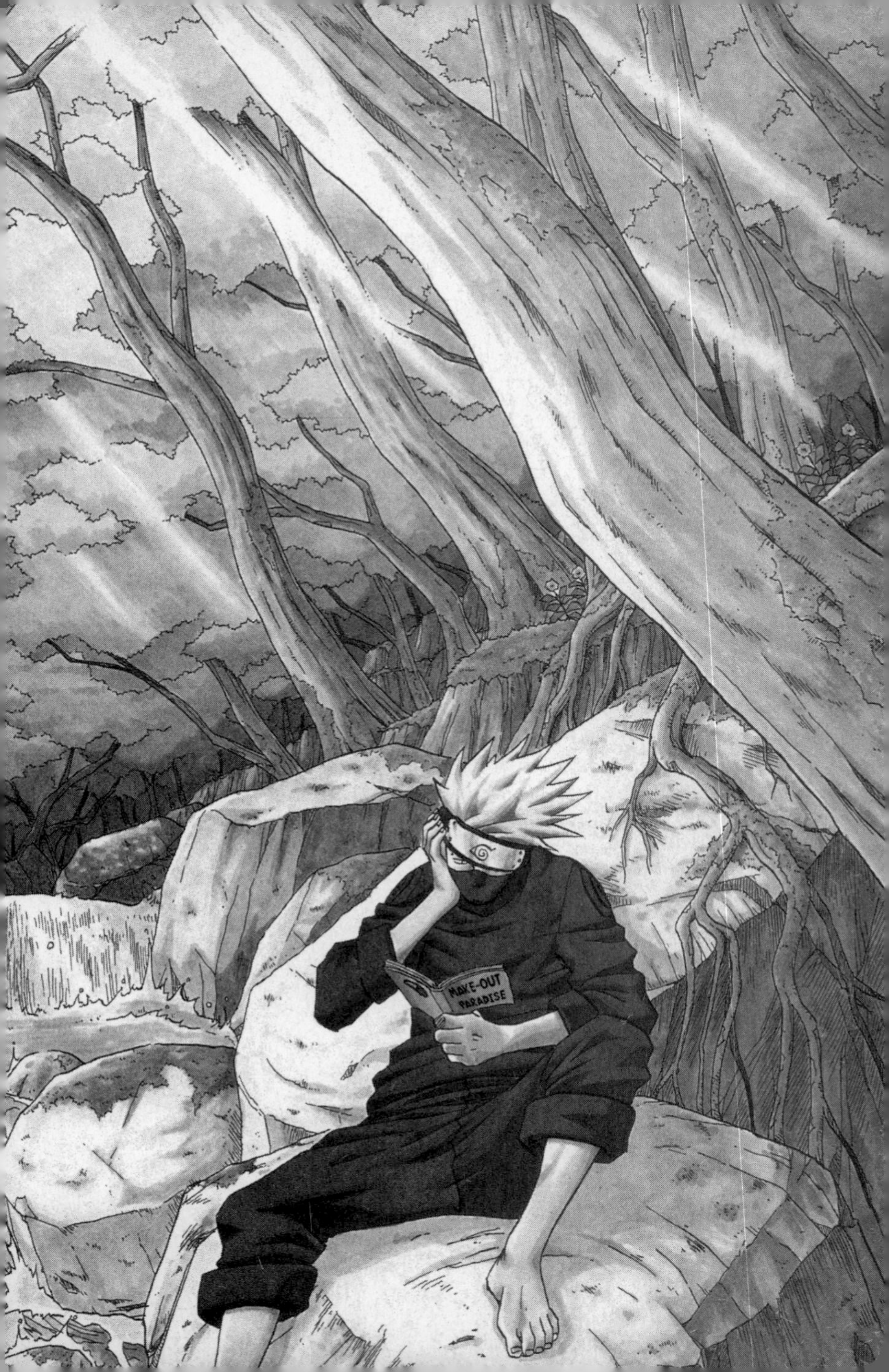
MAKE-OUT
PARADISE

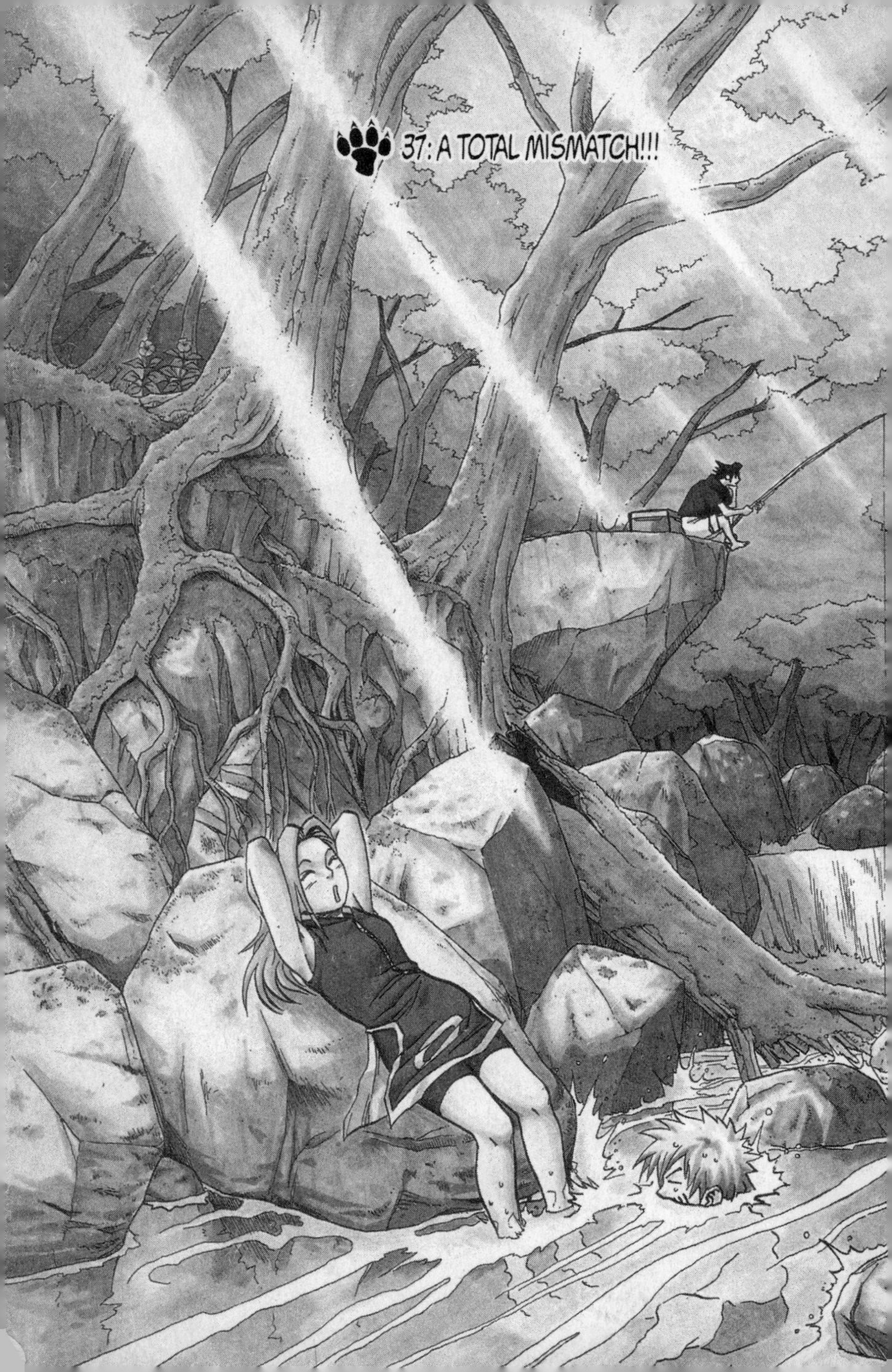
37: A TOTAL MISMATCH!!!

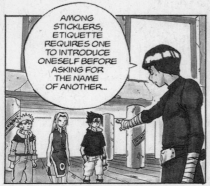

MY NAME IS ROCK LEE.
AMONG STICKLERS, ETIQUETTE REQUIRES ONE TO INTRODUCE ONESELF BEFORE ASKING FOR THE NAME OF ANOTHER...
...UCHIHA SASUKE.
HUH... SO YOU KNEW WHO I WAS ALL ALONG.
SHF
I'M CALLING YOU OUT!!
I WANT TO TEST THE EFFECTIVE-NESS OF MY TECHNIQUES...
...AGAINST THE LAST SURVIVING MEMBER OF YOUR LEGENDARY CLAN.
BESIDES...
THROB

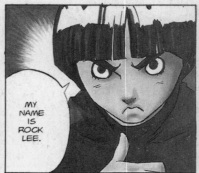

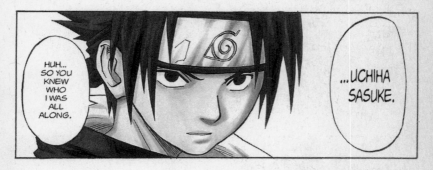

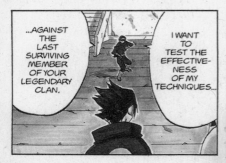

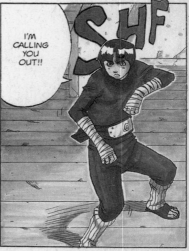

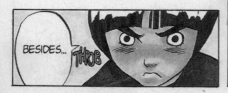

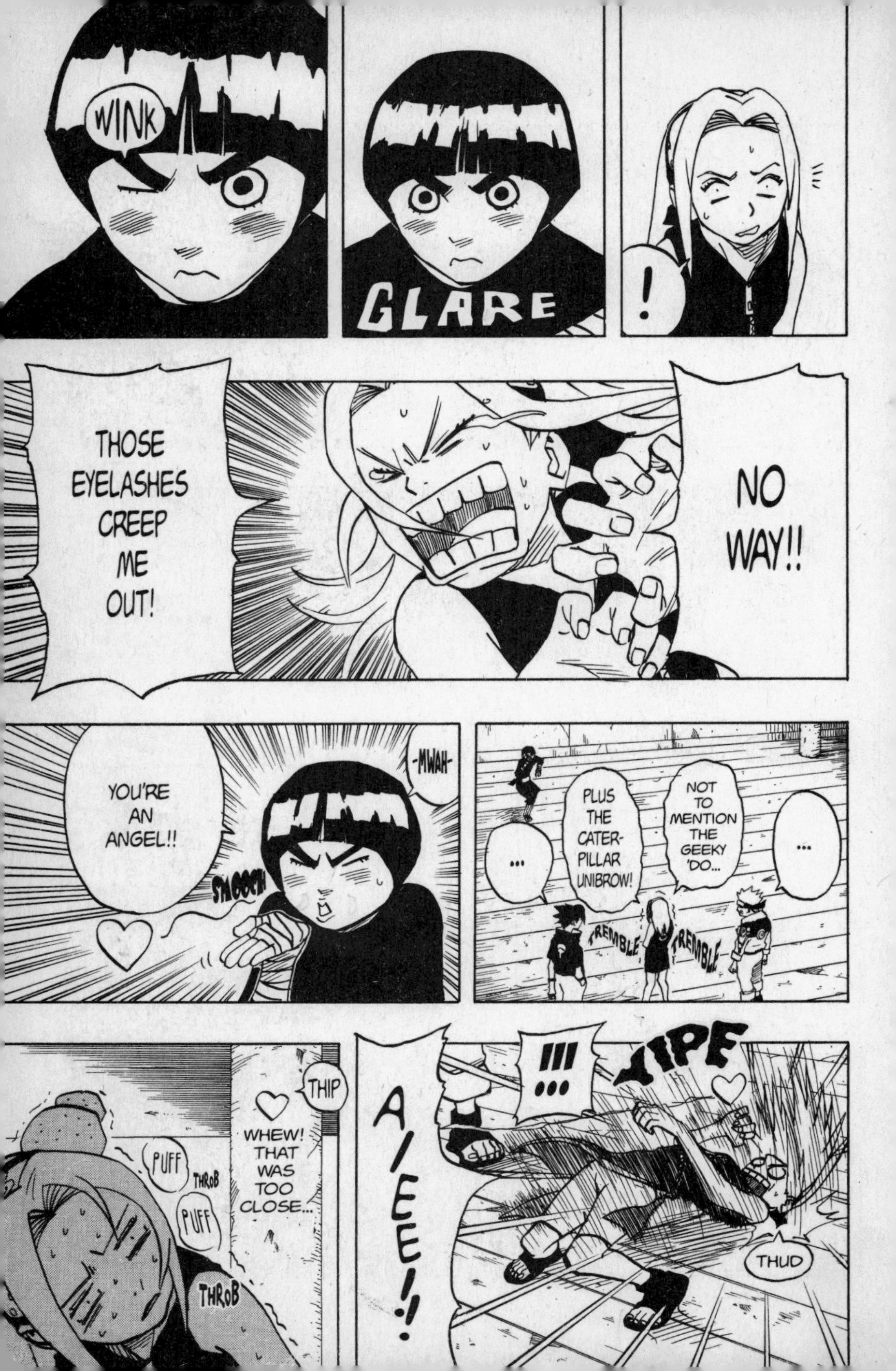
!
GLARE
WINK
NO WAY!!
THOSE EYELASHES CREEP ME OUT!
...
NOT TO MENTION THE GEEKY 'DO...
PLUS THE CATER-PILLAR UNIBROW!
...
TREMBLE
TREMBLE
-MWAH-
YOU'RE AN ANGEL!!
SMOOCH
YIPE
!!! ...
AIEE!!
THUD
THIP
WHEW! THAT WAS TOO CLOSE...
PUFF
THROB
PUFF
THROB

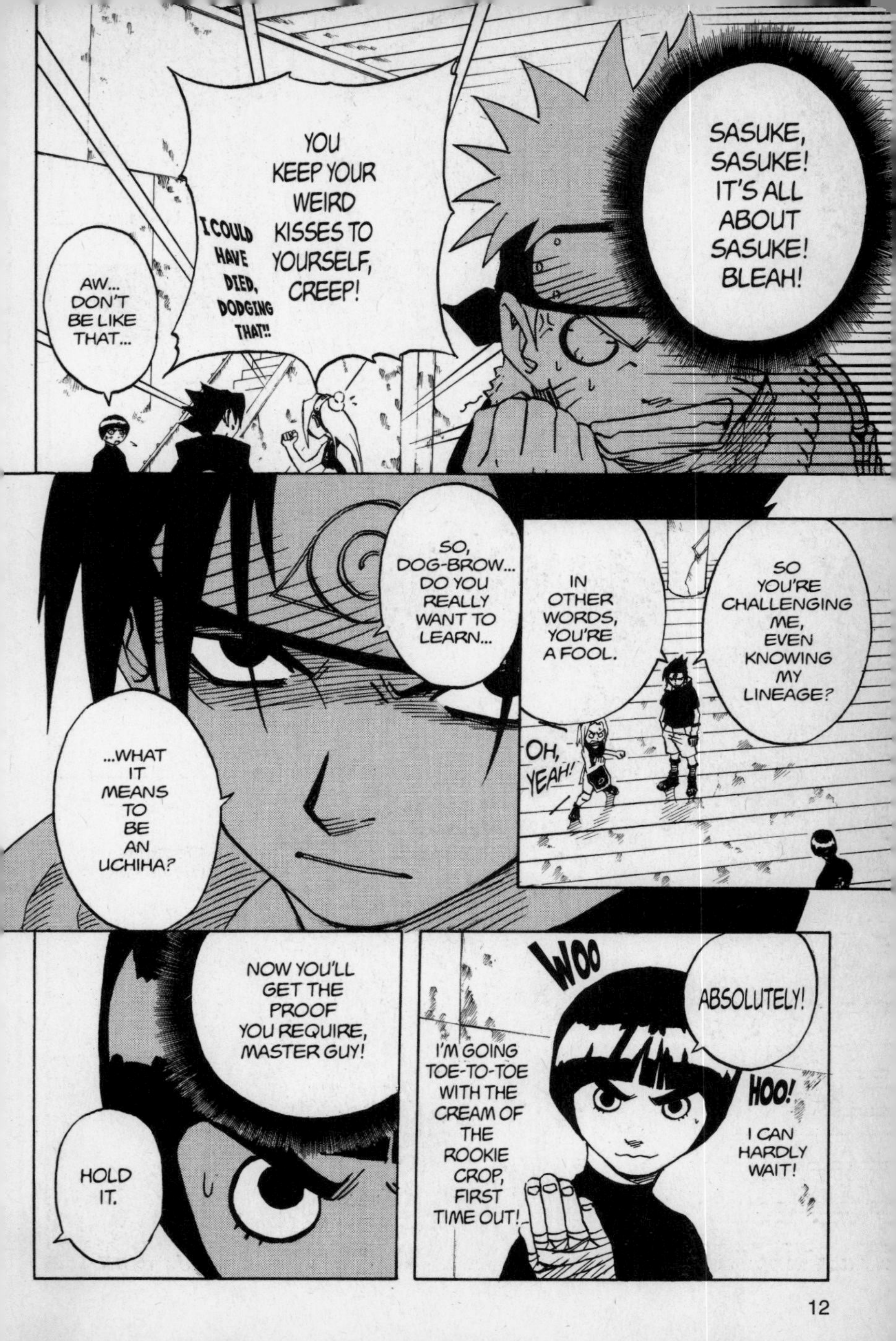
SASUKE, SASUKE! IT'S ALL ABOUT SASUKE! BLEAH!
YOU KEEP YOUR WEIRD KISSES TO YOURSELF, CREEP!
I COULD HAVE DIED, DODGING THAT!!
AW... DON'T BE LIKE THAT...
SO YOU'RE CHALLENGING ME, EVEN KNOWING MY LINEAGE?
IN OTHER WORDS, YOU'RE A FOOL.
OH, YEAH!
SO, DOG-BROW... DO YOU REALLY WANT TO LEARN...
...WHAT IT MEANS TO BE AN UCHIHA?
WOO
ABSOLUTELY!
HOO!
I CAN HARDLY WAIT!
I'M GOING TOE-TO-TOE WITH THE CREAM OF THE ROOKIE CROP, FIRST TIME OUT!
NOW YOU'LL GET THE PROOF YOU REQUIRE, MASTER GUY!
HOLD IT.

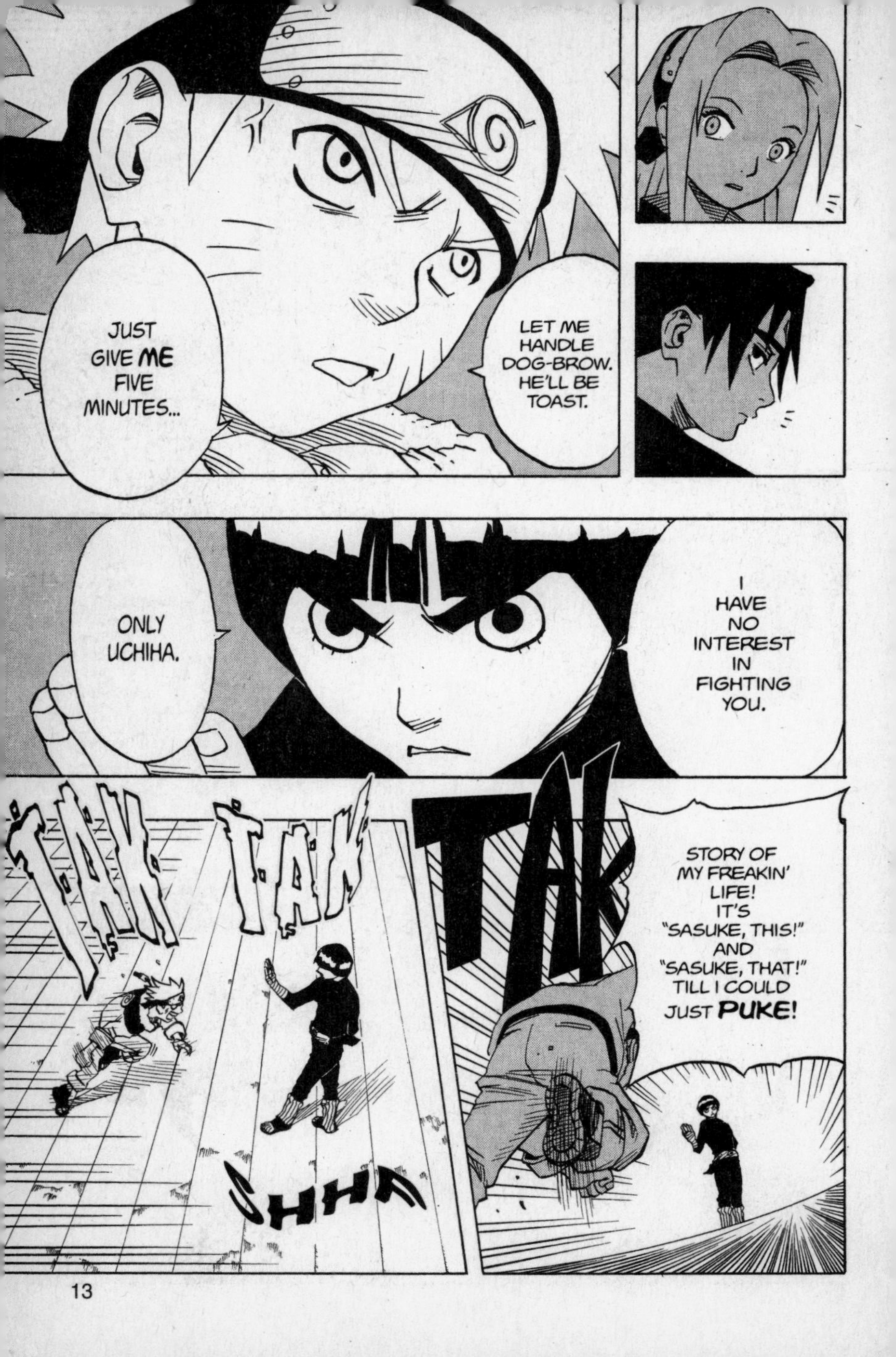

LET ME HANDLE DOG-BROW. HE'LL BE TOAST.
JUST GIVE ME FIVE MINUTES...
I HAVE NO INTEREST IN FIGHTING YOU.
ONLY UCHIHA.
STORY OF MY FREAKIN' LIFE! IT'S "SASUKE, THIS!" AND "SASUKE, THAT!" TILL I COULD JUST PUKE!
TAK
TAK
TAK
SHHF

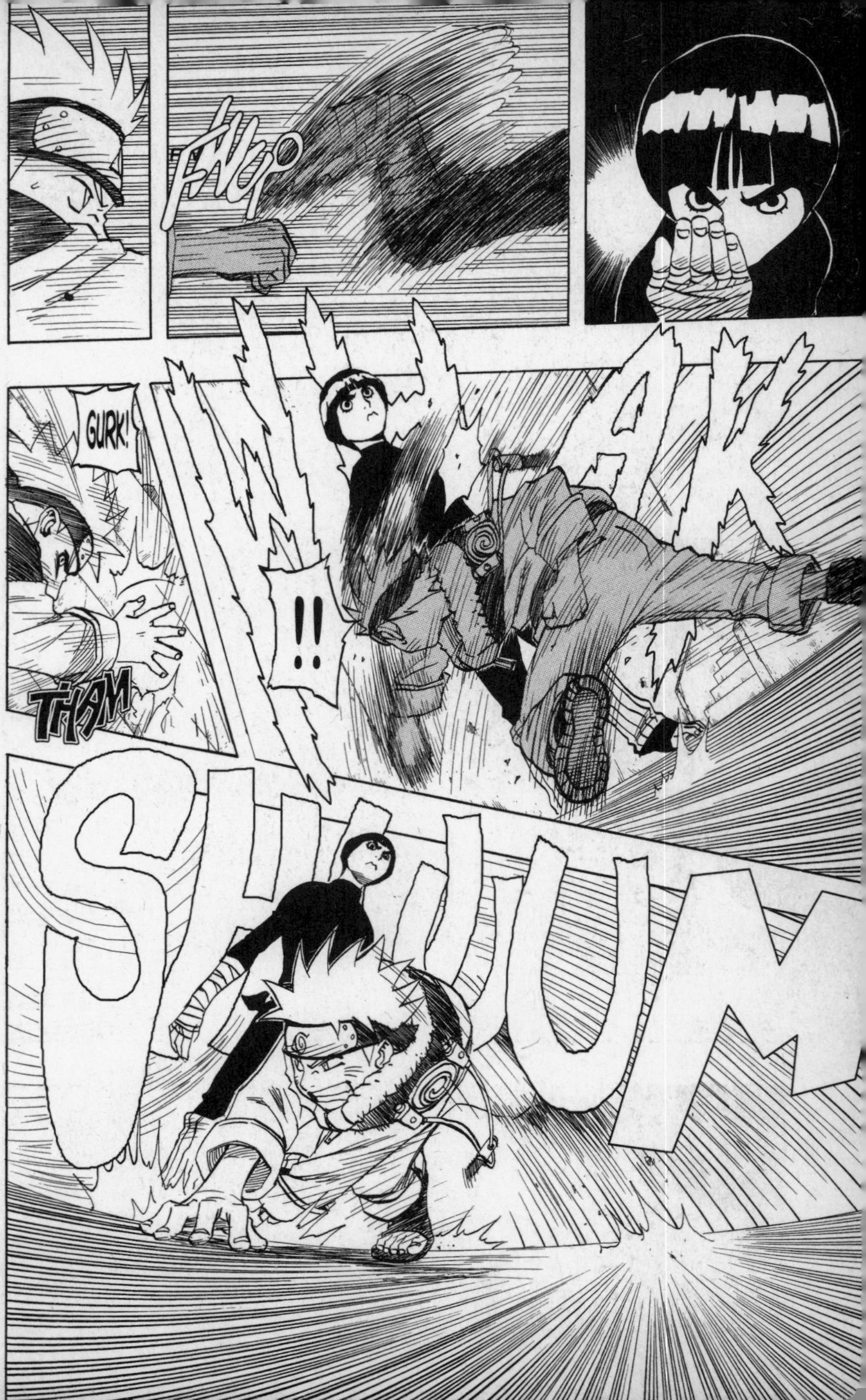
FWUP
WHAK
!!
GURK!
THAM
SHUUN

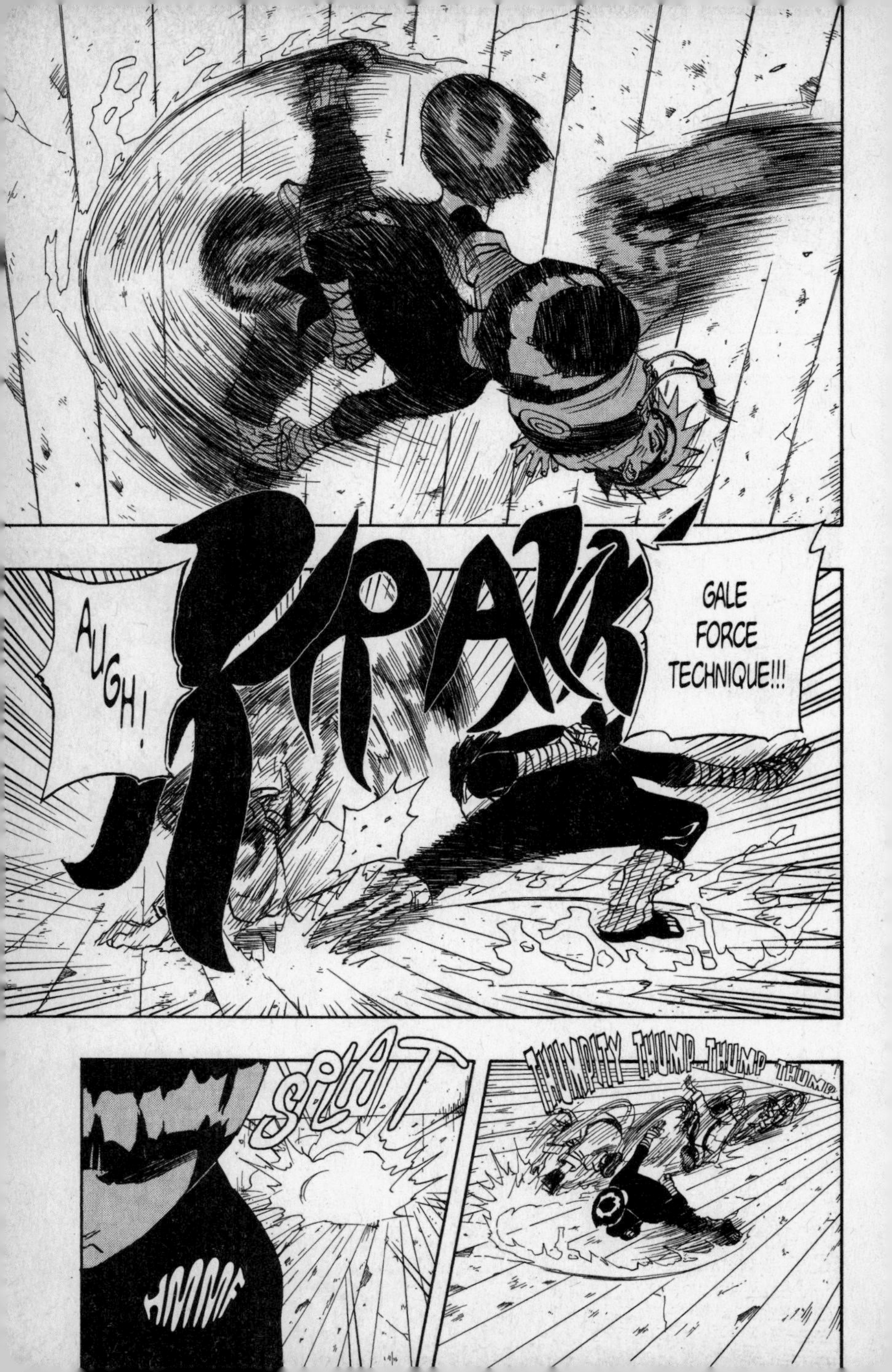
GALE FORCE TECHNIQUE!!!
AUGH!
THUMPITY THUMP THUMP THUMP
SPLAT

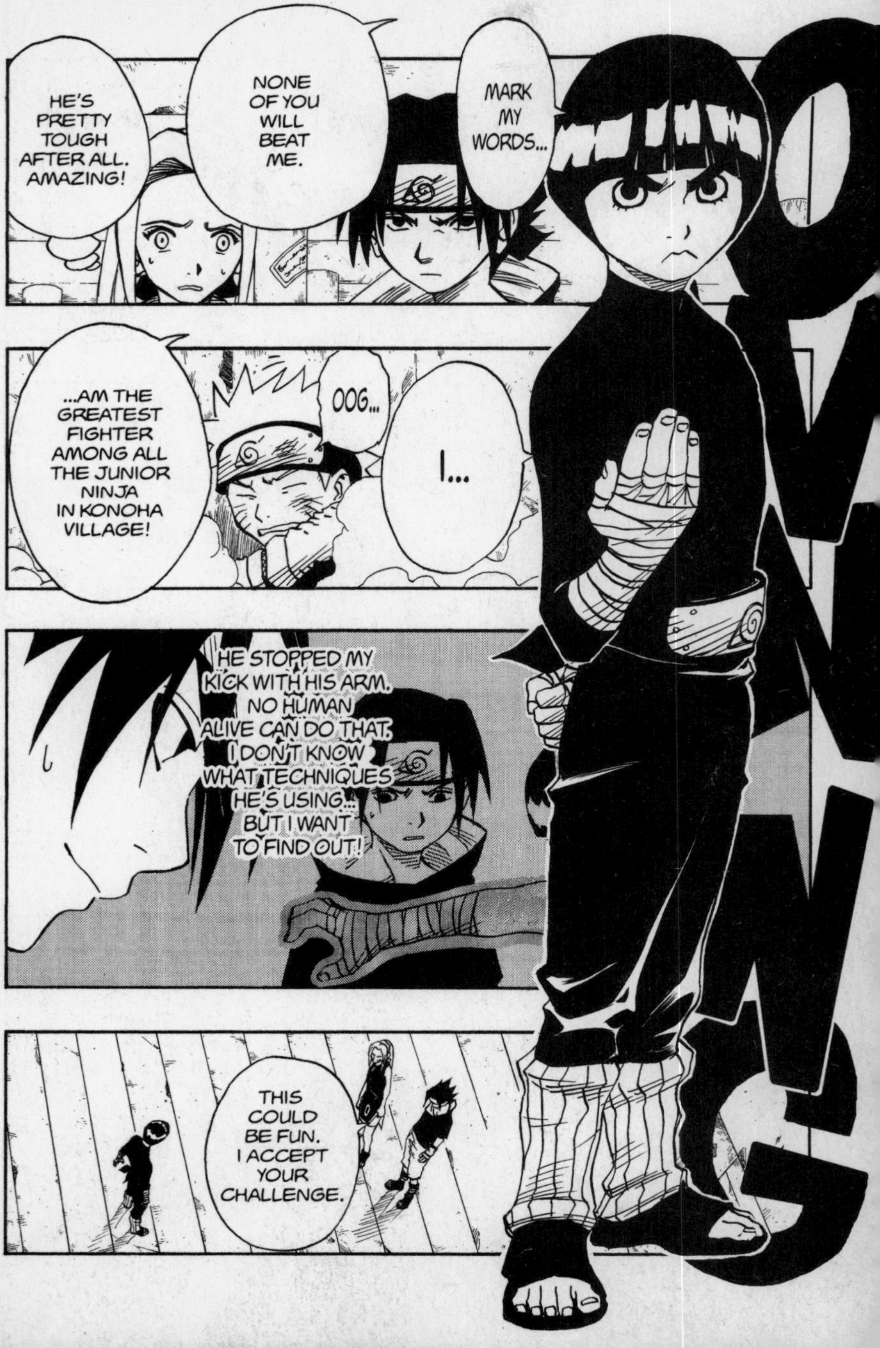

MARK MY WORDS...
NONE OF YOU WILL BEAT ME.
HE'S PRETTY TOUGH AFTER ALL. AMAZING!
I...
OOG...
...AM THE GREATEST FIGHTER AMONG ALL THE JUNIOR NINJA IN KONOHA VILLAGE!
HE STOPPED MY KICK WITH HIS ARM. NO HUMAN ALIVE CAN DO THAT. I DON'T KNOW WHAT TECHNIQUES HE'S USING... BUT I WANT TO FIND OUT!
THIS COULD BE FUN. I ACCEPT YOUR CHALLENGE.

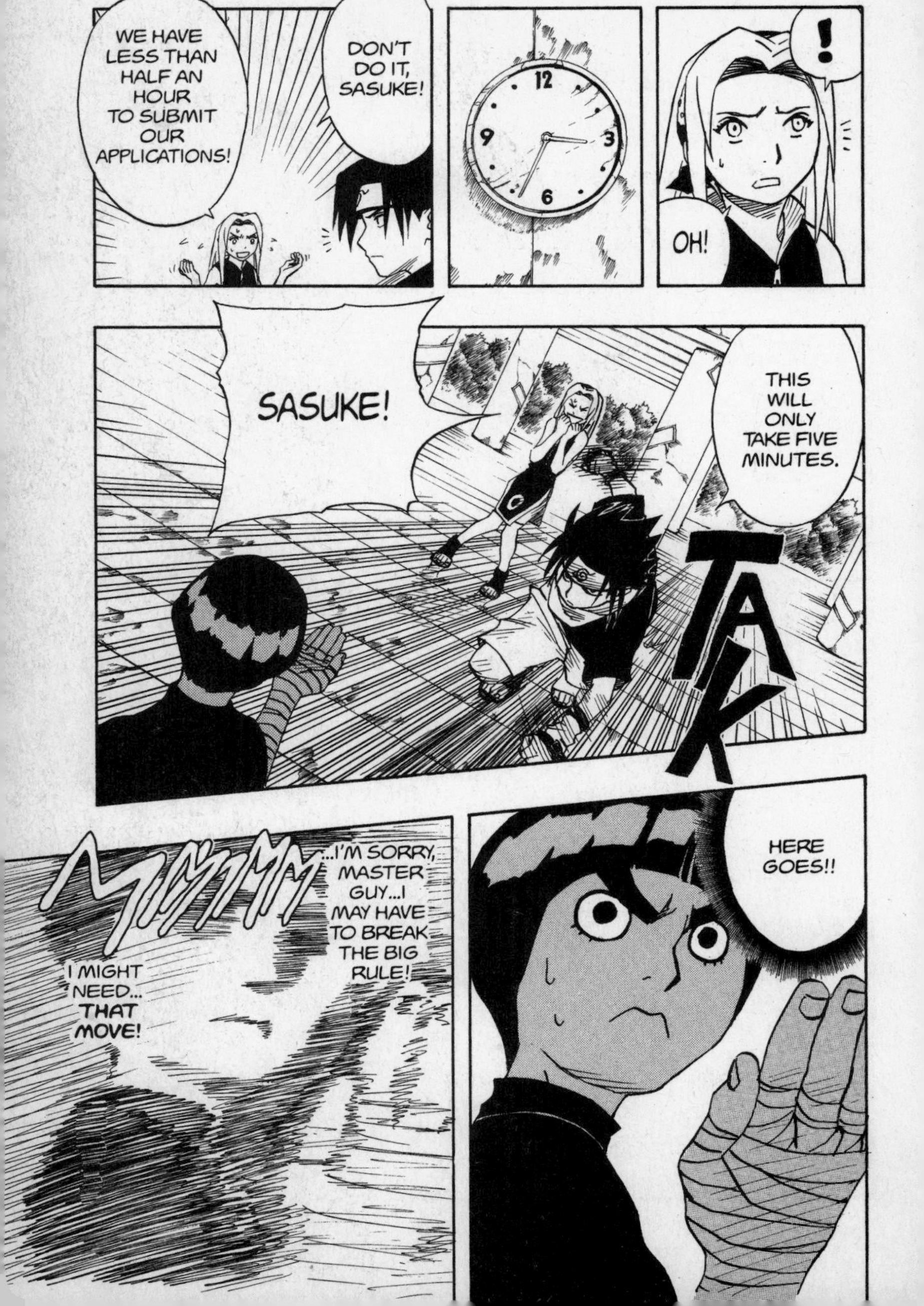
!
OH!
DON'T DO IT, SASUKE!
WE HAVE LESS THAN HALF AN HOUR TO SUBMIT OUR APPLICATIONS!
THIS WILL ONLY TAKE FIVE MINUTES.
TAK
SASUKE!
HERE GOES!!
...I'M SORRY, MASTER GUY...I MAY HAVE TO BREAK THE BIG RULE!
I MIGHT NEED... THAT MOVE!

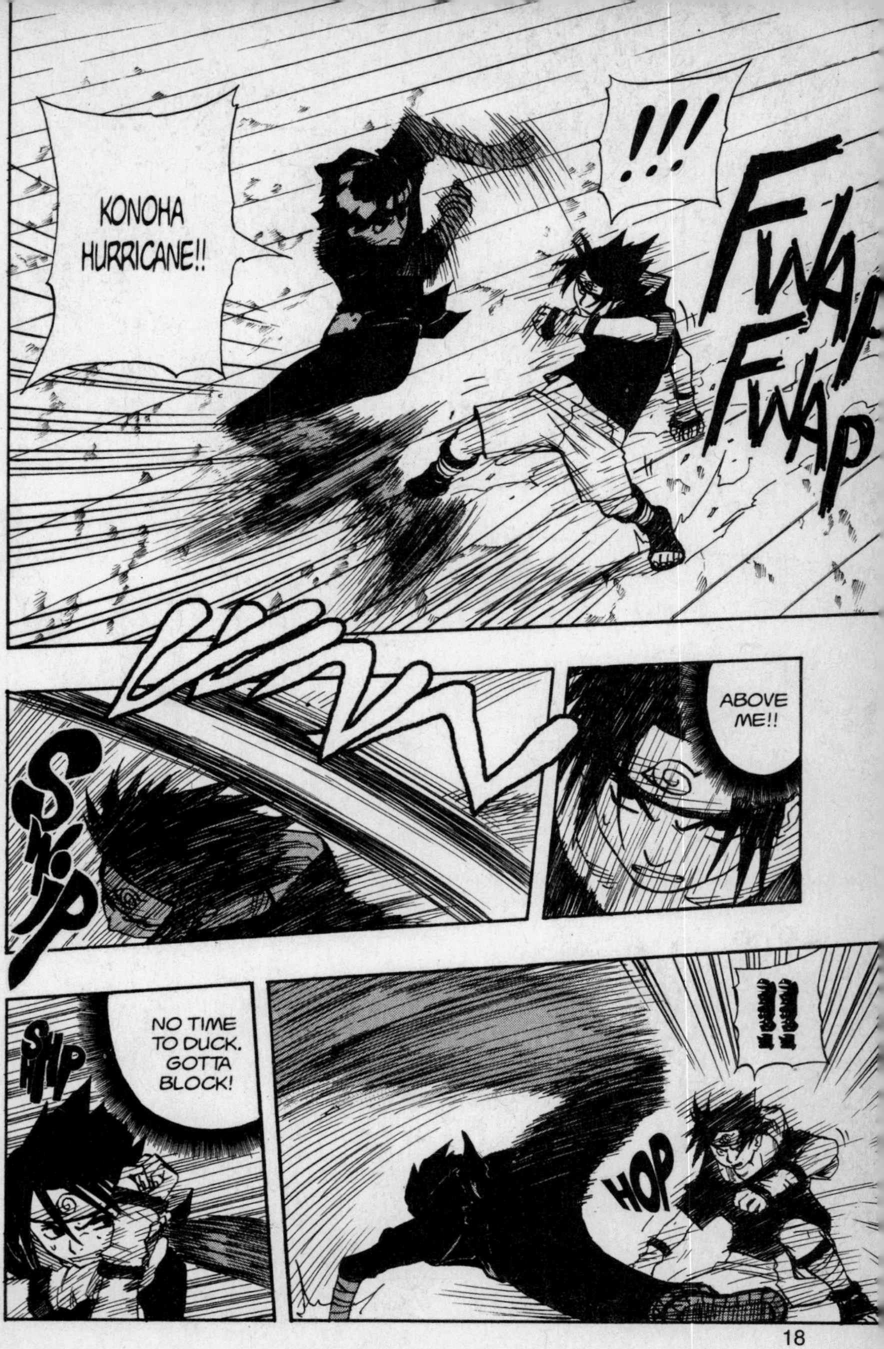
!!!
FWAP
FWAP
KONOHA HURRICANE!!
ABOVE ME!!
HOP
NO TIME TO DUCK. GOTTA BLOCK!

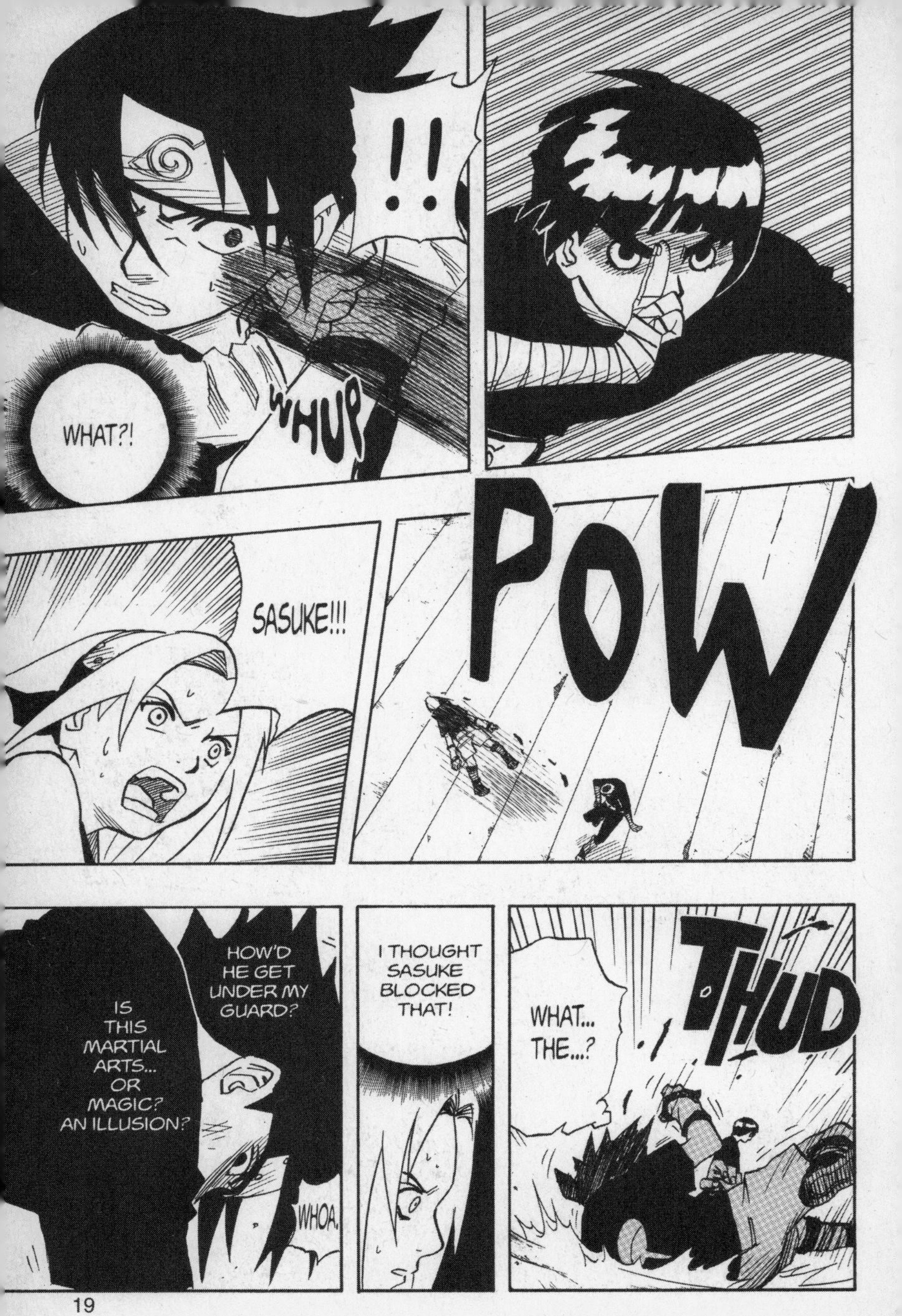
!!
WHUP
WHAT?!
POW
SASUKE!!!
THUD
WHAT... THE...?
I THOUGHT SASUKE BLOCKED THAT!
HOW'D HE GET UNDER MY GUARD?
IS THIS MARTIAL ARTS... OR MAGIC? AN ILLUSION?
WHOA.

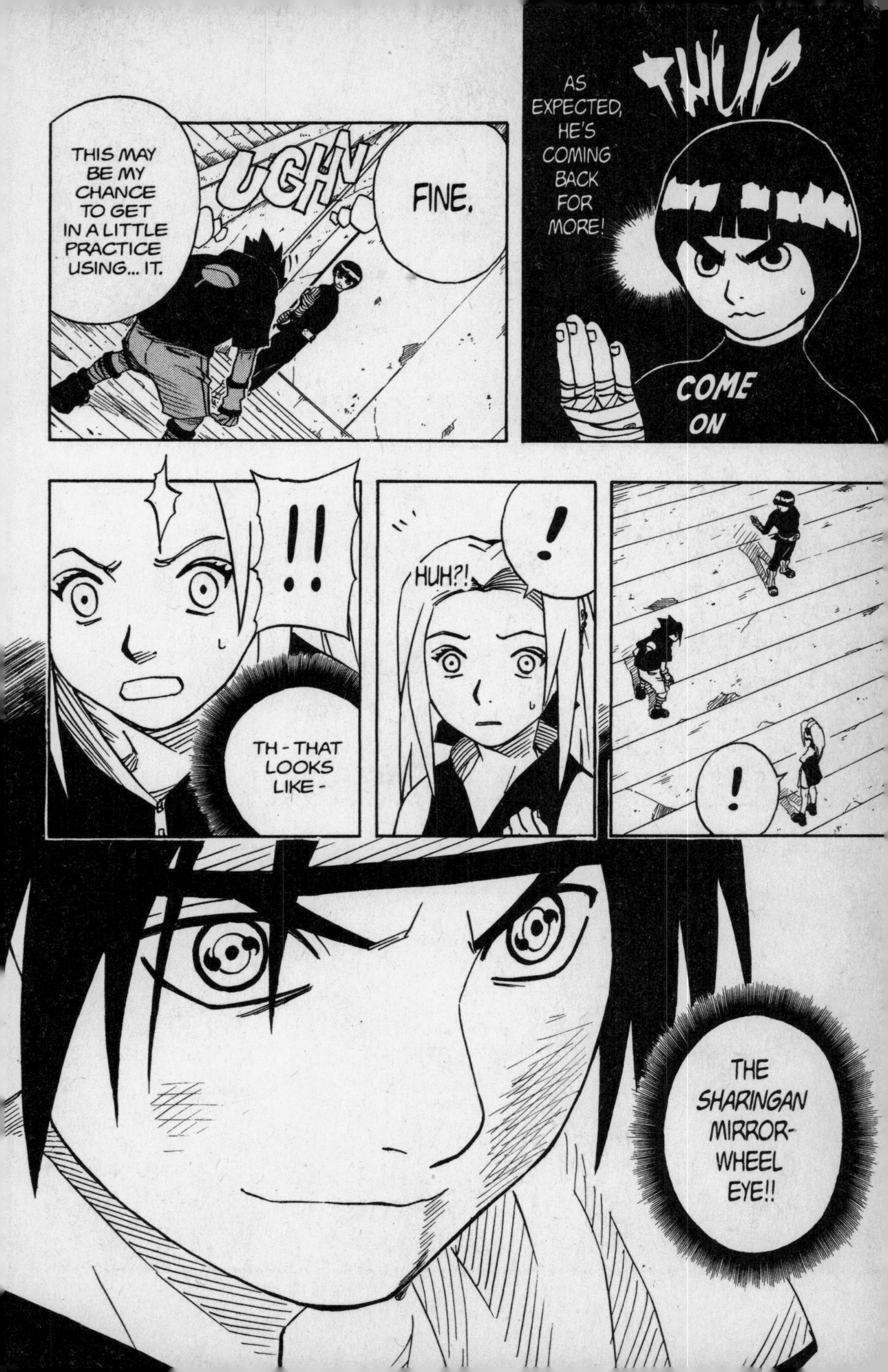
THUP
AS EXPECTED, HE'S COMING BACK FOR MORE!
COME ON
FINE.
UGHN
THIS MAY BE MY CHANCE TO GET IN A LITTLE PRACTICE USING... IT.
!
!
HUH?!
!!
TH - THAT LOOKS LIKE -
THE SHARINGAN MIRROR-WHEEL EYE!!

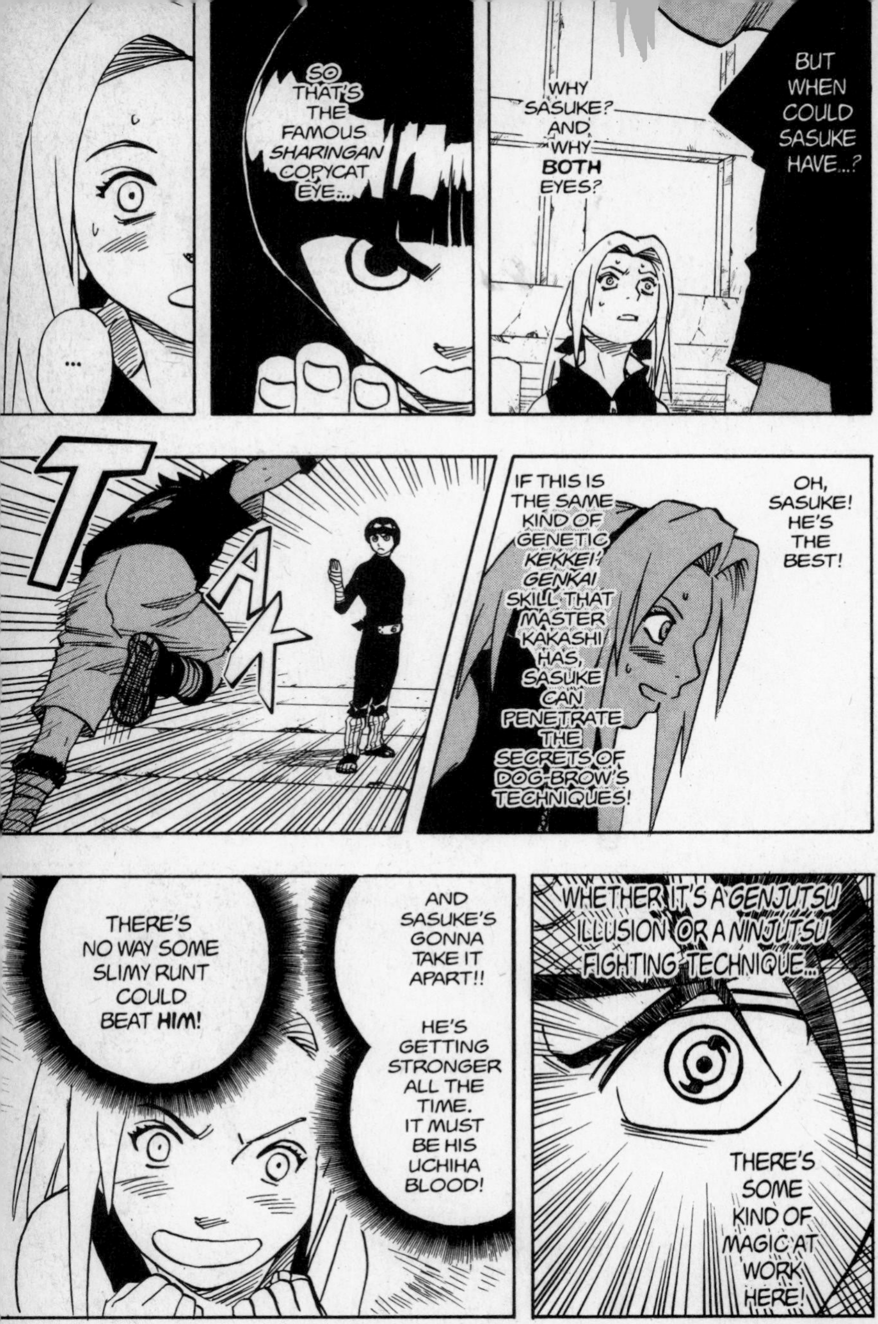
BUT WHEN COULD SASUKE HAVE...?
WHY SASUKE? AND WHY **BOTH** EYES?
SO THAT'S THE FAMOUS SHARINGAN COPYCAT EYE...
...
OH, SASUKE! HE'S THE BEST!
IF THIS IS THE SAME KIND OF GENETIC KEKKEI GENKAI SKILL THAT MASTER KAKASHI HAS, SASUKE CAN PENETRATE THE SECRETS OF DOG-BROW'S TECHNIQUES!
TAK
WHETHER IT'S A GENJUTSU ILLUSION OR A NINJUTSU FIGHTING TECHNIQUE...
THERE'S SOME KIND OF MAGIC AT WORK HERE!
AND SASUKE'S GONNA TAKE IT APART!!
THERE'S NO WAY SOME SLIMY RUNT COULD BEAT **HIM**!
HE'S GETTING STRONGER ALL THE TIME. IT MUST BE HIS UCHIHA BLOOD!

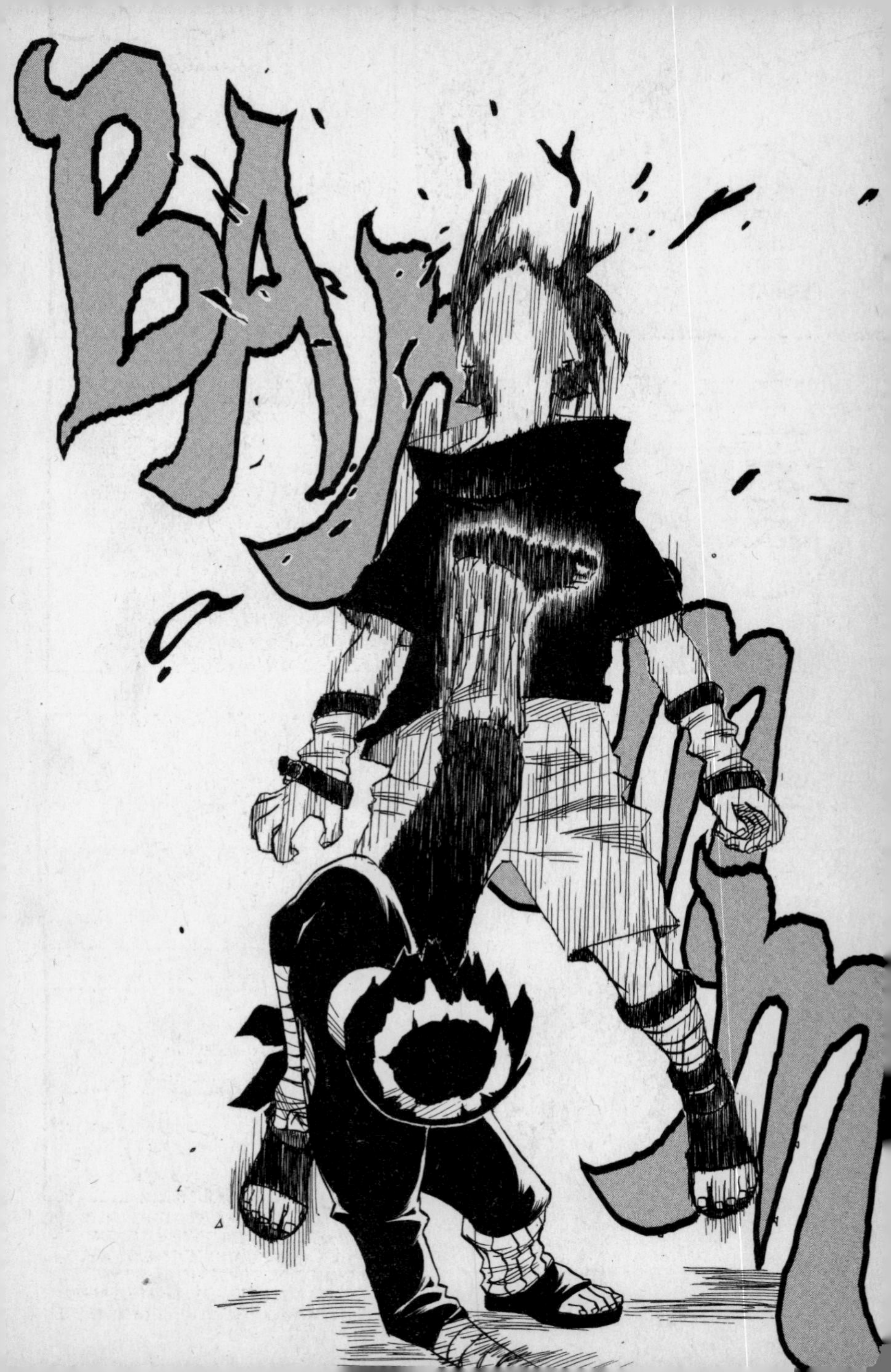
BAMM

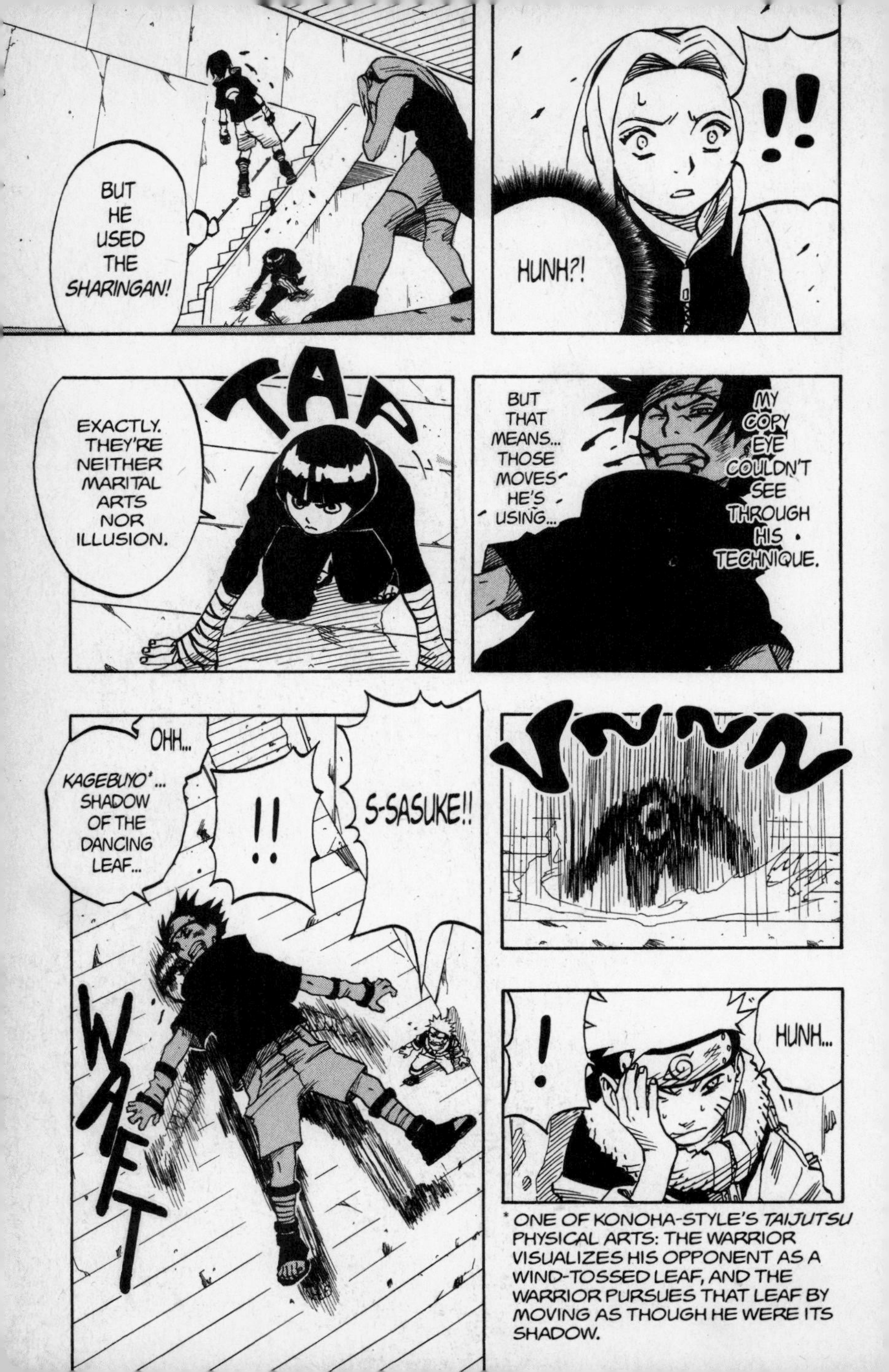
!!
HUNH?!
BUT HE USED THE SHARINGAN!
BUT THAT MEANS... THOSE MOVES HE'S USING...
MY COPY EYE COULDN'T SEE THROUGH HIS TECHNIQUE.
TAP
EXACTLY. THEY'RE NEITHER MARITAL ARTS NOR ILLUSION.
VNNN
HUNH...
!
S-SASUKE!!
!!
OHH...
KAGEBUYO*... SHADOW OF THE DANCING LEAF...
WAFT

* ONE OF KONOHA-STYLE'S *TAIJUTSU* PHYSICAL ARTS: THE WARRIOR VISUALIZES HIS OPPONENT AS A WIND-TOSSED LEAF, AND THE WARRIOR PURSUES THAT LEAF BY MOVING AS THOUGH HE WERE ITS SHADOW.

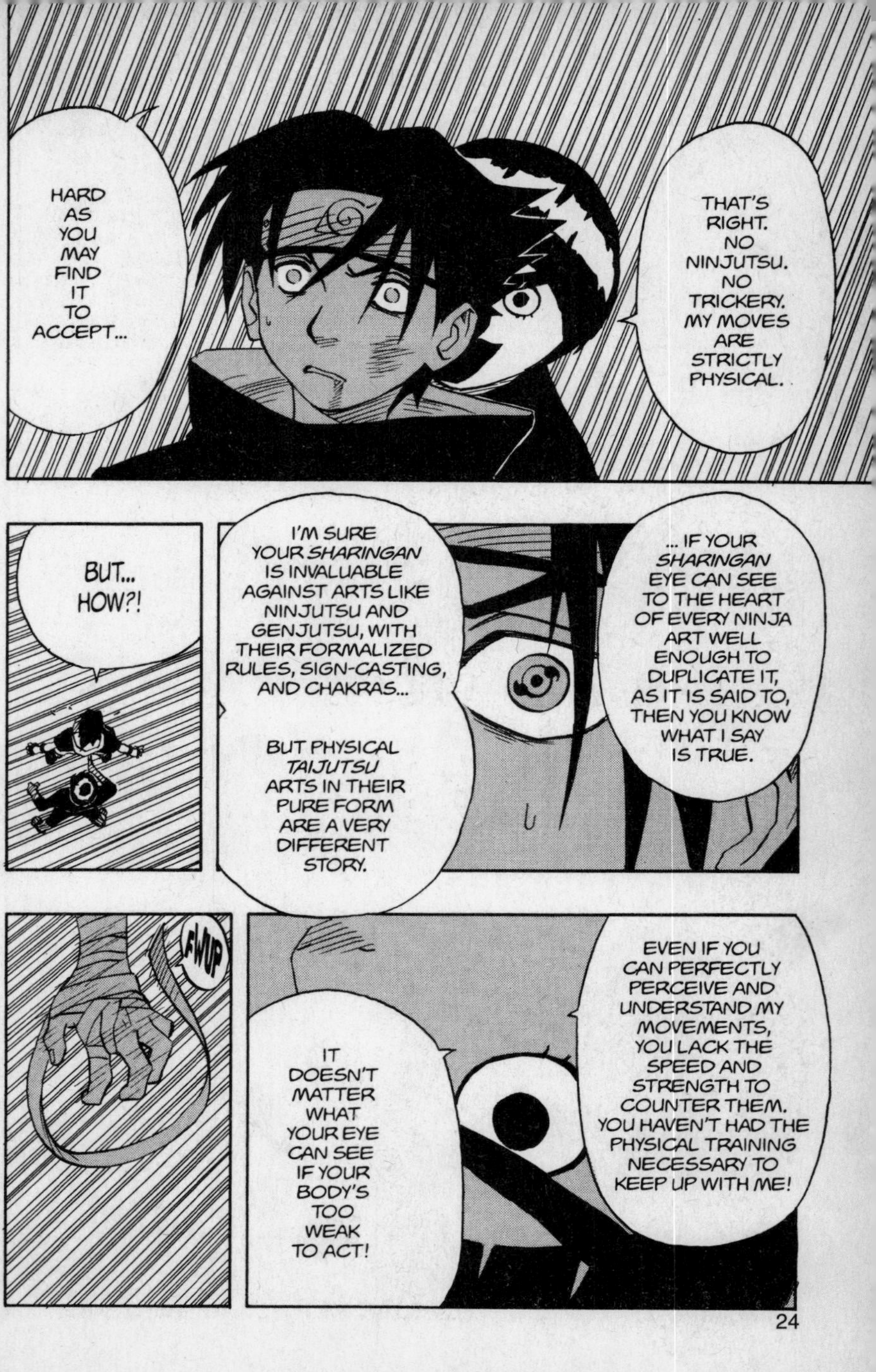
THAT'S RIGHT. NO NINJUTSU. NO TRICKERY. MY MOVES ARE STRICTLY PHYSICAL.
HARD AS YOU MAY FIND IT TO ACCEPT...
... IF YOUR *SHARINGAN* EYE CAN SEE TO THE HEART OF EVERY NINJA ART WELL ENOUGH TO DUPLICATE IT, AS IT IS SAID TO, THEN YOU KNOW WHAT I SAY IS TRUE.
I'M SURE YOUR *SHARINGAN* IS INVALUABLE AGAINST ARTS LIKE NINJUTSU AND GENJUTSU, WITH THEIR FORMALIZED RULES, SIGN-CASTING, AND CHAKRAS...
BUT PHYSICAL *TAIJUTSU* ARTS IN THEIR PURE FORM ARE A VERY DIFFERENT STORY.
BUT... HOW?!
EVEN IF YOU CAN PERFECTLY PERCEIVE AND UNDERSTAND MY MOVEMENTS, YOU LACK THE SPEED AND STRENGTH TO COUNTER THEM. YOU HAVEN'T HAD THE PHYSICAL TRAINING NECESSARY TO KEEP UP WITH ME!
IT DOESN'T MATTER WHAT YOUR EYE CAN SEE IF YOUR BODY'S TOO WEAK TO ACT!
FWUP

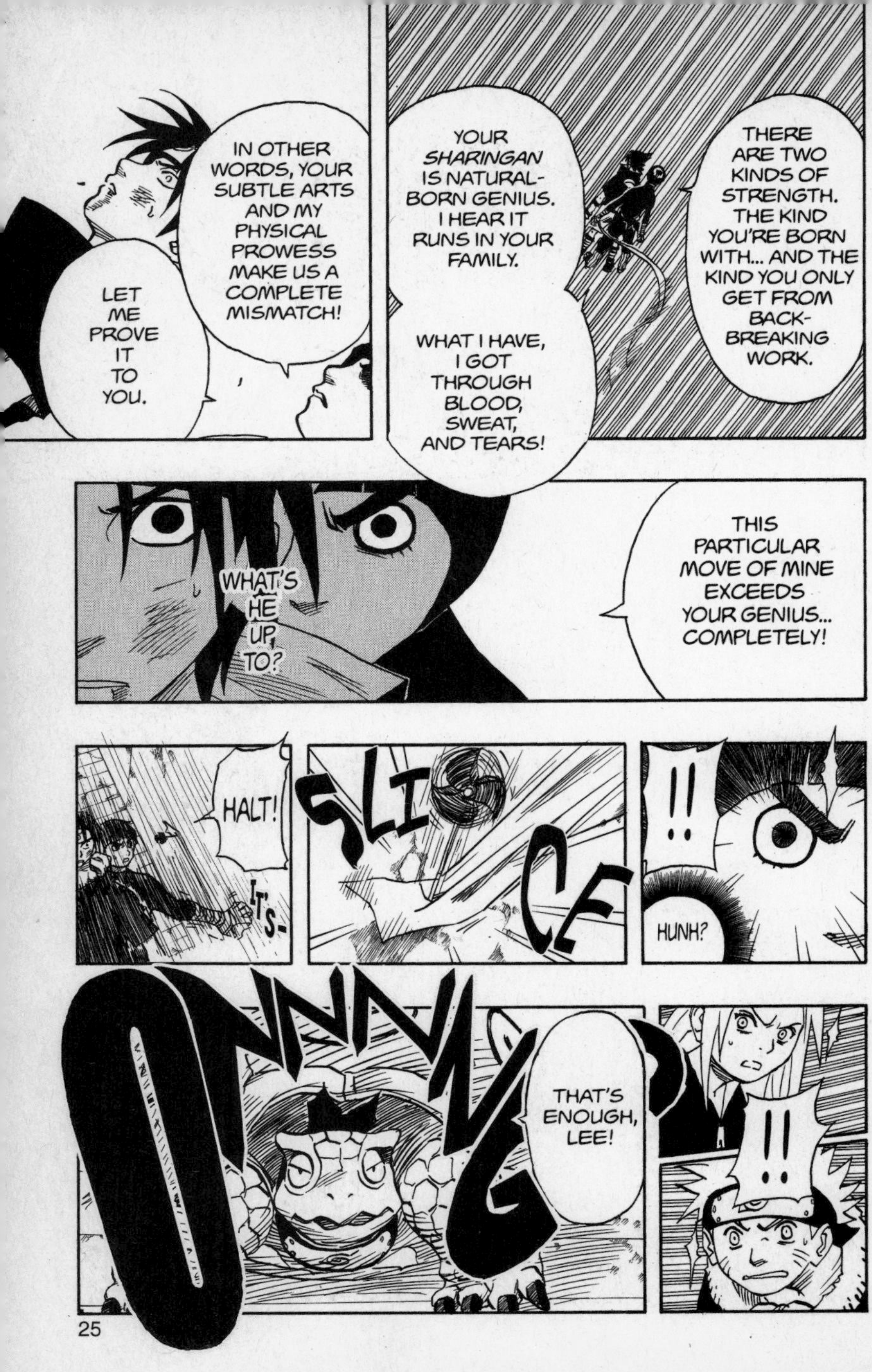
THERE ARE TWO KINDS OF STRENGTH. THE KIND YOU'RE BORN WITH... AND THE KIND YOU ONLY GET FROM BACK-BREAKING WORK.
YOUR SHARINGAN IS NATURAL-BORN GENIUS. I HEAR IT RUNS IN YOUR FAMILY.
WHAT I HAVE, I GOT THROUGH BLOOD, SWEAT, AND TEARS!
IN OTHER WORDS, YOUR SUBTLE ARTS AND MY PHYSICAL PROWESS MAKE US A COMPLETE MISMATCH!
LET ME PROVE IT TO YOU.
THIS PARTICULAR MOVE OF MINE EXCEEDS YOUR GENIUS... COMPLETELY!
WHAT'S HE UP TO?
!!
HUNH?
SLICE
HALT!
IT'S-
!!
THAT'S ENOUGH, LEE!
ONNNG

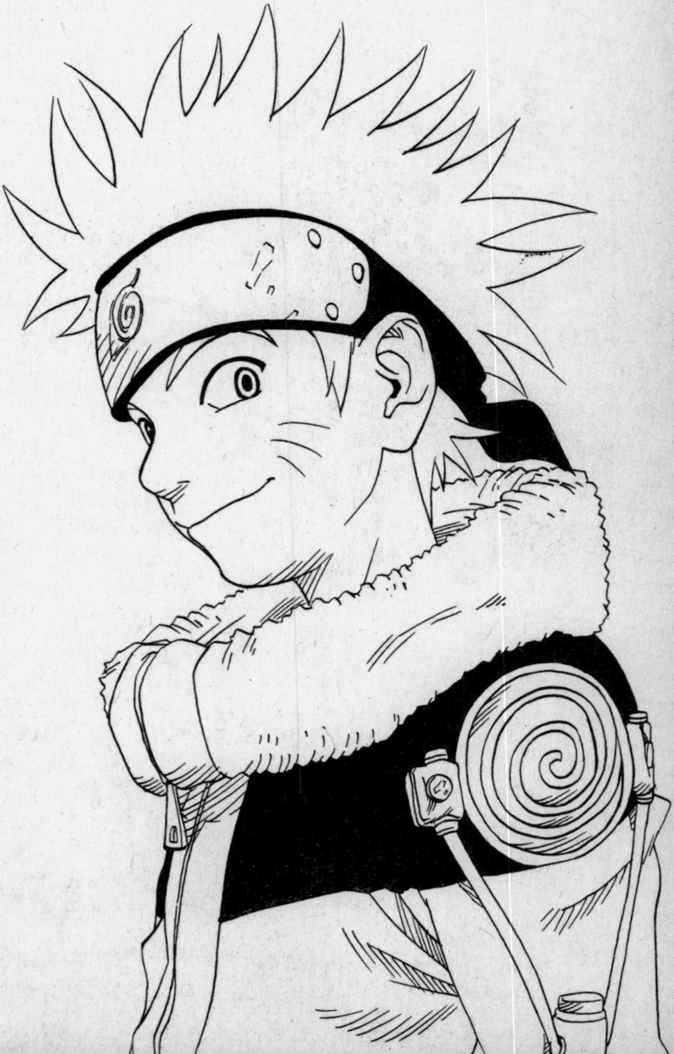

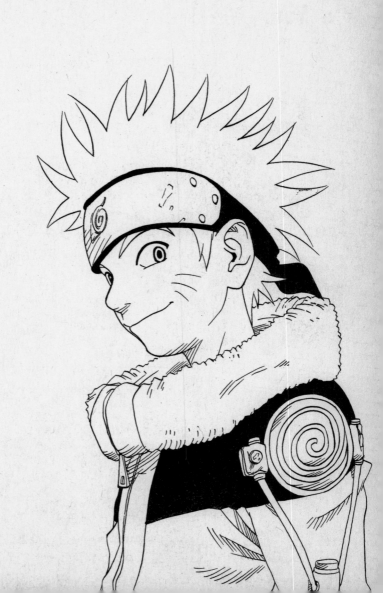

Number 38: On Your Mark

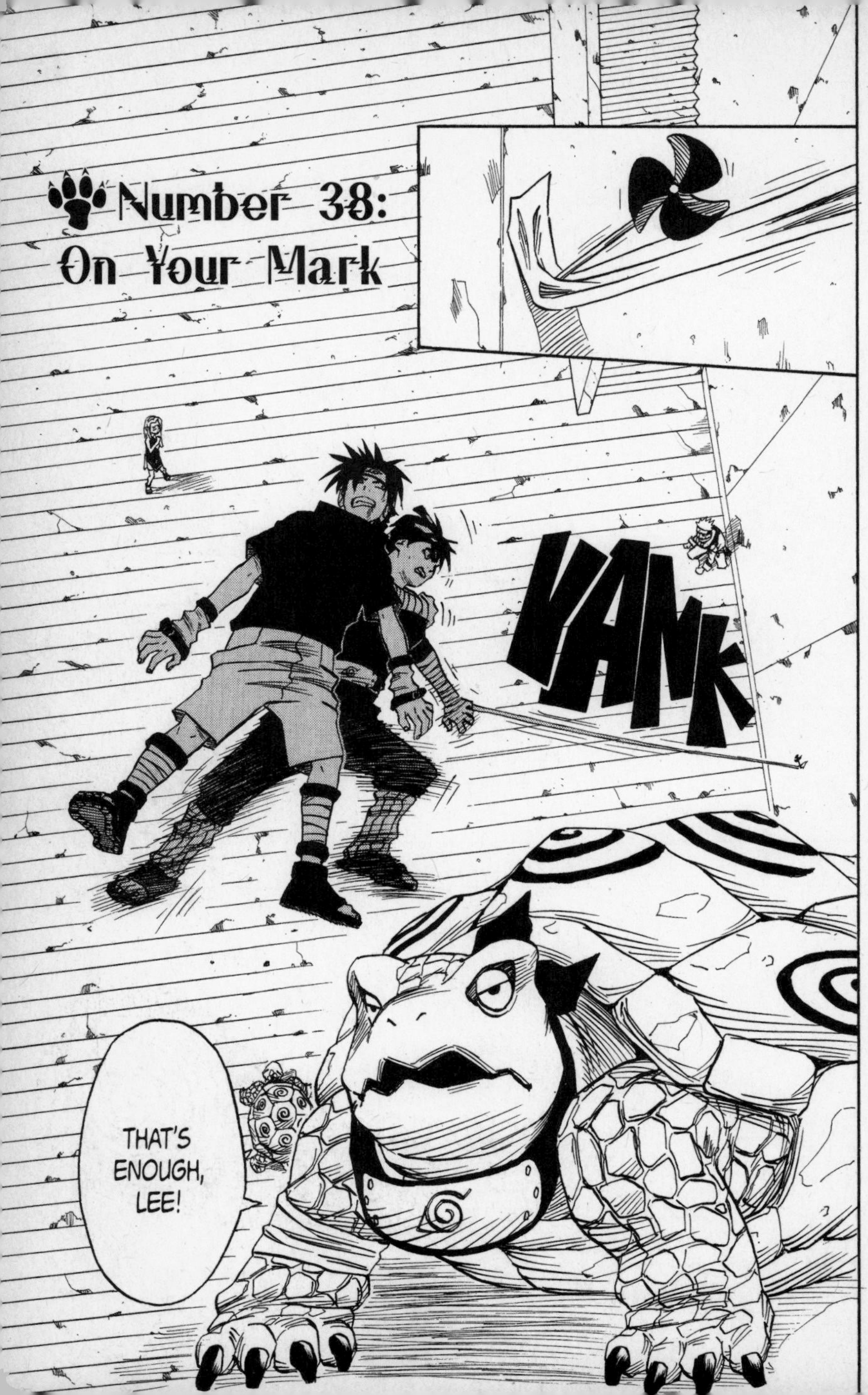
YANK
THAT'S ENOUGH, LEE!

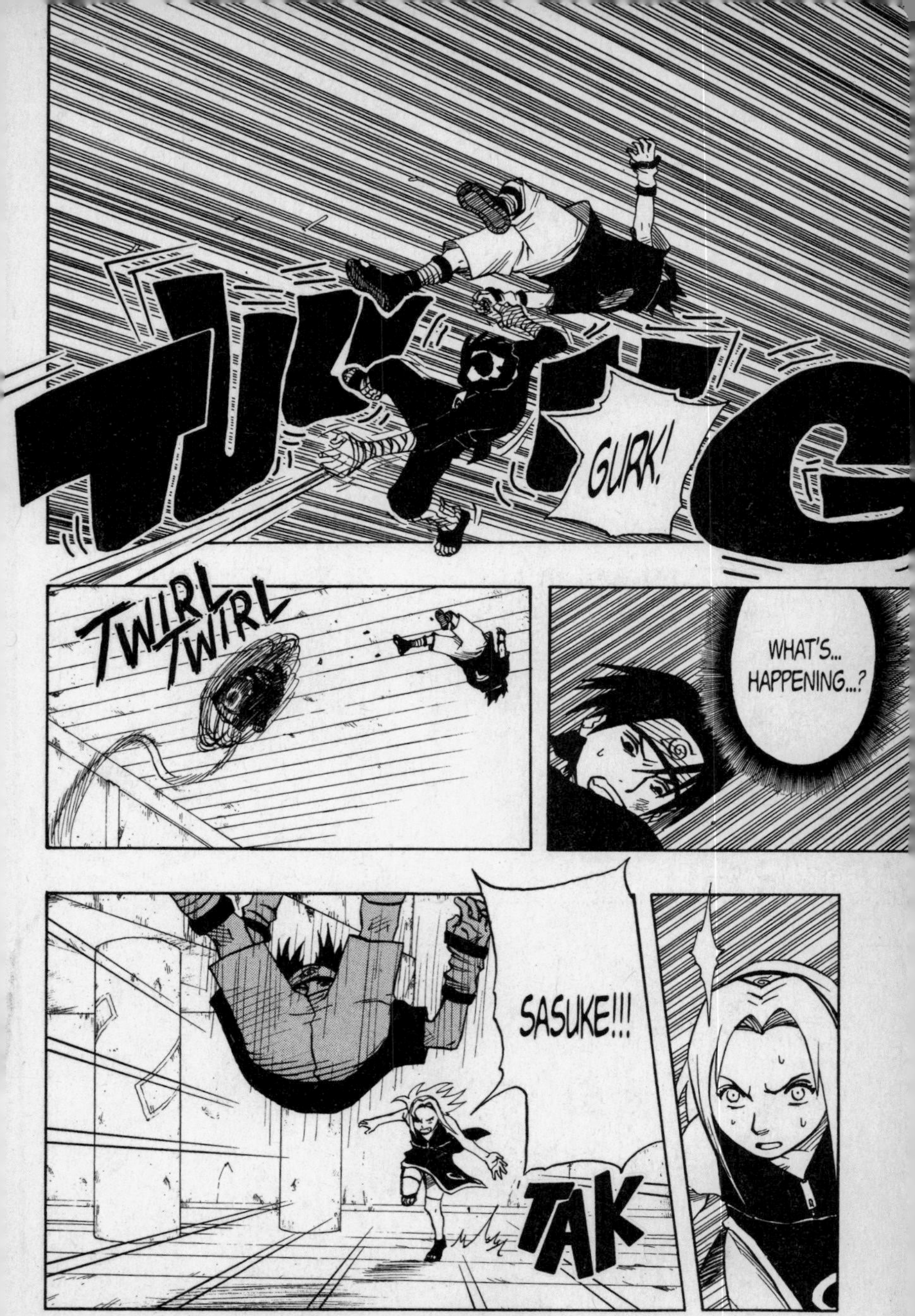
TUG
GURK!
WHAT'S... HAPPENING...?
TWIRL TWIRL
SASUKE!!!
TAK

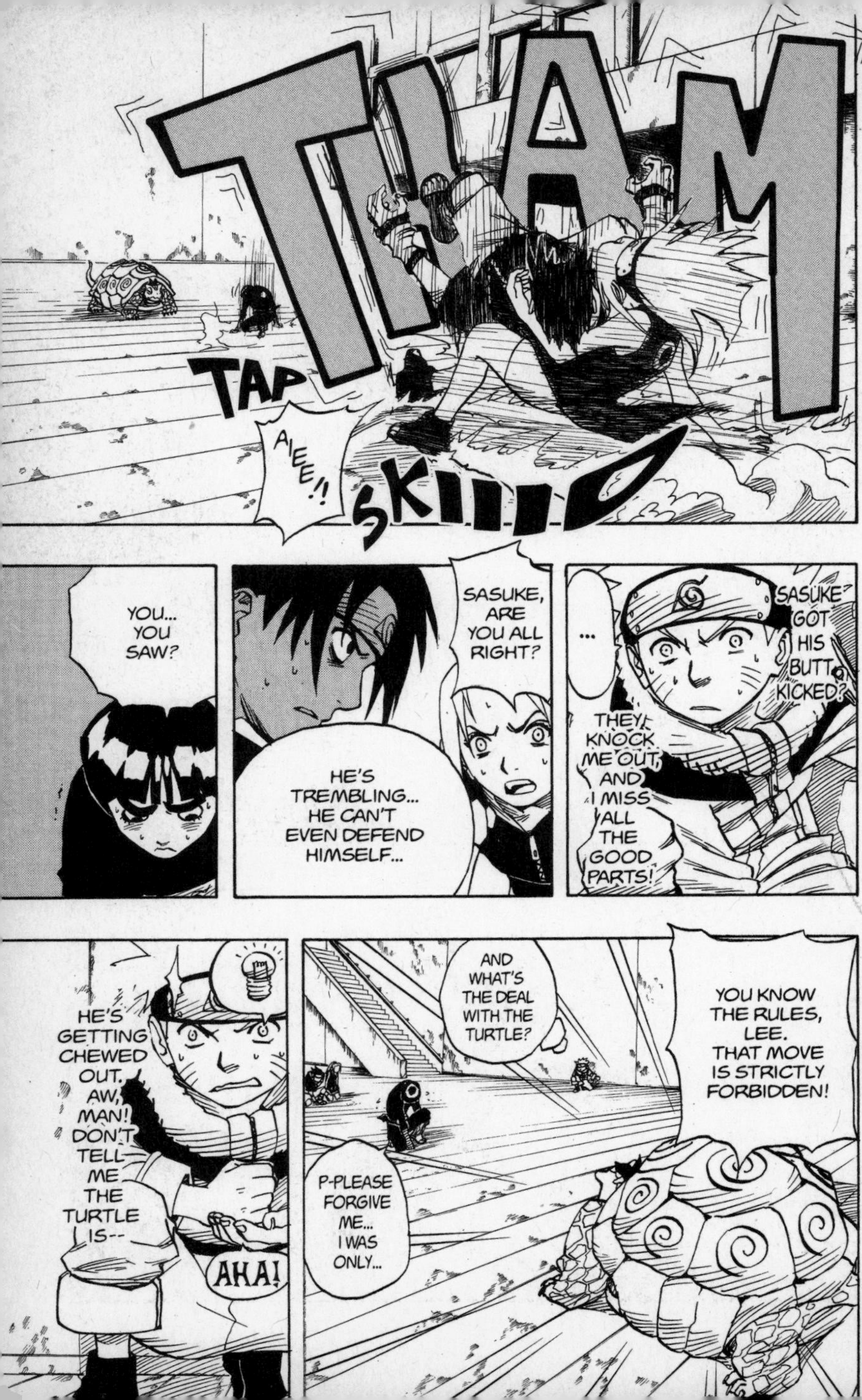
THAM
TAP
AIEE!!
SKIIIID
SASUKE GOT HIS BUTT KICKED?
...
THEY KNOCK ME OUT, AND I MISS ALL THE GOOD PARTS!
SASUKE, ARE YOU ALL RIGHT?
HE'S TREMBLING... HE CAN'T EVEN DEFEND HIMSELF...
YOU... YOU SAW?
YOU KNOW THE RULES, LEE. THAT MOVE IS STRICTLY FORBIDDEN!
AND WHAT'S THE DEAL WITH THE TURTLE?
P-PLEASE FORGIVE ME... I WAS ONLY...
HE'S GETTING CHEWED OUT. AW, MAN! DON'T TELL ME THE TURTLE IS--
AHA!

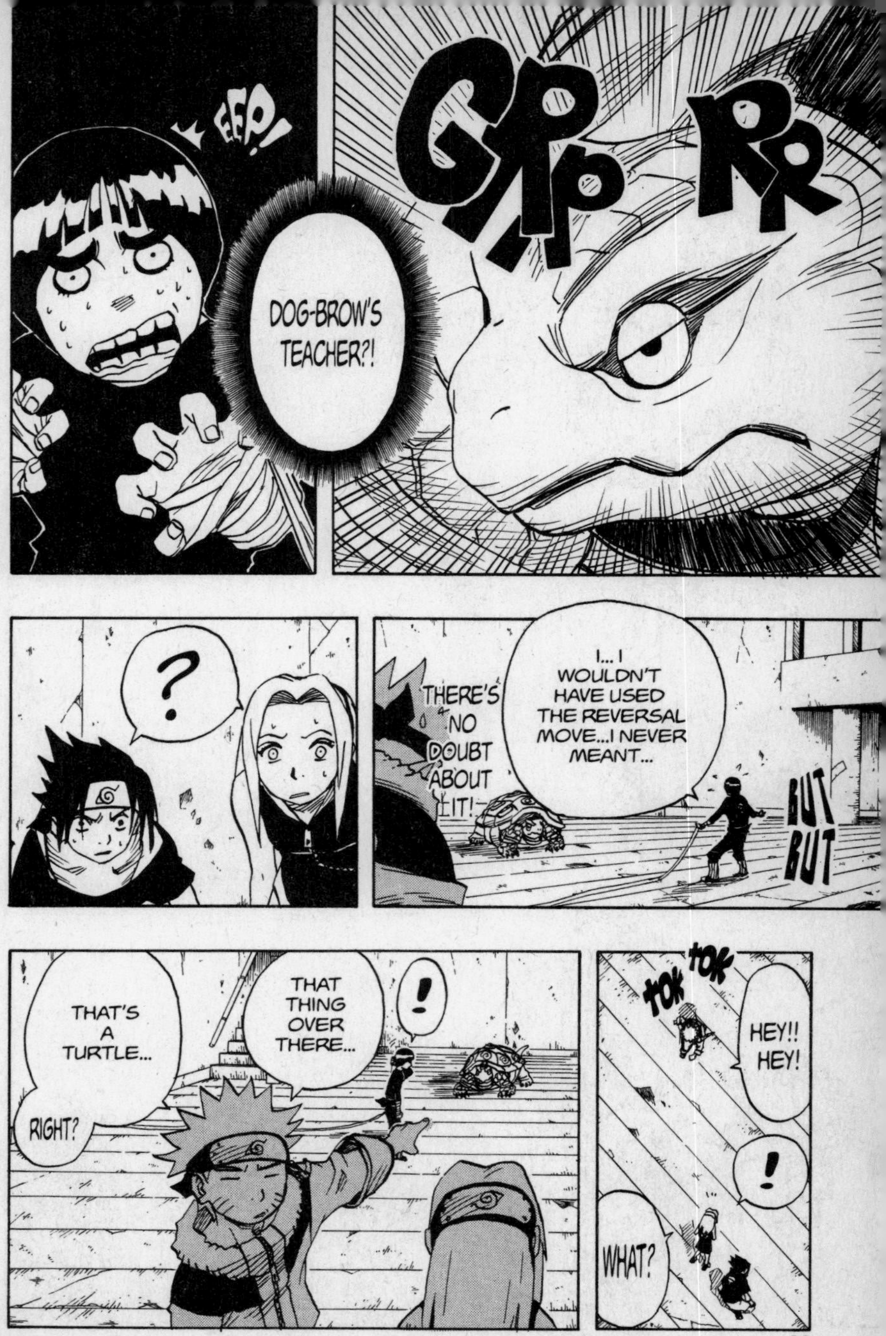
GRRRR
EEP!
DOG-BROW'S TEACHER?!
I... I WOULDN'T HAVE USED THE REVERSAL MOVE...I NEVER MEANT...
BUT BUT
THERE'S NO DOUBT ABOUT IT!
?
TOK TOK
HEY!! HEY!
!
WHAT?
!
THAT THING OVER THERE...
THAT'S A TURTLE...
RIGHT?

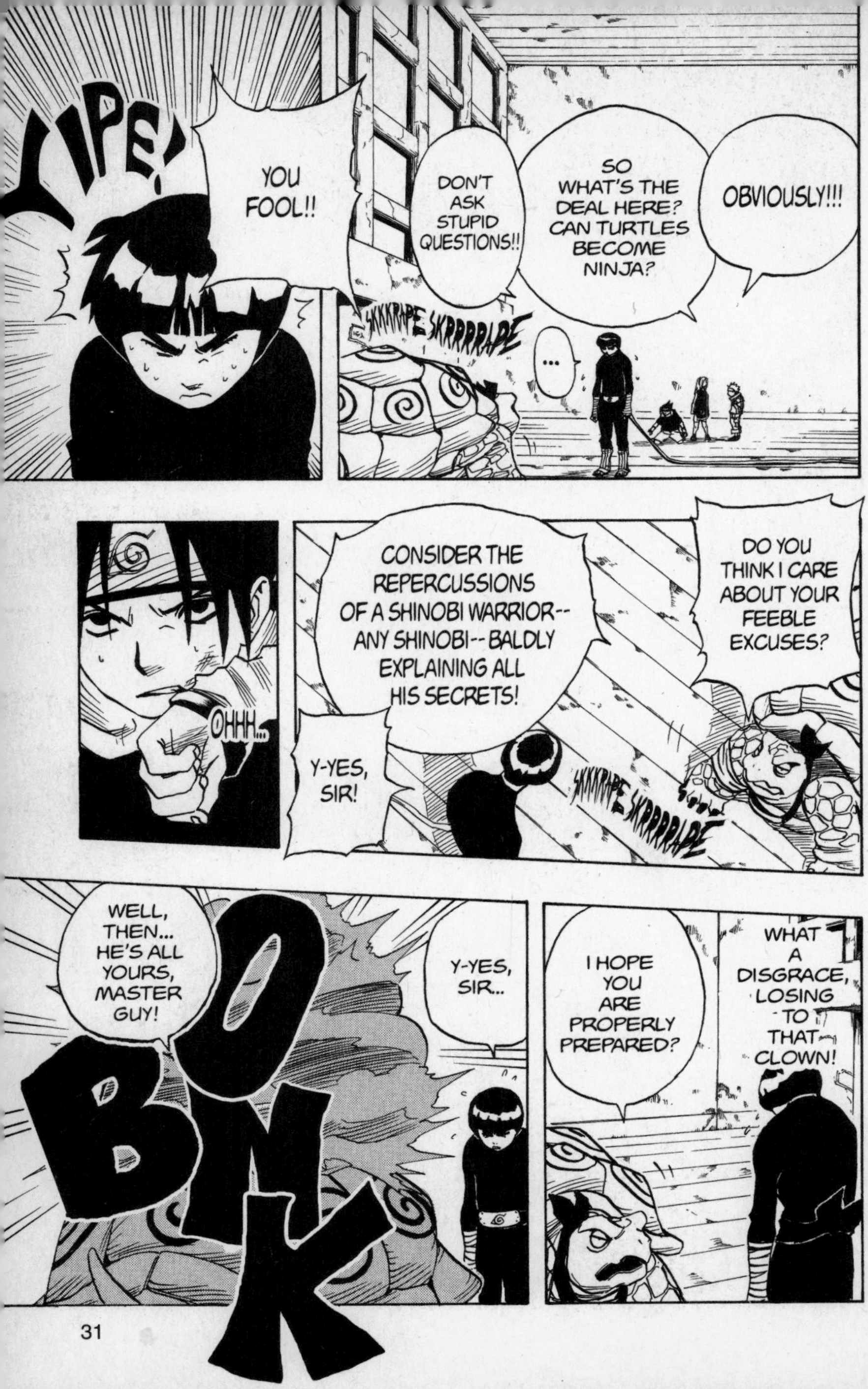
SO WHAT'S THE DEAL HERE? CAN TURTLES BECOME NINJA?
OBVIOUSLY!!!
DON'T ASK STUPID QUESTIONS!!
SKKKRAPE SKRRRRAPE
...
YOU FOOL!!
YIPE!
DO YOU THINK I CARE ABOUT YOUR FEEBLE EXCUSES?
CONSIDER THE REPERCUSSIONS OF A SHINOBI WARRIOR-- ANY SHINOBI-- BALDLY EXPLAINING ALL HIS SECRETS!
Y-YES, SIR!
SKKKRAPE SKRRRRAPE
OHHH...
WHAT A DISGRACE, LOSING TO THAT CLOWN!
I HOPE YOU ARE PROPERLY PREPARED?
Y-YES, SIR...
WELL, THEN... HE'S ALL YOURS, MASTER GUY!
BONK

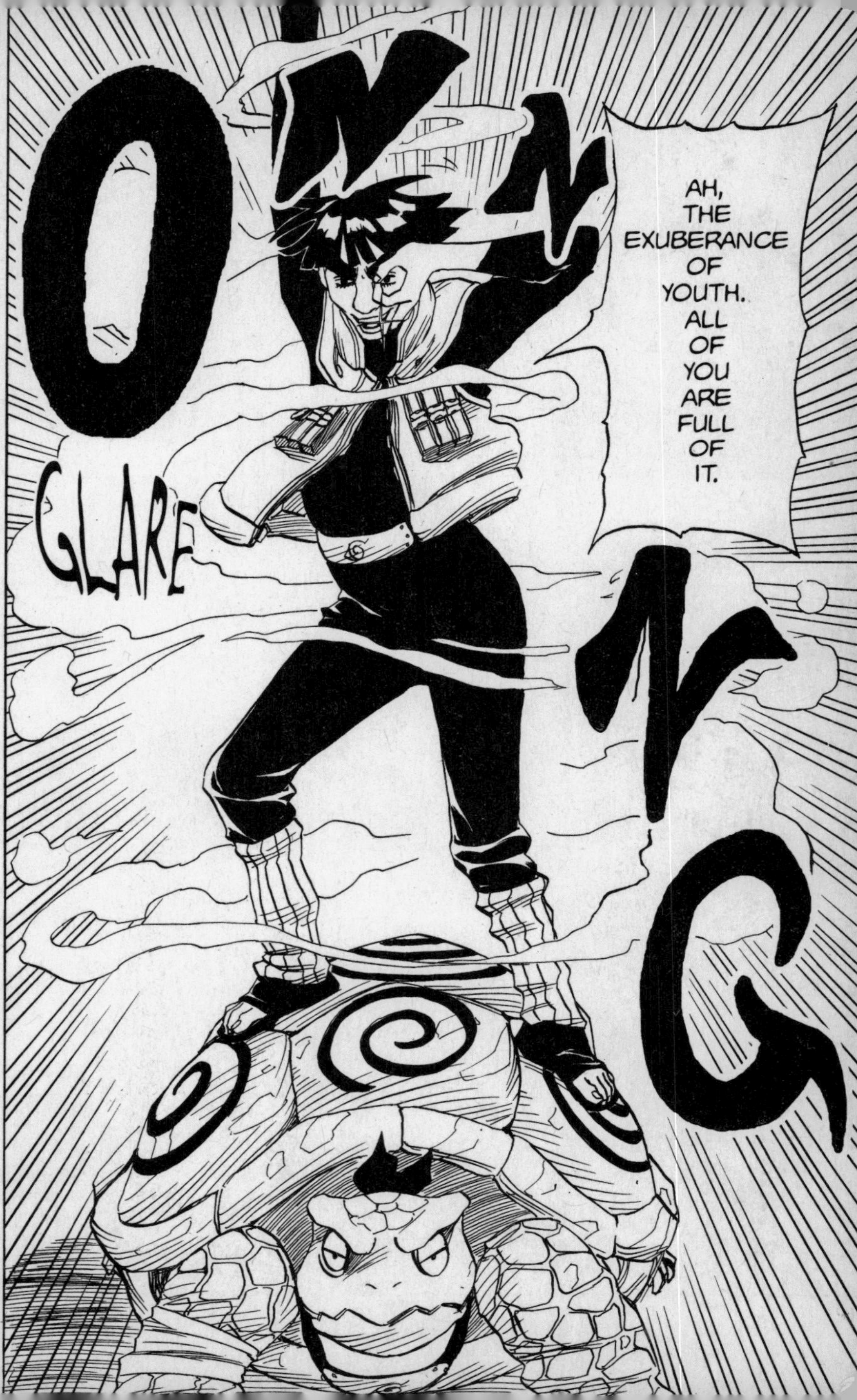
AH, THE EXUBERANCE OF YOUTH. ALL OF YOU ARE FULL OF IT.
GLARE

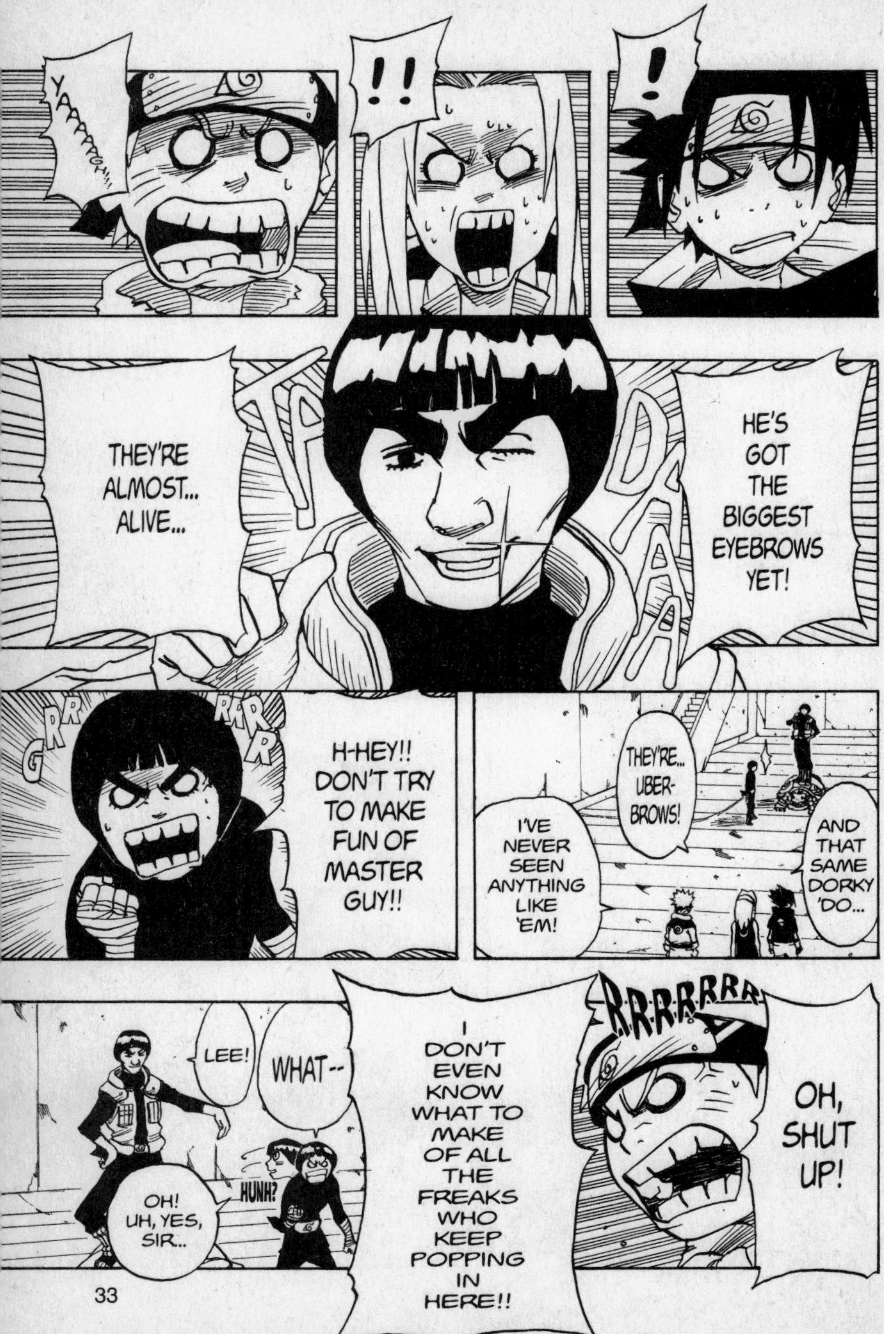
!
!!
YAAAAGH!!
HE'S GOT THE BIGGEST EYEBROWS YET!
TA DAAA
THEY'RE ALMOST... ALIVE...
AND THAT SAME DORKY 'DO...
THEY'RE... UBER-BROWS!
I'VE NEVER SEEN ANYTHING LIKE 'EM!
GRRRRR
H-HEY!! DON'T TRY TO MAKE FUN OF MASTER GUY!!
RRRRRRR
OH, SHUT UP!
I DON'T EVEN KNOW WHAT TO MAKE OF ALL THE FREAKS WHO KEEP POPPING IN HERE!!
WHAT--
LEE!
HUNH?
OH! UH, YES, SIR..

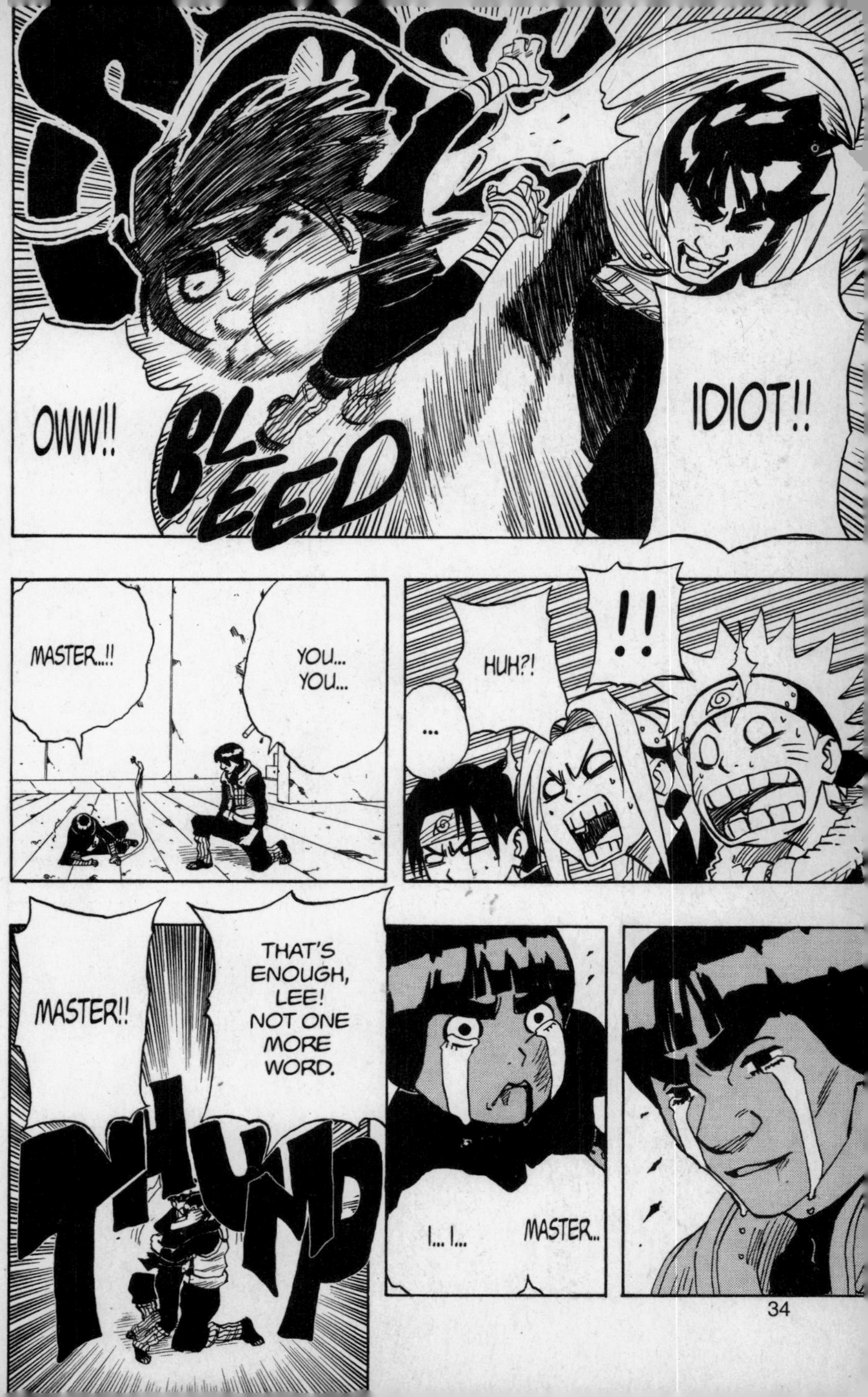
IDIOT!!
OWW!!
!!
HUH?!
...
YOU... YOU...
MASTER...!!
MASTER...
I... I...
THAT'S ENOUGH, LEE! NOT ONE MORE WORD.
MASTER!!
THUMP

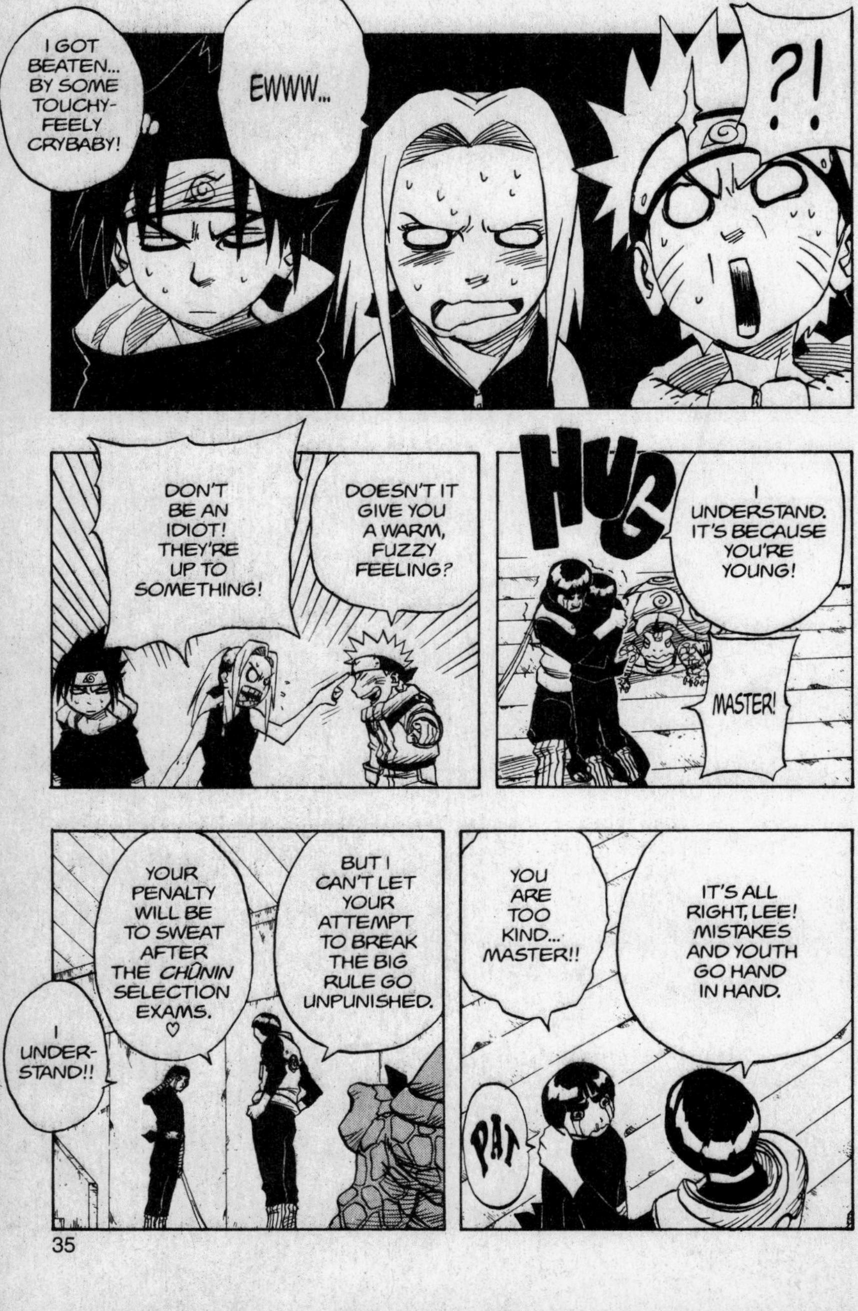
?!
EWWW...
I GOT BEATEN... BY SOME TOUCHY-FEELY CRYBABY!
HUG
I UNDERSTAND. IT'S BECAUSE YOU'RE YOUNG!
MASTER!
DOESN'T IT GIVE YOU A WARM, FUZZY FEELING?
DON'T BE AN IDIOT! THEY'RE UP TO SOMETHING!
IT'S ALL RIGHT, LEE! MISTAKES AND YOUTH GO HAND IN HAND.
YOU ARE TOO KIND... MASTER!!
PAT
BUT I CAN'T LET YOUR ATTEMPT TO BREAK THE BIG RULE GO UNPUNISHED.
YOUR PENALTY WILL BE TO SWEAT AFTER THE *CHŪNIN* SELECTION EXAMS. ♡
I UNDERSTAND!!

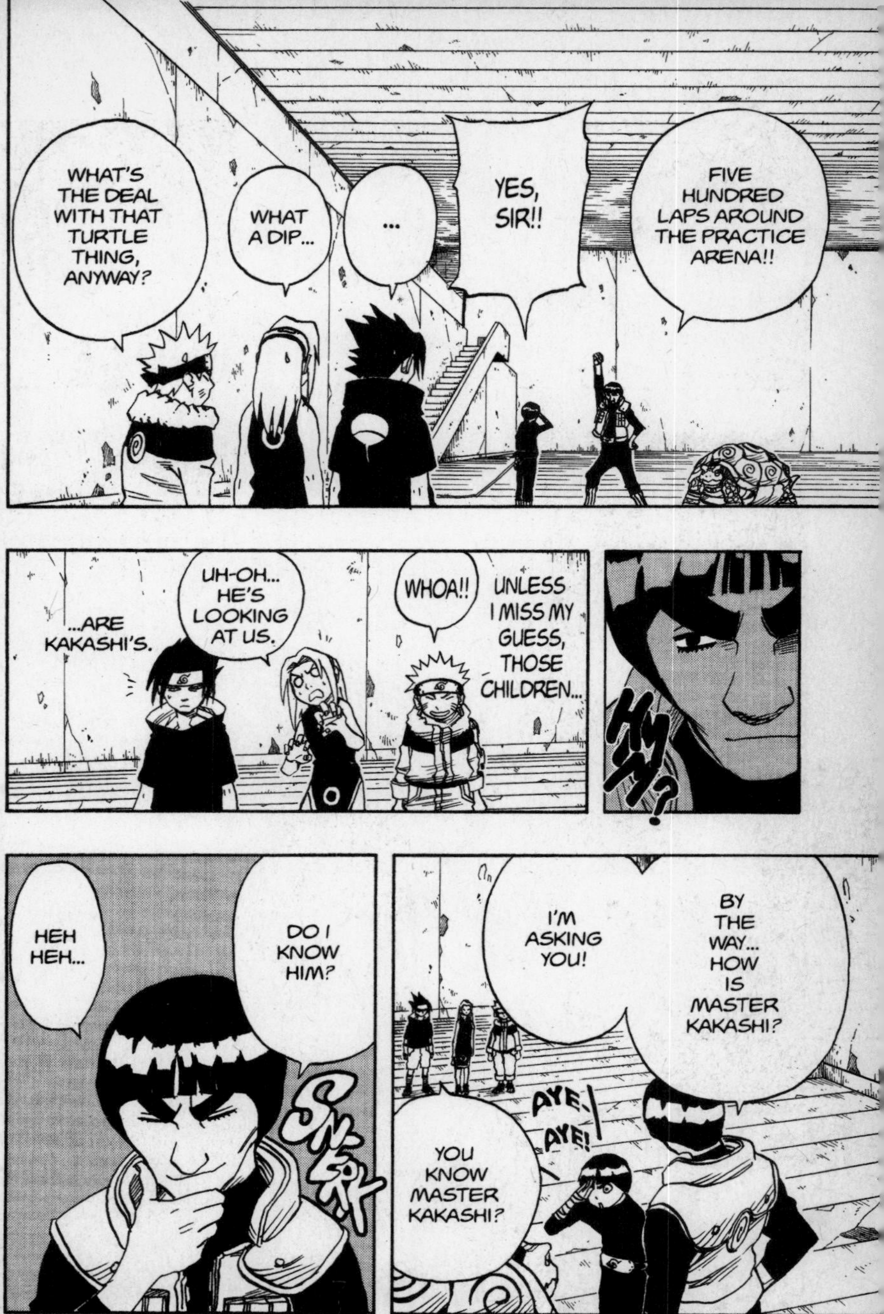
FIVE HUNDRED LAPS AROUND THE PRACTICE ARENA!!
YES, SIR!!
...
WHAT A DIP...
WHAT'S THE DEAL WITH THAT TURTLE THING, ANYWAY?
HMM?
UNLESS I MISS MY GUESS, THOSE CHILDREN...
WHOA!!
UH-OH... HE'S LOOKING AT US.
...ARE KAKASHI'S.
BY THE WAY... HOW IS MASTER KAKASHI?
I'M ASKING YOU!
AYE, AYE!
YOU KNOW MASTER KAKASHI?
DO I KNOW HIM?
SNERK
HEH HEH...

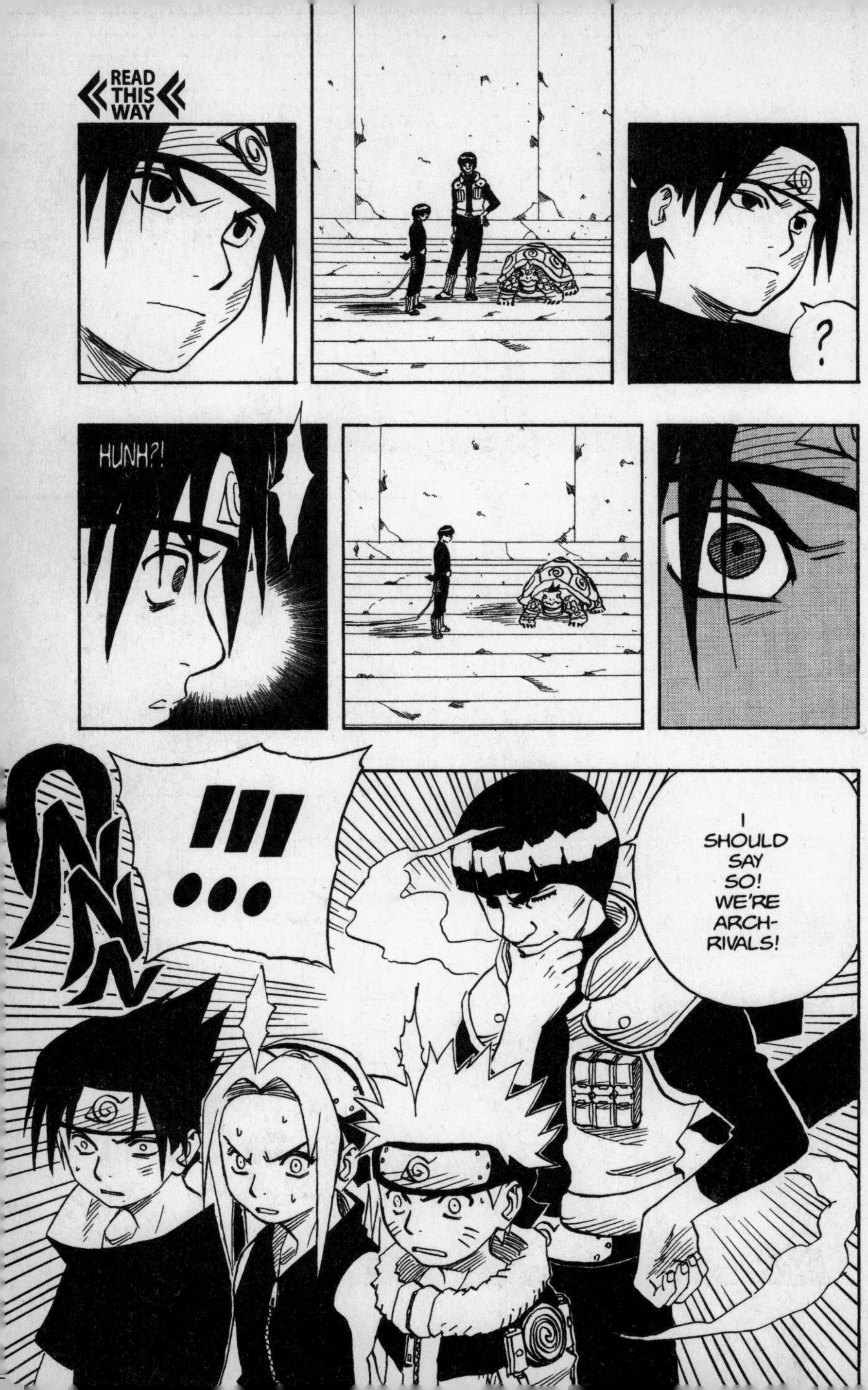
READ THIS WAY
?
HUNH?!
I SHOULD SAY SO! WE'RE ARCH-RIVALS!
!!!
...

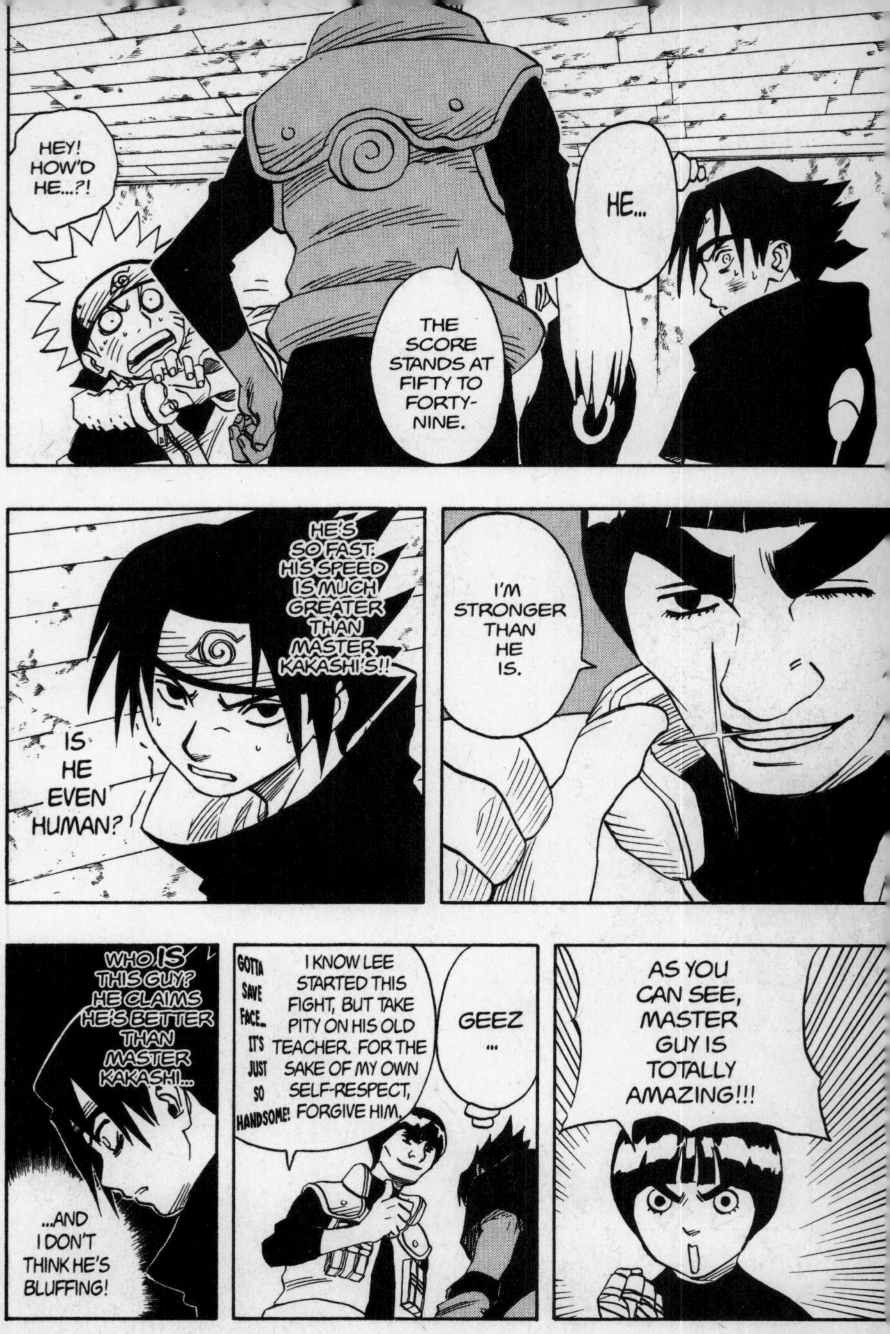

HE...
THE SCORE STANDS AT FIFTY TO FORTY-NINE.
HEY! HOW'D HE...?!
I'M STRONGER THAN HE IS.
HE'S SO FAST. HIS SPEED IS MUCH GREATER THAN MASTER KAKASHI'S!!
IS HE EVEN HUMAN?
AS YOU CAN SEE, MASTER GUY IS TOTALLY AMAZING!!!
GEEZ...
I KNOW LEE STARTED THIS FIGHT, BUT TAKE PITY ON HIS OLD TEACHER. FOR THE SAKE OF MY OWN SELF-RESPECT, FORGIVE HIM.
GOTTA SAVE FACE... IT'S JUST SO HANDSOME!
WHO IS THIS GUY? HE CLAIMS HE'S BETTER THAN MASTER KAKASHI...
...AND I DON'T THINK HE'S BLUFFING!

CHUK

!!!
!!!

YOU AND LEE SHOULD HEAD UP TO THE CLASSROOM NOW.

POW

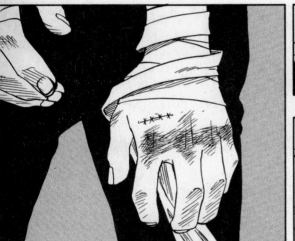

!

FLAP

FLUP
FLUP

!!

HE'S...

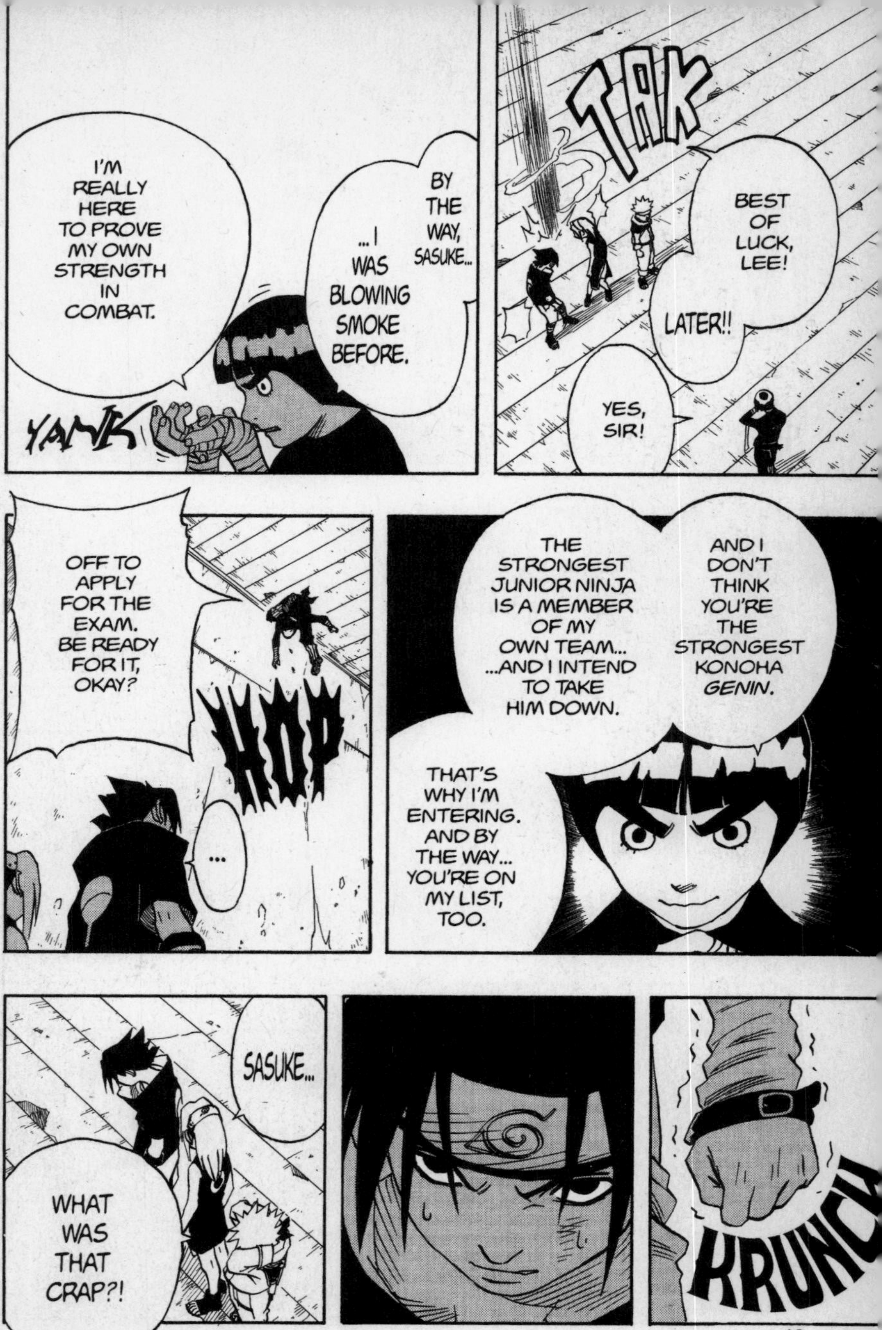

TAK
BEST OF LUCK, LEE!
LATER!!
YES, SIR!
BY THE WAY, SASUKE...
...I WAS BLOWING SMOKE BEFORE.
I'M REALLY HERE TO PROVE MY OWN STRENGTH IN COMBAT.
YANK
AND I DON'T THINK YOU'RE THE STRONGEST KONOHA GENIN.
THE STRONGEST JUNIOR NINJA IS A MEMBER OF MY OWN TEAM... ...AND I INTEND TO TAKE HIM DOWN.
THAT'S WHY I'M ENTERING. AND BY THE WAY... YOU'RE ON MY LIST, TOO.
OFF TO APPLY FOR THE EXAM. BE READY FOR IT, OKAY?
HOP
...
KRUNCH
SASUKE...
WHAT WAS THAT CRAP?!

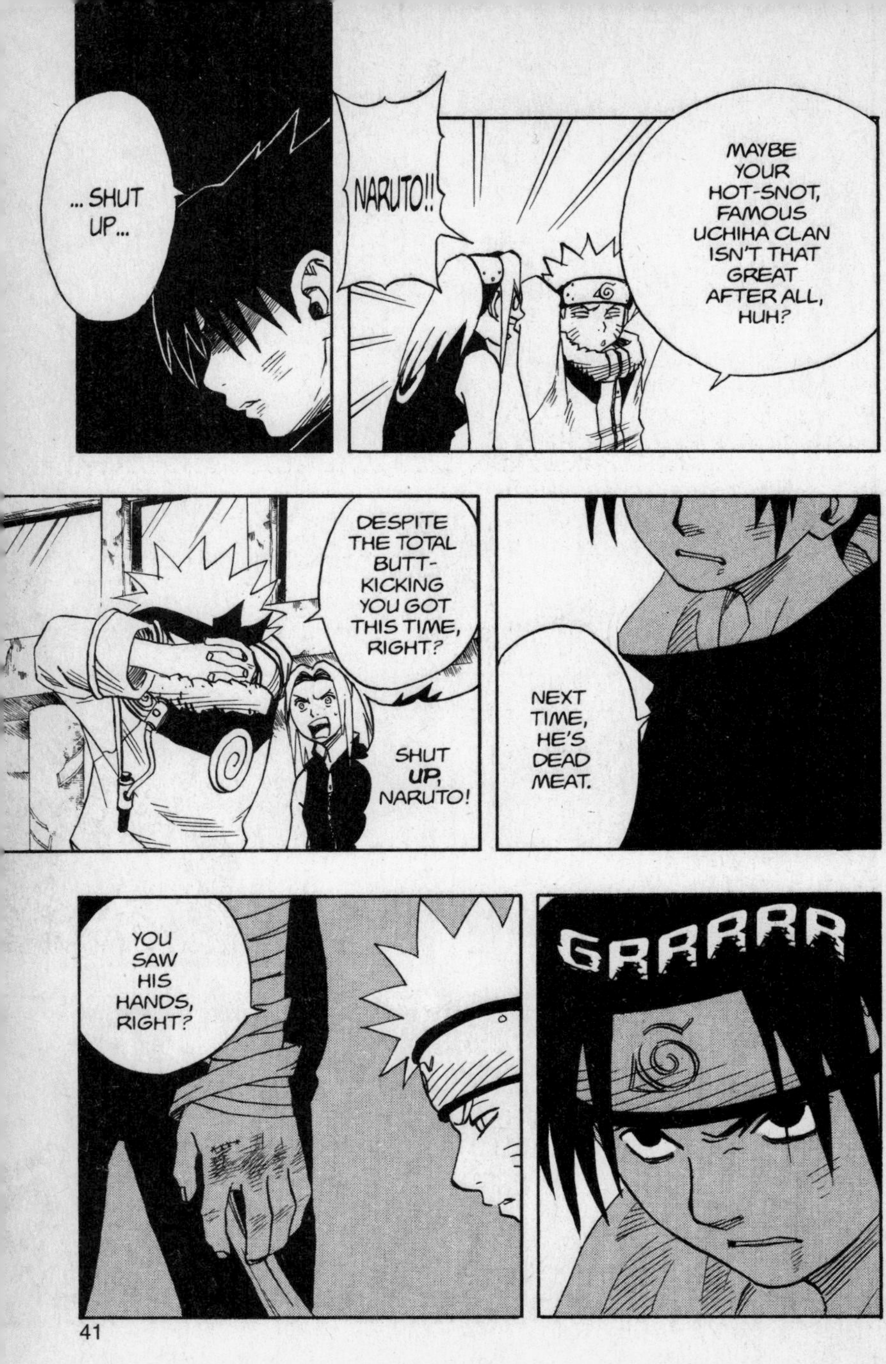
MAYBE YOUR HOT-SNOT, FAMOUS UCHIHA CLAN ISN'T THAT GREAT AFTER ALL, HUH?
NARUTO!!
... SHUT UP...
NEXT TIME, HE'S DEAD MEAT.
DESPITE THE TOTAL BUTT-KICKING YOU GOT THIS TIME, RIGHT?
SHUT UP, NARUTO!
GRRRRR
YOU SAW HIS HANDS, RIGHT?

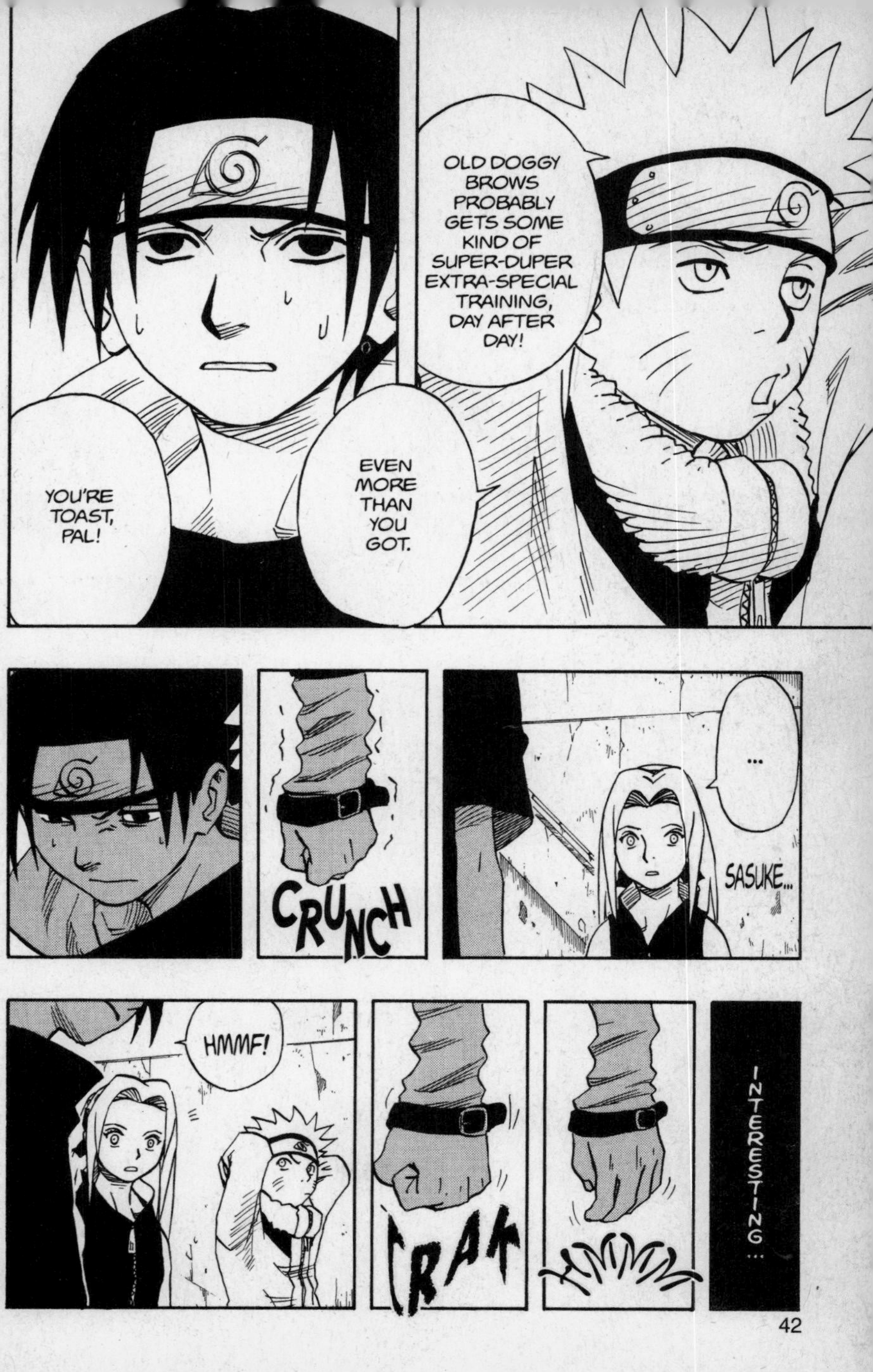
OLD DOGGY BROWS PROBABLY GETS SOME KIND OF SUPER-DUPER EXTRA-SPECIAL TRAINING, DAY AFTER DAY!
EVEN MORE THAN YOU GOT.
YOU'RE TOAST, PAL!
...
SASUKE...
CRUNCH
INTERESTING..
CRAK
HMMF!

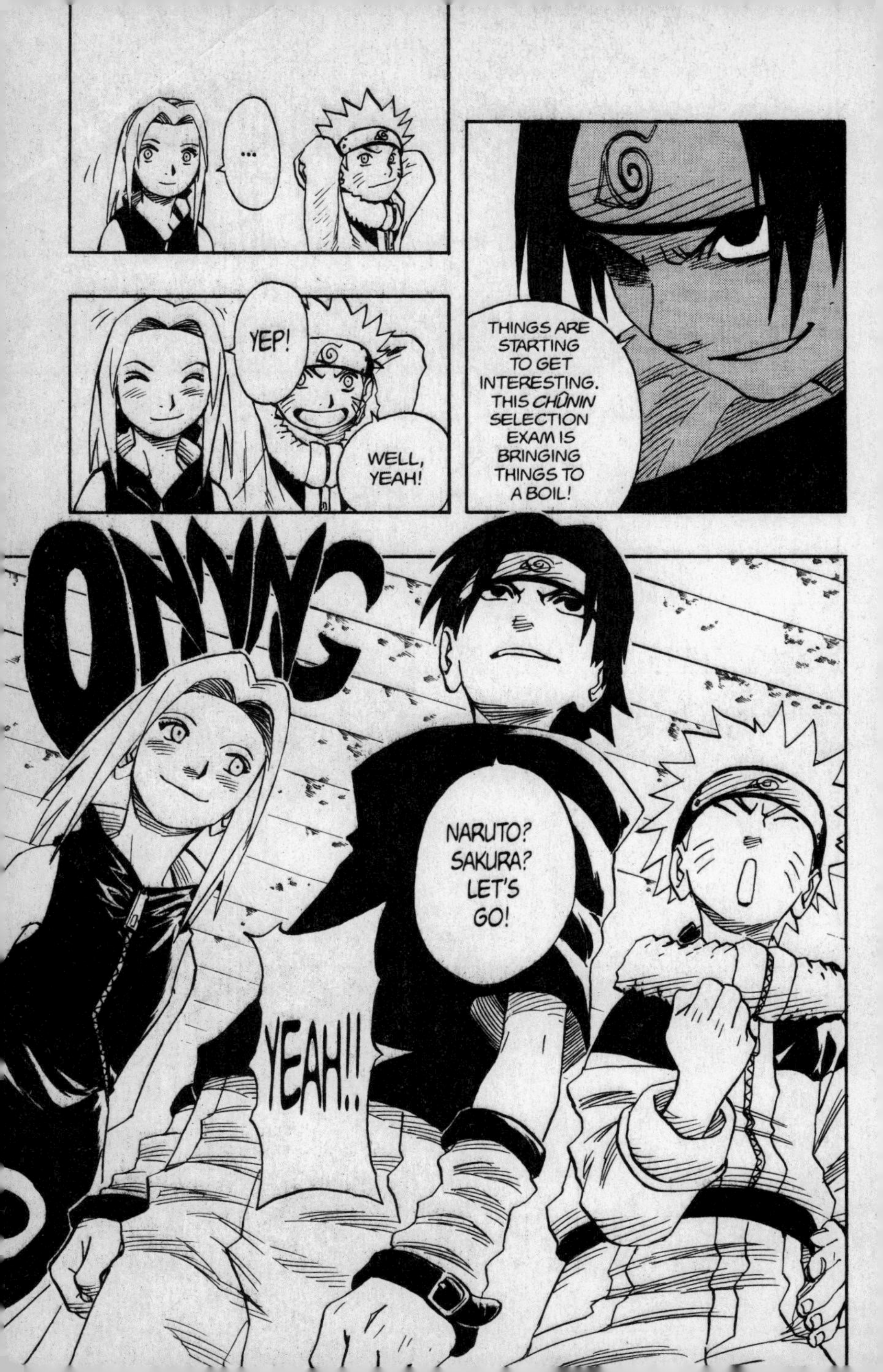
THINGS ARE STARTING TO GET INTERESTING. THIS *CHŪNIN* SELECTION EXAM IS BRINGING THINGS TO A BOIL!
...
WELL, YEAH!
YEP!
NARUTO? SAKURA? LET'S GO!
YEAH!!

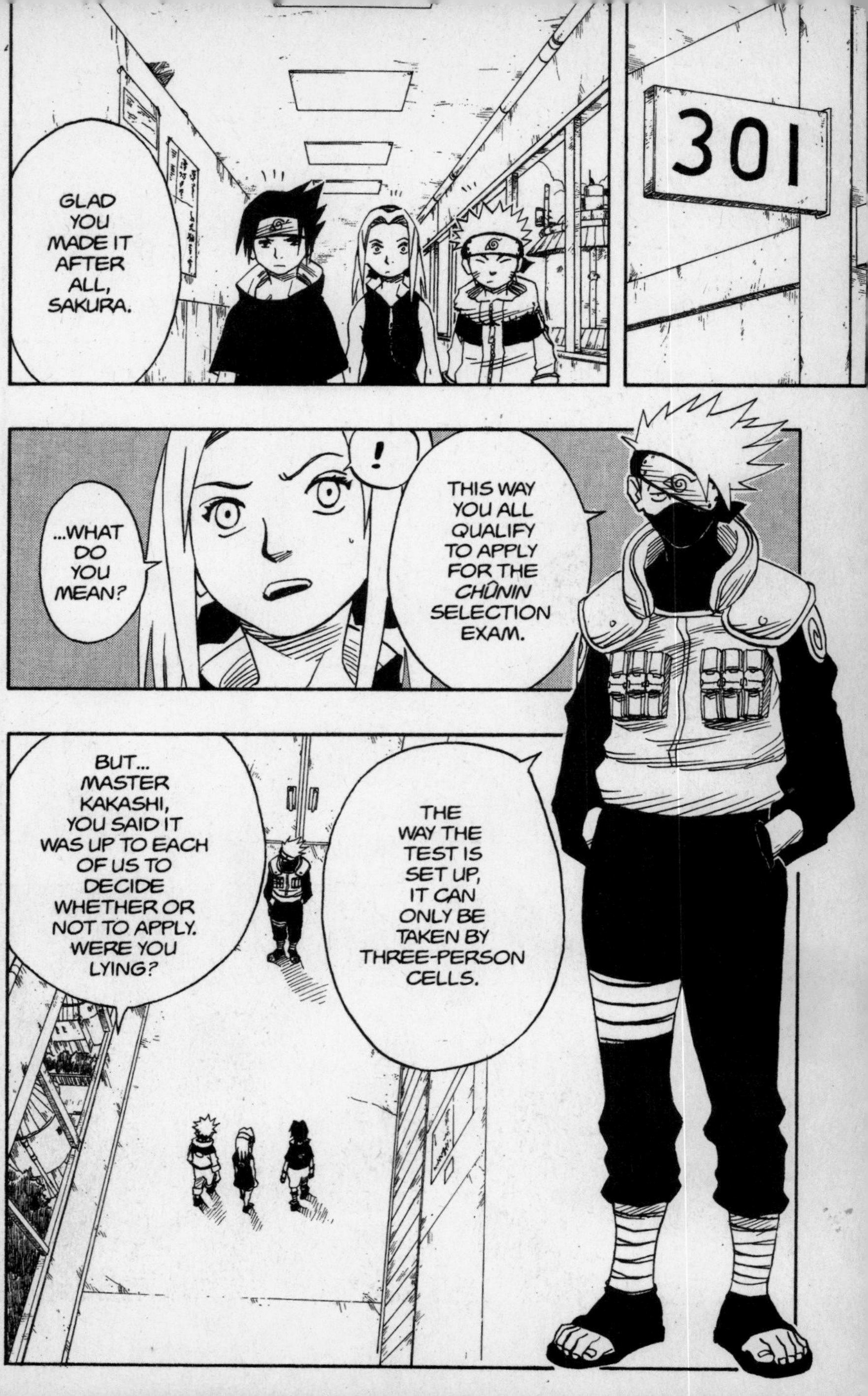
301
GLAD YOU MADE IT AFTER ALL, SAKURA.
THIS WAY YOU ALL QUALIFY TO APPLY FOR THE *CHŪNIN* SELECTION EXAM.
!
...WHAT DO YOU MEAN?
THE WAY THE TEST IS SET UP, IT CAN ONLY BE TAKEN BY THREE-PERSON CELLS.
BUT... MASTER KAKASHI, YOU SAID IT WAS UP TO EACH OF US TO DECIDE WHETHER OR NOT TO APPLY. WERE YOU LYING?

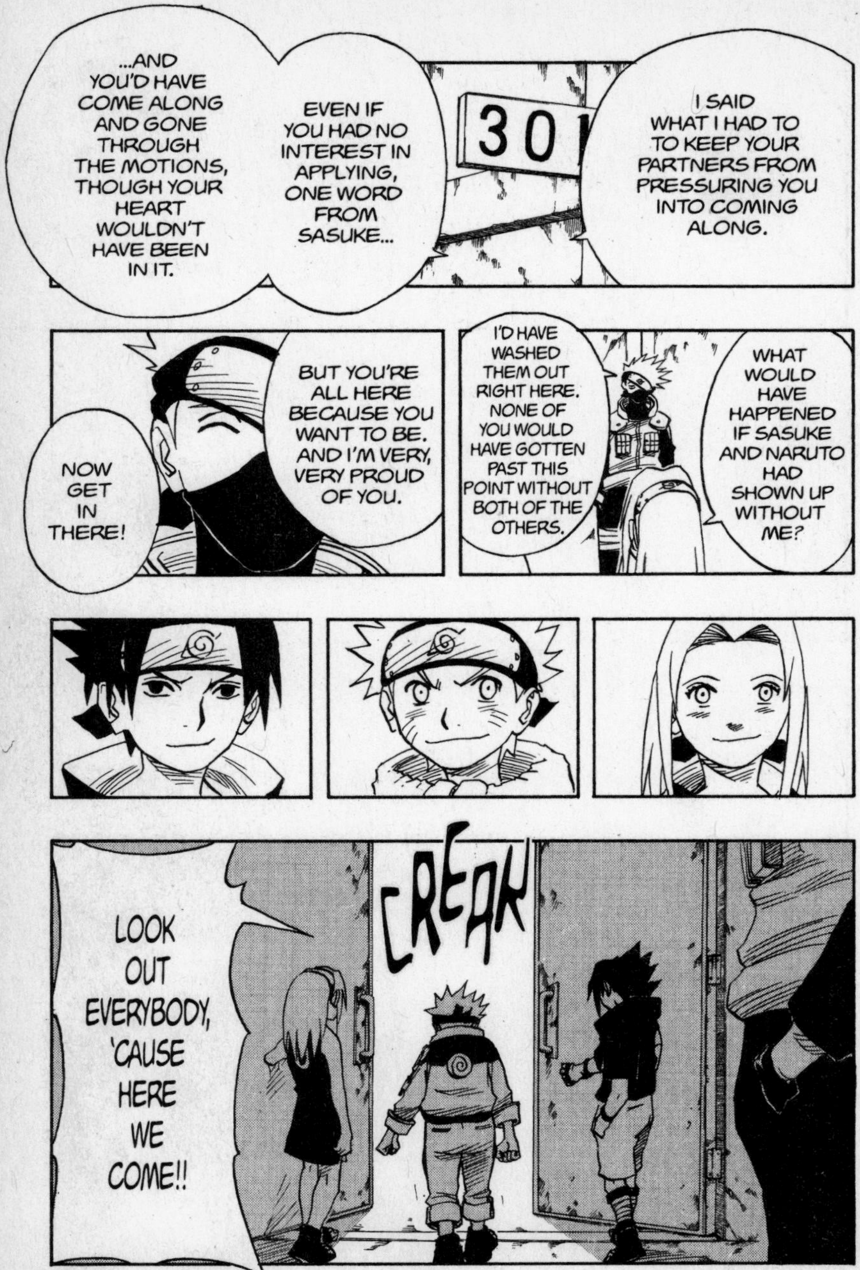
I SAID WHAT I HAD TO TO KEEP YOUR PARTNERS FROM PRESSURING YOU INTO COMING ALONG.
301
EVEN IF YOU HAD NO INTEREST IN APPLYING, ONE WORD FROM SASUKE...
...AND YOU'D HAVE COME ALONG AND GONE THROUGH THE MOTIONS, THOUGH YOUR HEART WOULDN'T HAVE BEEN IN IT.
WHAT WOULD HAVE HAPPENED IF SASUKE AND NARUTO HAD SHOWN UP WITHOUT ME?
I'D HAVE WASHED THEM OUT RIGHT HERE. NONE OF YOU WOULD HAVE GOTTEN PAST THIS POINT WITHOUT BOTH OF THE OTHERS.
BUT YOU'RE ALL HERE BECAUSE YOU WANT TO BE. AND I'M VERY, VERY PROUD OF YOU.
NOW GET IN THERE!
CREAK
LOOK OUT EVERYBODY, 'CAUSE HERE WE COME!!

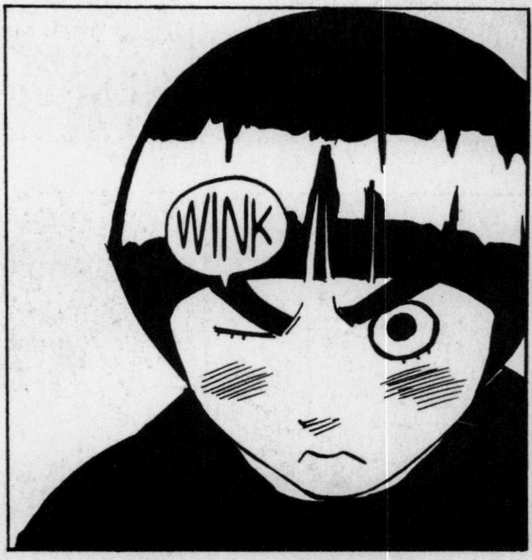
WINK

39: THE CHALLENGERS!!

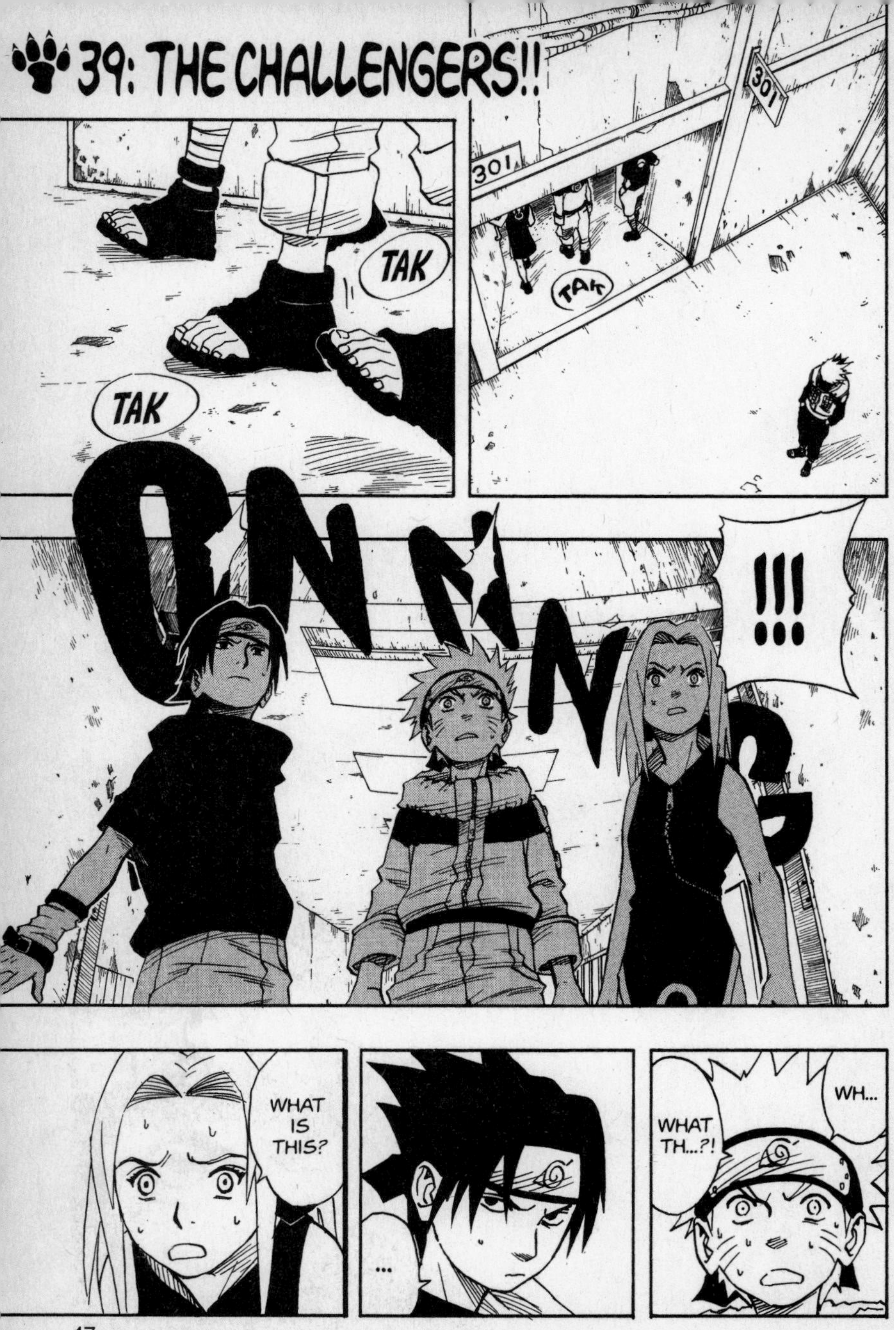
301
301
TAK
TAK
TAK
!!!
WH...
WHAT TH...?!
...
WHAT IS THIS?

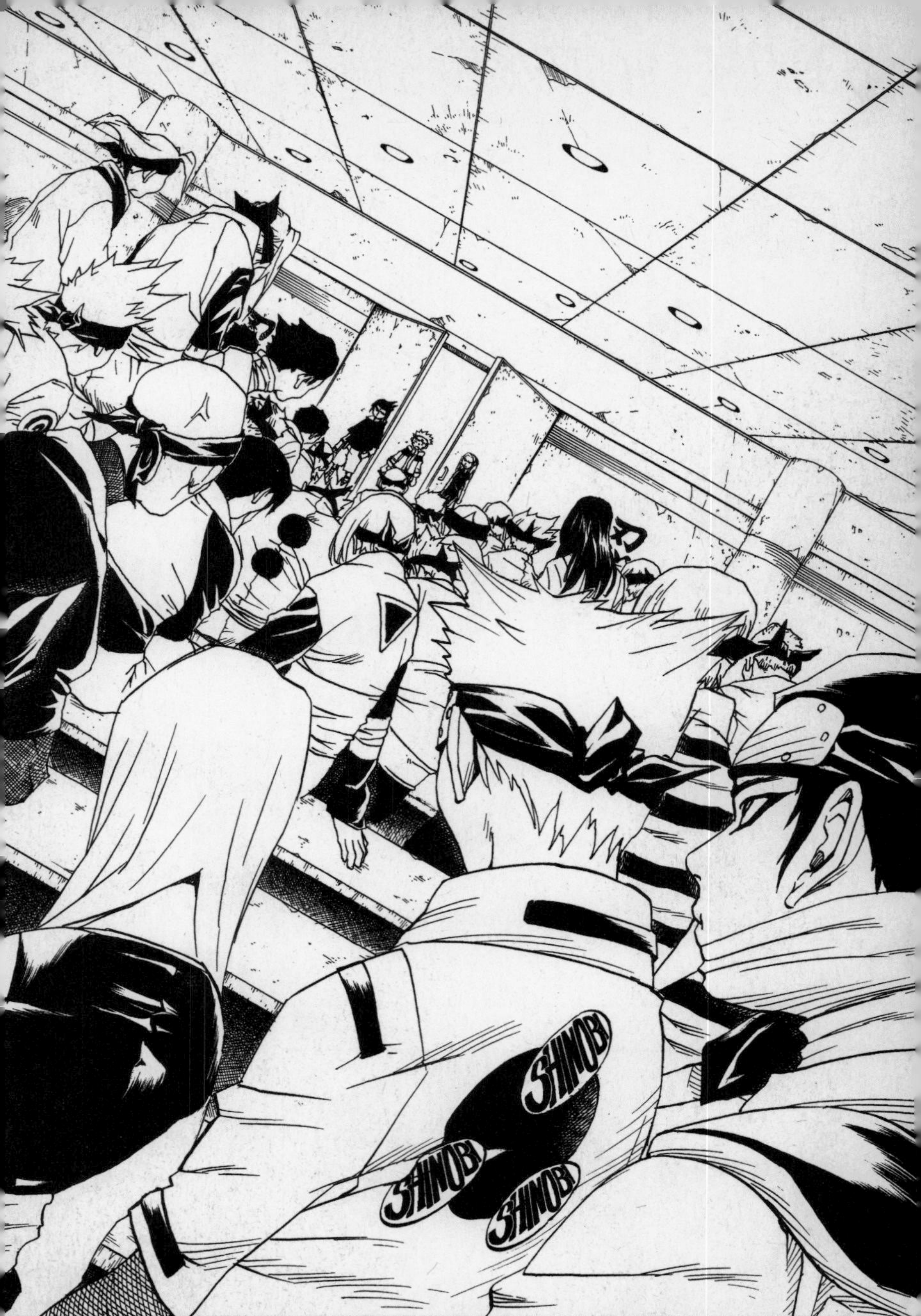
SHINOBI
SHINOBI
SHINOBI

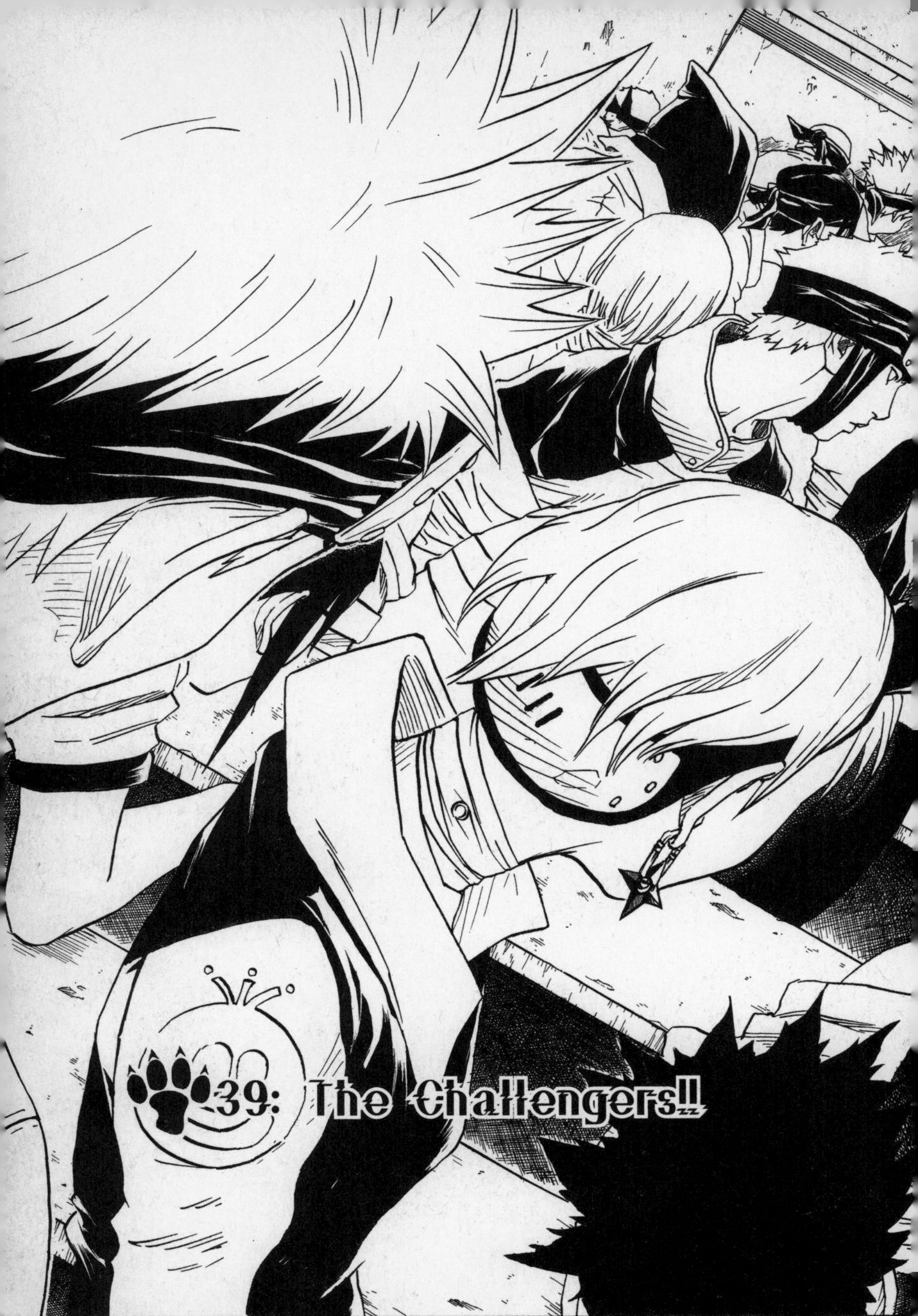
39: The Challengers!!

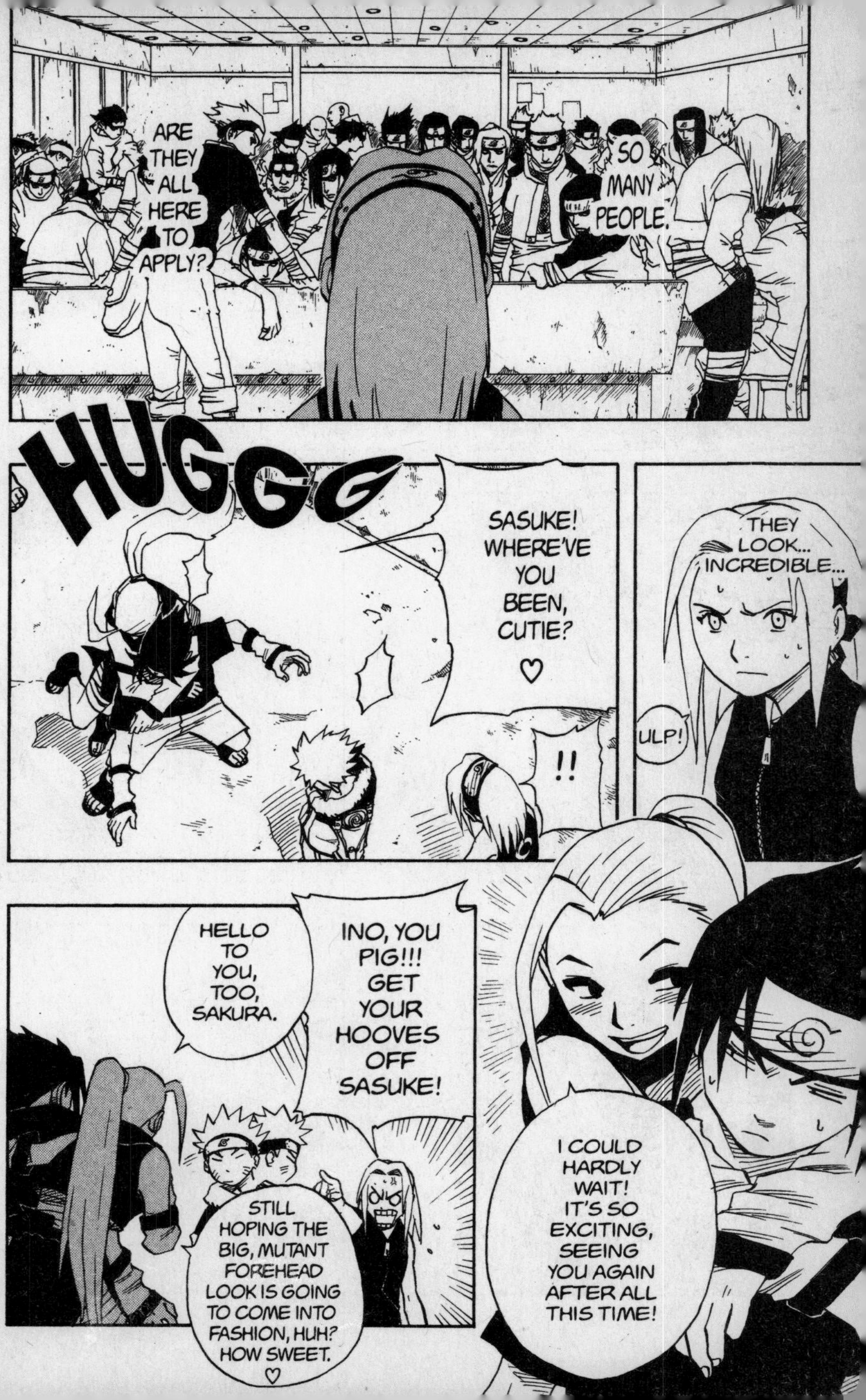

SO MANY PEOPLE.
ARE THEY ALL HERE TO APPLY?
THEY LOOK... INCREDIBLE...
ULP!
HUGGG
SASUKE! WHERE'VE YOU BEEN, CUTIE? ♡
!!
I COULD HARDLY WAIT! IT'S SO EXCITING, SEEING YOU AGAIN AFTER ALL THIS TIME!
INO, YOU PIG!!! GET YOUR HOOVES OFF SASUKE!
HELLO TO YOU, TOO, SAKURA.
STILL HOPING THE BIG, MUTANT FOREHEAD LOOK IS GOING TO COME INTO FASHION, HUH? HOW SWEET. ♡

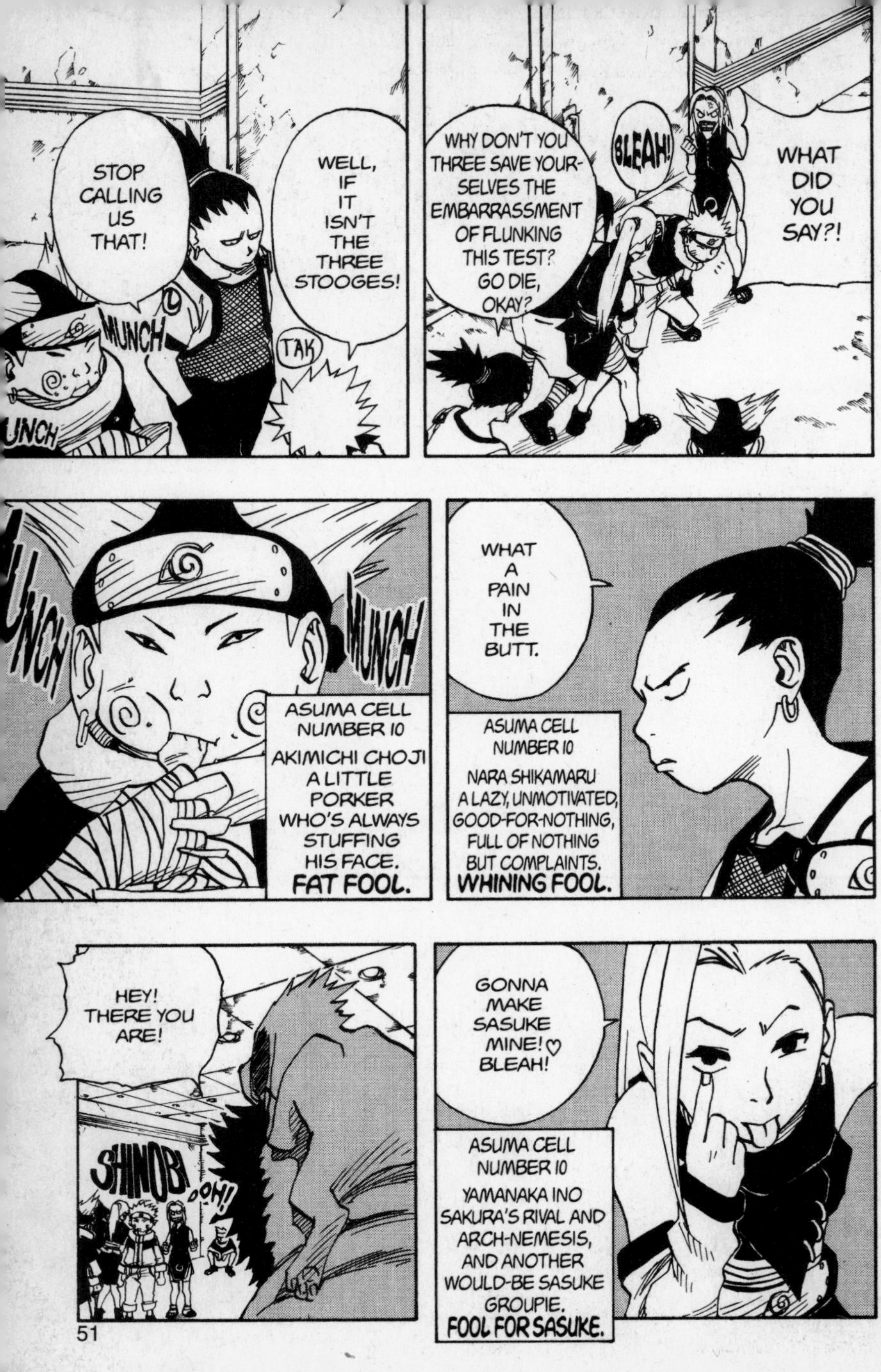
WHY DON'T YOU THREE SAVE YOURSELVES THE EMBARRASSMENT OF FLUNKING THIS TEST? GO DIE, OKAY?
BLEAH!
WHAT DID YOU SAY?!
WELL, IF IT ISN'T THE THREE STOOGES!
TAK
STOP CALLING US THAT!
MUNCH
UNCH
WHAT A PAIN IN THE BUTT.
ASUMA CELL NUMBER 10
NARA SHIKAMARU A LAZY, UNMOTIVATED, GOOD-FOR-NOTHING, FULL OF NOTHING BUT COMPLAINTS. WHINING FOOL.
MUNCH
UNCH
ASUMA CELL NUMBER 10
AKIMICHI CHOJI A LITTLE PORKER WHO'S ALWAYS STUFFING HIS FACE. FAT FOOL.
GONNA MAKE SASUKE MINE! ♡ BLEAH!
ASUMA CELL NUMBER 10
YAMANAKA INO SAKURA'S RIVAL AND ARCH-NEMESIS, AND ANOTHER WOULD-BE SASUKE GROUPIE. FOOL FOR SASUKE.
HEY! THERE YOU ARE!
SHINOBI
OOH!

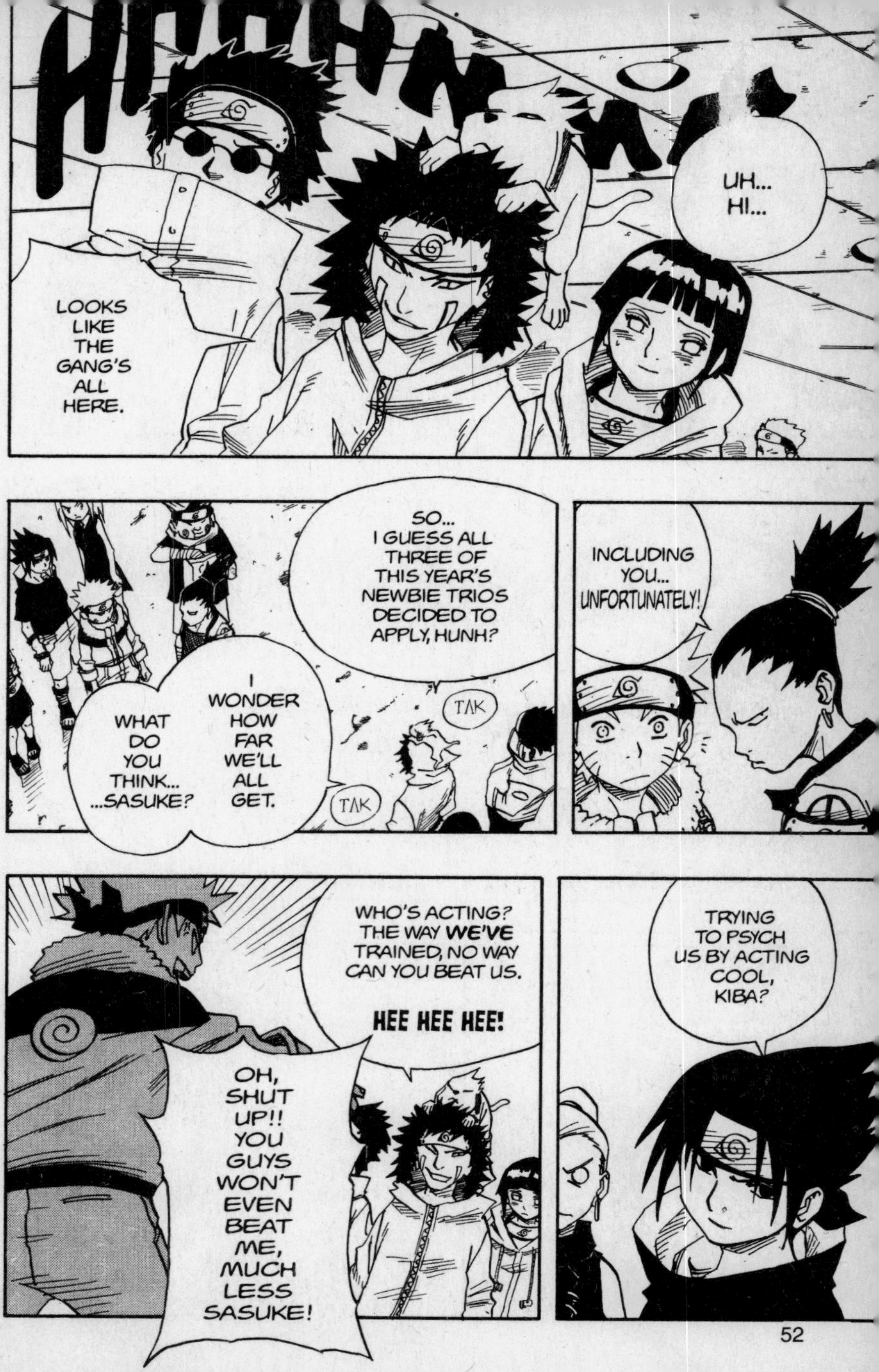
UH... HI...
LOOKS LIKE THE GANG'S ALL HERE.
INCLUDING YOU... UNFORTUNATELY!
SO... I GUESS ALL THREE OF THIS YEAR'S NEWBIE TRIOS DECIDED TO APPLY, HUNH?
TAK
TAK
I WONDER HOW FAR WE'LL ALL GET.
WHAT DO YOU THINK... ...SASUKE?
TRYING TO PSYCH US BY ACTING COOL, KIBA?
WHO'S ACTING? THE WAY WE'VE TRAINED, NO WAY CAN YOU BEAT US.
HEE HEE HEE!
OH, SHUT UP!! YOU GUYS WON'T EVEN BEAT ME, MUCH LESS SASUKE!

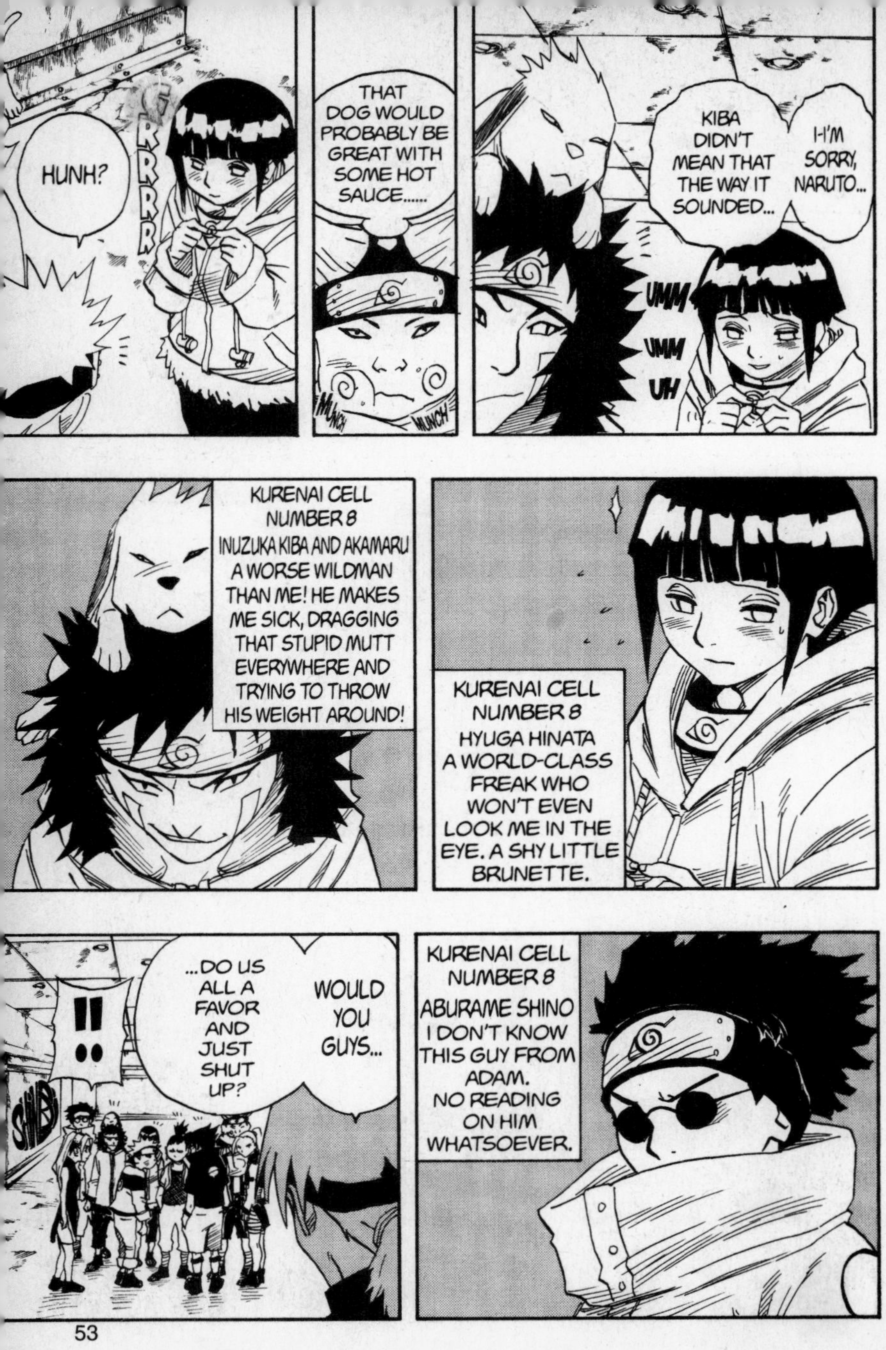
I-I'M SORRY, NARUTO...
KIBA DIDN'T MEAN THAT THE WAY IT SOUNDED...
UMM UMM UH
THAT DOG WOULD PROBABLY BE GREAT WITH SOME HOT SAUCE......
MUNCH
MUNCH
HUNH?
RRRR
KURENAI CELL NUMBER 8
HYUGA HINATA
A WORLD-CLASS FREAK WHO WON'T EVEN LOOK ME IN THE EYE. A SHY LITTLE BRUNETTE.
KURENAI CELL NUMBER 8
INUZUKA KIBA AND AKAMARU
A WORSE WILDMAN THAN ME! HE MAKES ME SICK, DRAGGING THAT STUPID MUTT EVERYWHERE AND TRYING TO THROW HIS WEIGHT AROUND!
KURENAI CELL NUMBER 8
ABURAME SHINO
I DON'T KNOW THIS GUY FROM ADAM. NO READING ON HIM WHATSOEVER.
WOULD YOU GUYS...
...DO US ALL A FAVOR AND JUST SHUT UP?
!!

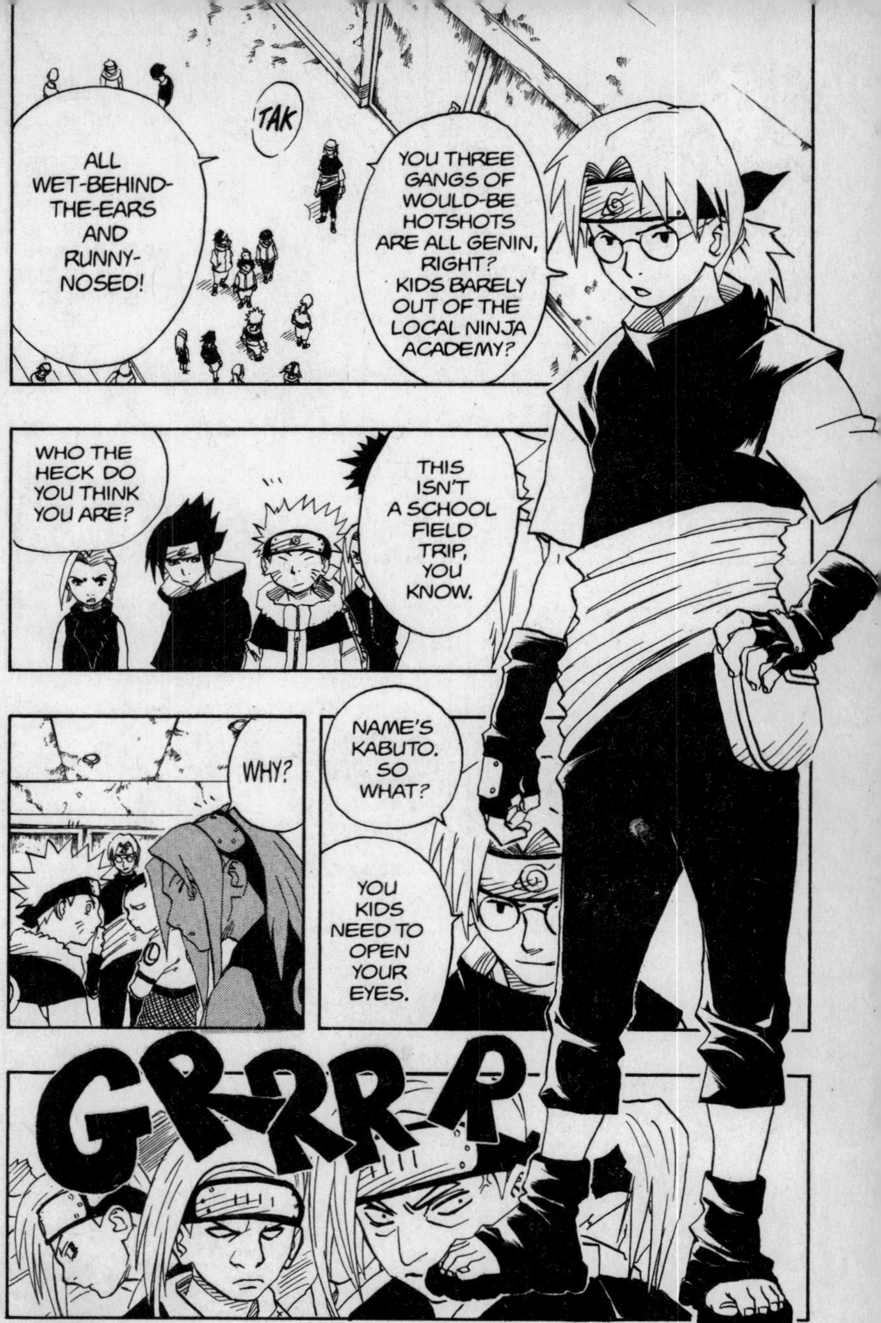
YOU THREE GANGS OF WOULD-BE HOTSHOTS ARE ALL GENIN, RIGHT? KIDS BARELY OUT OF THE LOCAL NINJA ACADEMY?
TAK
ALL WET-BEHIND-THE-EARS AND RUNNY-NOSED!
THIS ISN'T A SCHOOL FIELD TRIP, YOU KNOW.
WHO THE HECK DO YOU THINK YOU ARE?
NAME'S KABUTO. SO WHAT?
YOU KIDS NEED TO OPEN YOUR EYES.
WHY?
GRRRR

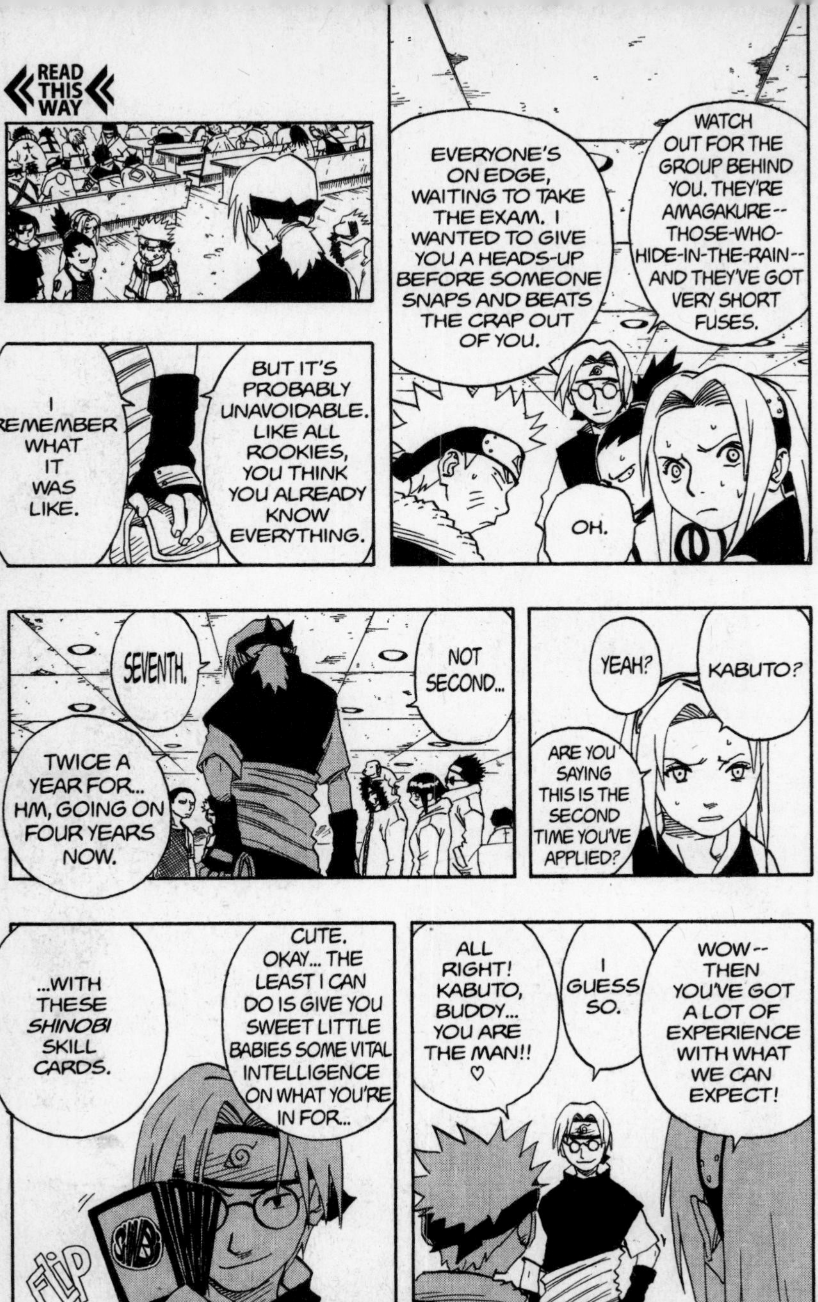
READ THIS WAY
WATCH OUT FOR THE GROUP BEHIND YOU. THEY'RE AMAGAKURE-- THOSE-WHO-HIDE-IN-THE-RAIN-- AND THEY'VE GOT VERY SHORT FUSES.
EVERYONE'S ON EDGE, WAITING TO TAKE THE EXAM. I WANTED TO GIVE YOU A HEADS-UP BEFORE SOMEONE SNAPS AND BEATS THE CRAP OUT OF YOU.
OH.
BUT IT'S PROBABLY UNAVOIDABLE. LIKE ALL ROOKIES, YOU THINK YOU ALREADY KNOW EVERYTHING.
I REMEMBER WHAT IT WAS LIKE.
KABUTO?
YEAH?
ARE YOU SAYING THIS IS THE SECOND TIME YOU'VE APPLIED?
NOT SECOND...
SEVENTH.
TWICE A YEAR FOR... HM, GOING ON FOUR YEARS NOW.
WOW-- THEN YOU'VE GOT A LOT OF EXPERIENCE WITH WHAT WE CAN EXPECT!
I GUESS SO.
ALL RIGHT! KABUTO, BUDDY... YOU ARE THE MAN!! ♡
CUTE. OKAY... THE LEAST I CAN DO IS GIVE YOU SWEET LITTLE BABIES SOME VITAL INTELLIGENCE ON WHAT YOU'RE IN FOR...
...WITH THESE *SHINOBI* SKILL CARDS.
FLIP

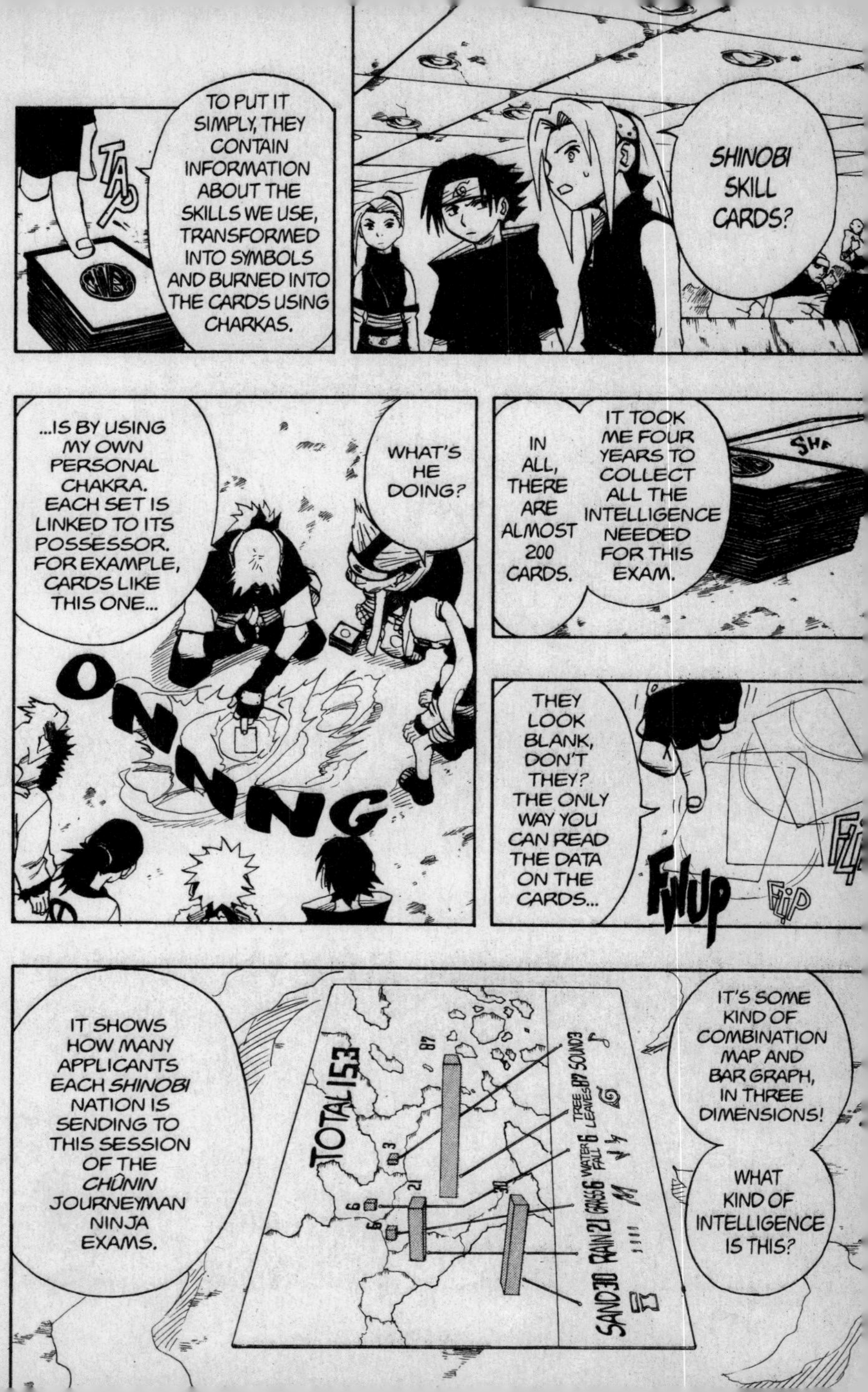
SHINOBI SKILL CARDS?
TO PUT IT SIMPLY, THEY CONTAIN INFORMATION ABOUT THE SKILLS WE USE, TRANSFORMED INTO SYMBOLS AND BURNED INTO THE CARDS USING CHARKAS.
TAP
SHF
IT TOOK ME FOUR YEARS TO COLLECT ALL THE INTELLIGENCE NEEDED FOR THIS EXAM.
IN ALL, THERE ARE ALMOST 200 CARDS.
FLIP
FLIP
FWUP
THEY LOOK BLANK, DON'T THEY? THE ONLY WAY YOU CAN READ THE DATA ON THE CARDS...
WHAT'S HE DOING?
...IS BY USING MY OWN PERSONAL CHAKRA. EACH SET IS LINKED TO ITS POSSESSOR. FOR EXAMPLE, CARDS LIKE THIS ONE...
ONNNNG
IT'S SOME KIND OF COMBINATION MAP AND BAR GRAPH, IN THREE DIMENSIONS!
WHAT KIND OF INTELLIGENCE IS THIS?
TOTAL 153
SAND 30
RAIN 21
GRASS 6
WATER FALL 6
TREE LEAVES 87
SOUND 3
IT SHOWS HOW MANY APPLICANTS EACH SHINOBI NATION IS SENDING TO THIS SESSION OF THE CHÛNIN JOURNEYMAN NINJA EXAMS.

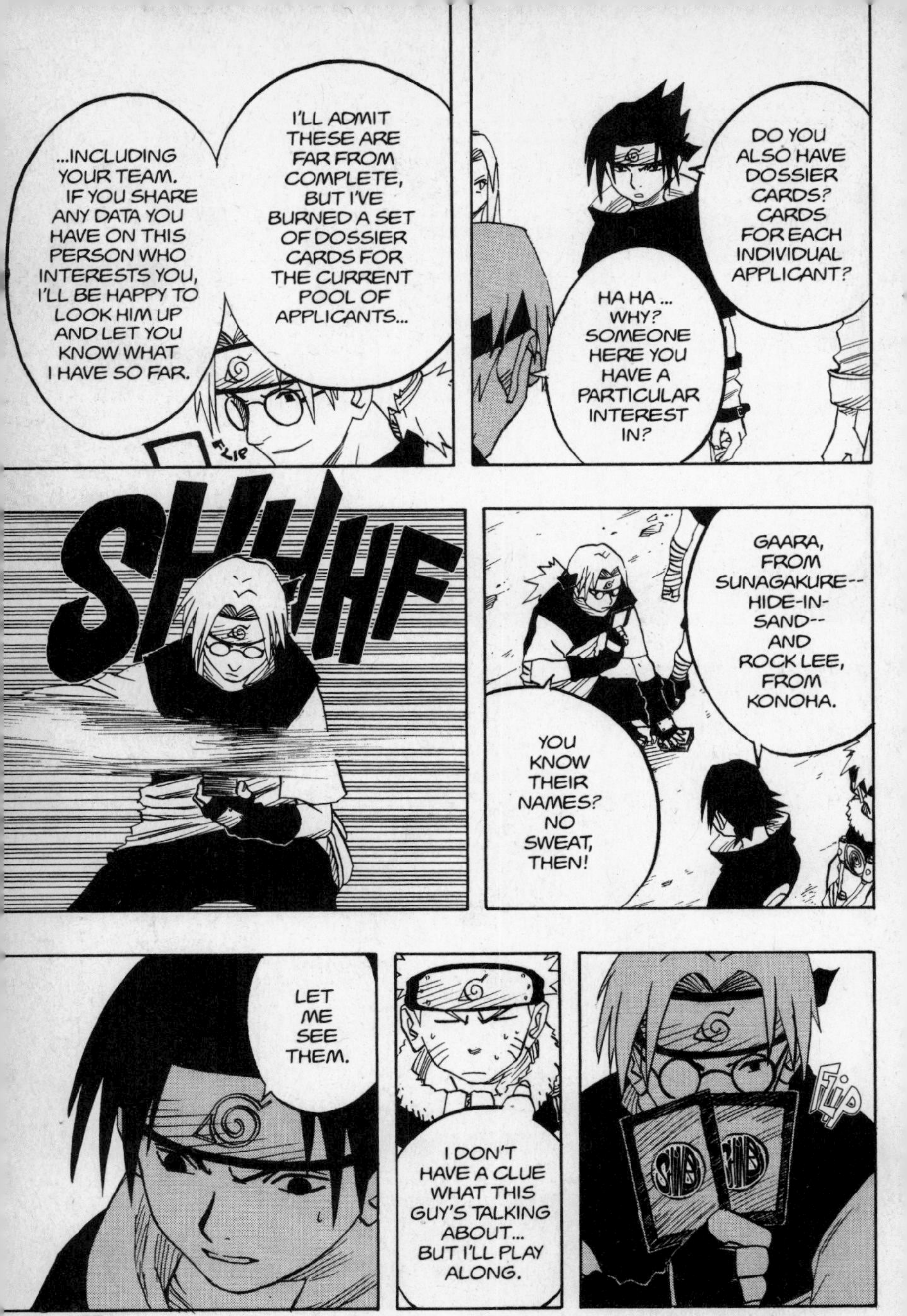
DO YOU ALSO HAVE DOSSIER CARDS? CARDS FOR EACH INDIVIDUAL APPLICANT?
HA HA ... WHY? SOMEONE HERE YOU HAVE A PARTICULAR INTEREST IN?
I'LL ADMIT THESE ARE FAR FROM COMPLETE, BUT I'VE BURNED A SET OF DOSSIER CARDS FOR THE CURRENT POOL OF APPLICANTS...
...INCLUDING YOUR TEAM. IF YOU SHARE ANY DATA YOU HAVE ON THIS PERSON WHO INTERESTS YOU, I'LL BE HAPPY TO LOOK HIM UP AND LET YOU KNOW WHAT I HAVE SO FAR.
FLIP
GAARA, FROM SUNAGAKURE--HIDE-IN-SAND--AND ROCK LEE, FROM KONOHA.
YOU KNOW THEIR NAMES? NO SWEAT, THEN!
SHHHF
FLIP
I DON'T HAVE A CLUE WHAT THIS GUY'S TALKING ABOUT... BUT I'LL PLAY ALONG.
LET ME SEE THEM.

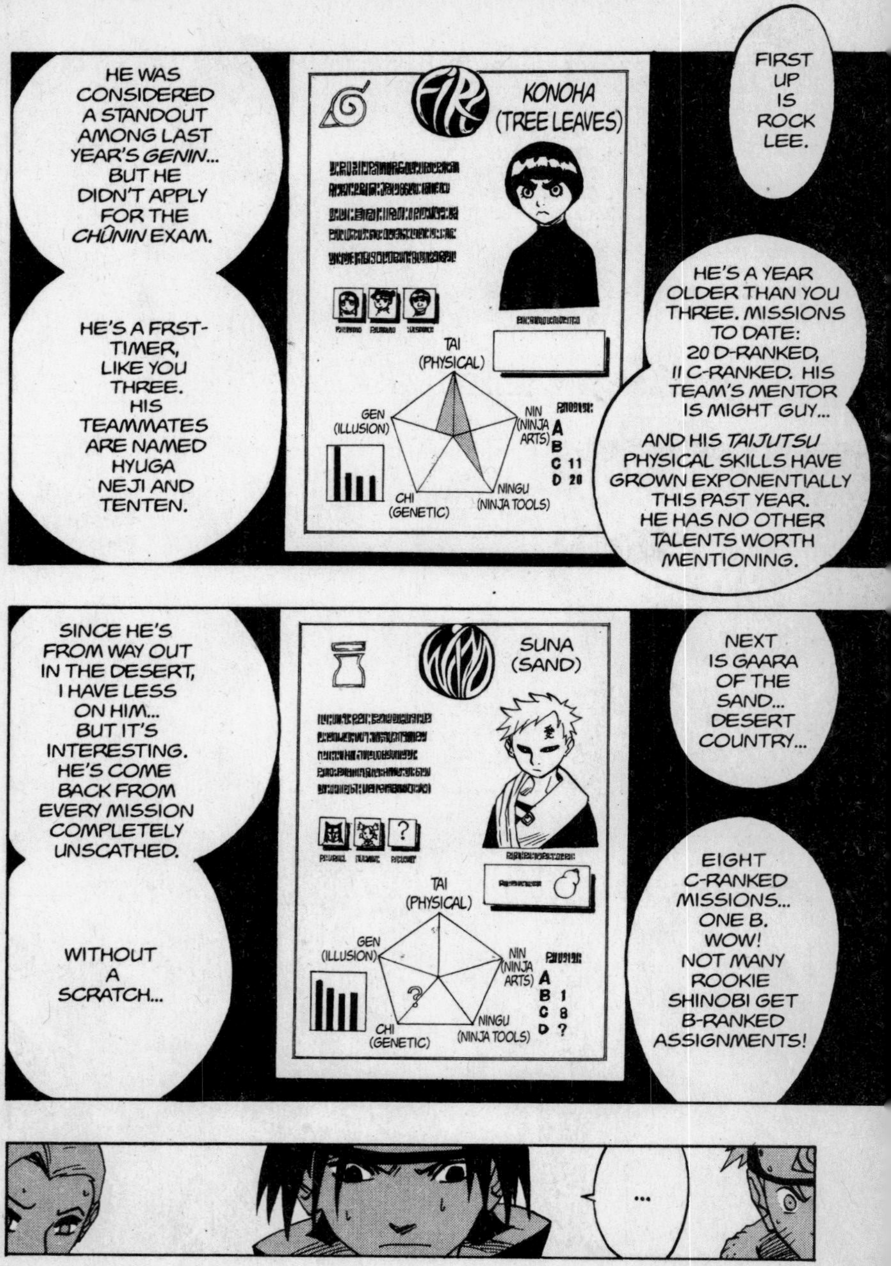

FIRST UP IS ROCK LEE.
KONOHA (TREE LEAVES)
TAI (PHYSICAL)
NIN (NINJA ARTS)
NINGU (NINJA TOOLS)
CHI (GENETIC)
GEN (ILLUSION)
A
B
C 11
D 20
HE'S A YEAR OLDER THAN YOU THREE. MISSIONS TO DATE: 20 D-RANKED, 11 C-RANKED. HIS TEAM'S MENTOR IS MIGHT GUY...
AND HIS *TAIJUTSU* PHYSICAL SKILLS HAVE GROWN EXPONENTIALLY THIS PAST YEAR. HE HAS NO OTHER TALENTS WORTH MENTIONING.
HE WAS CONSIDERED A STANDOUT AMONG LAST YEAR'S *GENIN*... BUT HE DIDN'T APPLY FOR THE *CHÛNIN* EXAM.
HE'S A FRST-TIMER, LIKE YOU THREE. HIS TEAMMATES ARE NAMED HYUGA NEJI AND TENTEN.
NEXT IS GAARA OF THE SAND... DESERT COUNTRY...
SUNA (SAND)
TAI (PHYSICAL)
NIN (NINJA ARTS)
NINGU (NINJA TOOLS)
CHI (GENETIC)
GEN (ILLUSION)
?
A
B 1
C 8
D ?
EIGHT C-RANKED MISSIONS... ONE B. WOW! NOT MANY ROOKIE SHINOBI GET B-RANKED ASSIGNMENTS!
SINCE HE'S FROM WAY OUT IN THE DESERT, I HAVE LESS ON HIM... BUT IT'S INTERESTING. HE'S COME BACK FROM EVERY MISSION COMPLETELY UNSCATHED.
WITHOUT A SCRATCH...
...

READ THIS WAY

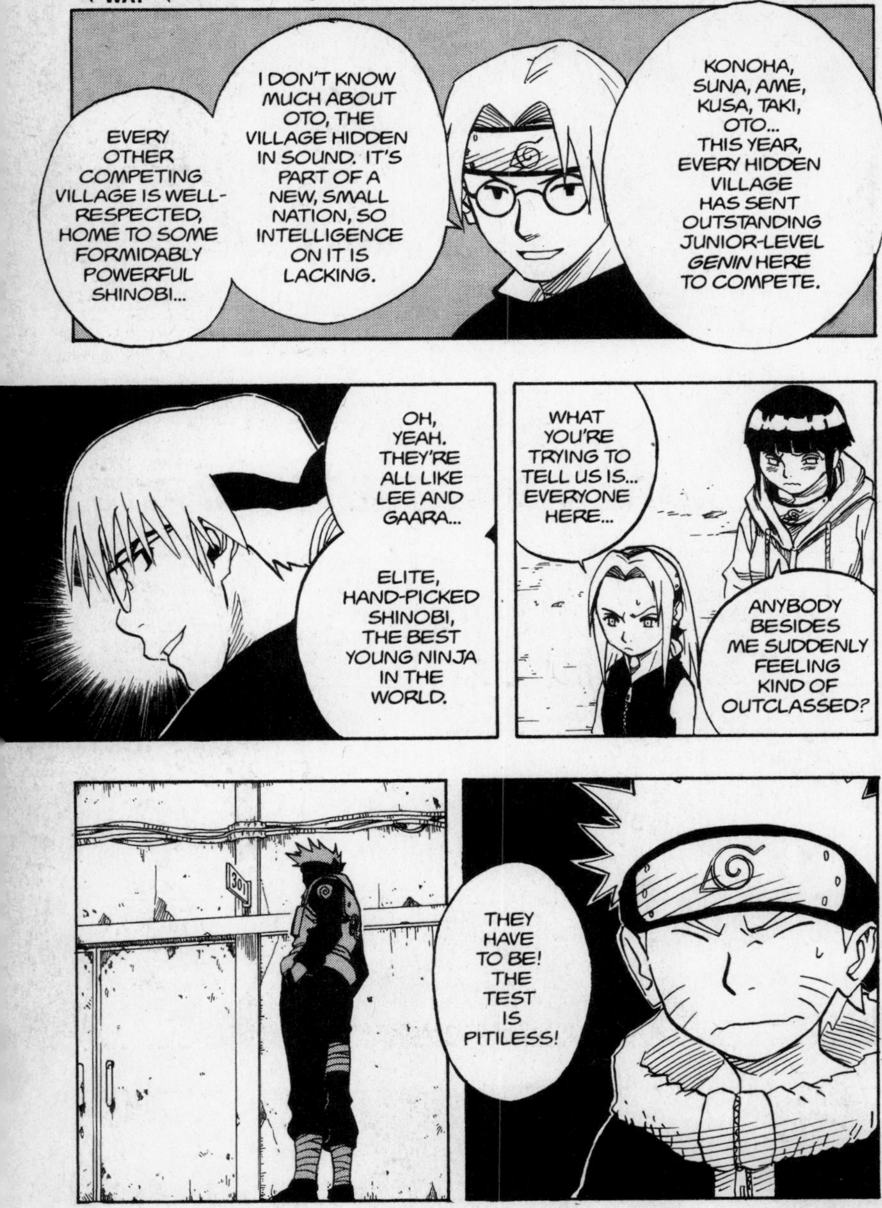
KONOHA, SUNA, AME, KUSA, TAKI, OTO... THIS YEAR, EVERY HIDDEN VILLAGE HAS SENT OUTSTANDING JUNIOR-LEVEL *GENIN* HERE TO COMPETE.
I DON'T KNOW MUCH ABOUT OTO, THE VILLAGE HIDDEN IN SOUND. IT'S PART OF A NEW, SMALL NATION, SO INTELLIGENCE ON IT IS LACKING.
EVERY OTHER COMPETING VILLAGE IS WELL-RESPECTED, HOME TO SOME FORMIDABLY POWERFUL SHINOBI...
WHAT YOU'RE TRYING TO TELL US IS... EVERYONE HERE...
ANYBODY BESIDES ME SUDDENLY FEELING KIND OF OUTCLASSED?
OH, YEAH. THEY'RE ALL LIKE LEE AND GAARA...
ELITE, HAND-PICKED SHINOBI, THE BEST YOUNG NINJA IN THE WORLD.
THEY HAVE TO BE! THE TEST IS PITILESS!
301

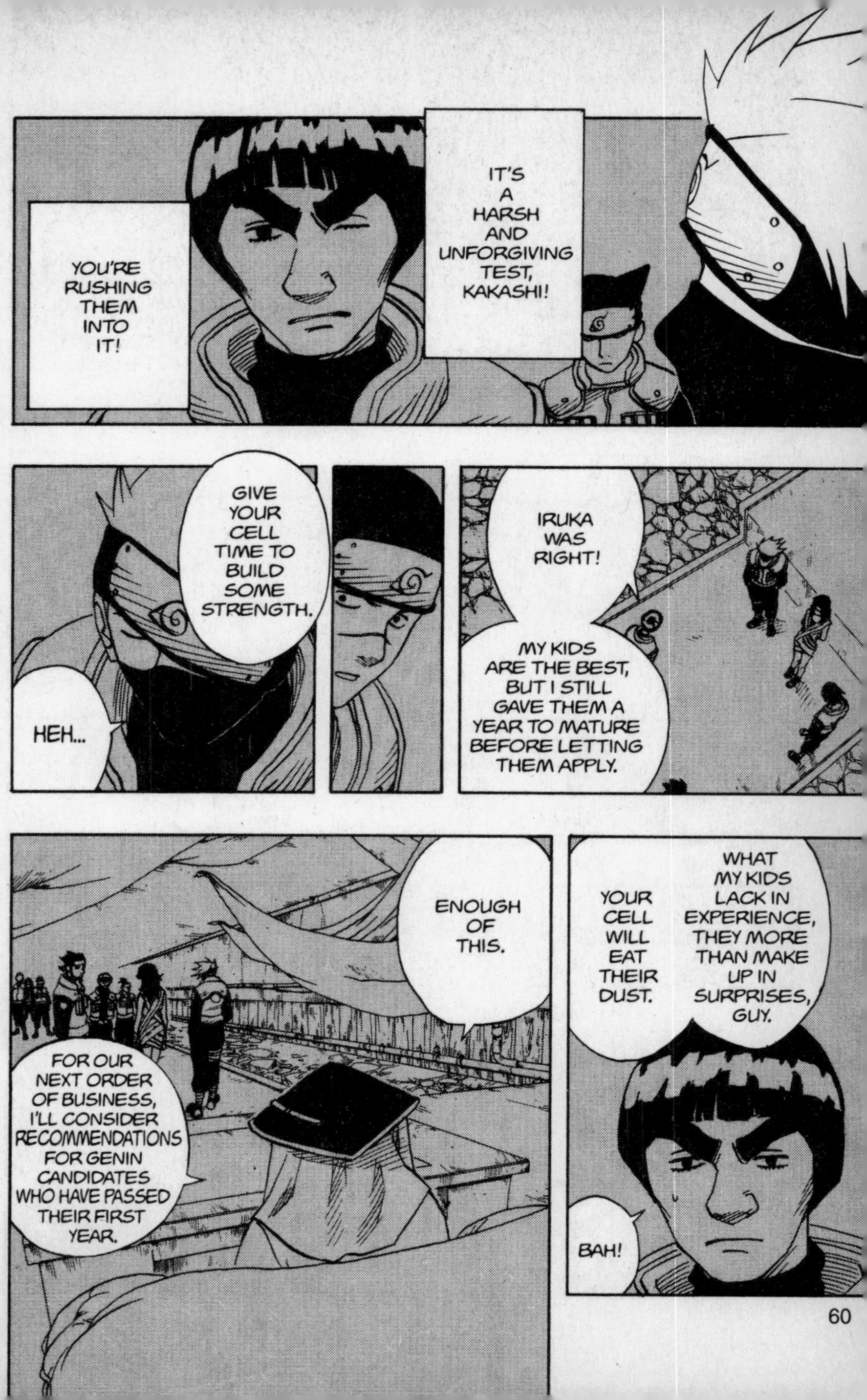
IT'S A HARSH AND UNFORGIVING TEST, KAKASHI!
YOU'RE RUSHING THEM INTO IT!
IRUKA WAS RIGHT!
MY KIDS ARE THE BEST, BUT I STILL GAVE THEM A YEAR TO MATURE BEFORE LETTING THEM APPLY.
GIVE YOUR CELL TIME TO BUILD SOME STRENGTH.
HEH...
WHAT MY KIDS LACK IN EXPERIENCE, THEY MORE THAN MAKE UP IN SURPRISES, GUY.
YOUR CELL WILL EAT THEIR DUST.
BAH!
ENOUGH OF THIS.
FOR OUR NEXT ORDER OF BUSINESS, I'LL CONSIDER RECOMMENDATIONS FOR GENIN CANDIDATES WHO HAVE PASSED THEIR FIRST YEAR.

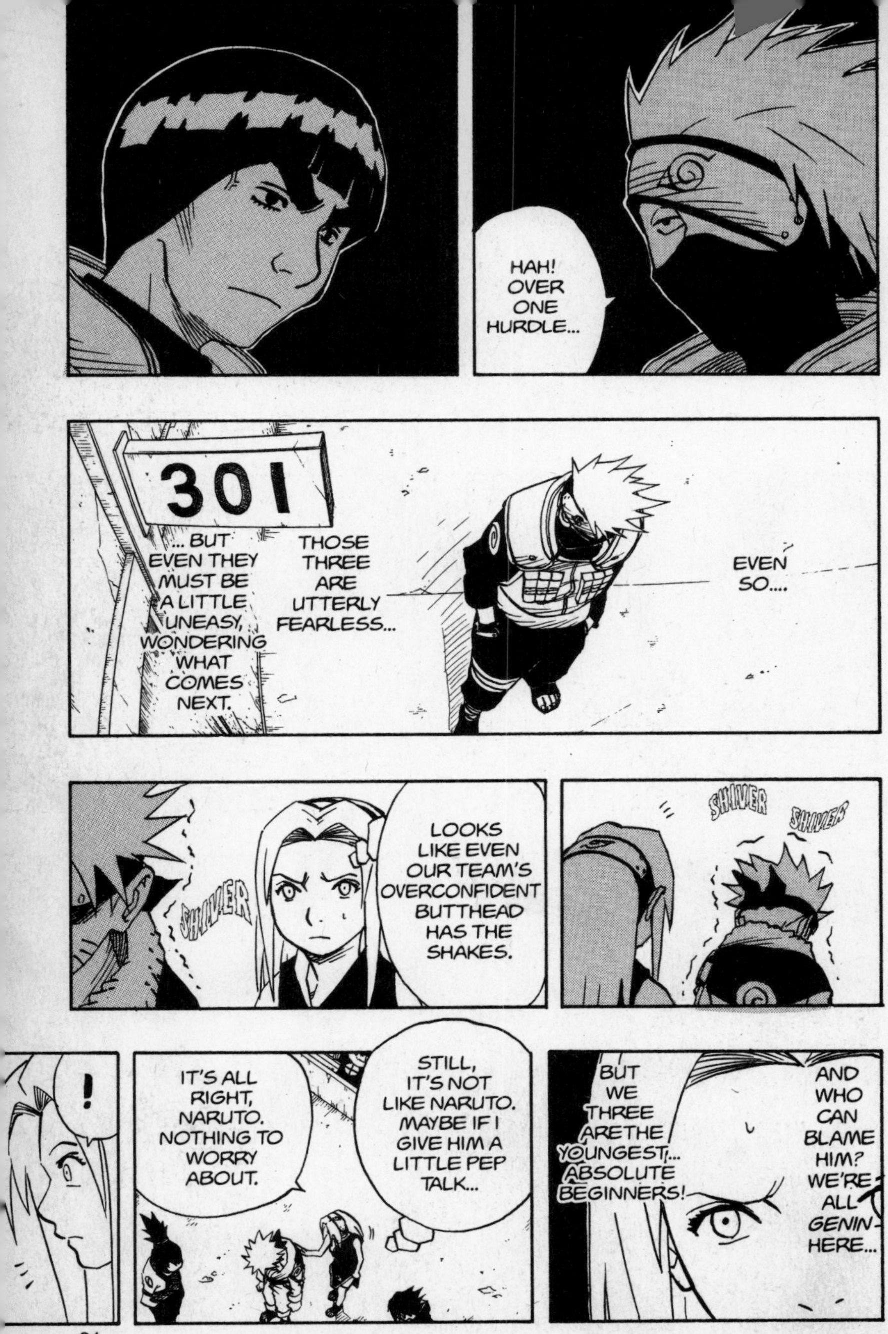
HAH! OVER ONE HURDLE...
EVEN SO....
THOSE THREE ARE UTTERLY FEARLESS...
... BUT EVEN THEY MUST BE A LITTLE UNEASY, WONDERING WHAT COMES NEXT.
301
SHIVER
SHIVER
LOOKS LIKE EVEN OUR TEAM'S OVERCONFIDENT BUTTHEAD HAS THE SHAKES.
SHIVER
AND WHO CAN BLAME HIM? WE'RE ALL GENIN HERE...
BUT WE THREE ARE THE YOUNGEST... ABSOLUTE BEGINNERS!
STILL, IT'S NOT LIKE NARUTO. MAYBE IF I GIVE HIM A LITTLE PEP TALK...
IT'S ALL RIGHT, NARUTO. NOTHING TO WORRY ABOUT.
!

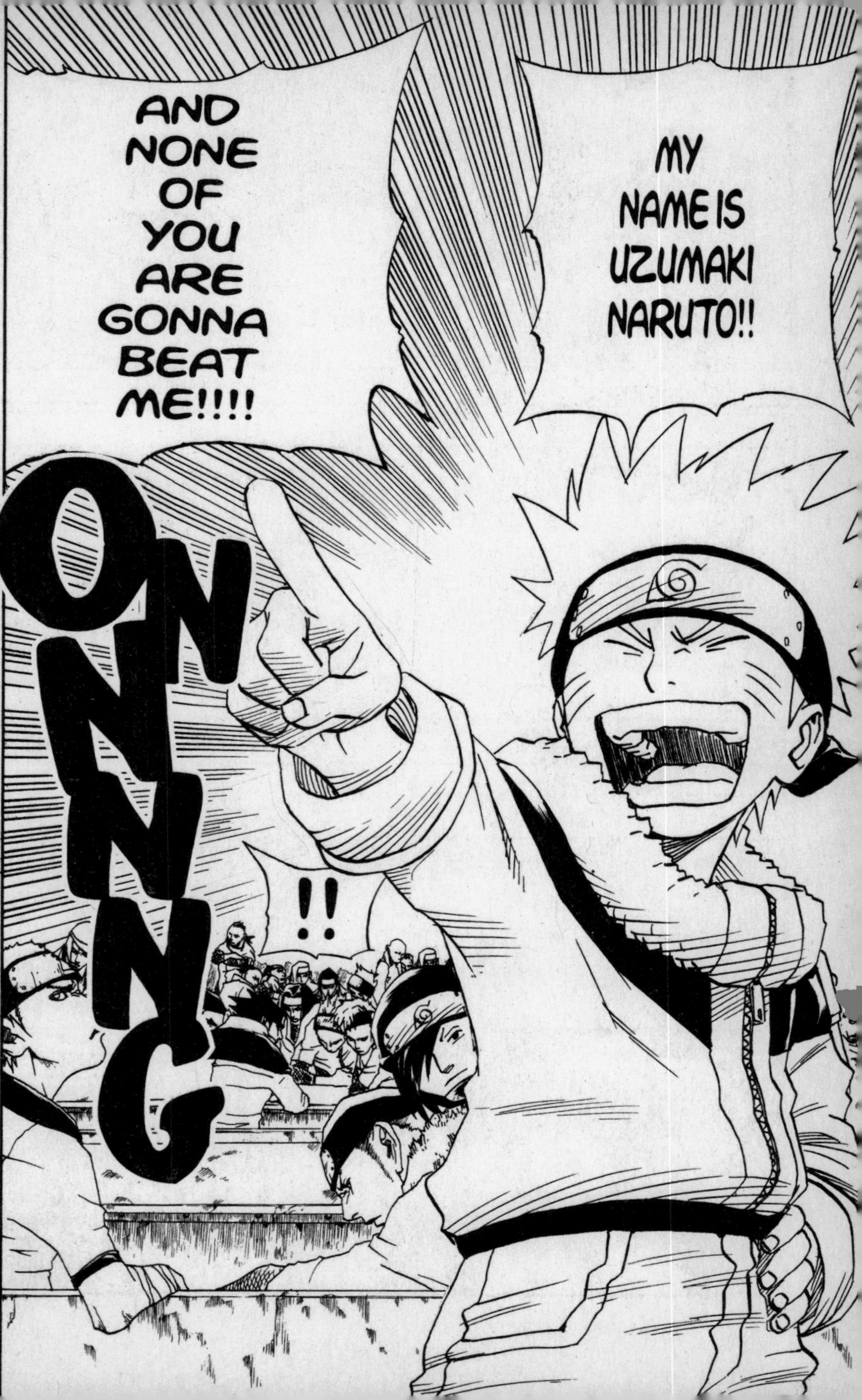
MY NAME IS UZUMAKI NARUTO!!
AND NONE OF YOU ARE GONNA BEAT ME!!!!
ONNNG
!!

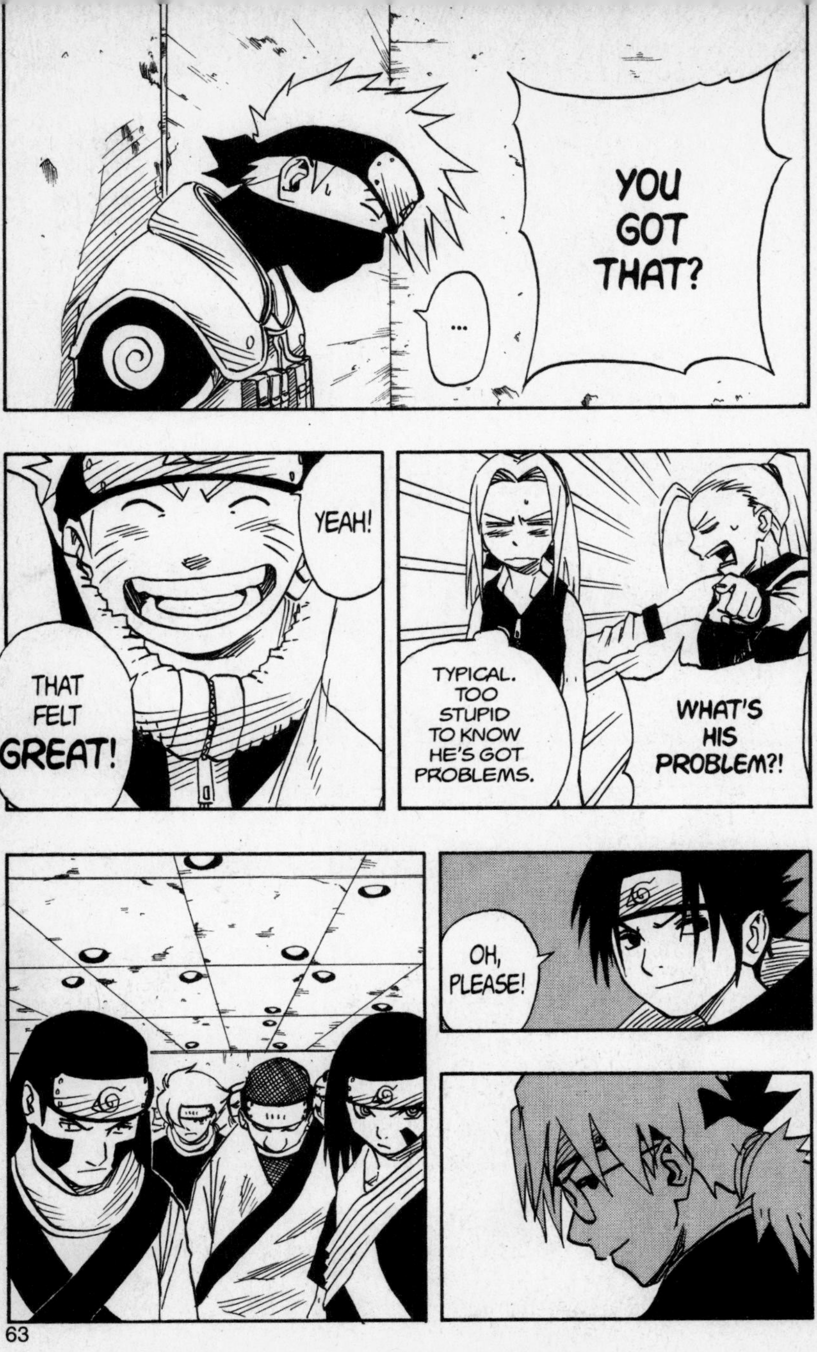
YOU GOT THAT?
...
WHAT'S HIS PROBLEM?!
TYPICAL. TOO STUPID TO KNOW HE'S GOT PROBLEMS.
YEAH!
THAT FELT GREAT!
OH, PLEASE!

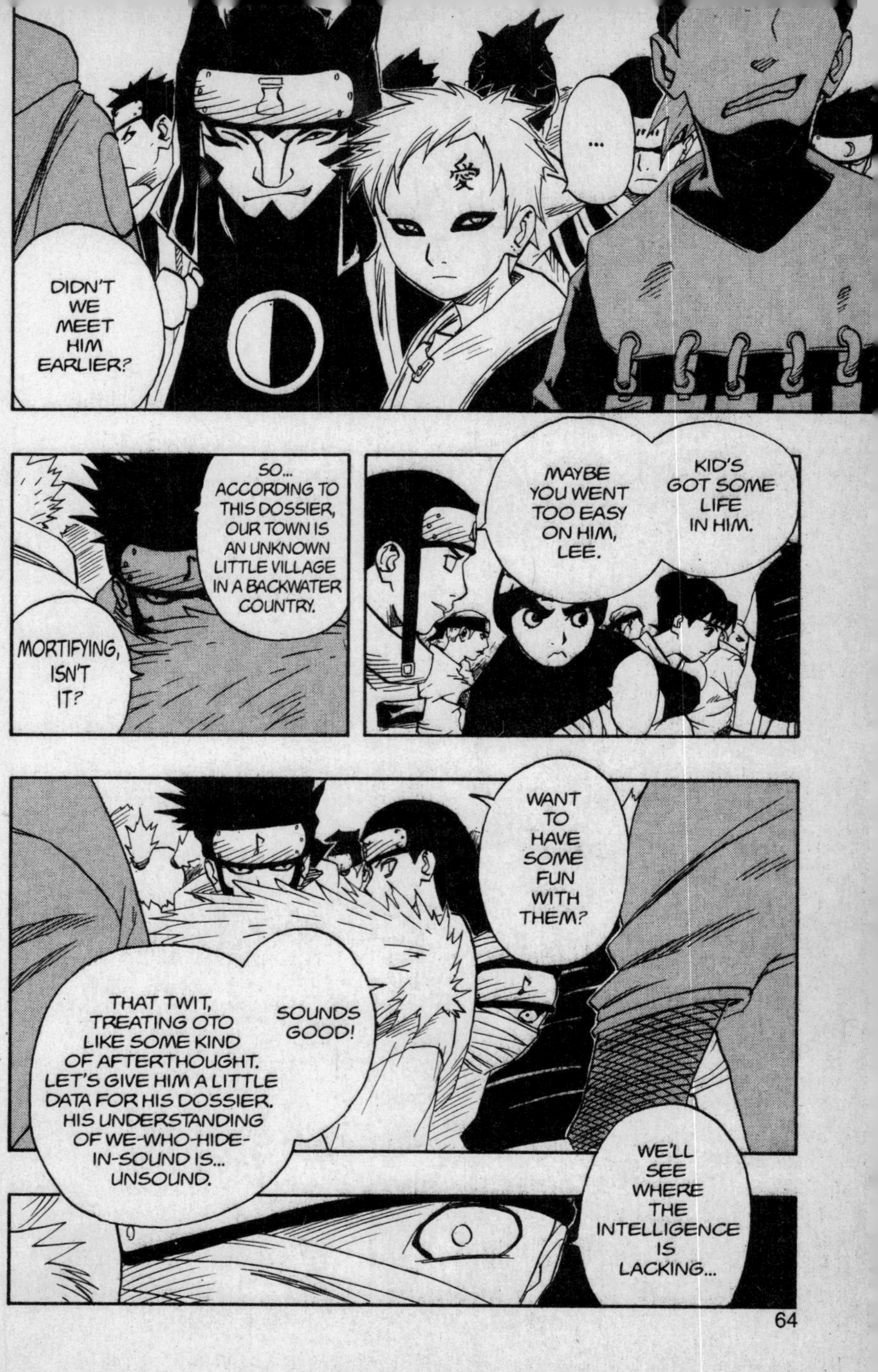
...
DIDN'T WE MEET HIM EARLIER?
KID'S GOT SOME LIFE IN HIM.
MAYBE YOU WENT TOO EASY ON HIM, LEE.
SO... ACCORDING TO THIS DOSSIER, OUR TOWN IS AN UNKNOWN LITTLE VILLAGE IN A BACKWATER COUNTRY.
MORTIFYING, ISN'T IT?
WANT TO HAVE SOME FUN WITH THEM?
SOUNDS GOOD!
THAT TWIT, TREATING OTO LIKE SOME KIND OF AFTERTHOUGHT. LET'S GIVE HIM A LITTLE DATA FOR HIS DOSSIER. HIS UNDERSTANDING OF WE-WHO-HIDE-IN-SOUND IS... UNSOUND.
WE'LL SEE WHERE THE INTELLIGENCE IS LACKING...

40: The First Test

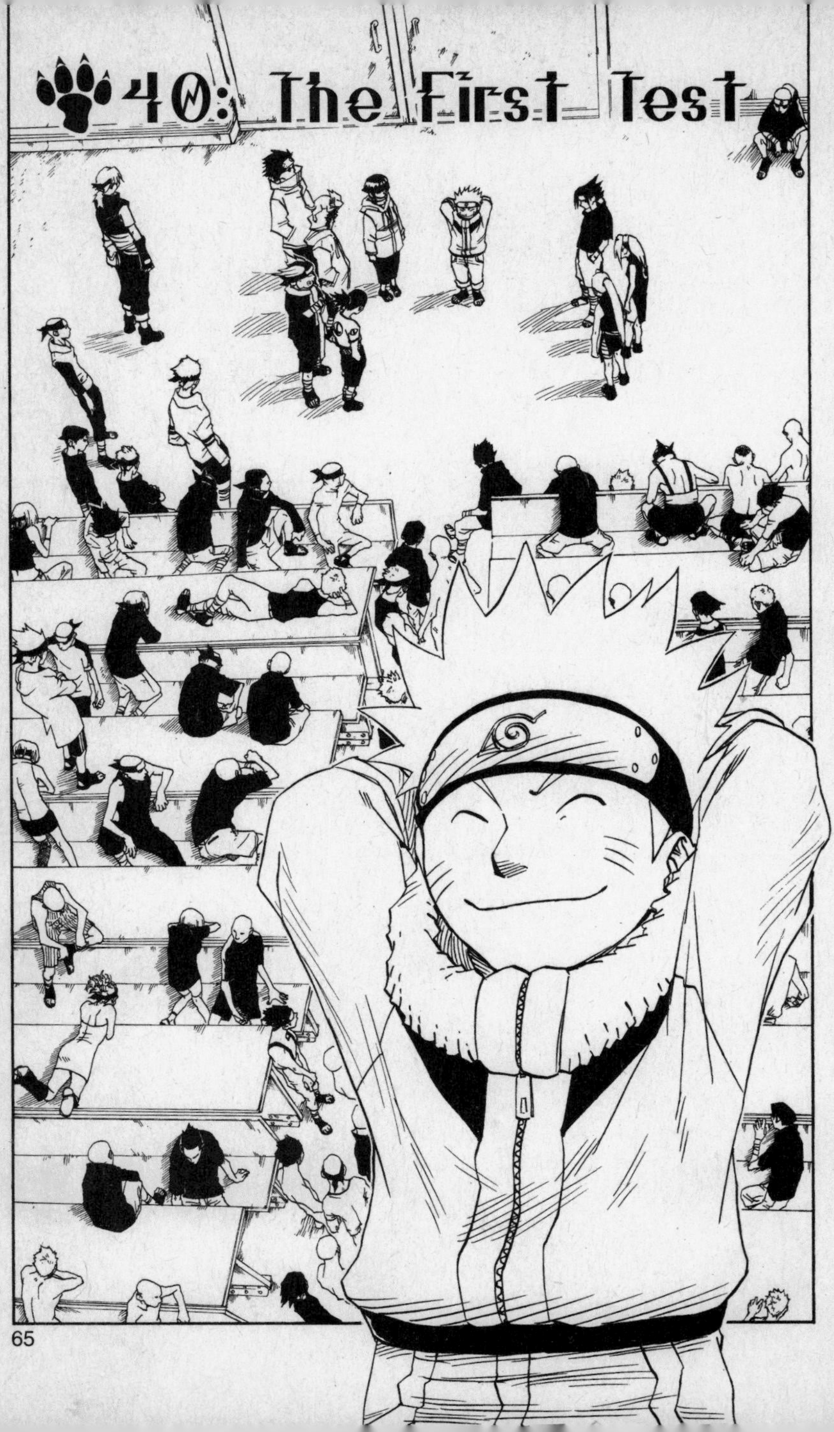

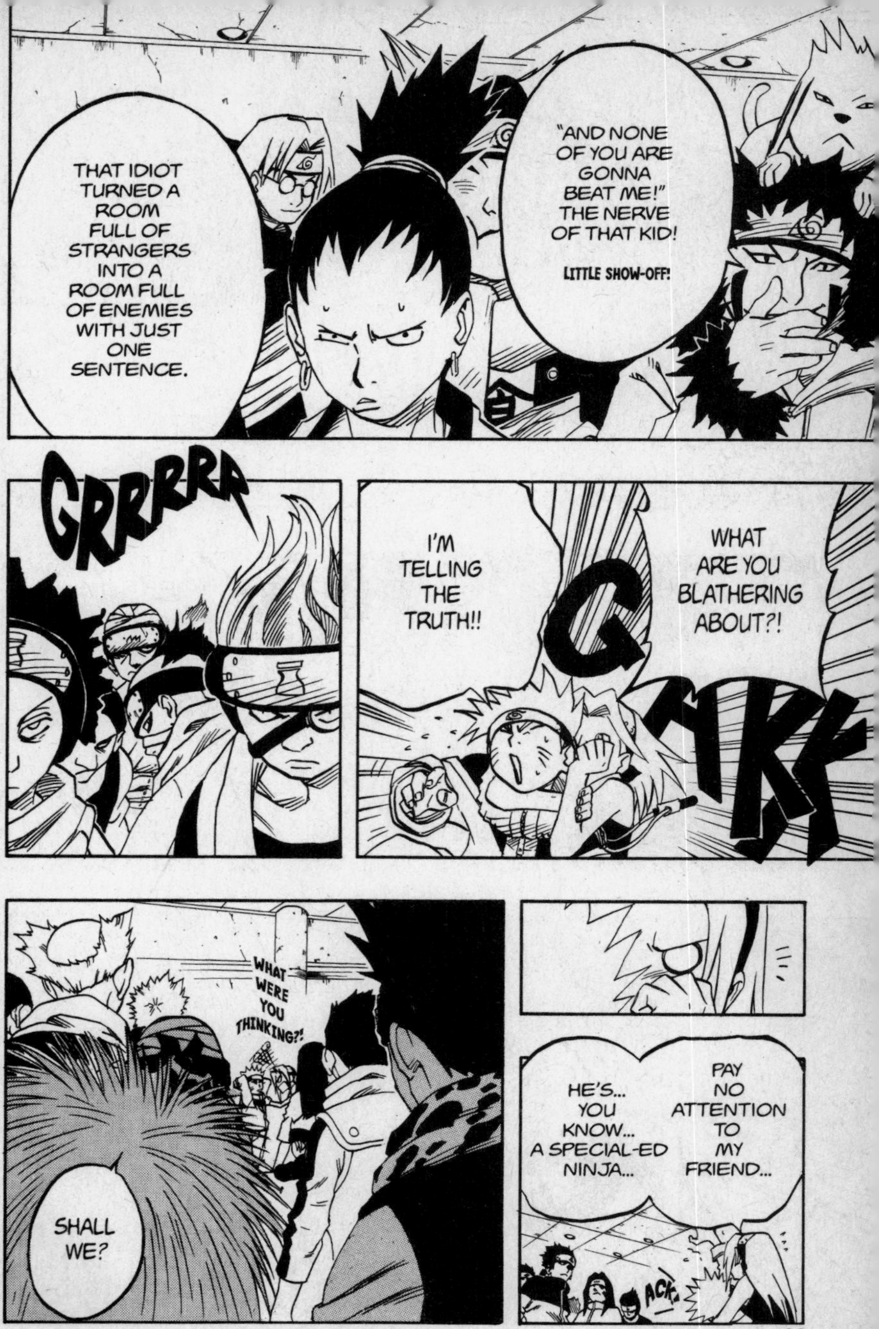
"AND NONE OF YOU ARE GONNA BEAT ME!" THE NERVE OF THAT KID!
LITTLE SHOW-OFF!
THAT IDIOT TURNED A ROOM FULL OF STRANGERS INTO A ROOM FULL OF ENEMIES WITH JUST ONE SENTENCE.
WHAT ARE YOU BLATHERING ABOUT?!
I'M TELLING THE TRUTH!!
GRRRRR
PAY NO ATTENTION TO MY FRIEND...
HE'S... YOU KNOW... A SPECIAL-ED NINJA...
ACK!
WHAT WERE YOU THINKING?!
SHALL WE?

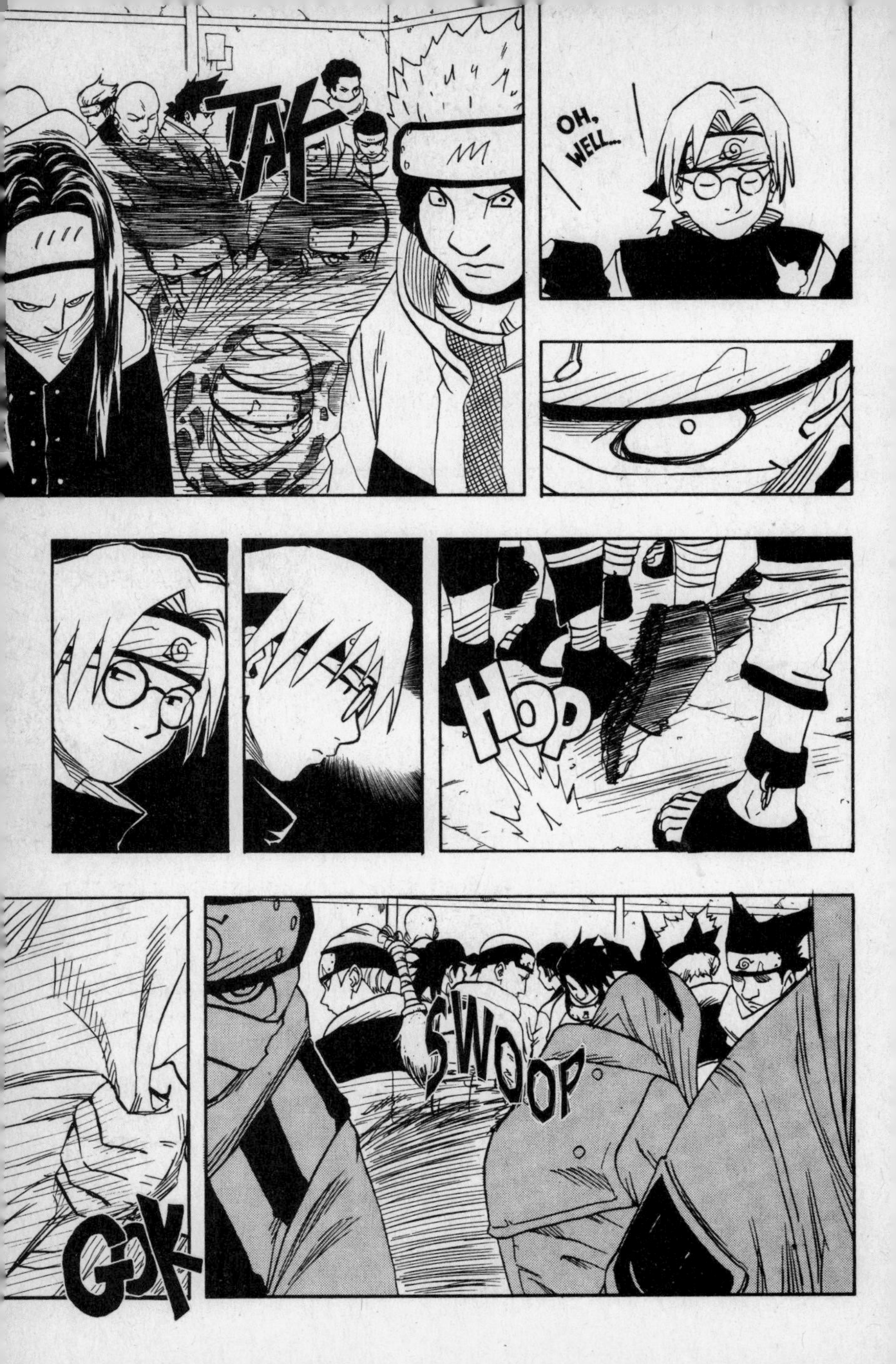
OH, WELL...
TAK
HOP
SWOOP
GOK

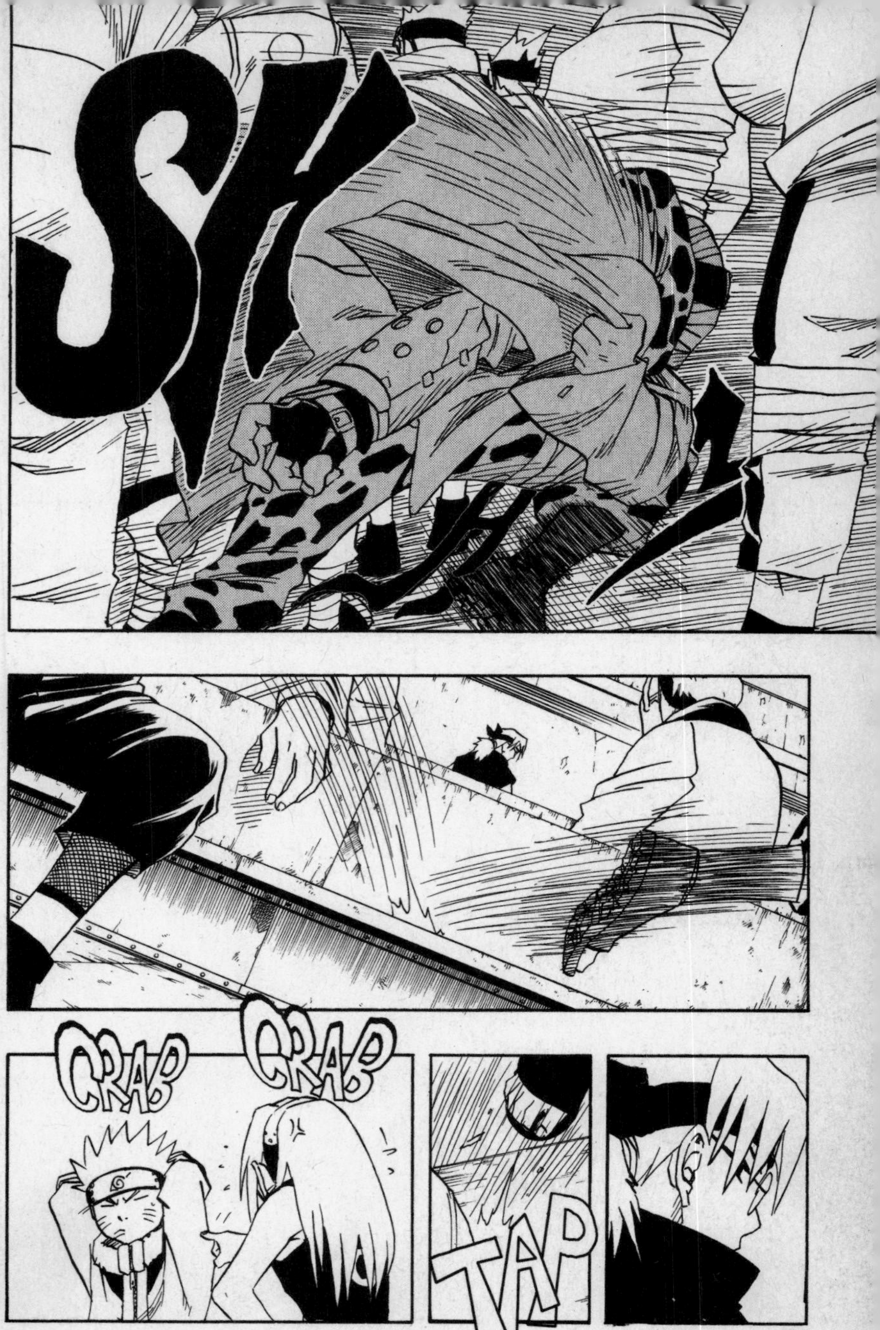
SHH!
TAP
CRAB
CRAB

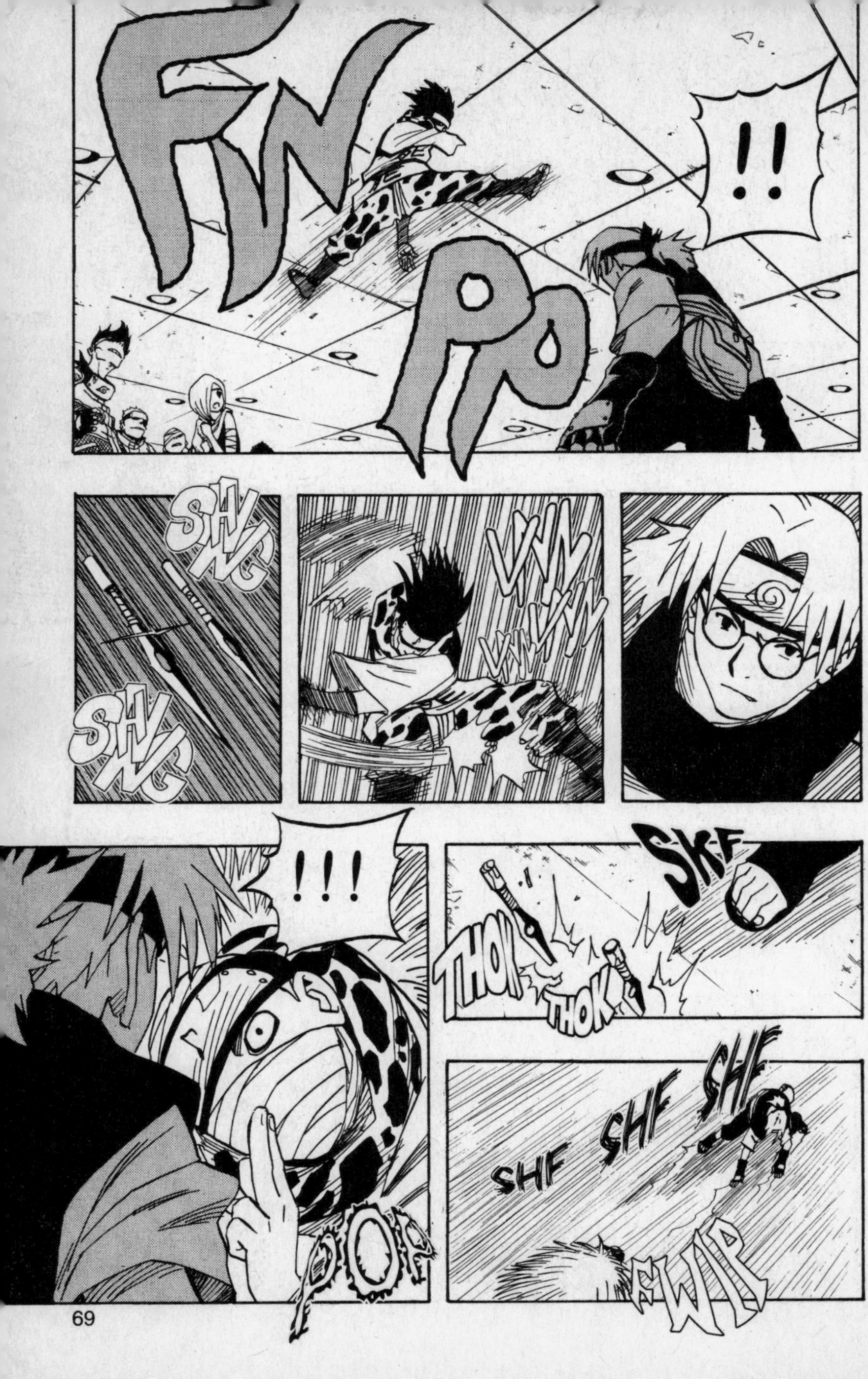
!!
SHF
THOK
THOK
SHF SHF SHF
FWIP
!!!
POOF

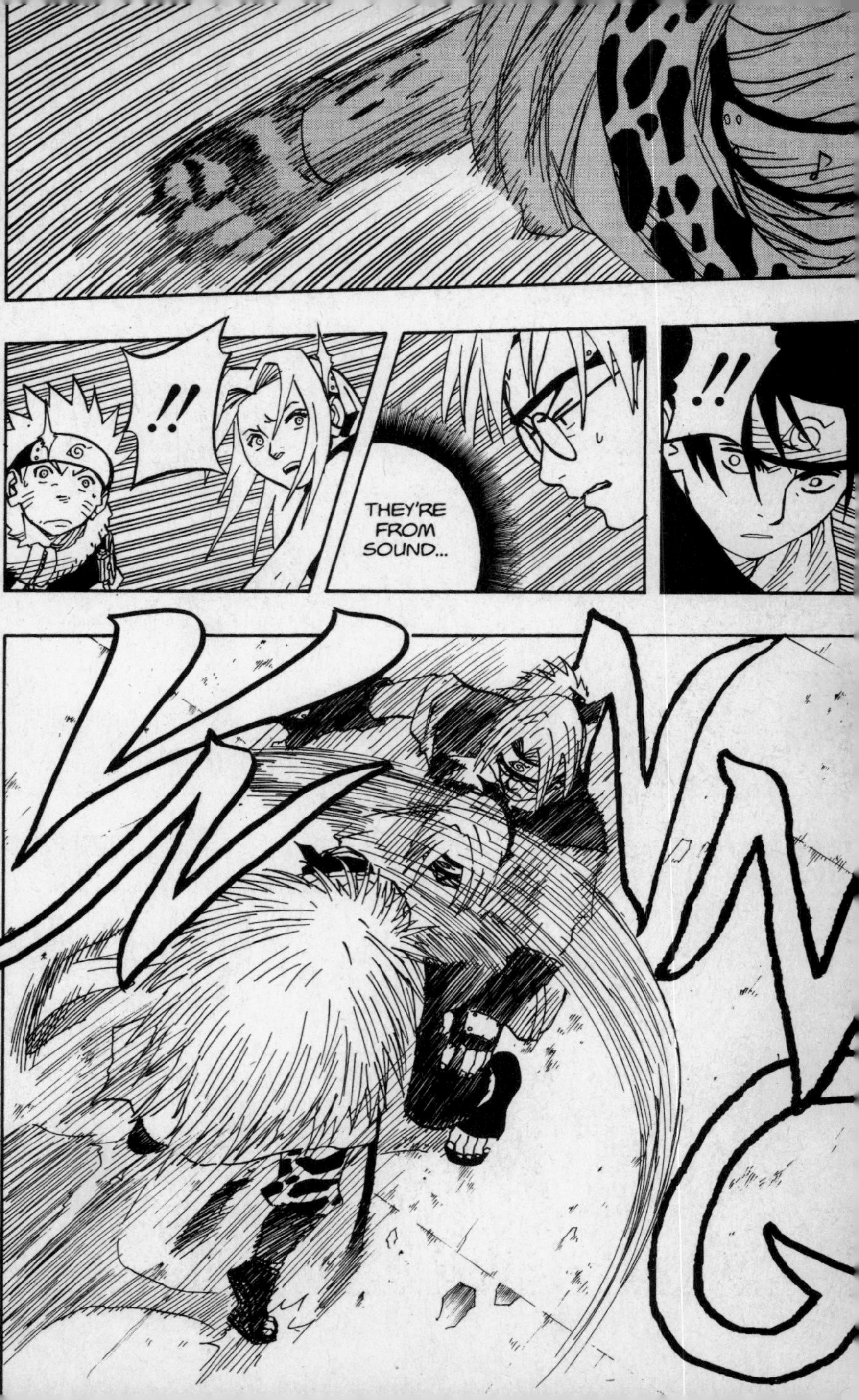
!!
THEY'RE FROM SOUND...
!!

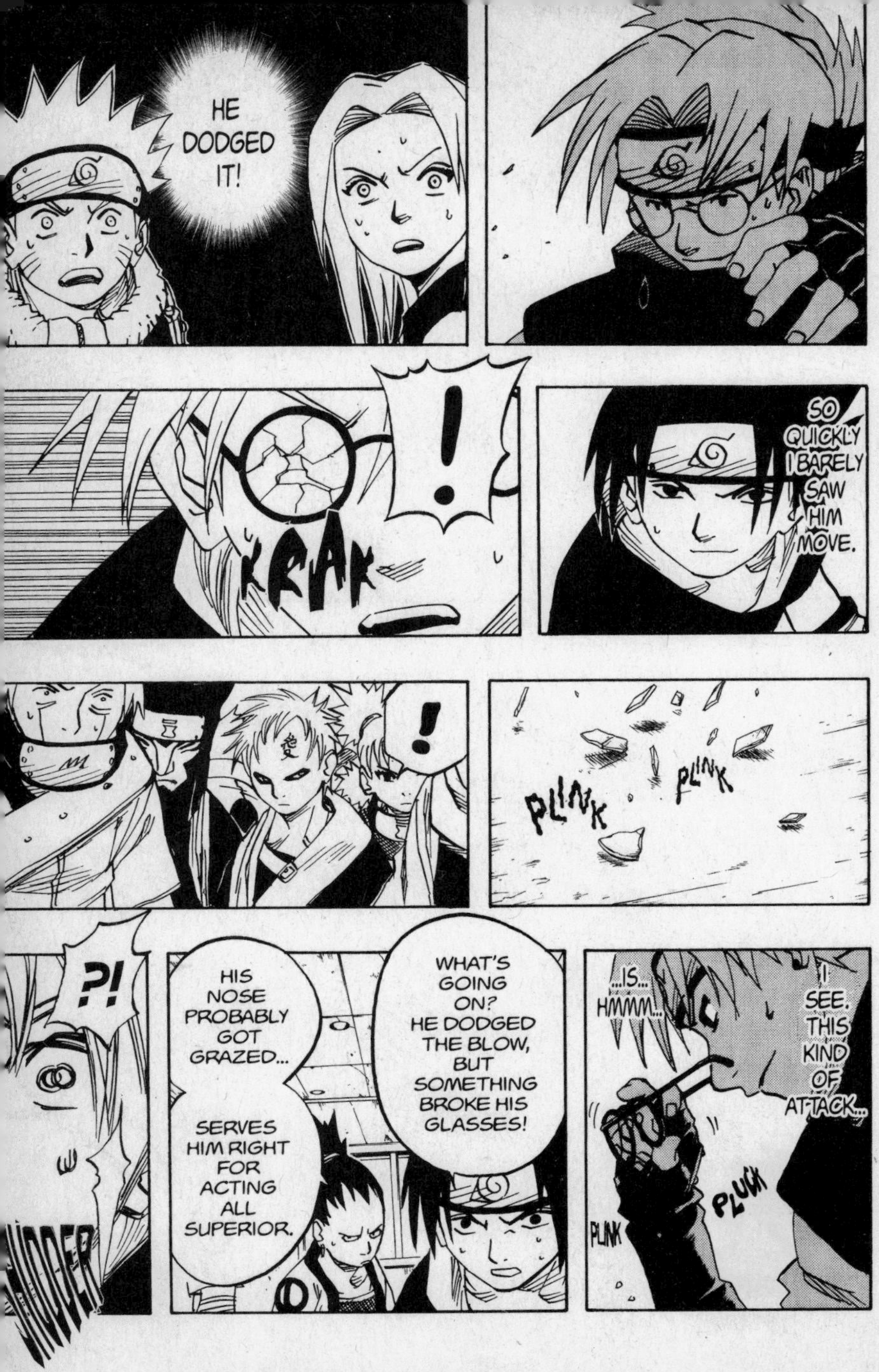
HE DODGED IT!
SO QUICKLY I BARELY SAW HIM MOVE.
!
KRAK
PLINK
PLINK
!
I SEE. THIS KIND OF ATTACK...
...IS... HMMM...
PLUCK
PLINK
WHAT'S GOING ON? HE DODGED THE BLOW, BUT SOMETHING BROKE HIS GLASSES!
HIS NOSE PROBABLY GOT GRAZED...
SERVES HIM RIGHT FOR ACTING ALL SUPERIOR.
?!
SHUDDER

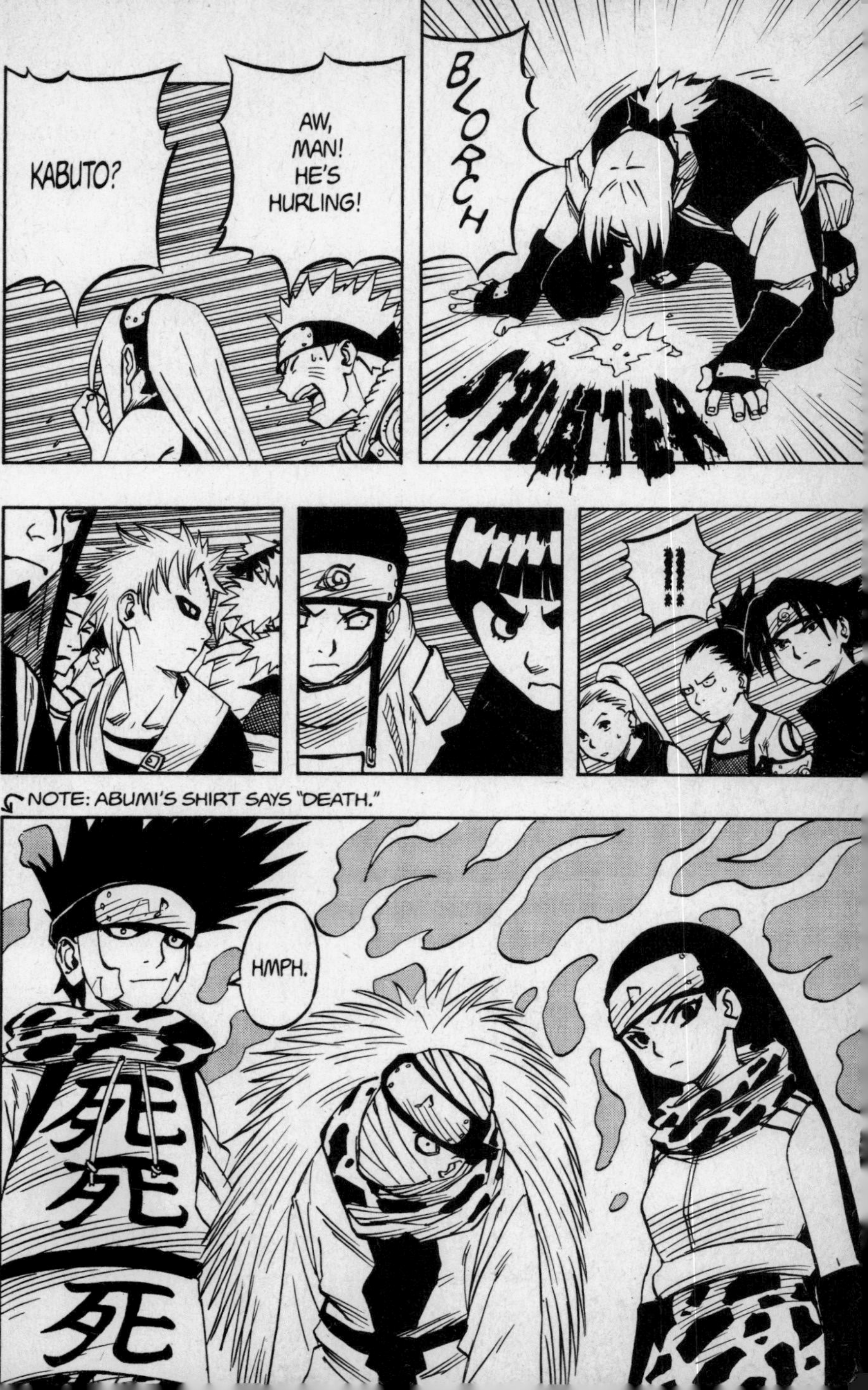
BLORCH
SPLATTER
AW, MAN! HE'S HURLING!
KABUTO?
!!
NOTE: ABUMI'S SHIRT SAYS "DEATH."
HMPH.
死 死 死

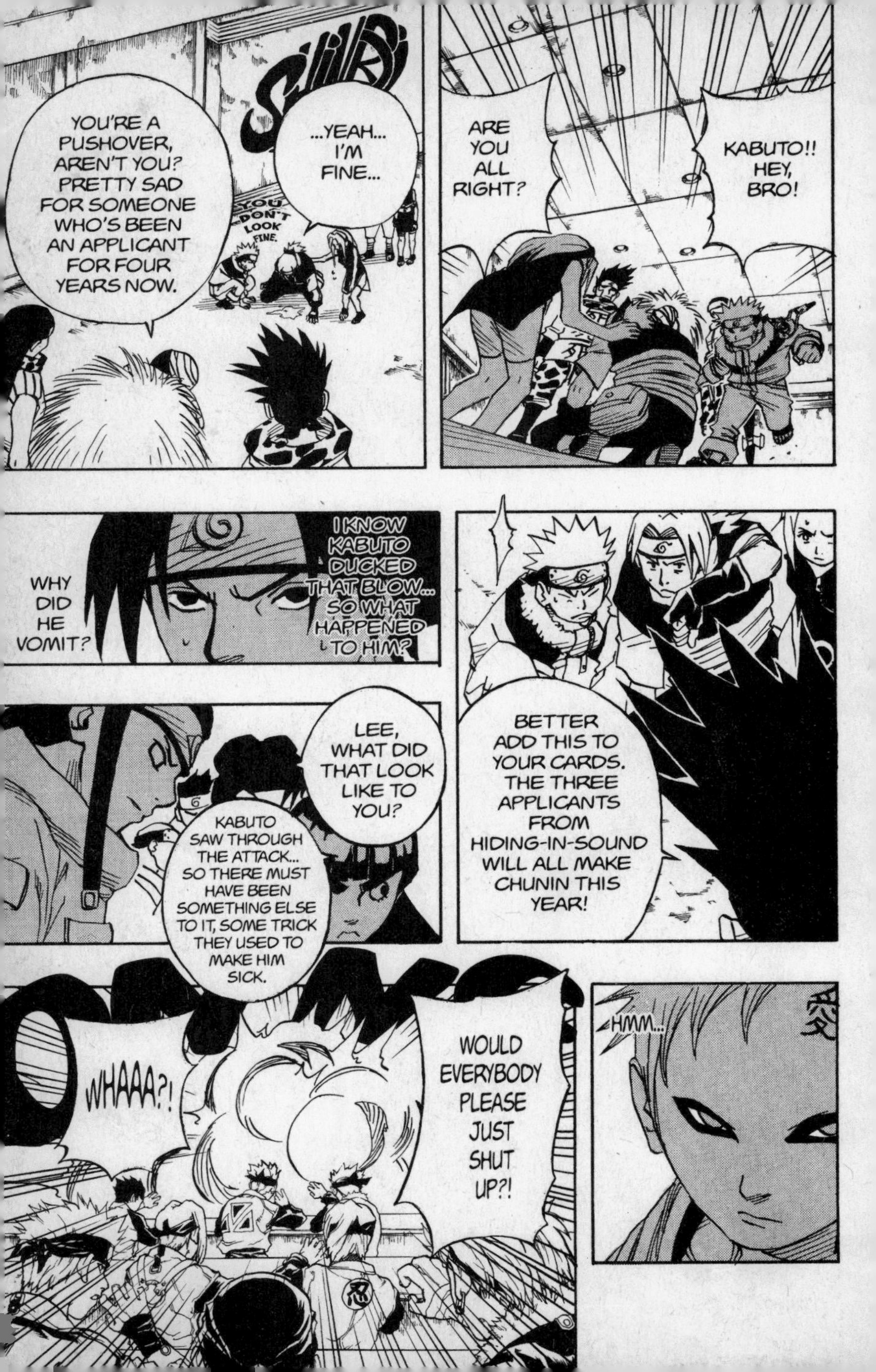
KABUTO!! HEY, BRO!
ARE YOU ALL RIGHT?
...YEAH... I'M FINE...
YOU DON'T LOOK FINE.
YOU'RE A PUSHOVER, AREN'T YOU? PRETTY SAD FOR SOMEONE WHO'S BEEN AN APPLICANT FOR FOUR YEARS NOW.
I KNOW KABUTO DUCKED THAT BLOW... SO WHAT HAPPENED TO HIM?
WHY DID HE VOMIT?
BETTER ADD THIS TO YOUR CARDS. THE THREE APPLICANTS FROM HIDING-IN-SOUND WILL ALL MAKE CHUNIN THIS YEAR!
LEE, WHAT DID THAT LOOK LIKE TO YOU?
KABUTO SAW THROUGH THE ATTACK... SO THERE MUST HAVE BEEN SOMETHING ELSE TO IT, SOME TRICK THEY USED TO MAKE HIM SICK.
HMM...
WOULD EVERYBODY PLEASE JUST SHUT UP?!
WHAAA?!

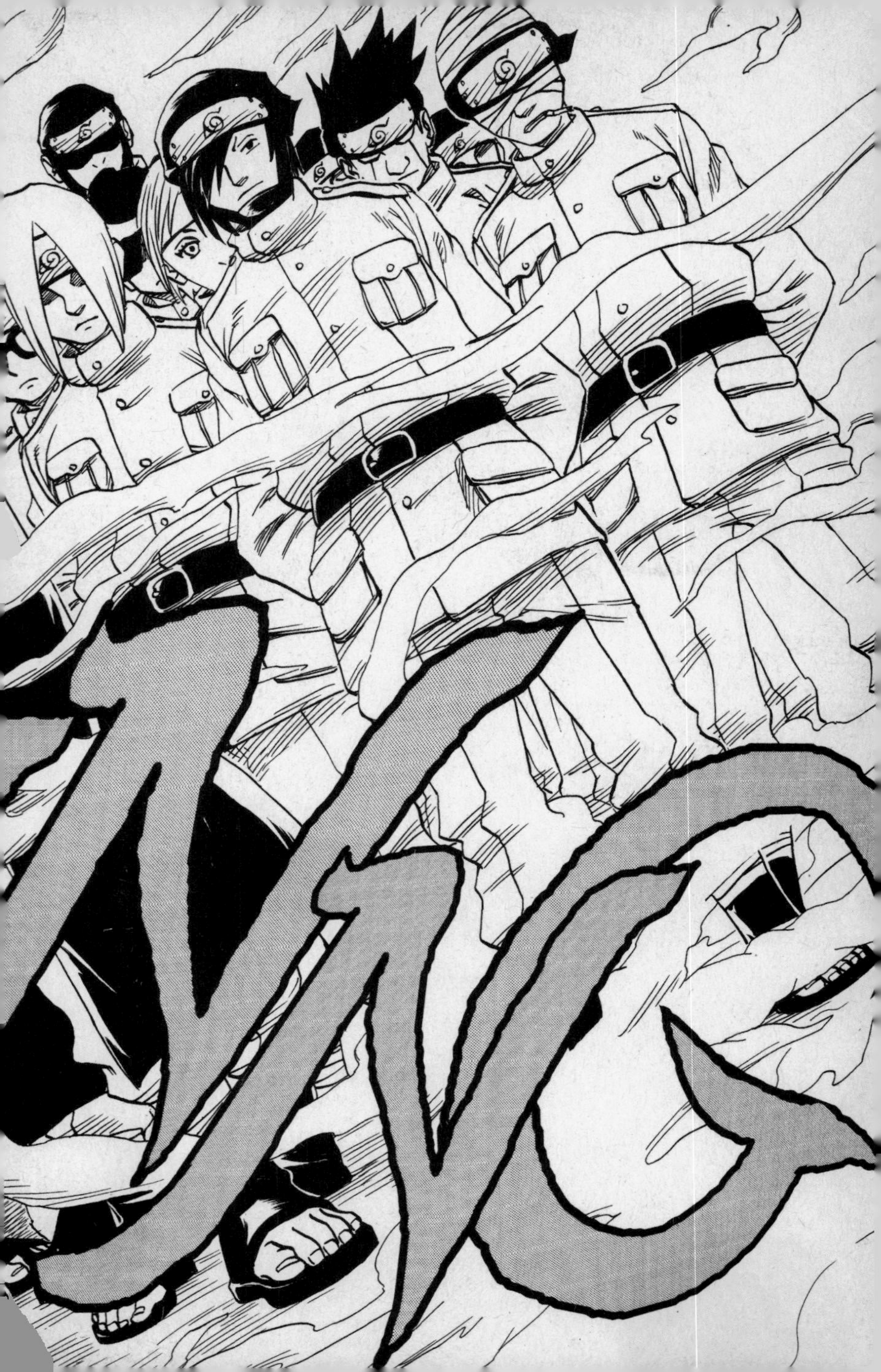

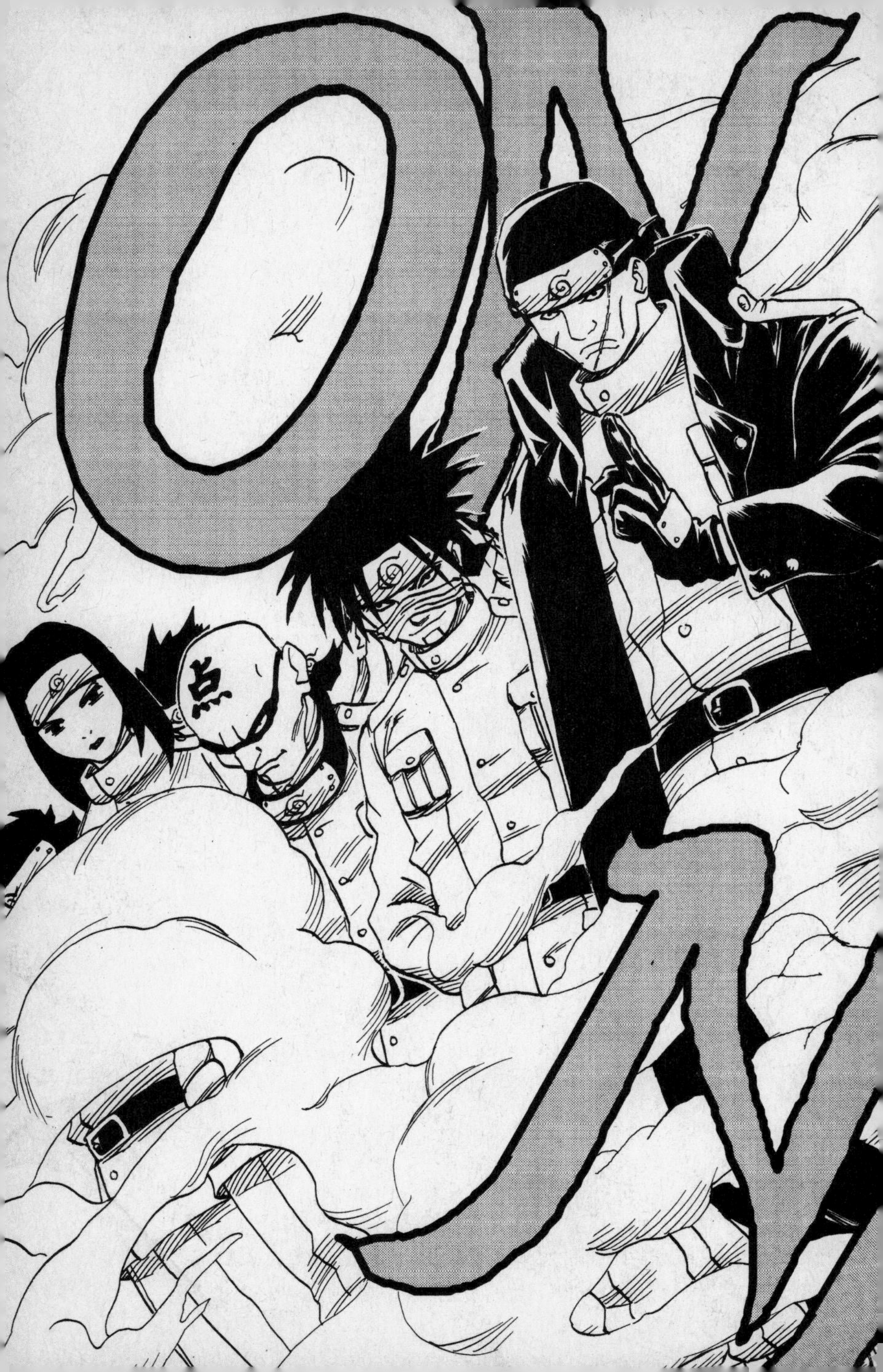

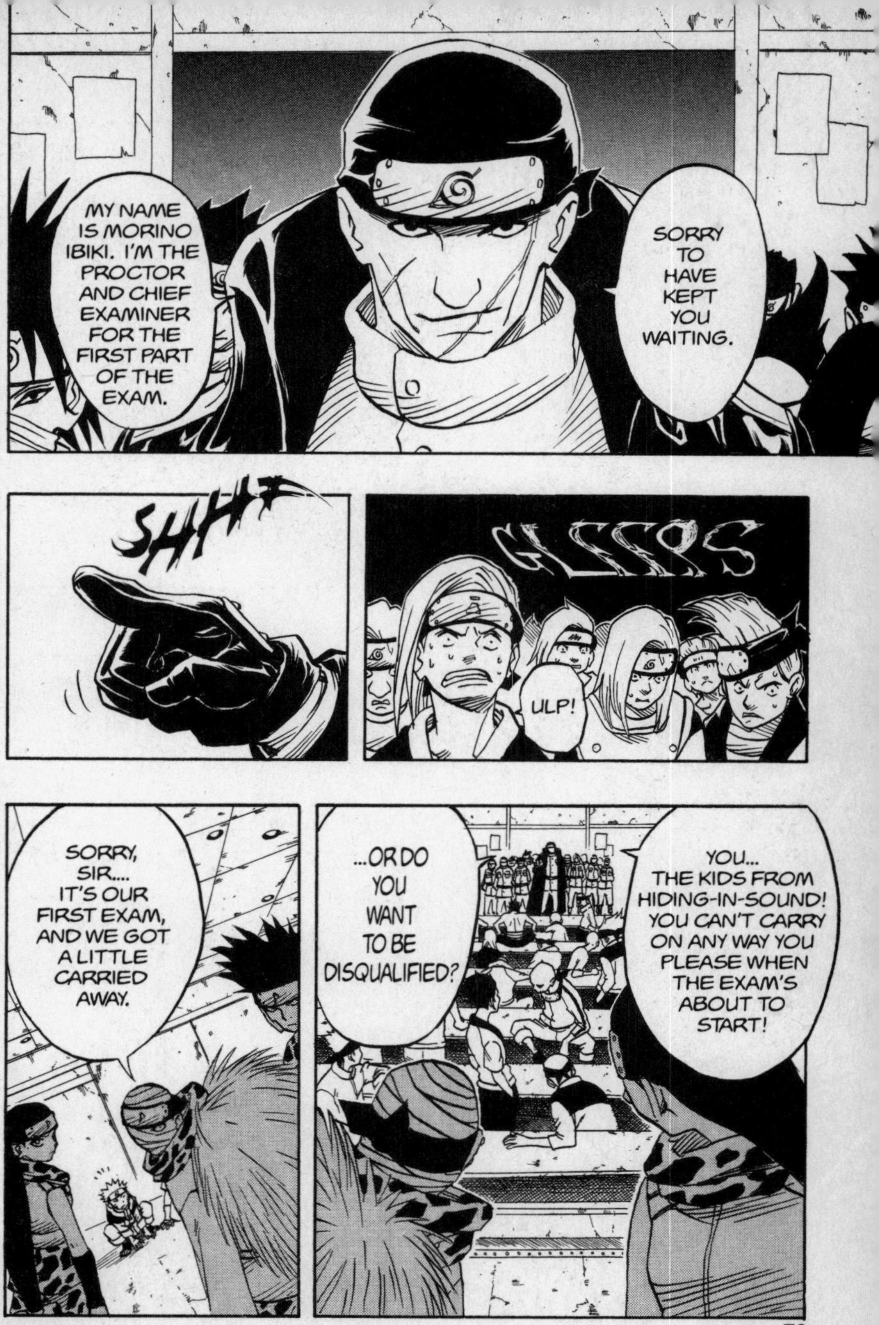
SORRY TO HAVE KEPT YOU WAITING.
MY NAME IS MORINO IBIKI. I'M THE PROCTOR AND CHIEF EXAMINER FOR THE FIRST PART OF THE EXAM.
ULP!
YOU... THE KIDS FROM HIDING-IN-SOUND! YOU CAN'T CARRY ON ANY WAY YOU PLEASE WHEN THE EXAM'S ABOUT TO START!
...OR DO YOU WANT TO BE DISQUALIFIED?
SORRY, SIR.... IT'S OUR FIRST EXAM, AND WE GOT A LITTLE CARRIED AWAY.

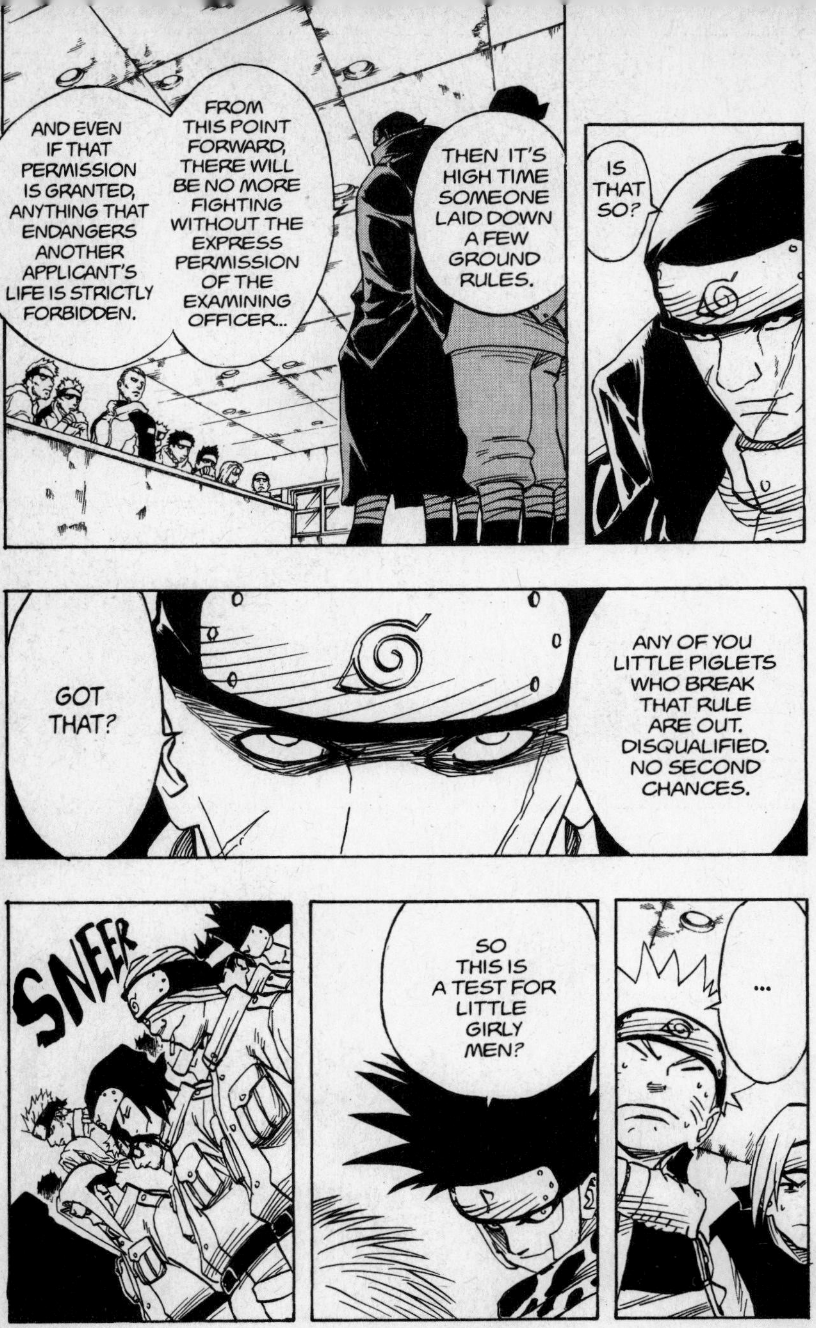
IS THAT SO?
THEN IT'S HIGH TIME SOMEONE LAID DOWN A FEW GROUND RULES.
FROM THIS POINT FORWARD, THERE WILL BE NO MORE FIGHTING WITHOUT THE EXPRESS PERMISSION OF THE EXAMINING OFFICER...
AND EVEN IF THAT PERMISSION IS GRANTED, ANYTHING THAT ENDANGERS ANOTHER APPLICANT'S LIFE IS STRICTLY FORBIDDEN.
ANY OF YOU LITTLE PIGLETS WHO BREAK THAT RULE ARE OUT. DISQUALIFIED. NO SECOND CHANCES.
GOT THAT?
...
SO THIS IS A TEST FOR LITTLE GIRLY MEN?
SNEER

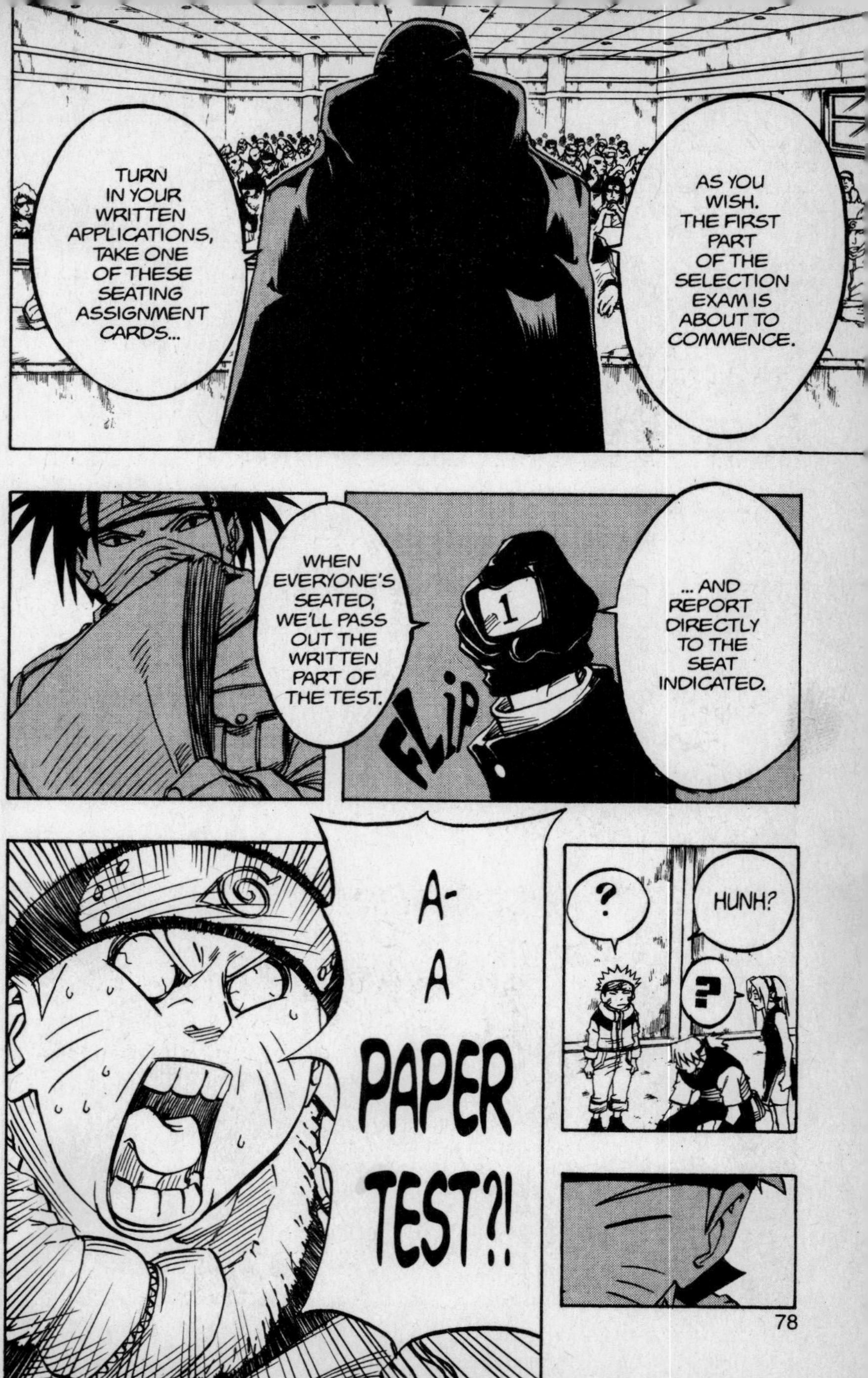
AS YOU WISH. THE FIRST PART OF THE SELECTION EXAM IS ABOUT TO COMMENCE.
TURN IN YOUR WRITTEN APPLICATIONS, TAKE ONE OF THESE SEATING ASSIGNMENT CARDS...
... AND REPORT DIRECTLY TO THE SEAT INDICATED.
WHEN EVERYONE'S SEATED, WE'LL PASS OUT THE WRITTEN PART OF THE TEST.
1
FLIP
HUNH?
?
?
A- A PAPER TEST?!

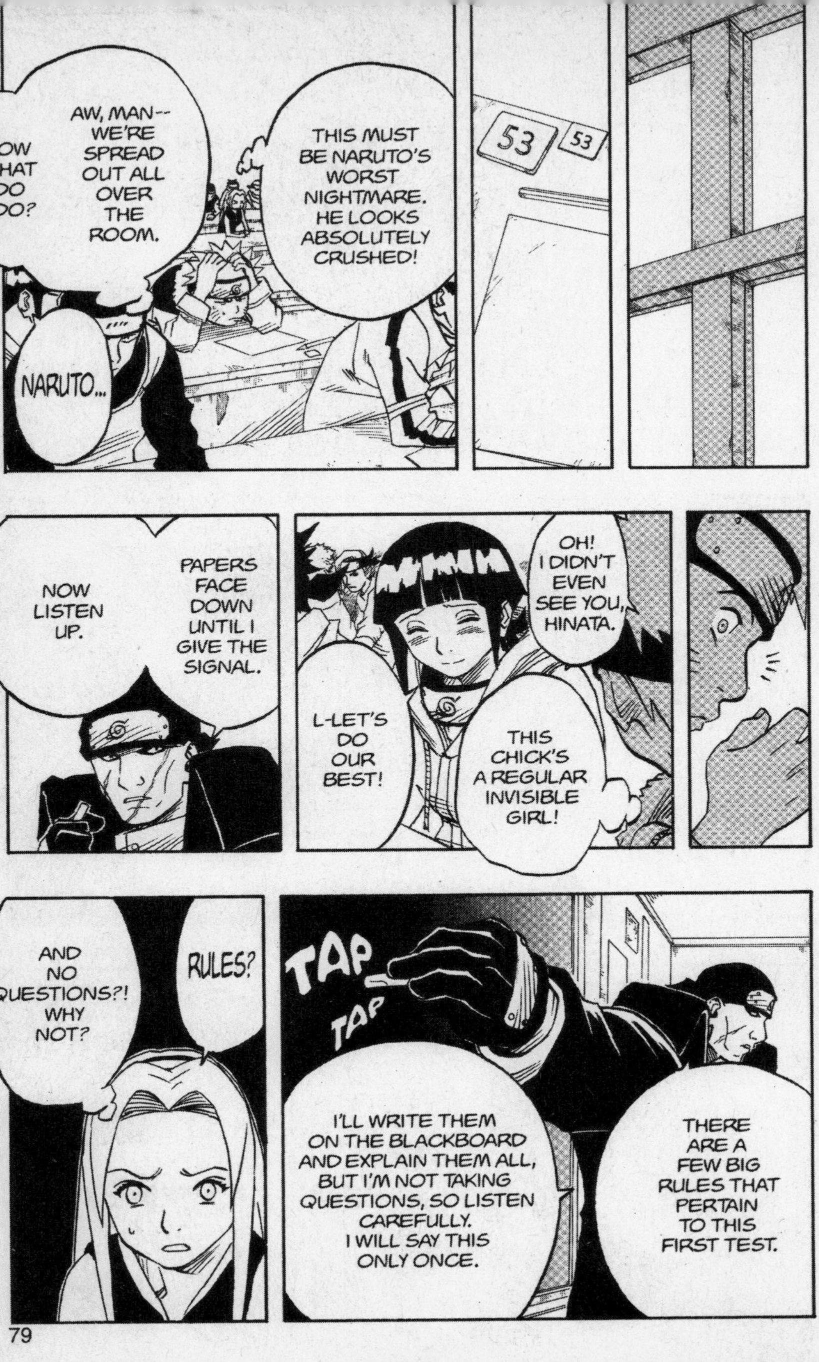
THIS MUST BE NARUTO'S WORST NIGHTMARE. HE LOOKS ABSOLUTELY CRUSHED!
AW, MAN-- WE'RE SPREAD OUT ALL OVER THE ROOM.
NOW WHAT DO I DO?
NARUTO...
OH! I DIDN'T EVEN SEE YOU, HINATA.
THIS CHICK'S A REGULAR INVISIBLE GIRL!
L-LET'S DO OUR BEST!
PAPERS FACE DOWN UNTIL I GIVE THE SIGNAL.
NOW LISTEN UP.
TAP TAP
THERE ARE A FEW BIG RULES THAT PERTAIN TO THIS FIRST TEST.
I'LL WRITE THEM ON THE BLACKBOARD AND EXPLAIN THEM ALL, BUT I'M NOT TAKING QUESTIONS, SO LISTEN CAREFULLY. I WILL SAY THIS ONLY ONCE.
RULES?
AND NO QUESTIONS?! WHY NOT?

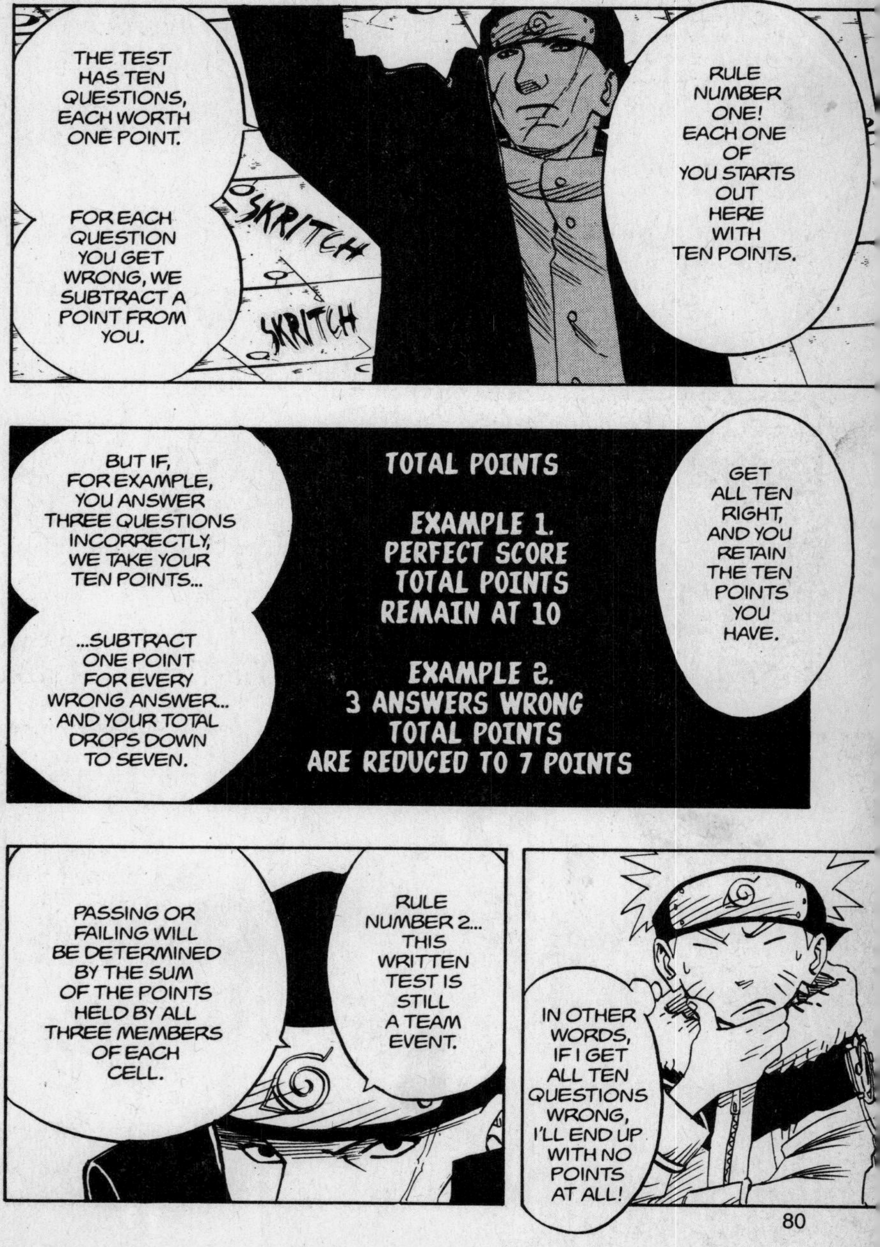
RULE NUMBER ONE! EACH ONE OF YOU STARTS OUT HERE WITH TEN POINTS.
THE TEST HAS TEN QUESTIONS, EACH WORTH ONE POINT.
FOR EACH QUESTION YOU GET WRONG, WE SUBTRACT A POINT FROM YOU.
SKRITCH
SKRITCH
GET ALL TEN RIGHT, AND YOU RETAIN THE TEN POINTS YOU HAVE.
TOTAL POINTS
EXAMPLE 1. PERFECT SCORE TOTAL POINTS REMAIN AT 10
EXAMPLE 2. 3 ANSWERS WRONG TOTAL POINTS ARE REDUCED TO 7 POINTS
BUT IF, FOR EXAMPLE, YOU ANSWER THREE QUESTIONS INCORRECTLY, WE TAKE YOUR TEN POINTS...
...SUBTRACT ONE POINT FOR EVERY WRONG ANSWER... AND YOUR TOTAL DROPS DOWN TO SEVEN.
IN OTHER WORDS, IF I GET ALL TEN QUESTIONS WRONG, I'LL END UP WITH NO POINTS AT ALL!
RULE NUMBER 2... THIS WRITTEN TEST IS STILL A TEAM EVENT.
PASSING OR FAILING WILL BE DETERMINED BY THE SUM OF THE POINTS HELD BY ALL THREE MEMBERS OF EACH CELL.

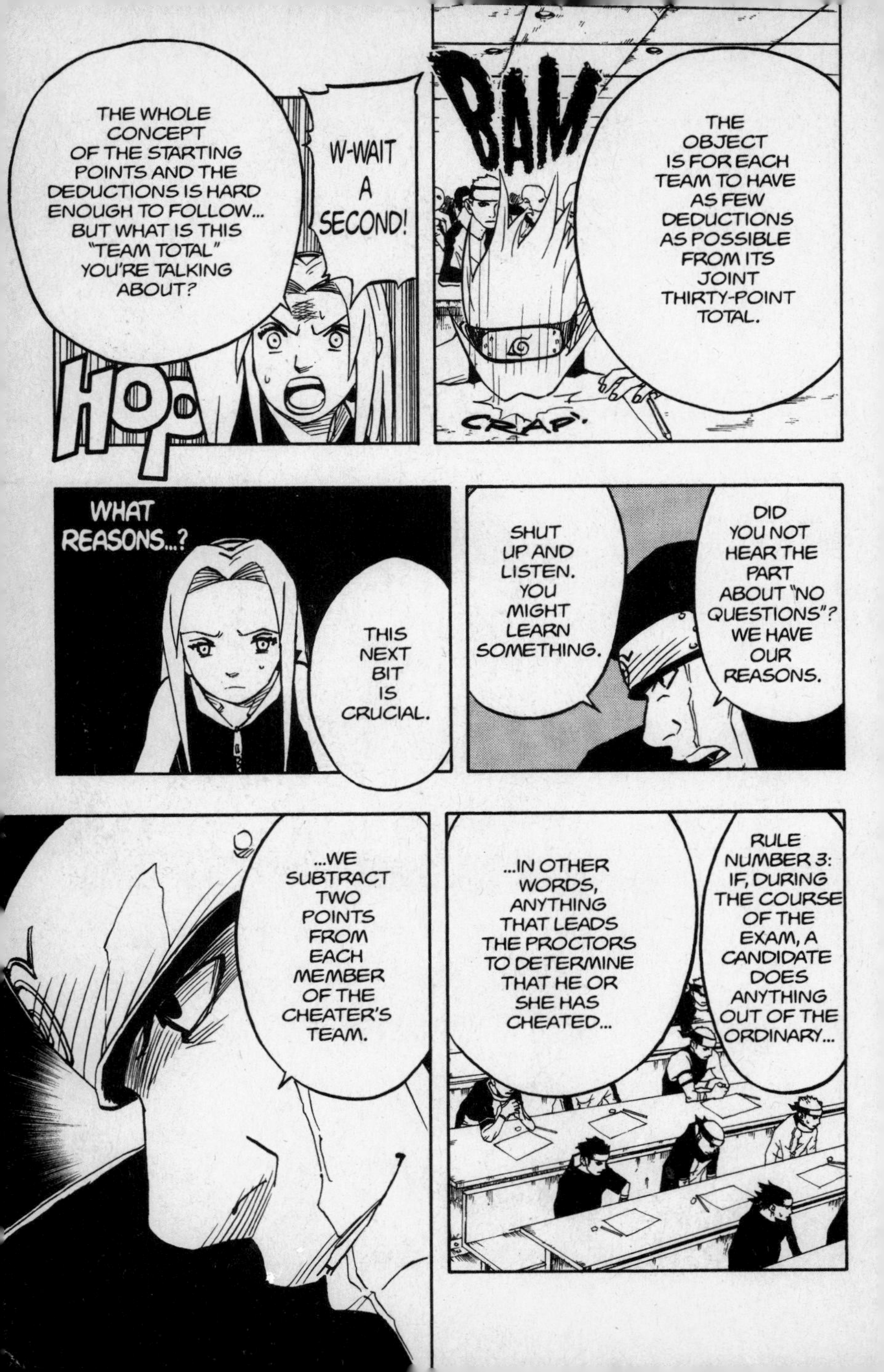
BAM
THE OBJECT IS FOR EACH TEAM TO HAVE AS FEW DEDUCTIONS AS POSSIBLE FROM ITS JOINT THIRTY-POINT TOTAL.
CRAP
W-WAIT A SECOND!
THE WHOLE CONCEPT OF THE STARTING POINTS AND THE DEDUCTIONS IS HARD ENOUGH TO FOLLOW... BUT WHAT IS THIS "TEAM TOTAL" YOU'RE TALKING ABOUT?
HOP
DID YOU NOT HEAR THE PART ABOUT "NO QUESTIONS"? WE HAVE OUR REASONS.
SHUT UP AND LISTEN. YOU MIGHT LEARN SOMETHING.
WHAT REASONS...?
THIS NEXT BIT IS CRUCIAL.
RULE NUMBER 3: IF, DURING THE COURSE OF THE EXAM, A CANDIDATE DOES ANYTHING OUT OF THE ORDINARY...
...IN OTHER WORDS, ANYTHING THAT LEADS THE PROCTORS TO DETERMINE THAT HE OR SHE HAS CHEATED...
...WE SUBTRACT TWO POINTS FROM EACH MEMBER OF THE CHEATER'S TEAM.

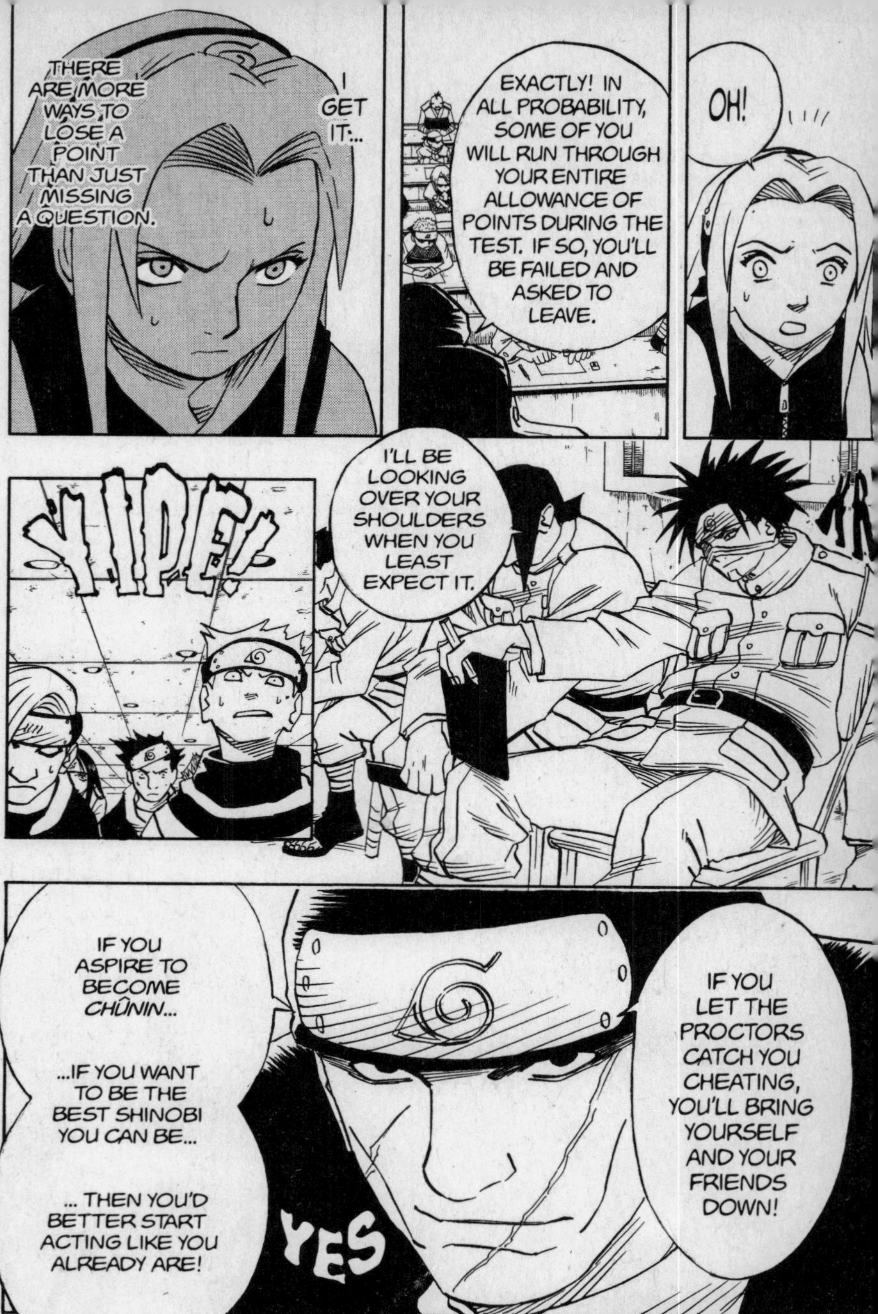
OH!
EXACTLY! IN ALL PROBABILITY, SOME OF YOU WILL RUN THROUGH YOUR ENTIRE ALLOWANCE OF POINTS DURING THE TEST. IF SO, YOU'LL BE FAILED AND ASKED TO LEAVE.
I GET IT...
THERE ARE MORE WAYS TO LOSE A POINT THAN JUST MISSING A QUESTION.
I'LL BE LOOKING OVER YOUR SHOULDERS WHEN YOU LEAST EXPECT IT.
YIPE!!
IF YOU LET THE PROCTORS CATCH YOU CHEATING, YOU'LL BRING YOURSELF AND YOUR FRIENDS DOWN!
IF YOU ASPIRE TO BECOME *CHŪNIN*...
...IF YOU WANT TO BE THE BEST SHINOBI YOU CAN BE...
... THEN YOU'D BETTER START ACTING LIKE YOU ALREADY ARE!
YES

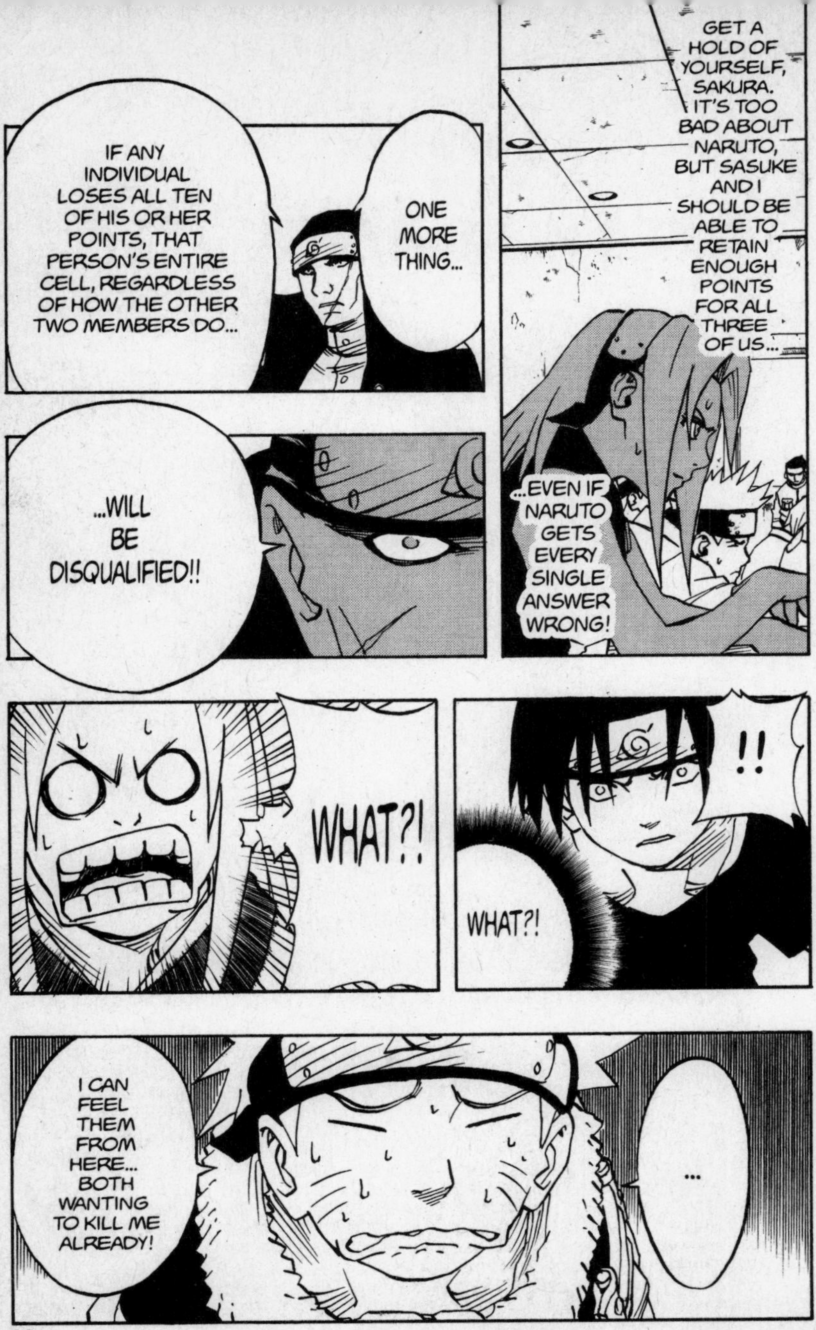
GET A HOLD OF YOURSELF, SAKURA. IT'S TOO BAD ABOUT NARUTO, BUT SASUKE AND I SHOULD BE ABLE TO RETAIN ENOUGH POINTS FOR ALL THREE OF US...
...EVEN IF NARUTO GETS EVERY SINGLE ANSWER WRONG!
ONE MORE THING...
IF ANY INDIVIDUAL LOSES ALL TEN OF HIS OR HER POINTS, THAT PERSON'S ENTIRE CELL, REGARDLESS OF HOW THE OTHER TWO MEMBERS DO...
...WILL BE DISQUALIFIED!!
!!
WHAT?!
WHAT?!
...
I CAN FEEL THEM FROM HERE... BOTH WANTING TO KILL ME ALREADY!

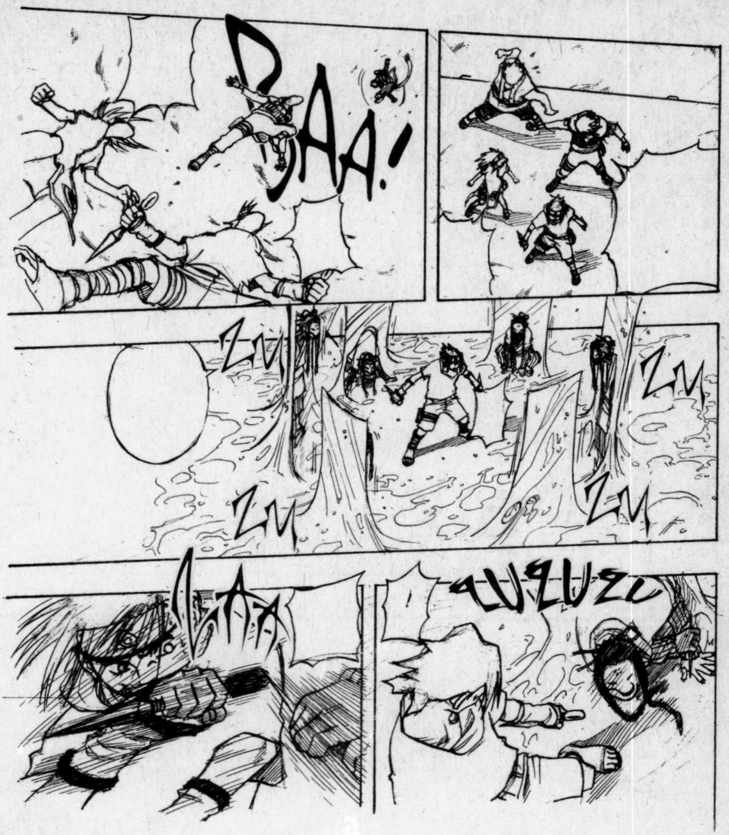
BAA!
ZU
ZU
ZU
ZU

KISHIMOTO MASASHI'S "I ONLY SHOW YOU THESE THINGS SO YOU'LL UNDERSTAND HOW MUCH I LOVE MANGA" REJECTS CORNER...

THE MANGA PAGE ABOVE IS A REJECTED PAGE FROM NARUTO. THIS PAGE HAD BEEN THUMBNAILED, BROKEN DOWN IN PENCIL, AND THEN FINISHED IN INK... BUT I STILL REDREW IT, BECAUSE I JUST DIDN'T FEEL IT WAS UP TO SNUFF. THE LAYOUT WAS TOO STATIC, AND THE PANELS WERE TOO SMALL FOR THE KIND OF DYNAMIC, IMPORTANT ACTION THIS SEQUENCE CALLED FOR. TRYING TO MAINTAIN A WEEKLY PUBLISHING SCHEDULE LEAVES ME VERY LITTLE TIME FOR THE LUXURY OF FUSSING OVER ART, SO IT'S PRETTY RARE TO REDO ANYTHING ONCE IT'S DOWN ON PAPER... BUT IF SOMETHING FEELS SO WRONG THAT I KNOW IT NEEDS FIXING, THEN I COMMIT TO THE CHANGE, NO MATTER HOW SET IN STONE I THINK MY STORY OUTLINE AND THUMBNAIL DRAWINGS ARE, AND NO MATTER HOW FAR ALONG I'VE GOTTEN IN THE FINISHED ART. IF SOMETHING REALLY FEELS WRONG, I'VE GOT TO RESPECT MY OWN CREATIVE GUT INSTINCTS. YOU KNOW... SEEING IT IN WRITING... I THINK I MAY HAVE JUST FIGURED OUT WHY I SOMETIMES HAVE TROUBLE MEETING DEADLINES!

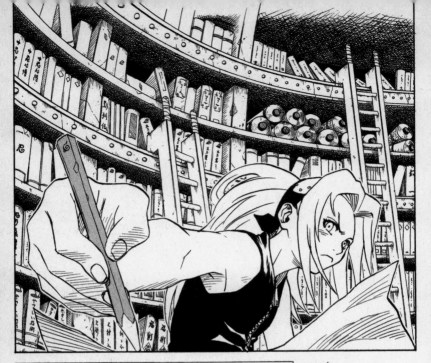

Number 41: The Whisper of Demons

THE *CHÛNIN* JOURNEYMAN NINJA SELECTION EXAM
RULES FOR PART ONE

(1) EACH APPLICANT BEGINS WITH A PERFECT SCORE OF TEN POINTS. THERE ARE TEN QUESTIONS WORTH ONE POINT APIECE. A POINT IS SUBTRACTED FOR EVERY INCORRECT ANSWER. THE GRADING SYSTEM IS ENTIRELY BASED ON A PRINCIPLE OF PENALIZATION.

(2) THE EXAM IS A TEAM EVENT. WHAT MATTERS IS HOW CLOSE EACH THREE-NINJA CELL CAN COME TO RETAINING ITS INITIAL THIRTY POINTS.

(3) ANYONE CAUGHT ATTEMPTING TO CHEAT OR AIDING AND ABETTING A CHEATER WILL LOSE TWO POINTS FOR EACH OFFENSE.

(4) ANYONE WHO HAS NO POINTS LEFT AT THE TEST'S END--WHETHER DUE TO BEING CAUGHT CHEATING OR TO AN INABILITY TO ANSWER ANY OF THE QUESTIONS CORRECTLY--WILL AUTOMATICALLY FAIL; IF A SINGLE INDIVIDUAL FAILS, THE REMAINING TWO MEMBERS OF THAT PERSON'S CELL WILL BE FAILED AS WELL.

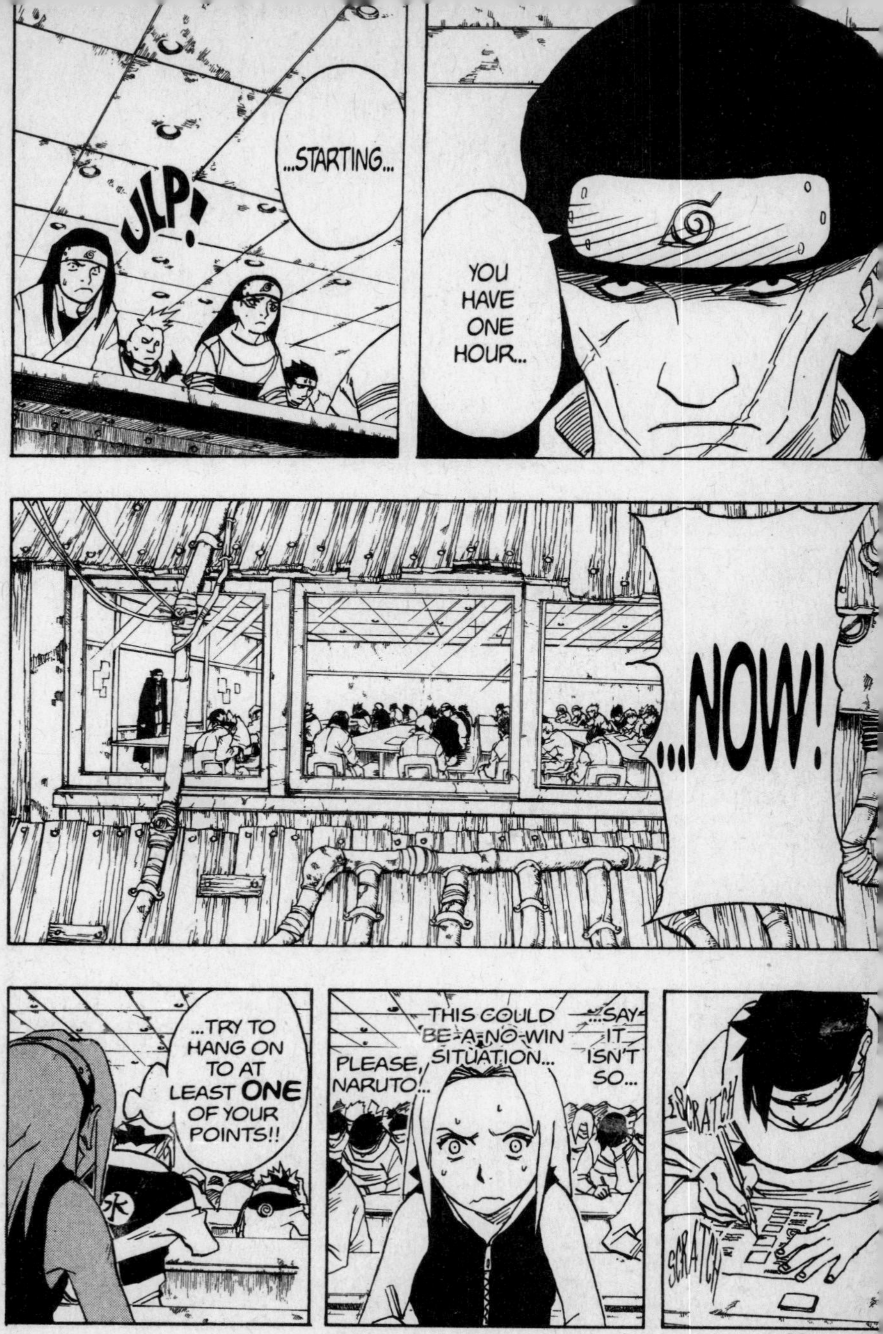
YOU HAVE ONE HOUR...
...STARTING...
JLP!
...NOW!
SCRATCH
SCRATCH
...SAY IT ISN'T SO...
THIS COULD BE A NO-WIN SITUATION...
PLEASE, NARUTO...
...TRY TO HANG ON TO AT LEAST ONE OF YOUR POINTS!!

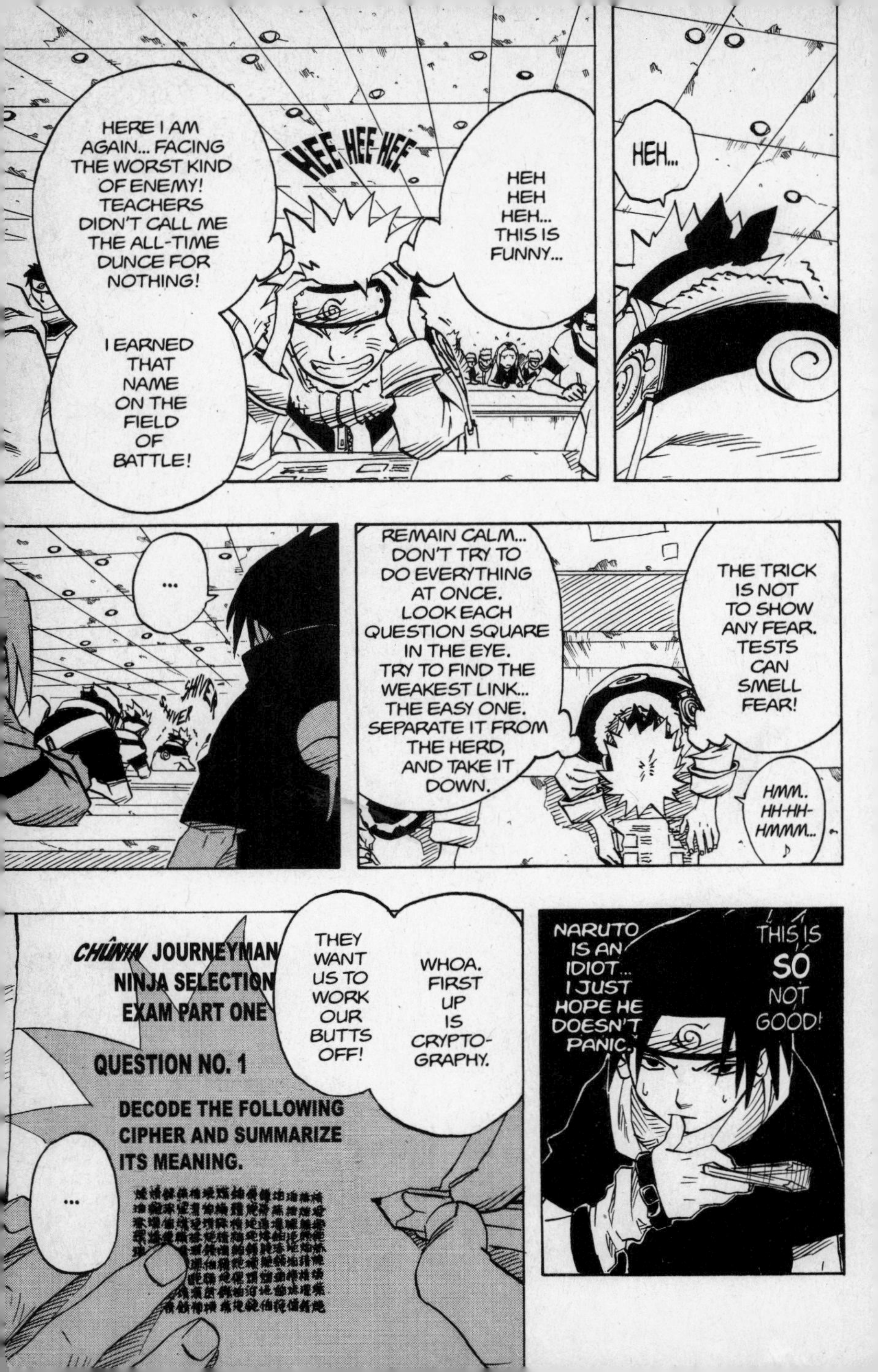
HEH...
HEH HEH HEH... THIS IS FUNNY...
HEE HEE HEE
HERE I AM AGAIN... FACING THE WORST KIND OF ENEMY! TEACHERS DIDN'T CALL ME THE ALL-TIME DUNCE FOR NOTHING!
I EARNED THAT NAME ON THE FIELD OF BATTLE!
THE TRICK IS NOT TO SHOW ANY FEAR. TESTS CAN SMELL FEAR!
REMAIN CALM... DON'T TRY TO DO EVERYTHING AT ONCE. LOOK EACH QUESTION SQUARE IN THE EYE. TRY TO FIND THE WEAKEST LINK... THE EASY ONE. SEPARATE IT FROM THE HERD, AND TAKE IT DOWN.
HMM.. HH-HH-HMMM... ♪
...
SHIVER SHIVER
THIS IS SO NOT GOOD!
NARUTO IS AN IDIOT... I JUST HOPE HE DOESN'T PANIC.
WHOA. FIRST UP IS CRYPTOGRAPHY.
THEY WANT US TO WORK OUR BUTTS OFF!
CHÛNIN JOURNEYMAN NINJA SELECTION EXAM PART ONE
QUESTION NO. 1
DECODE THE FOLLOWING CIPHER AND SUMMARIZE ITS MEANING.
...

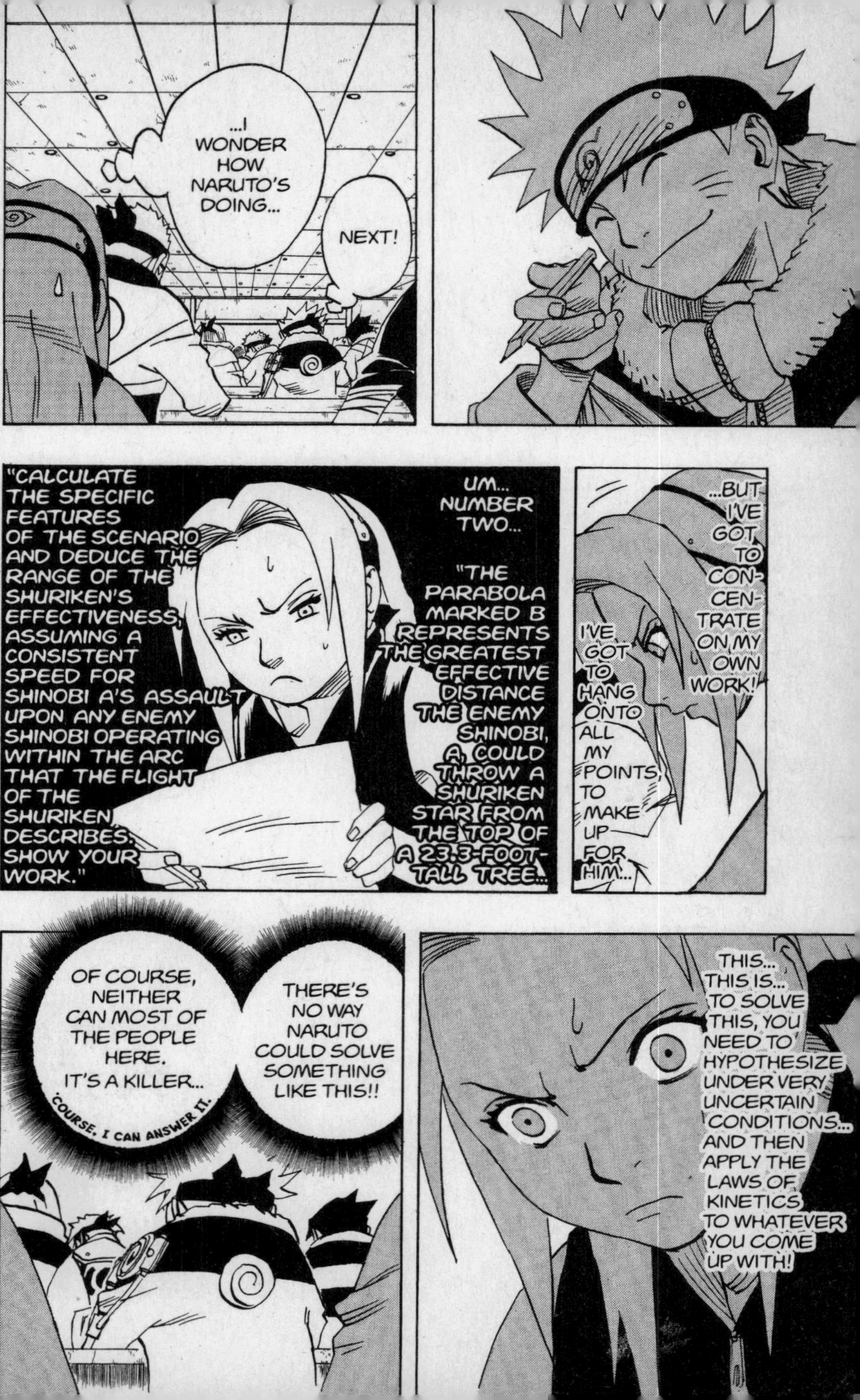
...I WONDER HOW NARUTO'S DOING...
NEXT!
...BUT I'VE GOT TO CONCENTRATE ON MY OWN WORK!
I'VE GOT TO HANG ONTO ALL MY POINTS, TO MAKE UP FOR HIM...
UM... NUMBER TWO...
"THE PARABOLA MARKED B REPRESENTS THE GREATEST EFFECTIVE DISTANCE THE ENEMY SHINOBI, A, COULD THROW A SHURIKEN STAR FROM THE TOP OF A 23.3-FOOT-TALL TREE...
"CALCULATE THE SPECIFIC FEATURES OF THE SCENARIO AND DEDUCE THE RANGE OF THE SHURIKEN'S EFFECTIVENESS, ASSUMING A CONSISTENT SPEED FOR SHINOBI A'S ASSAULT UPON ANY ENEMY SHINOBI OPERATING WITHIN THE ARC THAT THE FLIGHT OF THE SHURIKEN DESCRIBES. SHOW YOUR WORK."
THIS... THIS IS... TO SOLVE THIS, YOU NEED TO HYPOTHESIZE UNDER VERY UNCERTAIN CONDITIONS... AND THEN APPLY THE LAWS OF KINETICS TO WHATEVER YOU COME UP WITH!
THERE'S NO WAY NARUTO COULD SOLVE SOMETHING LIKE THIS!!
OF COURSE, NEITHER CAN MOST OF THE PEOPLE HERE. IT'S A KILLER...
'COURSE, I CAN ANSWER IT.

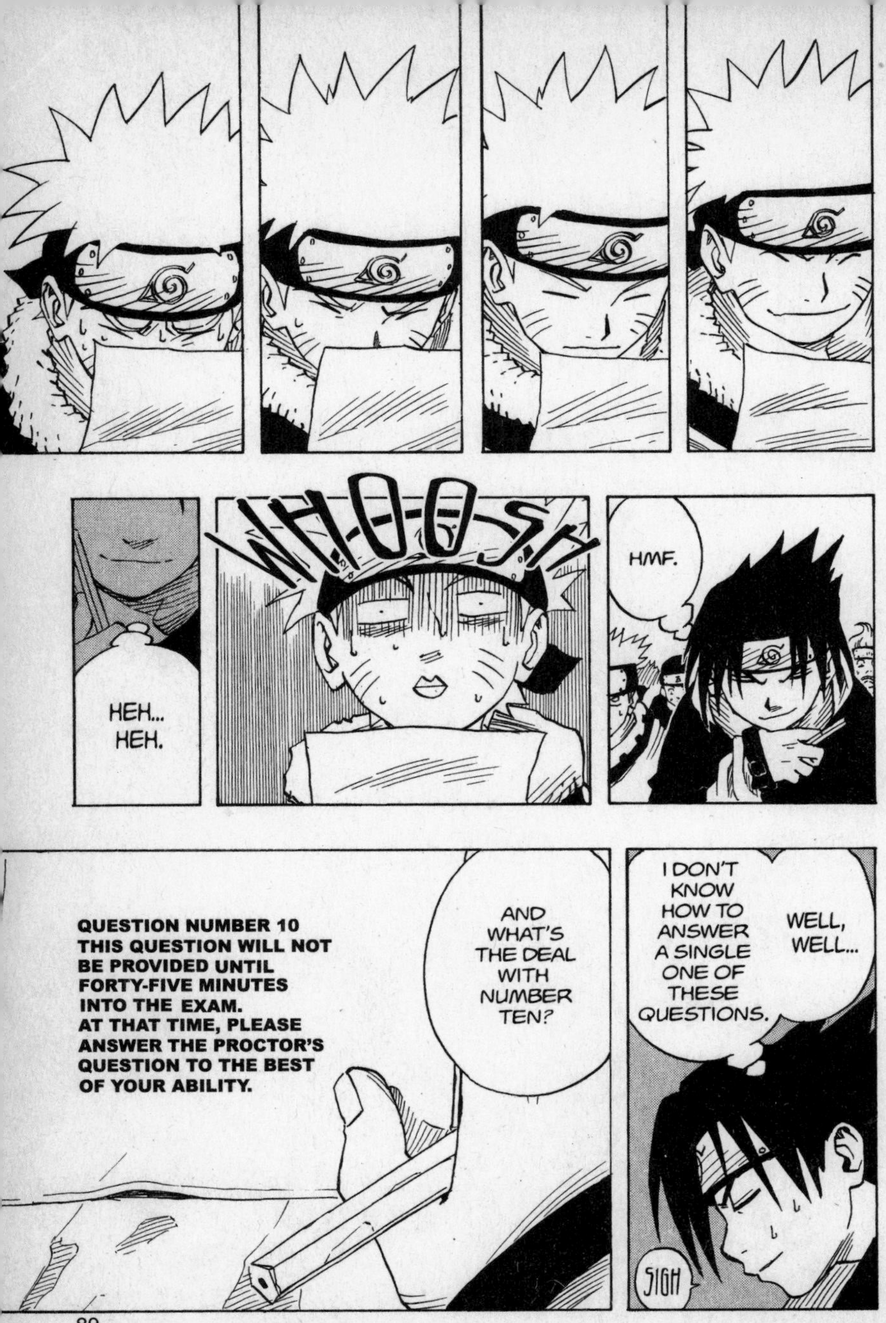
HMF.
WHOOSH
HEH... HEH.
WELL, WELL...
I DON'T KNOW HOW TO ANSWER A SINGLE ONE OF THESE QUESTIONS.
SIGH
AND WHAT'S THE DEAL WITH NUMBER TEN?
QUESTION NUMBER 10
THIS QUESTION WILL NOT BE PROVIDED UNTIL FORTY-FIVE MINUTES INTO THE EXAM.
AT THAT TIME, PLEASE ANSWER THE PROCTOR'S QUESTION TO THE BEST OF YOUR ABILITY.

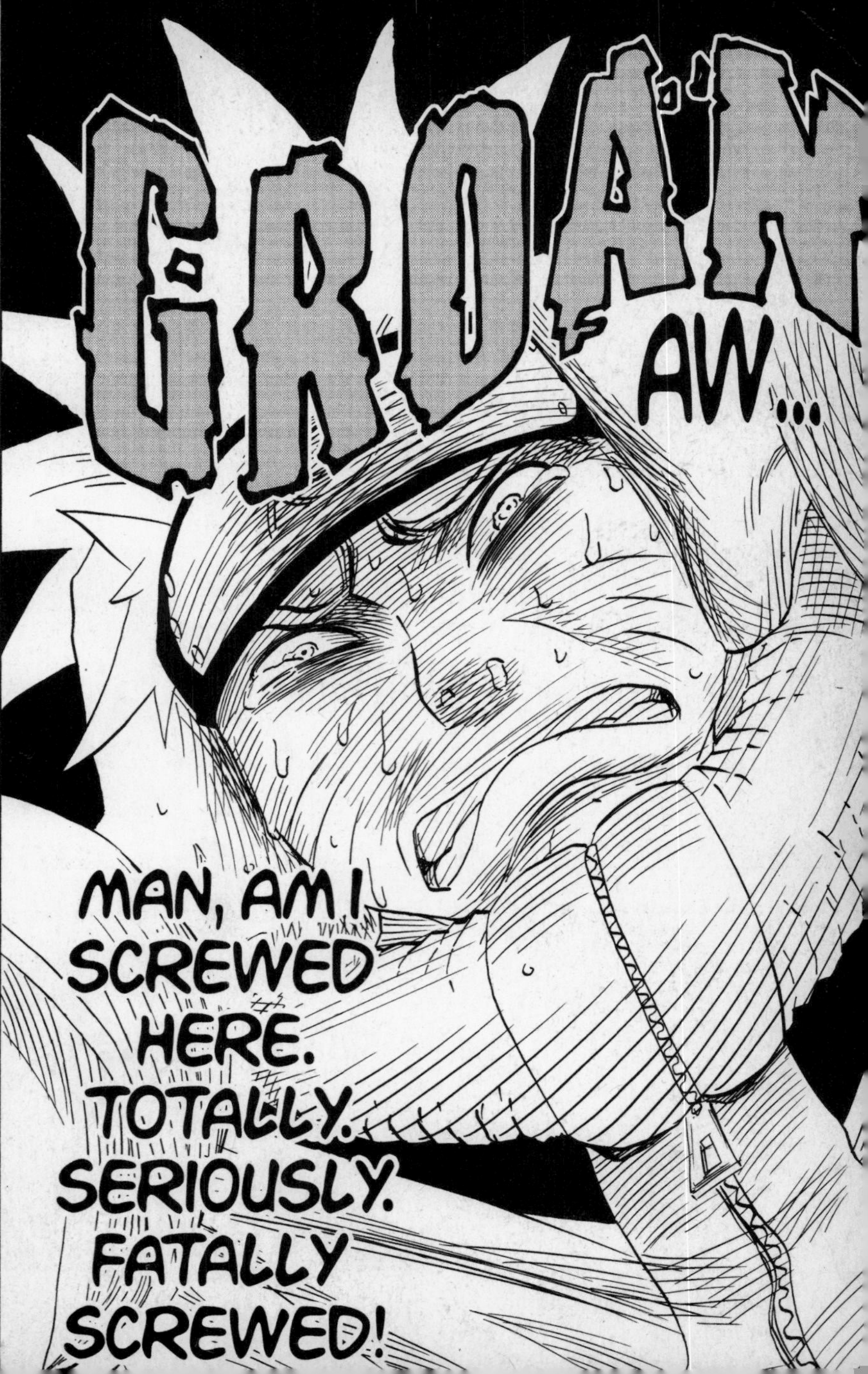
G-R-O-A-N
AW...
MAN, AM I SCREWED HERE. TOTALLY. SERIOUSLY. FATALLY SCREWED!

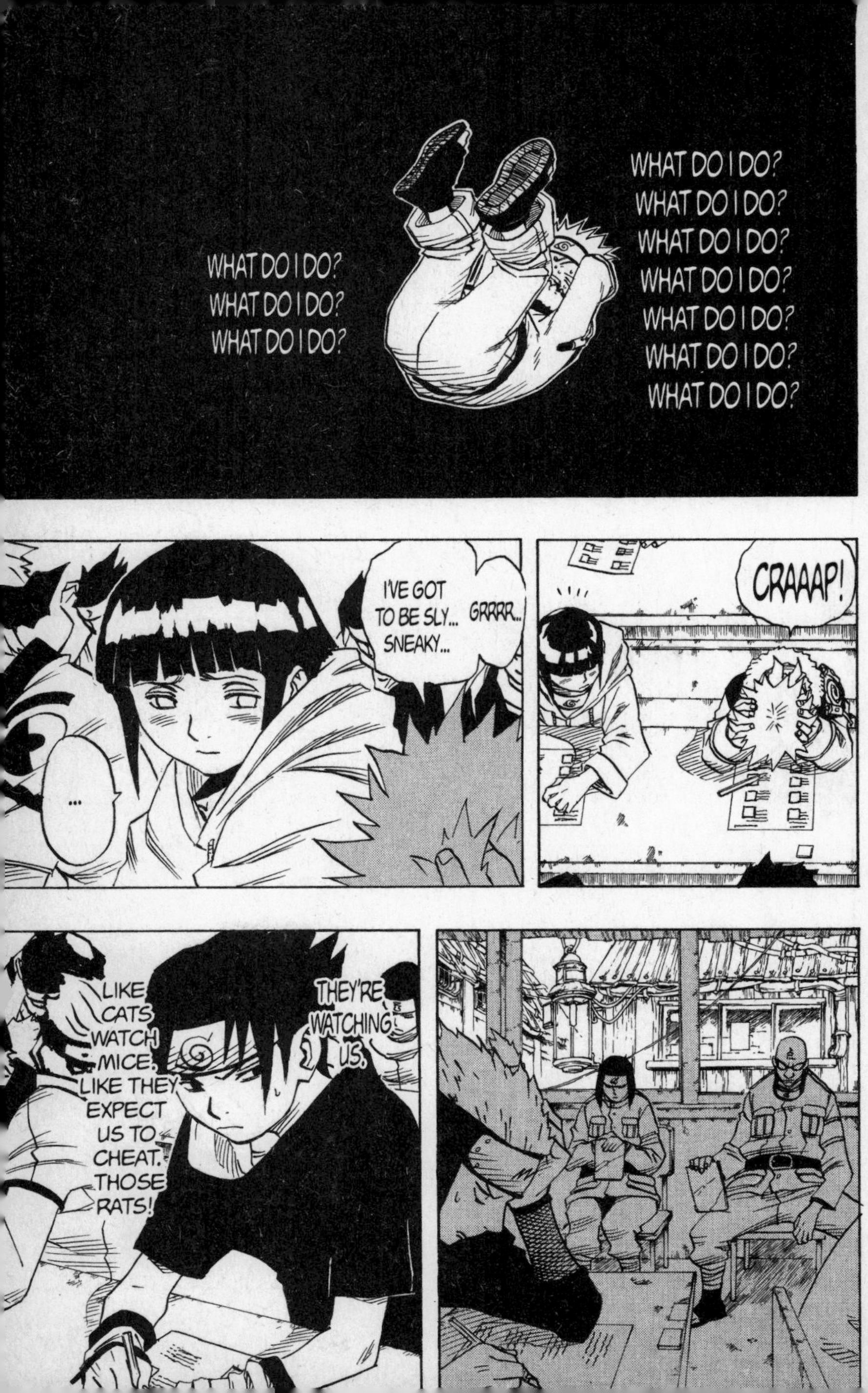
WHAT DO I DO?
WHAT DO I DO?
WHAT DO I DO?
WHAT DO I DO?
WHAT DO I DO?
WHAT DO I DO?
WHAT DO I DO?
WHAT DO I DO?
WHAT DO I DO?
WHAT DO I DO?
CRAAAP!
I'VE GOT TO BE SLY... SNEAKY...
GRRRR...
...
THEY'RE WATCHING US.
LIKE CATS WATCH MICE. LIKE THEY EXPECT US TO CHEAT. THOSE RATS!

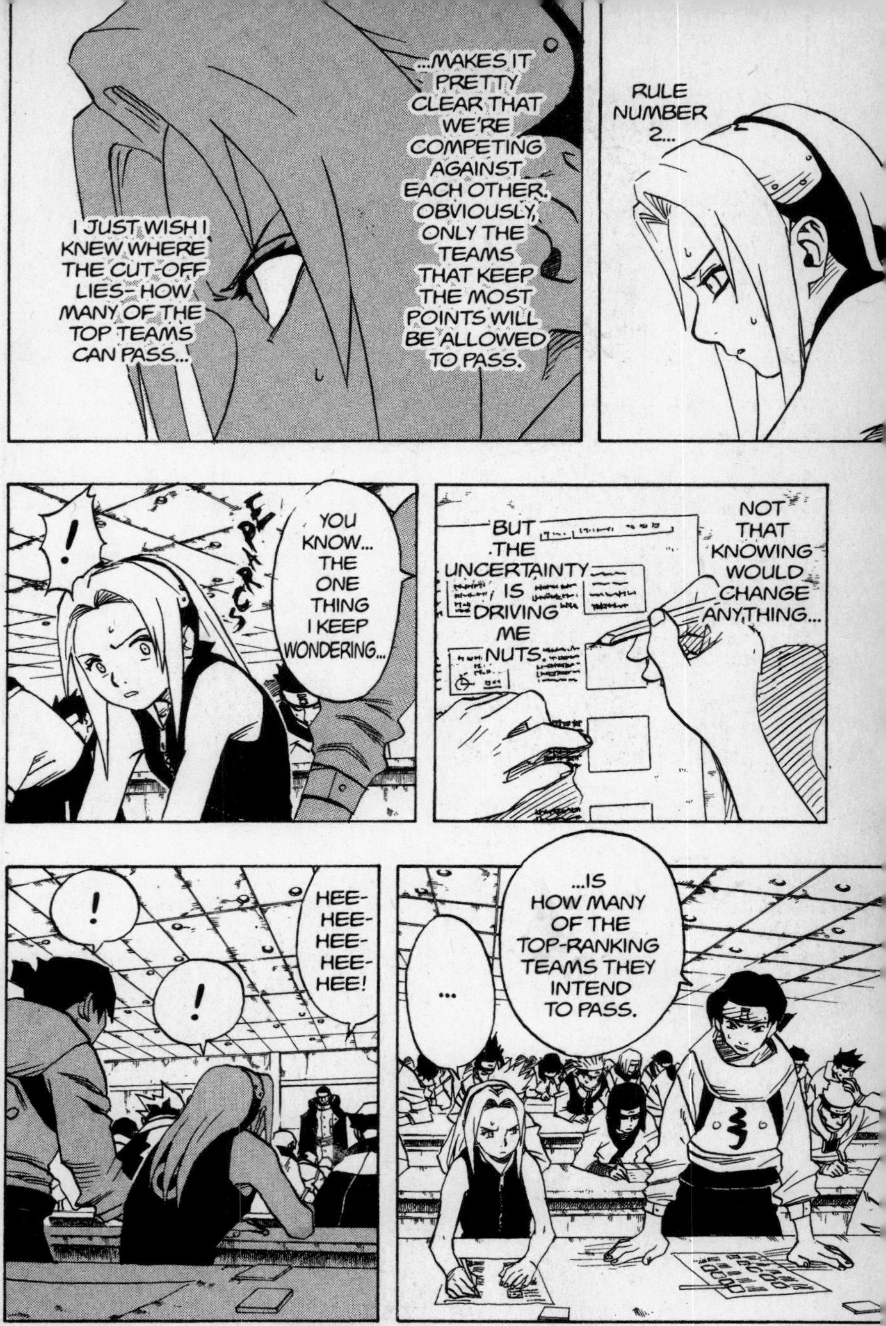
RULE NUMBER 2...
...MAKES IT PRETTY CLEAR THAT WE'RE COMPETING AGAINST EACH OTHER. OBVIOUSLY, ONLY THE TEAMS THAT KEEP THE MOST POINTS WILL BE ALLOWED TO PASS.
I JUST WISH I KNEW WHERE THE CUT-OFF LIES- HOW MANY OF THE TOP TEAMS CAN PASS...
NOT THAT KNOWING WOULD CHANGE ANYTHING...
BUT THE UNCERTAINTY IS DRIVING ME NUTS.
YOU KNOW... THE ONE THING I KEEP WONDERING...
SCRAPE
!
...IS HOW MANY OF THE TOP-RANKING TEAMS THEY INTEND TO PASS.
...
HEE-HEE-HEE-HEE-HEE!
!
!

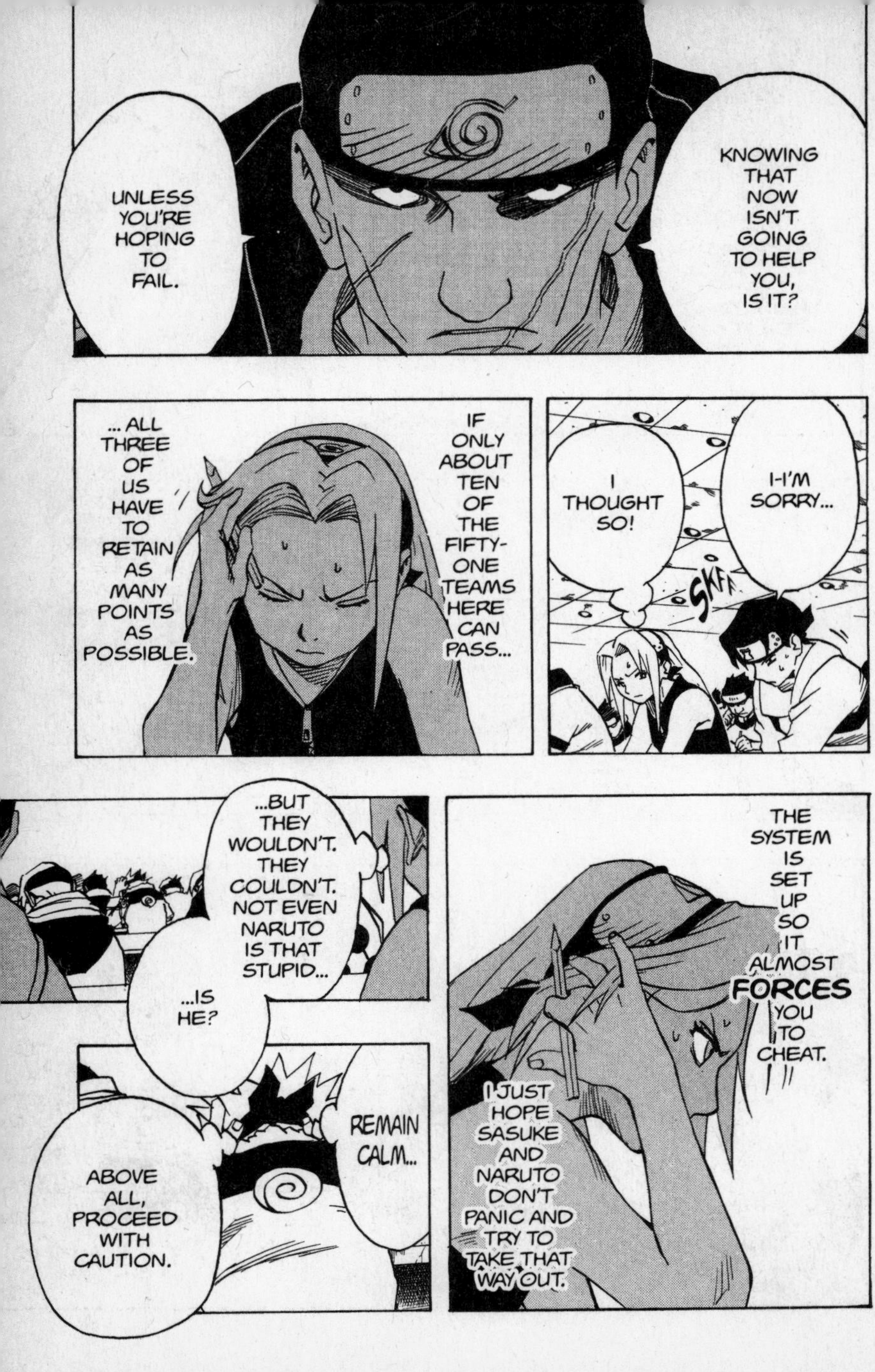
KNOWING THAT NOW ISN'T GOING TO HELP YOU, IS IT?
UNLESS YOU'RE HOPING TO FAIL.
I-I'M SORRY...
I THOUGHT SO!
SKFF
IF ONLY ABOUT TEN OF THE FIFTY-ONE TEAMS HERE CAN PASS...
...ALL THREE OF US HAVE TO RETAIN AS MANY POINTS AS POSSIBLE.
THE SYSTEM IS SET UP SO IT ALMOST **FORCES** YOU TO CHEAT.
I JUST HOPE SASUKE AND NARUTO DON'T PANIC AND TRY TO TAKE THAT WAY OUT.
...BUT THEY WOULDN'T. THEY COULDN'T. NOT EVEN NARUTO IS THAT STUPID...
...IS HE?
REMAIN CALM...
ABOVE ALL, PROCEED WITH CAUTION.

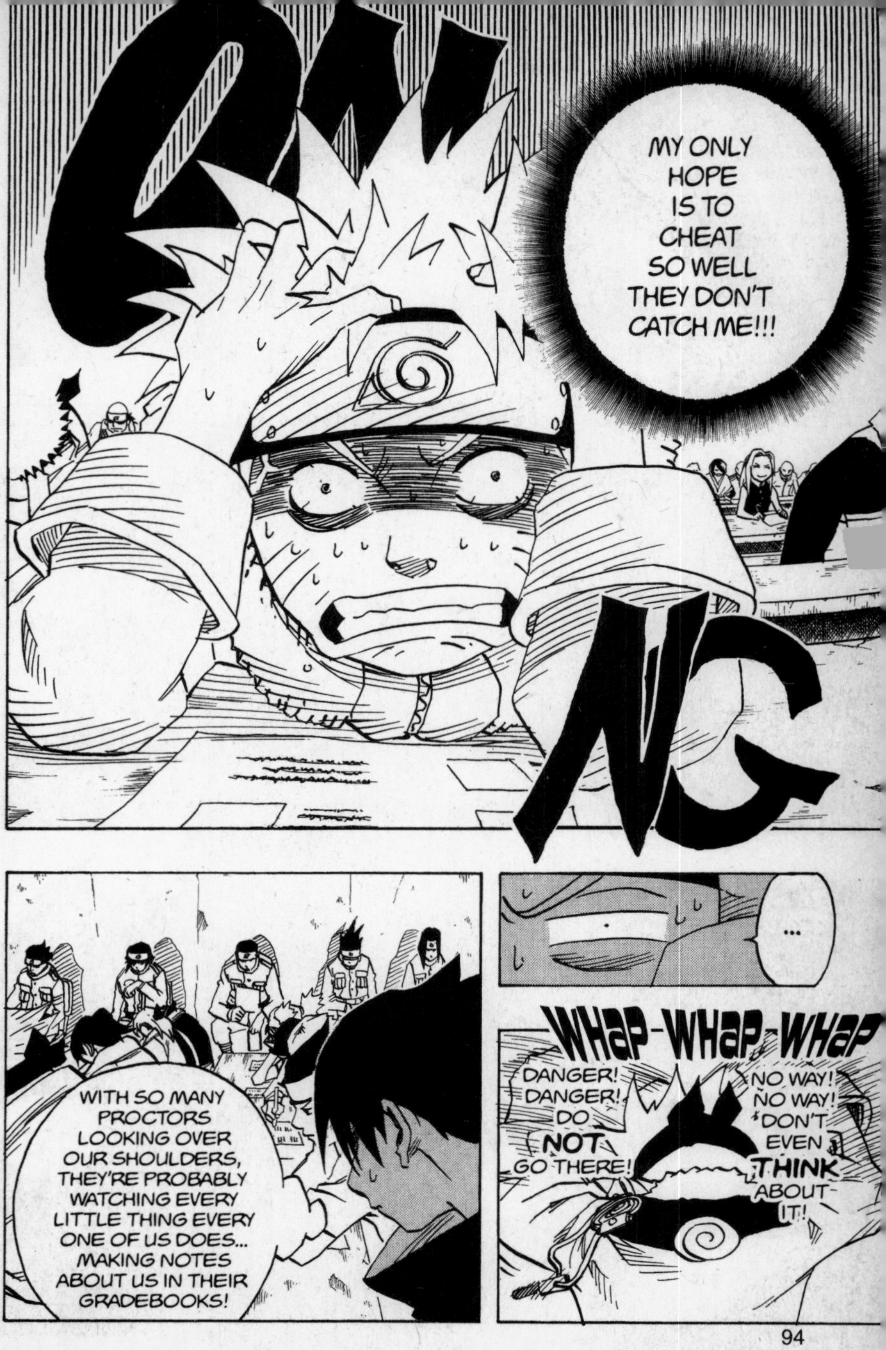
MY ONLY HOPE IS TO CHEAT SO WELL THEY DON'T CATCH ME!!!
...
WHAP-WHAP-WHAP
NO WAY! NO WAY! DON'T EVEN THINK ABOUT IT!
DANGER! DANGER! DO NOT GO THERE!
WITH SO MANY PROCTORS LOOKING OVER OUR SHOULDERS, THEY'RE PROBABLY WATCHING EVERY LITTLE THING EVERY ONE OF US DOES... MAKING NOTES ABOUT US IN THEIR GRADEBOOKS!

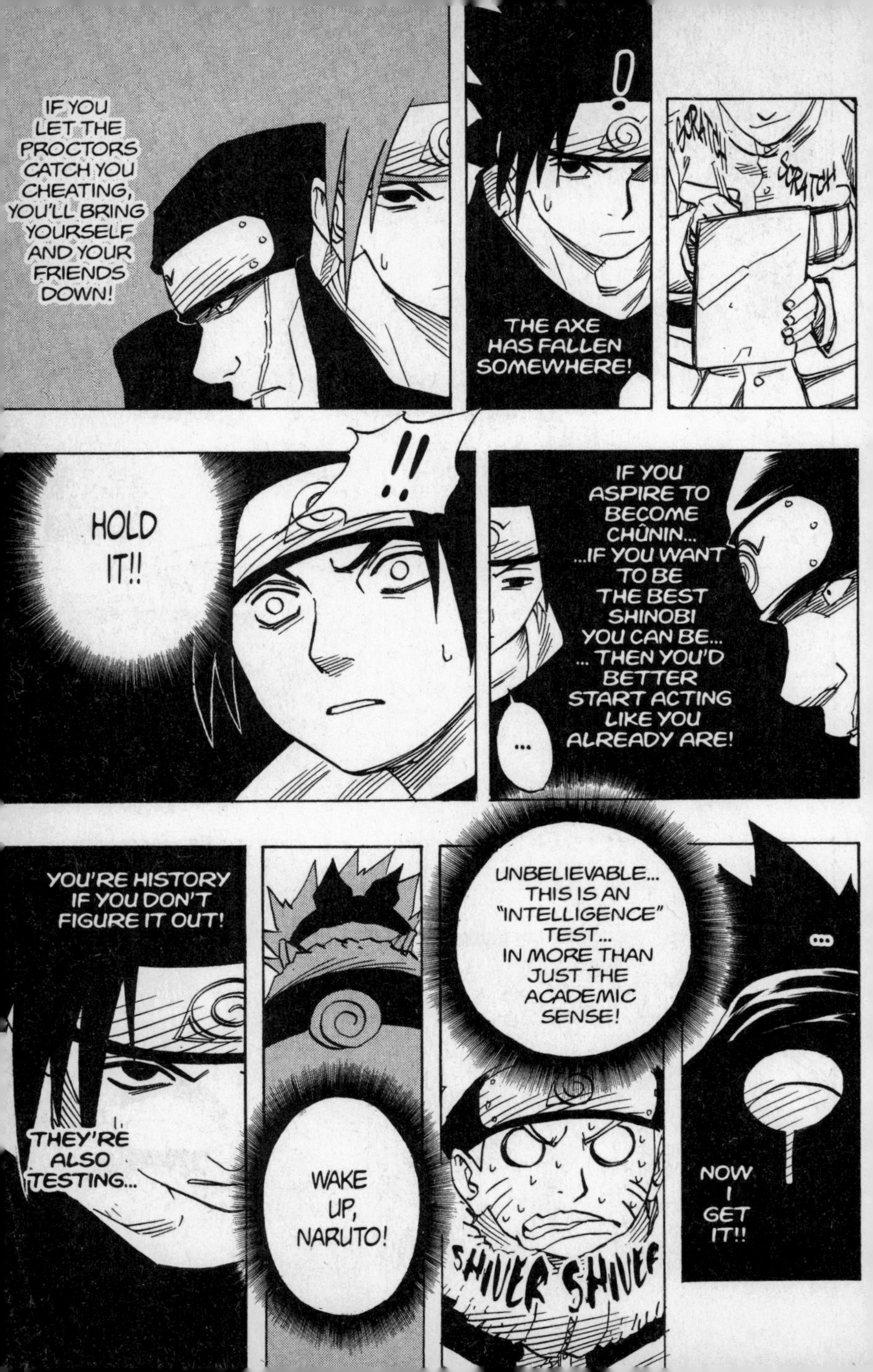
SCRATCH
SCRATCH
!
THE AXE HAS FALLEN SOMEWHERE!
IF YOU LET THE PROCTORS CATCH YOU CHEATING, YOU'LL BRING YOURSELF AND YOUR FRIENDS DOWN!
IF YOU ASPIRE TO BECOME CHÛNIN... ...IF YOU WANT TO BE THE BEST SHINOBI YOU CAN BE... ... THEN YOU'D BETTER START ACTING LIKE YOU ALREADY ARE!
...
!!
HOLD IT!!
...
NOW I GET IT!!
UNBELIEVABLE... THIS IS AN "INTELLIGENCE" TEST... IN MORE THAN JUST THE ACADEMIC SENSE!
SHIVER SHIVER
WAKE UP, NARUTO!
YOU'RE HISTORY IF YOU DON'T FIGURE IT OUT!
THEY'RE ALSO TESTING...

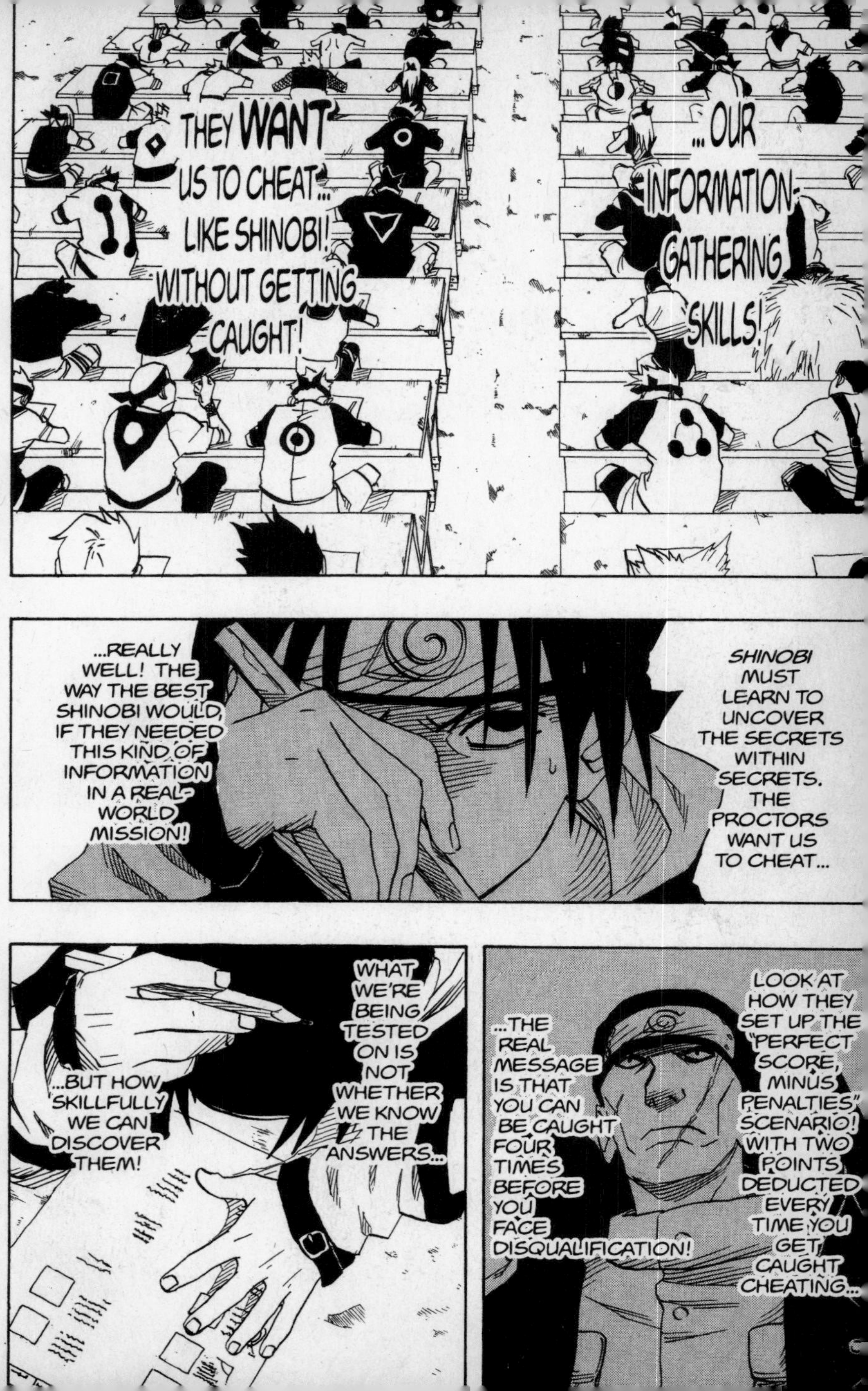
...OUR INFORMATION-GATHERING SKILLS!
THEY WANT US TO CHEAT... LIKE SHINOBI! WITHOUT GETTING CAUGHT!
SHINOBI MUST LEARN TO UNCOVER THE SECRETS WITHIN SECRETS. THE PROCTORS WANT US TO CHEAT...
...REALLY WELL! THE WAY THE BEST SHINOBI WOULD, IF THEY NEEDED THIS KIND OF INFORMATION IN A REAL-WORLD MISSION!
LOOK AT HOW THEY SET UP THE "PERFECT SCORE, MINUS PENALTIES" SCENARIO! WITH TWO POINTS DEDUCTED EVERY TIME YOU GET CAUGHT CHEATING...
...THE REAL MESSAGE IS THAT YOU CAN BE CAUGHT FOUR TIMES BEFORE YOU FACE DISQUALIFICATION!
WHAT WE'RE BEING TESTED ON IS NOT WHETHER WE KNOW THE ANSWERS...
...BUT HOW SKILLFULLY WE CAN DISCOVER THEM!

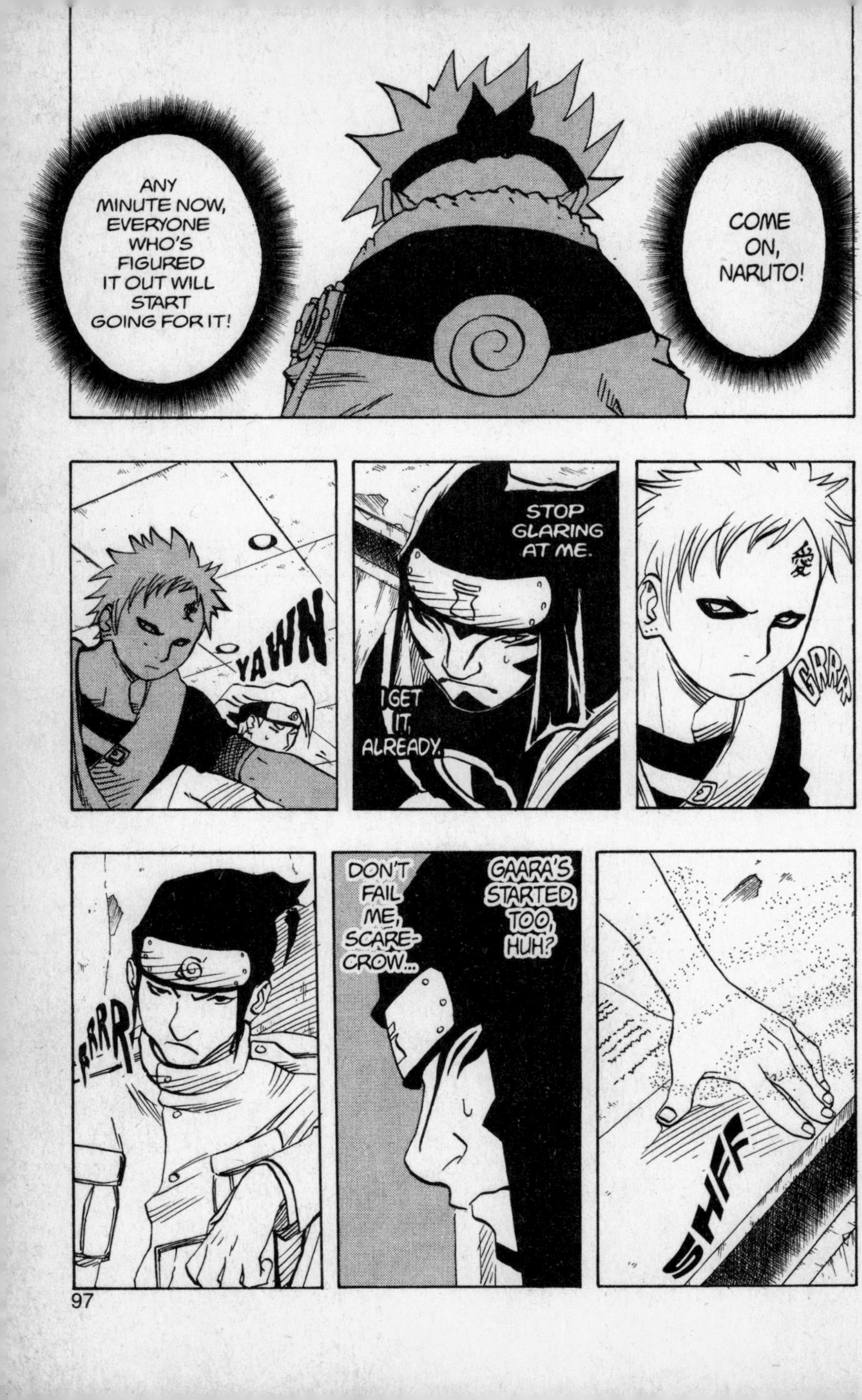
COME ON, NARUTO!
ANY MINUTE NOW, EVERYONE WHO'S FIGURED IT OUT WILL START GOING FOR IT!
STOP GLARING AT ME.
I GET IT, ALREADY.
YAWN
SHFF
GAARA'S STARTED, TOO, HUH?
DON'T FAIL ME, SCARE-CROW...

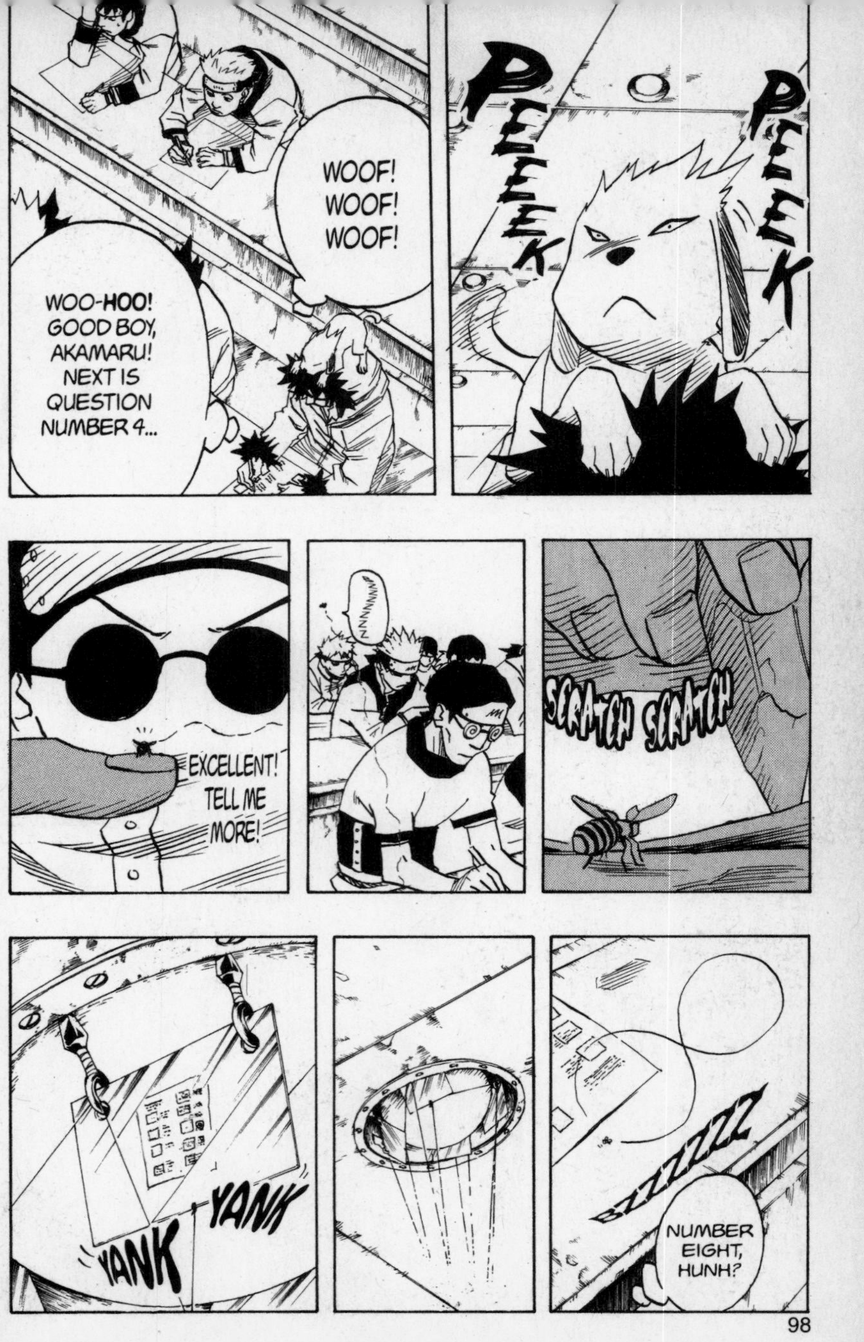
PEEEK
PEEEK
WOOF! WOOF! WOOF!
WOO-HOO! GOOD BOY, AKAMARU! NEXT IS QUESTION NUMBER 4...
SCRATCH SCRATCH
EXCELLENT! TELL ME MORE!
NUMBER EIGHT, HUNH?
YANK
YANK

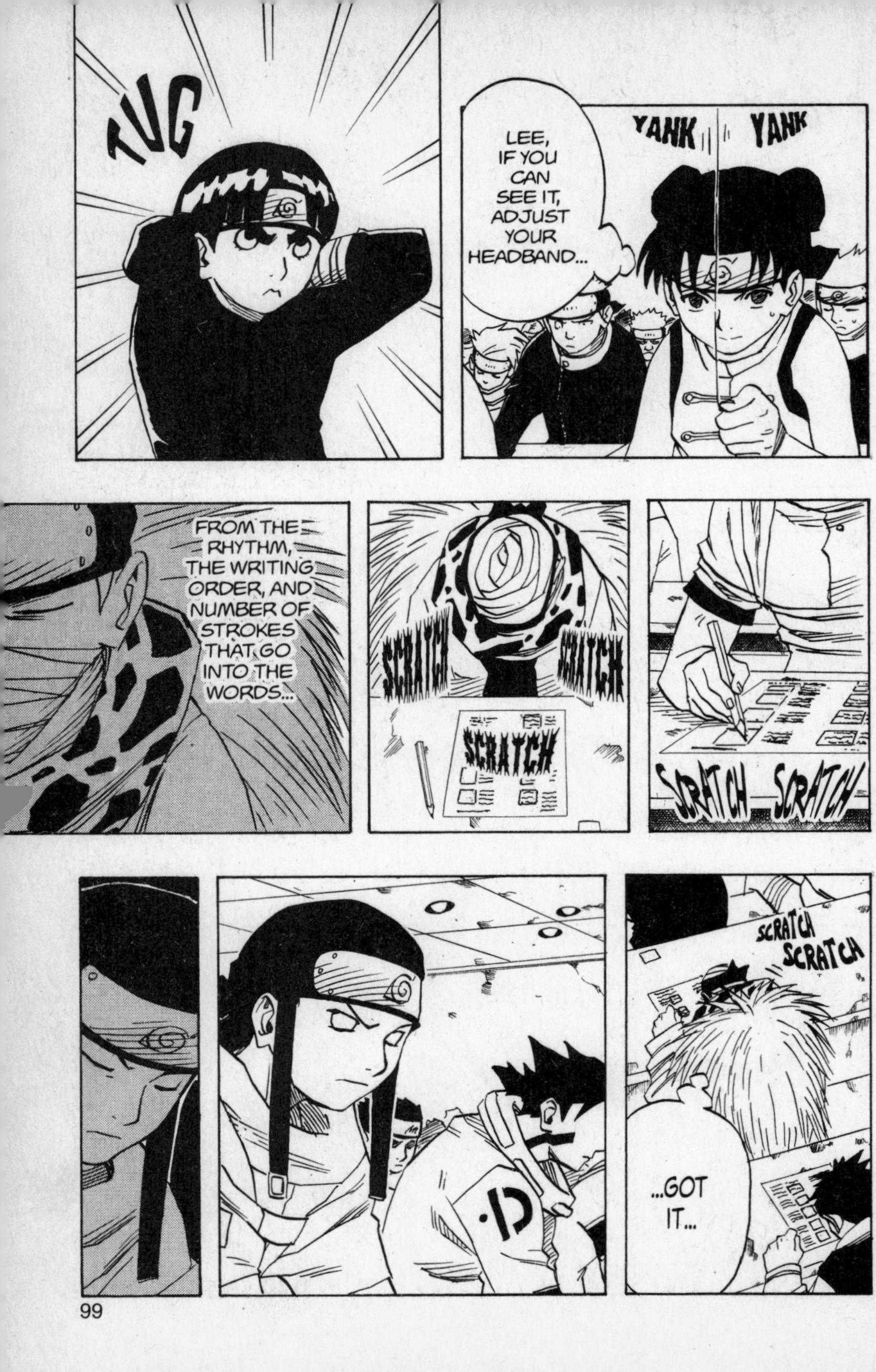
YANK
YANK
LEE, IF YOU CAN SEE IT, ADJUST YOUR HEADBAND...
TUG
SCRATCH
SCRATCH
SCRATCH
SCRATCH
SCRATCH
FROM THE RHYTHM, THE WRITING ORDER, AND NUMBER OF STROKES THAT GO INTO THE WORDS...
SCRATCH
SCRATCH
...GOT IT...

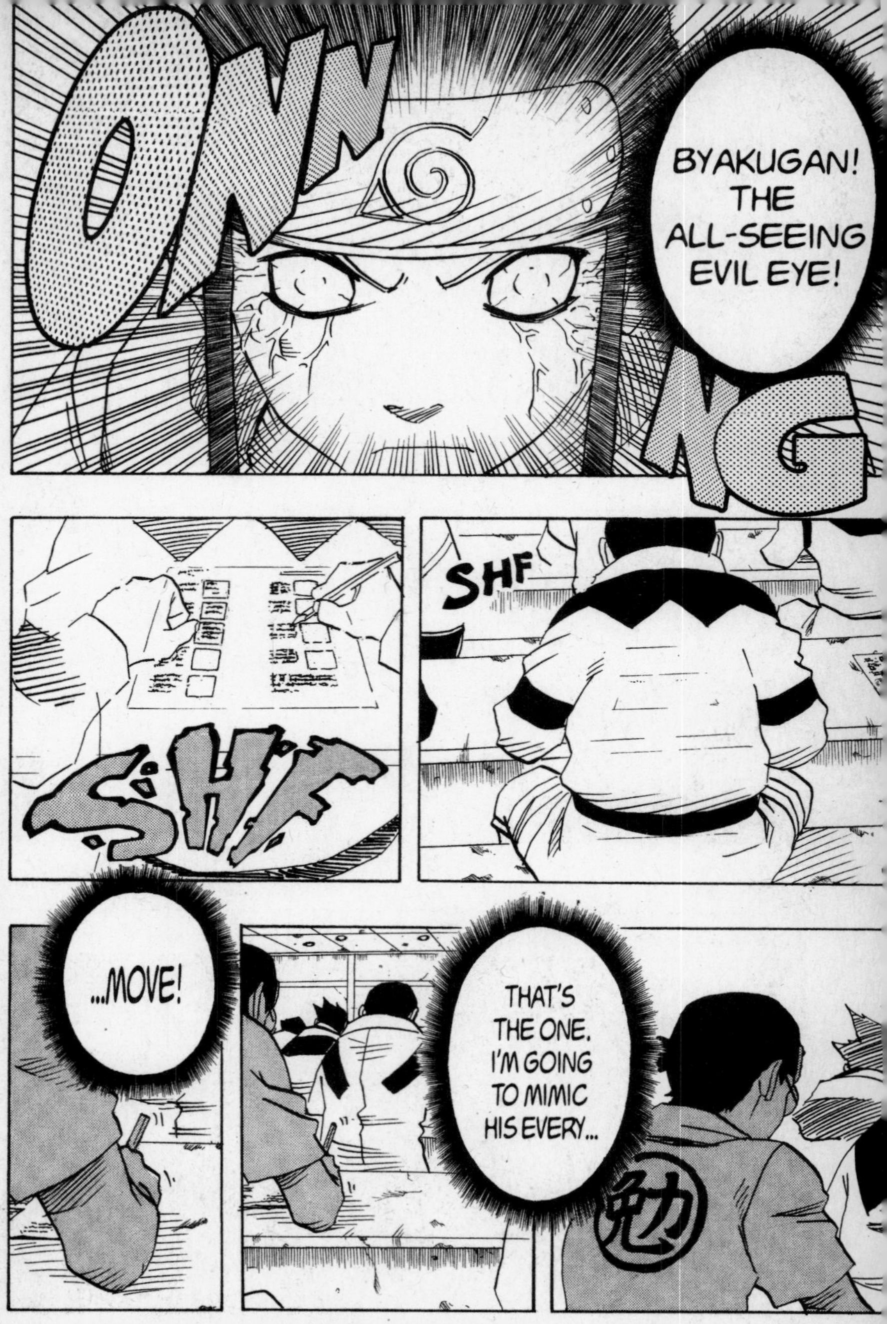
BYAKUGAN! THE ALL-SEEING EVIL EYE!
OWNNG
SHF
SHF
THAT'S THE ONE. I'M GOING TO MIMIC HIS EVERY...
...MOVE!

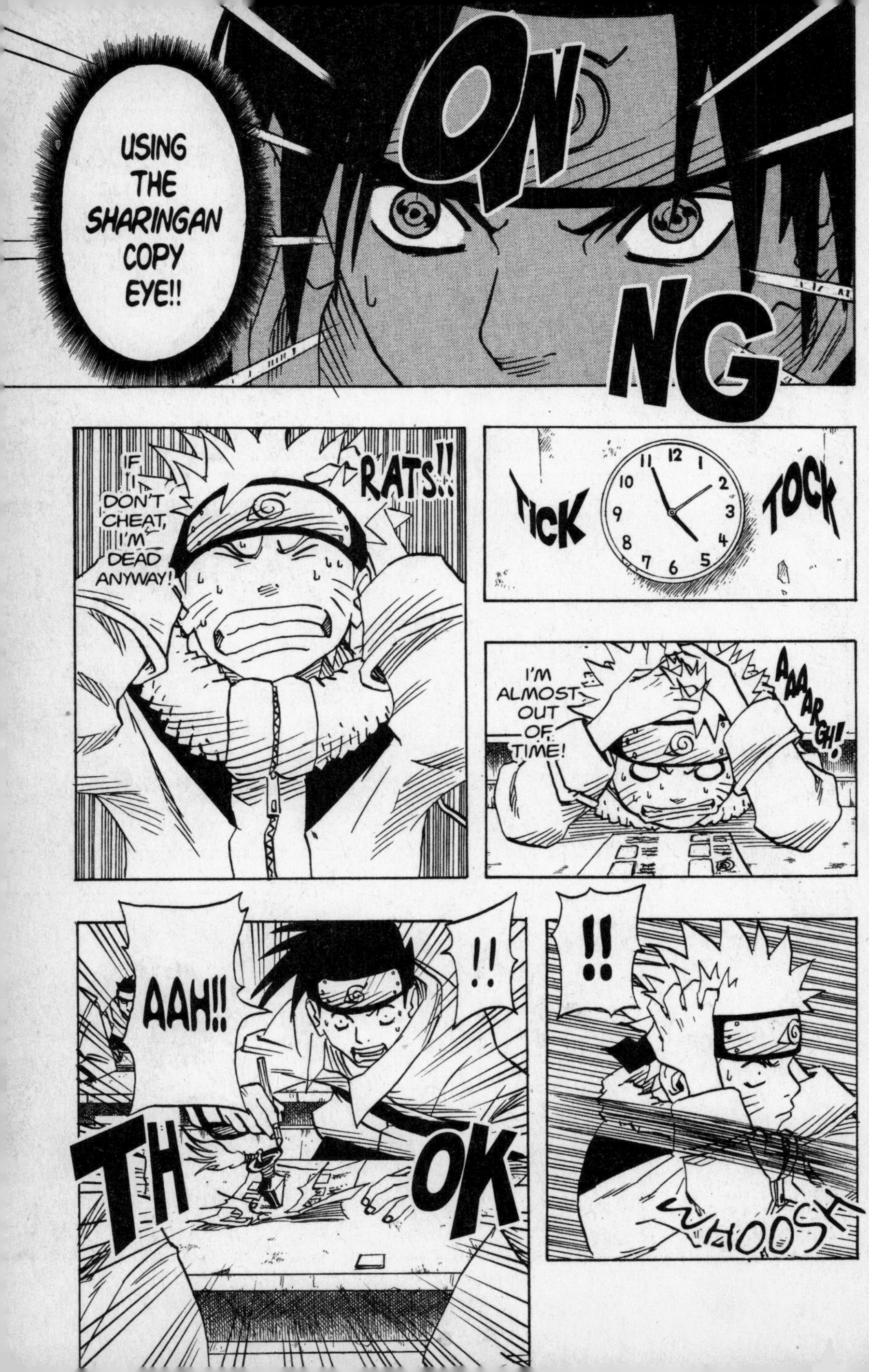
USING THE SHARINGAN COPY EYE!!
ONNG
TICK TOCK
I'M ALMOST OUT OF TIME!
AAAARGH!
IF I DON'T CHEAT, I'M DEAD ANYWAY!
RATS!!
!!
WHOOSH
!!
AAH!!
THOK

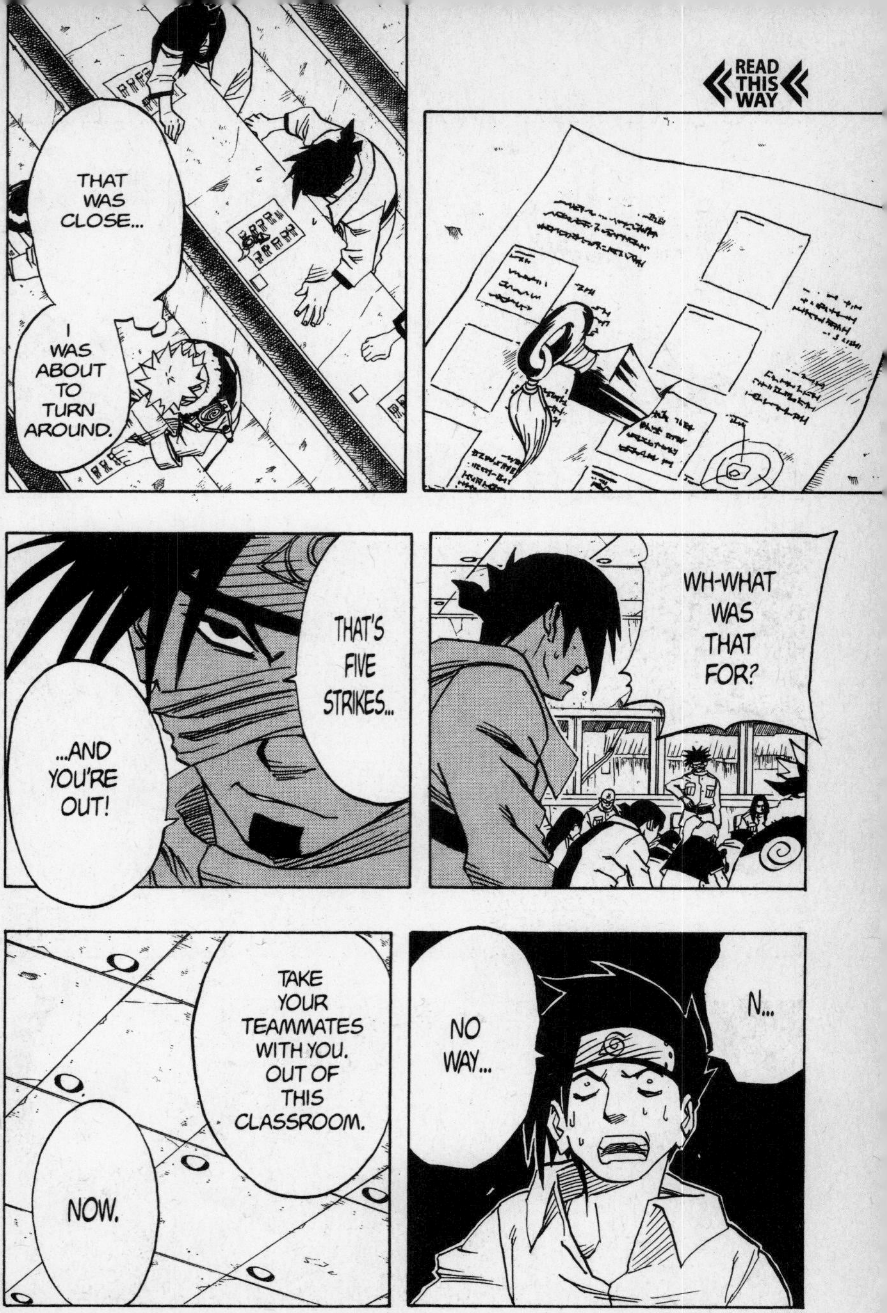
READ THIS WAY
THAT WAS CLOSE...
I WAS ABOUT TO TURN AROUND.
WH-WHAT WAS THAT FOR?
THAT'S FIVE STRIKES...
...AND YOU'RE OUT!
N...
NO WAY...
TAKE YOUR TEAMMATES WITH YOU. OUT OF THIS CLASSROOM.
NOW.

READ THIS WAY

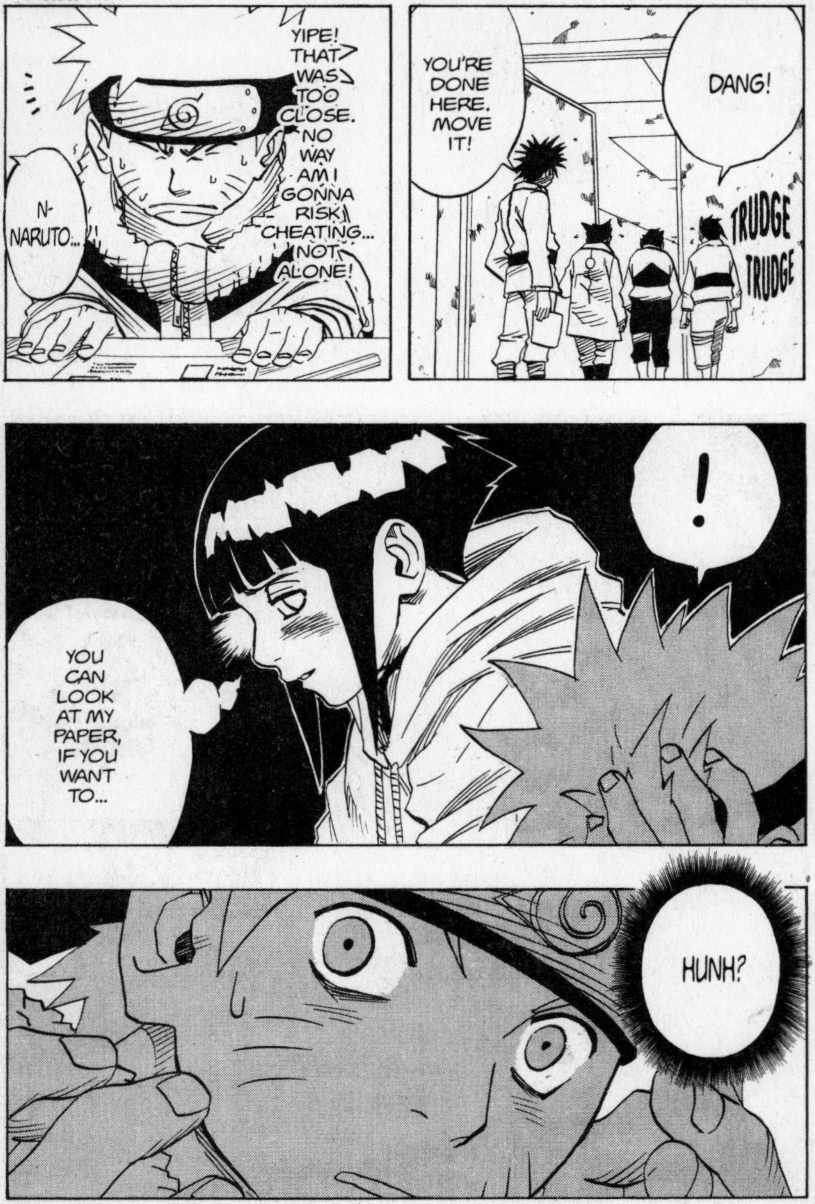
DANG!
YOU'RE DONE HERE. MOVE IT!
TRUDGE TRUDGE
YIPE! THAT WAS TOO CLOSE. NO WAY AM I GONNA RISK CHEATING... NOT ALONE!
N-NARUTO...
!
YOU CAN LOOK AT MY PAPER, IF YOU WANT TO...
HUNH?

HUNH?

Number 42:

To Each His Own

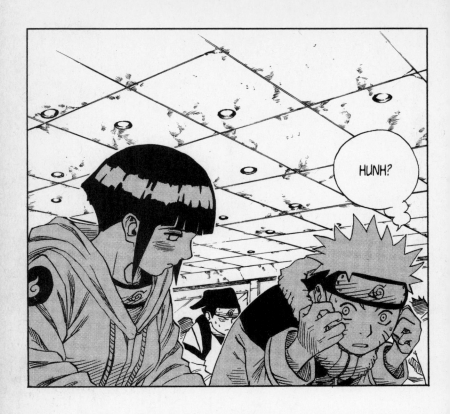

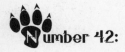

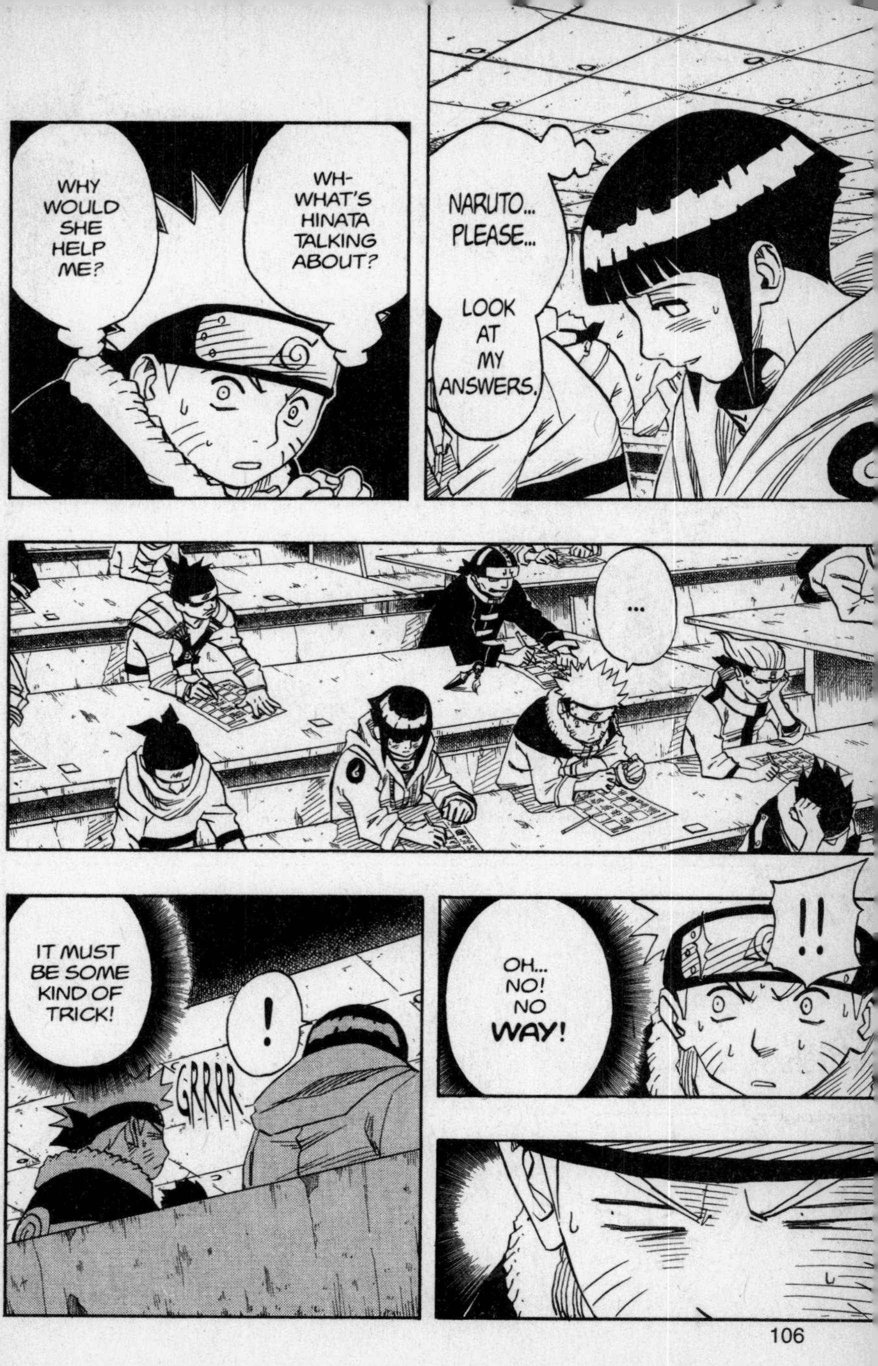
NARUTO... PLEASE...
LOOK AT MY ANSWERS.
WH- WHAT'S HINATA TALKING ABOUT?
WHY WOULD SHE HELP ME?
...
!!
OH... NO! NO **WAY!**
IT MUST BE SOME KIND OF TRICK!
!
GRRRR

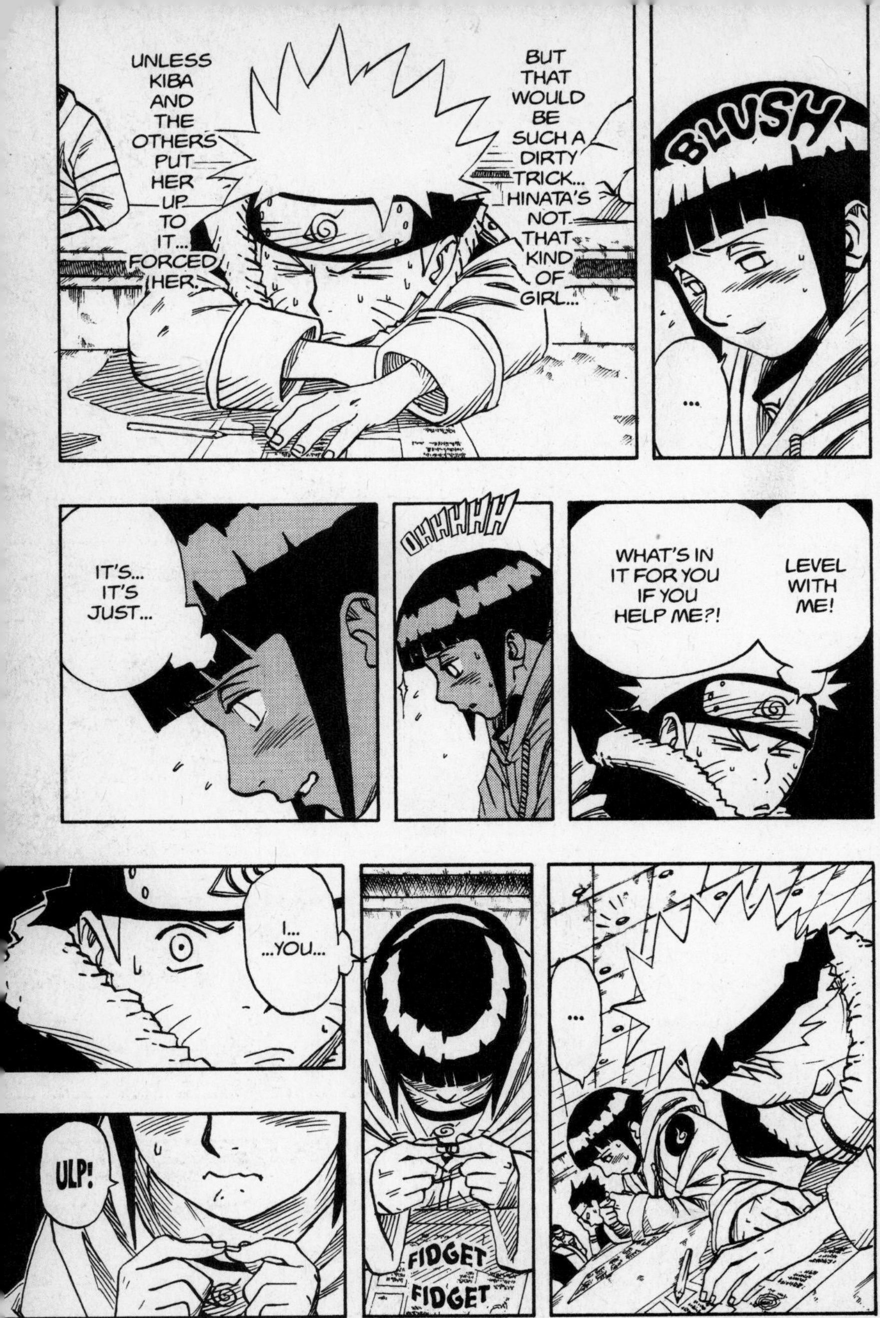
BLUSH
...
BUT THAT WOULD BE SUCH A DIRTY TRICK... HINATA'S NOT THAT KIND OF GIRL...
UNLESS KIBA AND THE OTHERS PUT HER UP TO IT... FORCED HER.
LEVEL WITH ME!
WHAT'S IN IT FOR YOU IF YOU HELP ME?!
OHHHHHH
IT'S... IT'S JUST...
...
FIDGET
FIDGET
I... ...YOU...
ULP!

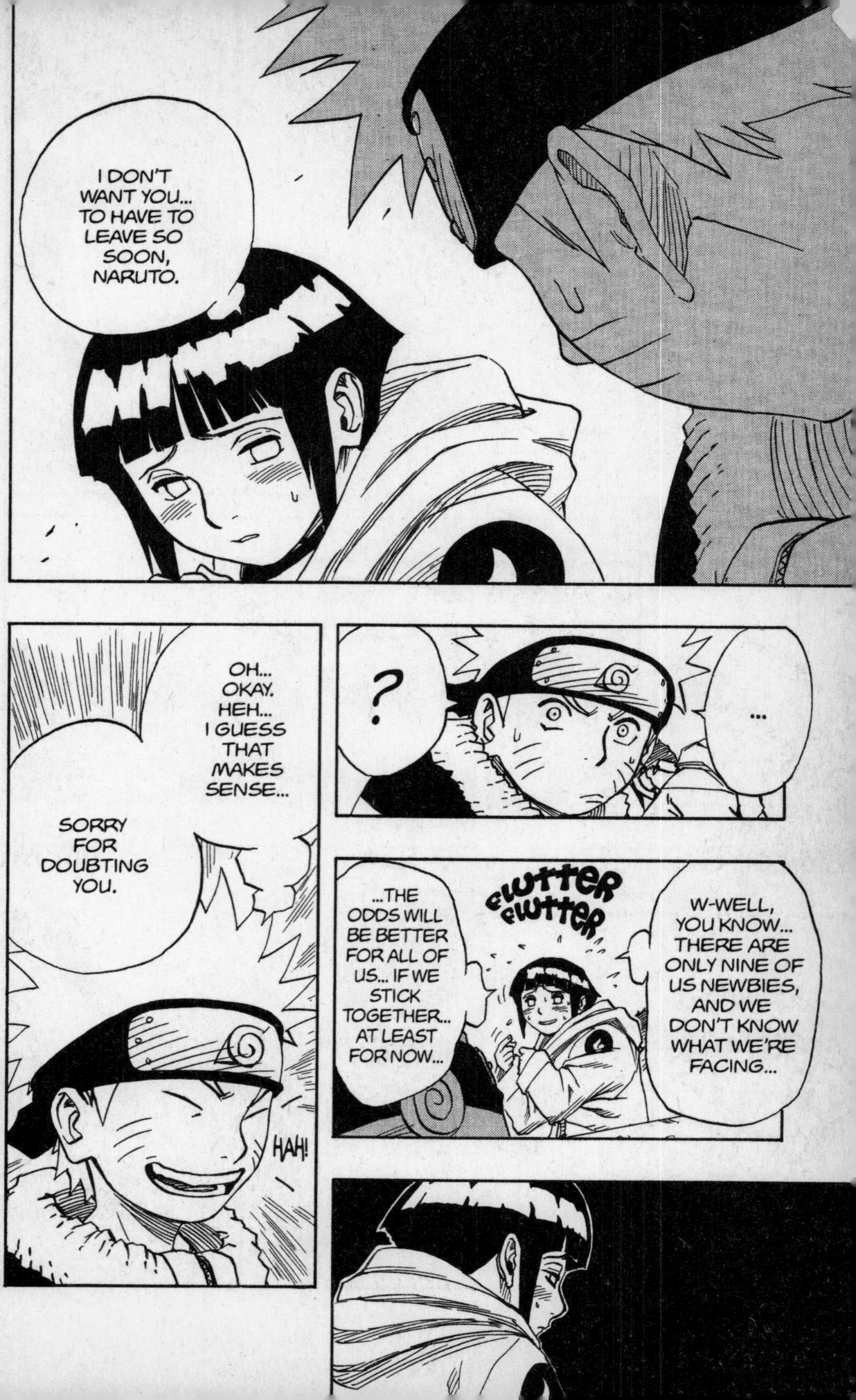
I DON'T WANT YOU... TO HAVE TO LEAVE SO SOON, NARUTO.
...
?
W-WELL, YOU KNOW... THERE ARE ONLY NINE OF US NEWBIES, AND WE DON'T KNOW WHAT WE'RE FACING...
FLUTTER FLUTTER
...THE ODDS WILL BE BETTER FOR ALL OF US... IF WE STICK TOGETHER.. AT LEAST FOR NOW...
OH... OKAY. HEH... I GUESS THAT MAKES SENSE...
SORRY FOR DOUBTING YOU.
HAH!

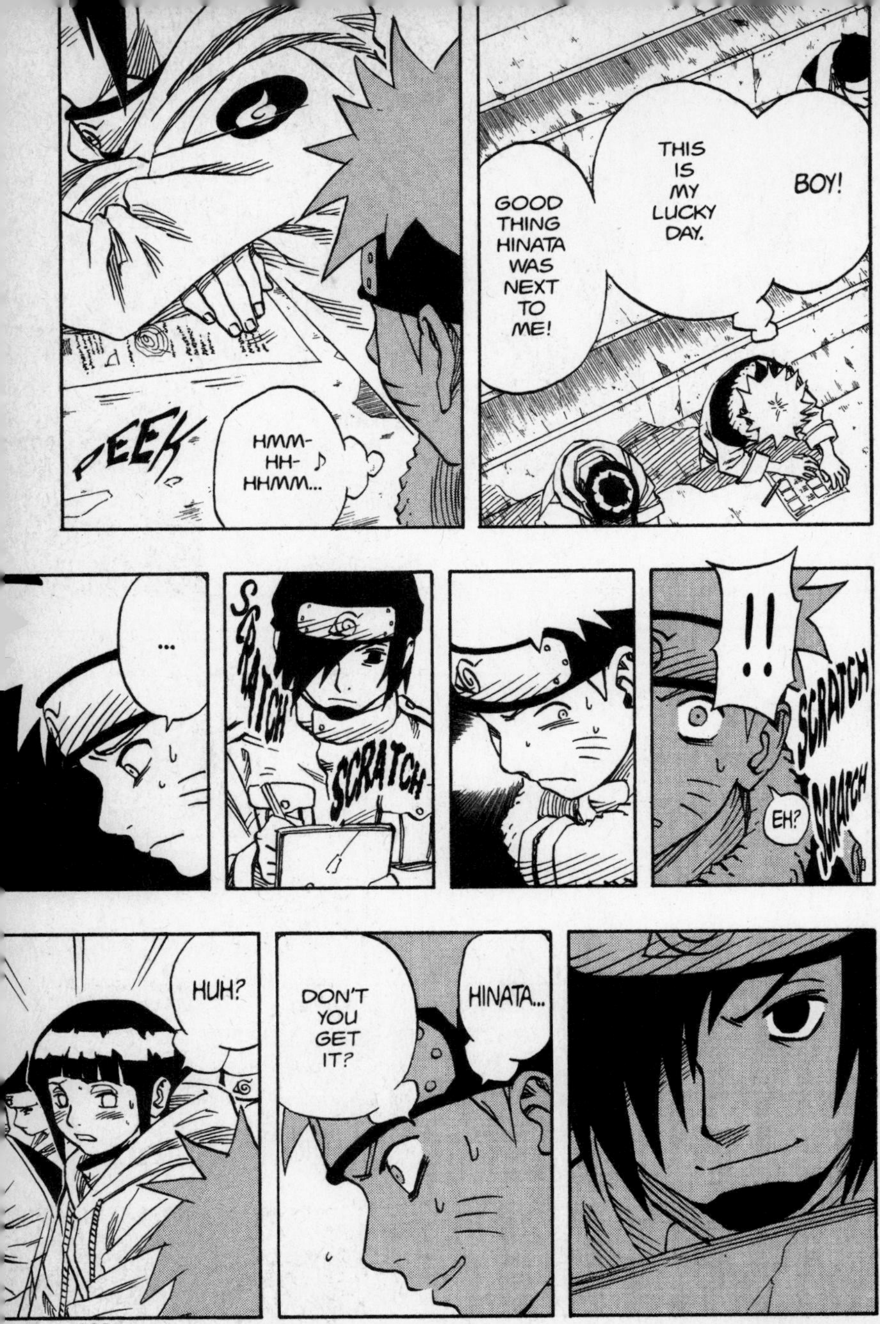
BOY!
THIS IS MY LUCKY DAY.
GOOD THING HINATA WAS NEXT TO ME!
PEEK
HMM-HH-HHMM... ♪
!!
SCRATCH
SCRATCH
EH?
SCRATCH
SCRATCH
...
HINATA...
DON'T YOU GET IT?
HUH?

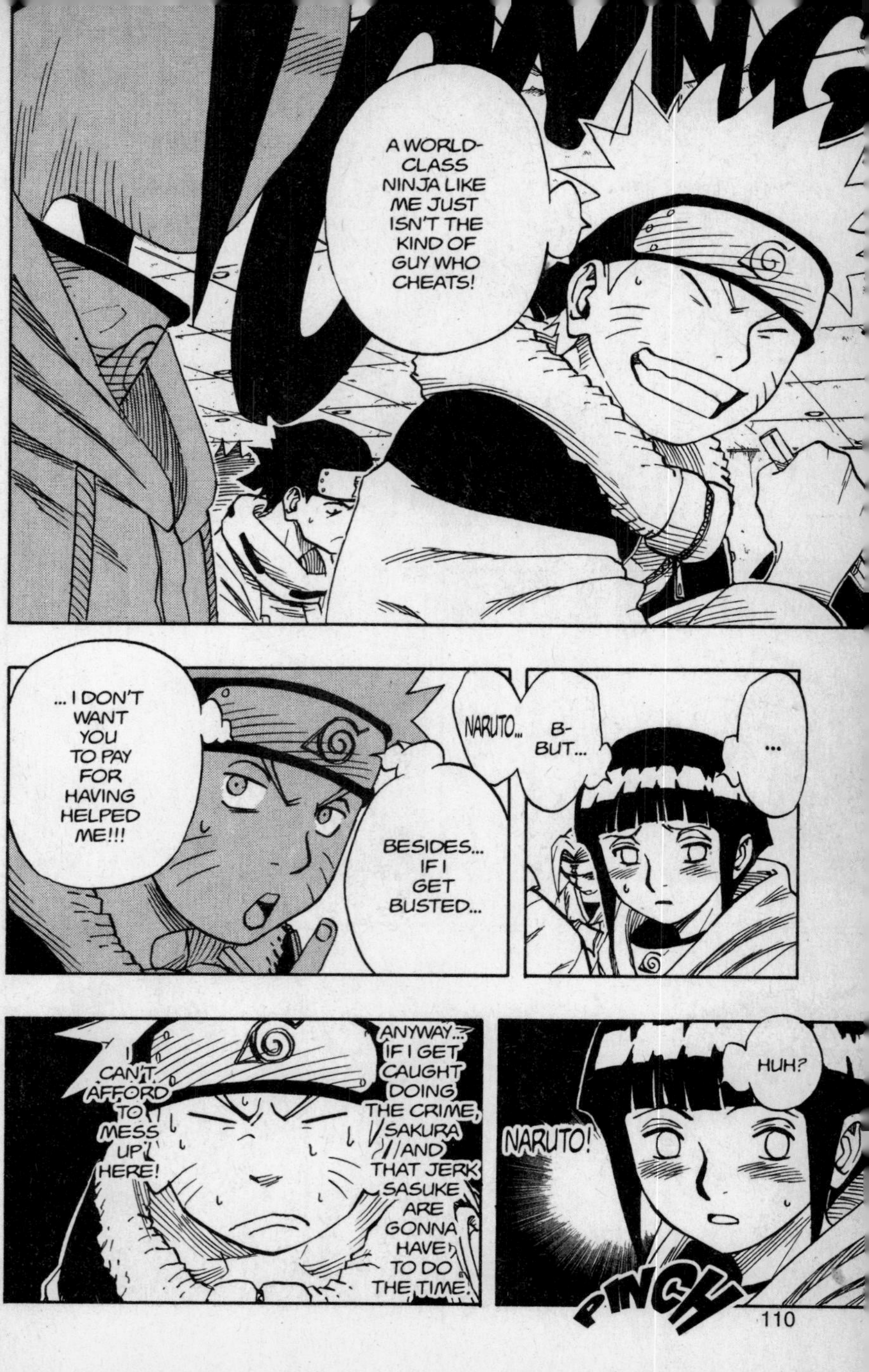
A WORLD-CLASS NINJA LIKE ME JUST ISN'T THE KIND OF GUY WHO CHEATS!
...
B-BUT...
NARUTO...
BESIDES... IF I GET BUSTED...
... I DON'T WANT YOU TO PAY FOR HAVING HELPED ME!!!
HUH?
NARUTO!
PINCH
ANYWAY... IF I GET CAUGHT DOING THE CRIME, SAKURA AND THAT JERK SASUKE ARE GONNA HAVE TO DO THE TIME.
I CAN'T AFFORD TO MESS UP HERE!

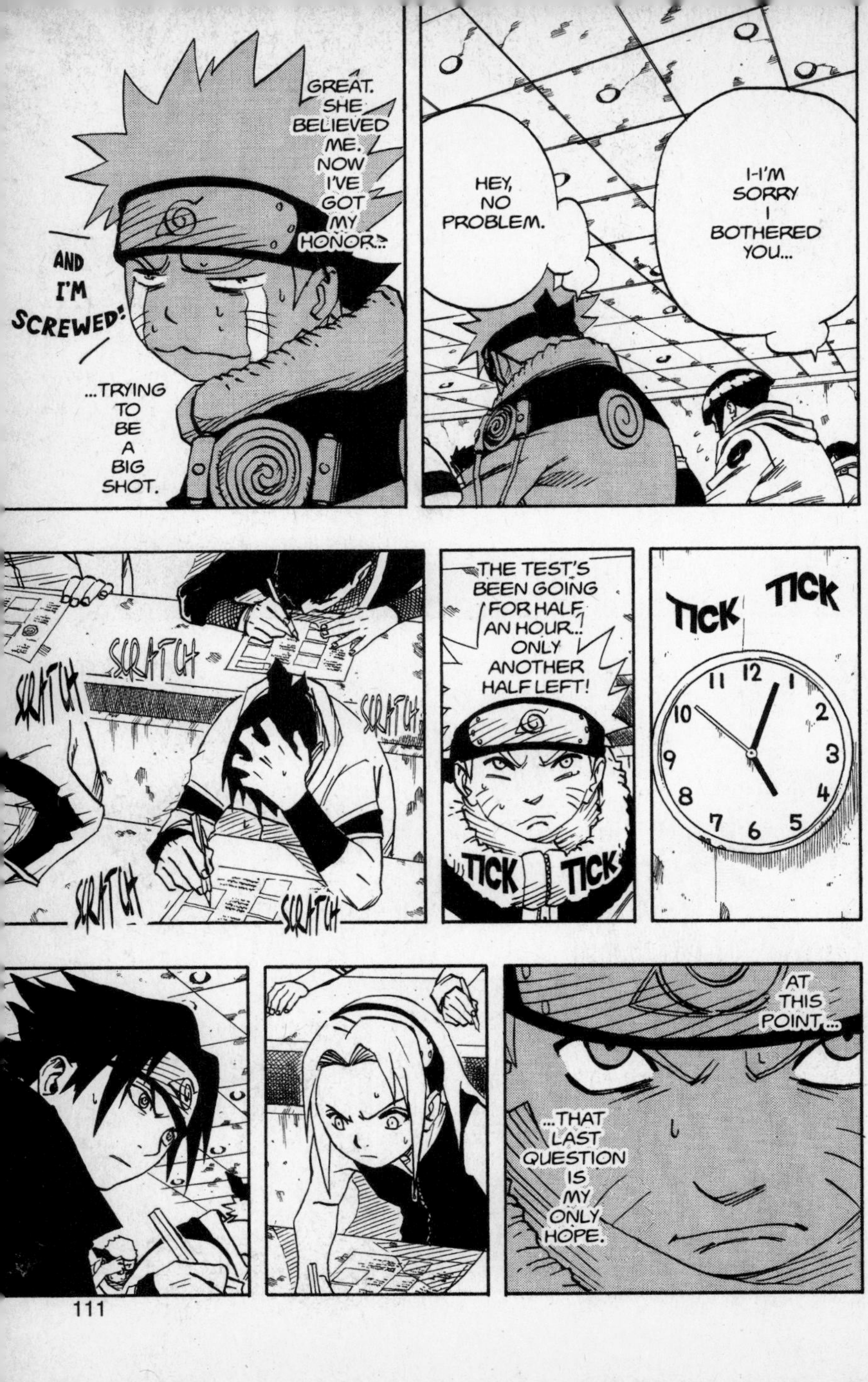
I-I'M SORRY I BOTHERED YOU...
HEY, NO PROBLEM.
GREAT. SHE BELIEVED ME. NOW I'VE GOT MY HONOR...
AND I'M SCREWED!
...TRYING TO BE A BIG SHOT.
TICK
TICK
THE TEST'S BEEN GOING FOR HALF AN HOUR... ONLY ANOTHER HALF LEFT!
TICK
TICK
SCRATCH
SCRATCH
SCRATCH
SCRATCH
SCRATCH
AT THIS POINT...
...THAT LAST QUESTION IS MY ONLY HOPE.

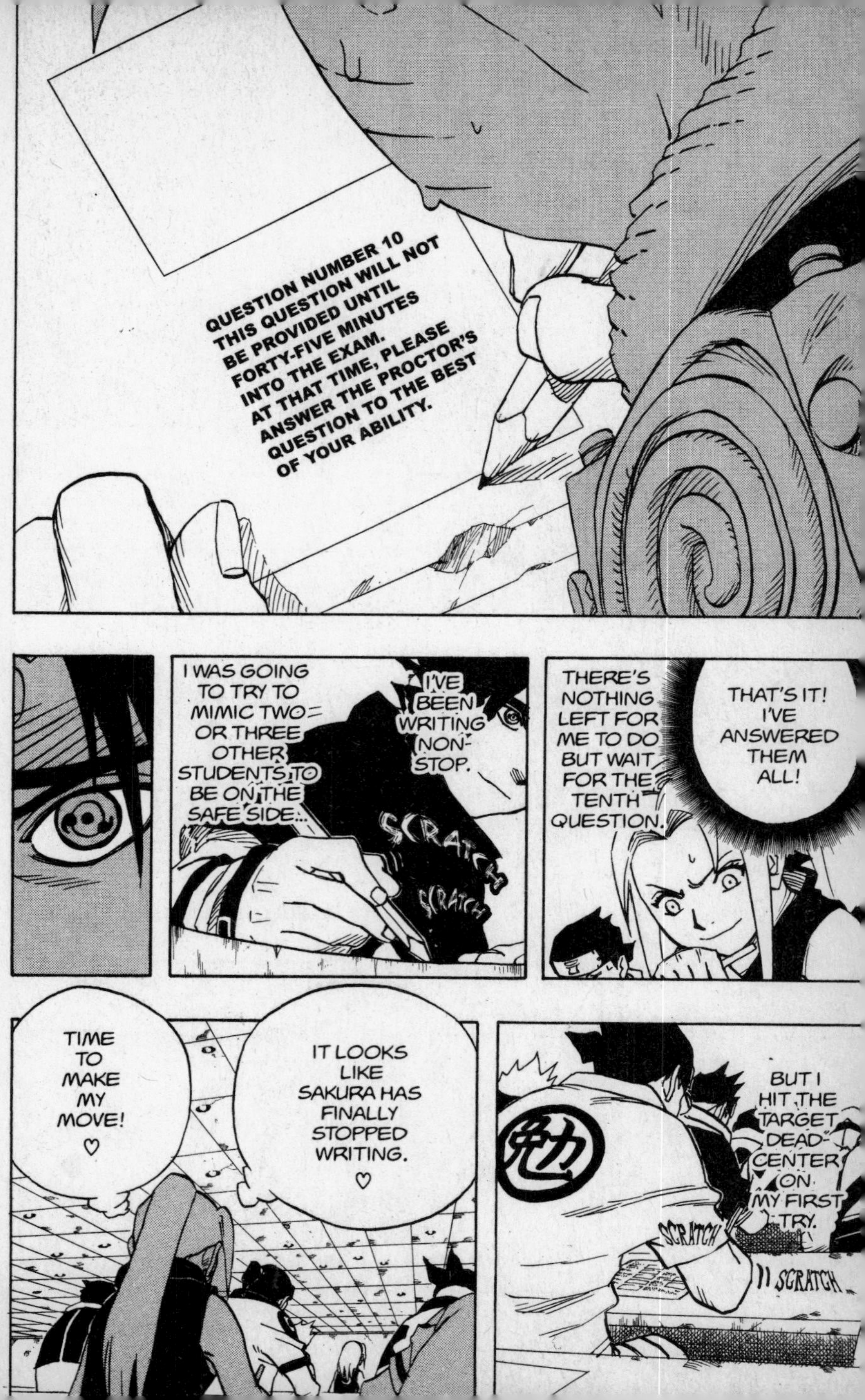
QUESTION NUMBER 10
THIS QUESTION WILL NOT BE PROVIDED UNTIL FORTY-FIVE MINUTES INTO THE EXAM. AT THAT TIME, PLEASE ANSWER THE PROCTOR'S QUESTION TO THE BEST OF YOUR ABILITY.
THAT'S IT! I'VE ANSWERED THEM ALL!
THERE'S NOTHING LEFT FOR ME TO DO BUT WAIT FOR THE TENTH QUESTION.
I'VE BEEN WRITING NON-STOP.
I WAS GOING TO TRY TO MIMIC TWO OR THREE OTHER STUDENTS TO BE ON THE SAFE SIDE...
SCRATCH
SCRATCH
BUT I HIT THE TARGET DEAD-CENTER ON MY FIRST TRY.
SCRATCH
SCRATCH
IT LOOKS LIKE SAKURA HAS FINALLY STOPPED WRITING. ♡
TIME TO MAKE MY MOVE! ♡

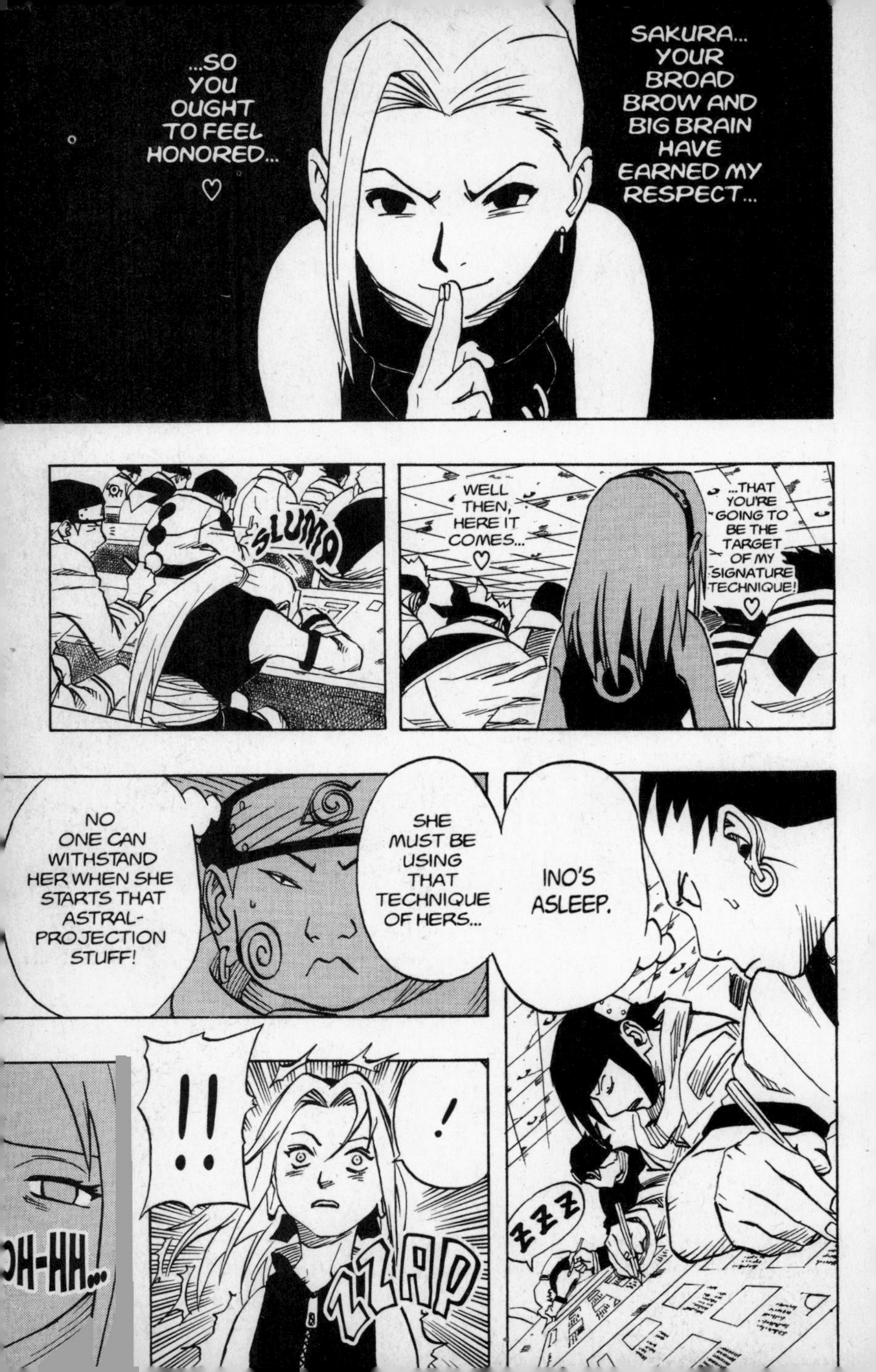
SAKURA... YOUR BROAD BROW AND BIG BRAIN HAVE EARNED MY RESPECT...
...SO YOU OUGHT TO FEEL HONORED... ♡
...THAT YOU'RE GOING TO BE THE TARGET OF MY SIGNATURE TECHNIQUE! ♡
WELL THEN, HERE IT COMES... ♡
SLUMP
INO'S ASLEEP.
SHE MUST BE USING THAT TECHNIQUE OF HERS...
NO ONE CAN WITHSTAND HER WHEN SHE STARTS THAT ASTRAL-PROJECTION STUFF!
ZZZ
!
!!
ZZAP
OH-HH...

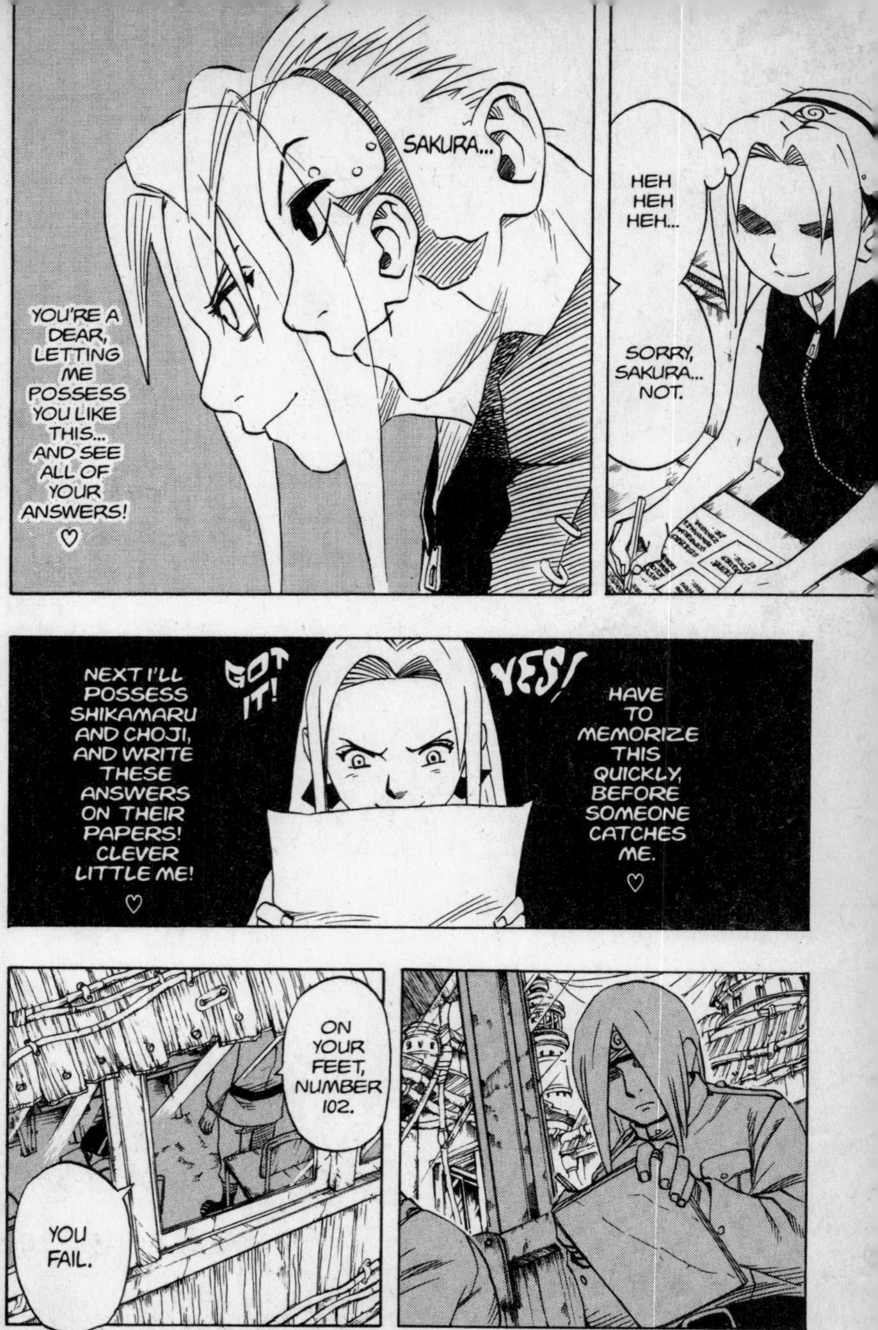
HEH HEH HEH...
SORRY, SAKURA... NOT.
SAKURA...
YOU'RE A DEAR, LETTING ME POSSESS YOU LIKE THIS... AND SEE ALL OF YOUR ANSWERS! ♡
HAVE TO MEMORIZE THIS QUICKLY, BEFORE SOMEONE CATCHES ME. ♡
YES!
GOT IT!
NEXT I'LL POSSESS SHIKAMARU AND CHOJI, AND WRITE THESE ANSWERS ON THEIR PAPERS! CLEVER LITTLE ME! ♡
ON YOUR FEET, NUMBER 102.
YOU FAIL.

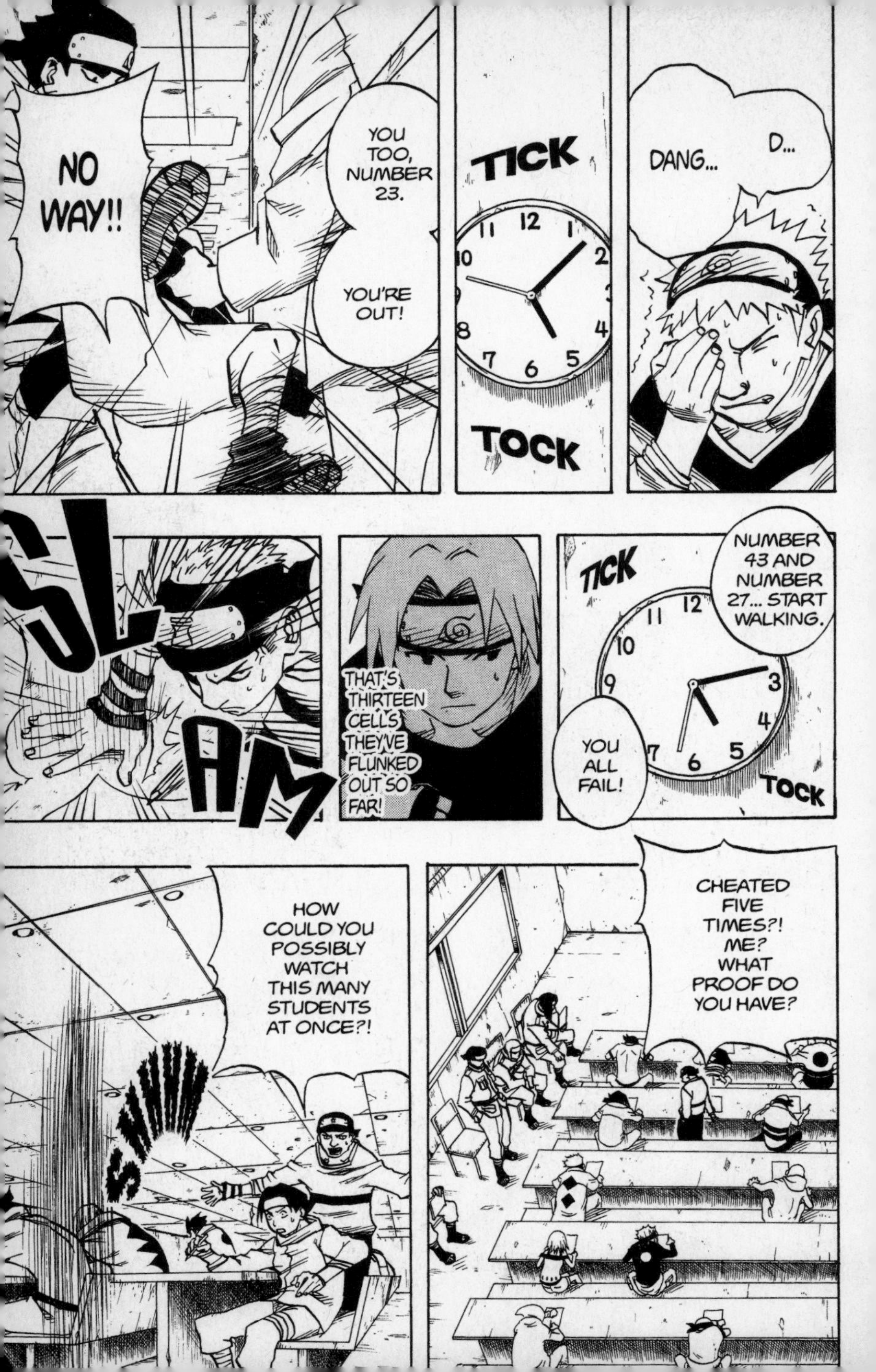
D...
DANG...
TICK
TOCK
YOU TOO, NUMBER 23.
YOU'RE OUT!
NO WAY!!
NUMBER 43 AND NUMBER 27... START WALKING.
TICK
YOU ALL FAIL!
TOCK
THAT'S THIRTEEN CELLS THEY'VE FLUNKED OUT SO FAR!
SLAM
CHEATED FIVE TIMES?! ME? WHAT PROOF DO YOU HAVE?
HOW COULD YOU POSSIBLY WATCH THIS MANY STUDENTS AT ONCE?!

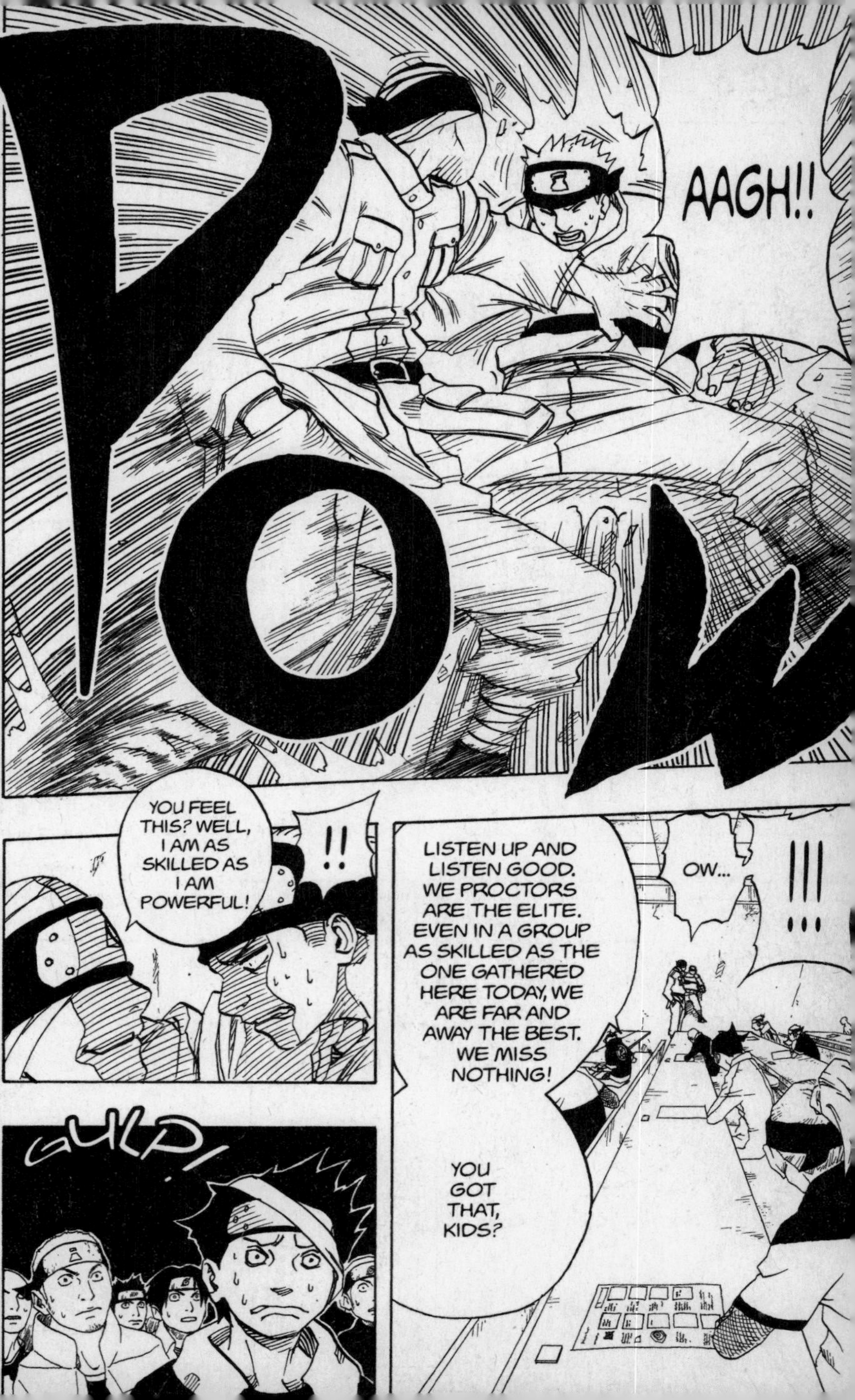
AAGH!!
POW
!!!
OW...
LISTEN UP AND LISTEN GOOD. WE PROCTORS ARE THE ELITE. EVEN IN A GROUP AS SKILLED AS THE ONE GATHERED HERE TODAY, WE ARE FAR AND AWAY THE BEST. WE MISS NOTHING!
YOU GOT THAT, KIDS?
!!
YOU FEEL THIS? WELL, I AM AS SKILLED AS I AM POWERFUL!
GULP!

READ THIS WAY

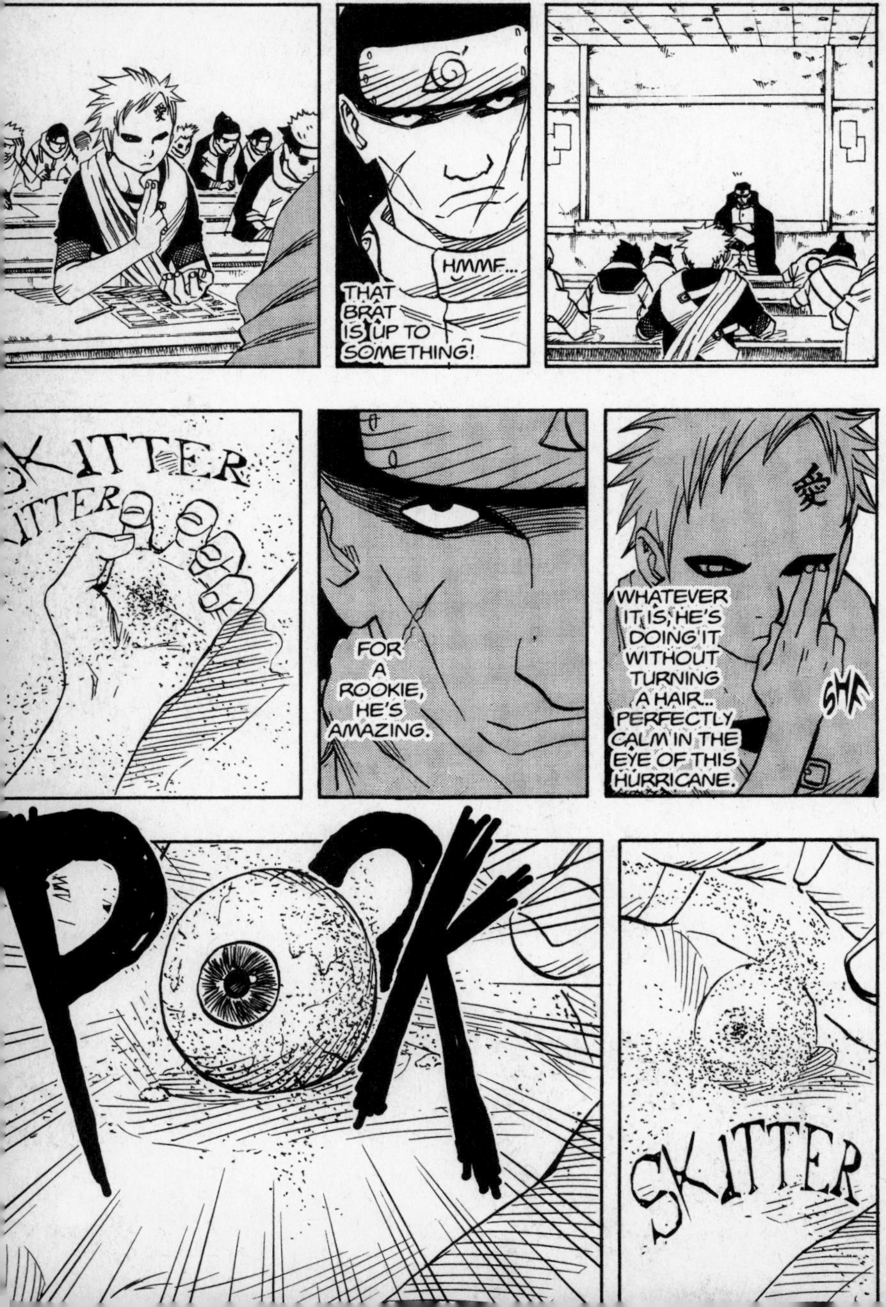
HMMF...
THAT BRAT IS UP TO SOMETHING!
WHATEVER IT IS, HE'S DOING IT WITHOUT TURNING A HAIR... PERFECTLY CALM IN THE EYE OF THIS HURRICANE.
SHF
FOR A ROOKIE, HE'S AMAZING.
SKITTER
SKITTER
POP

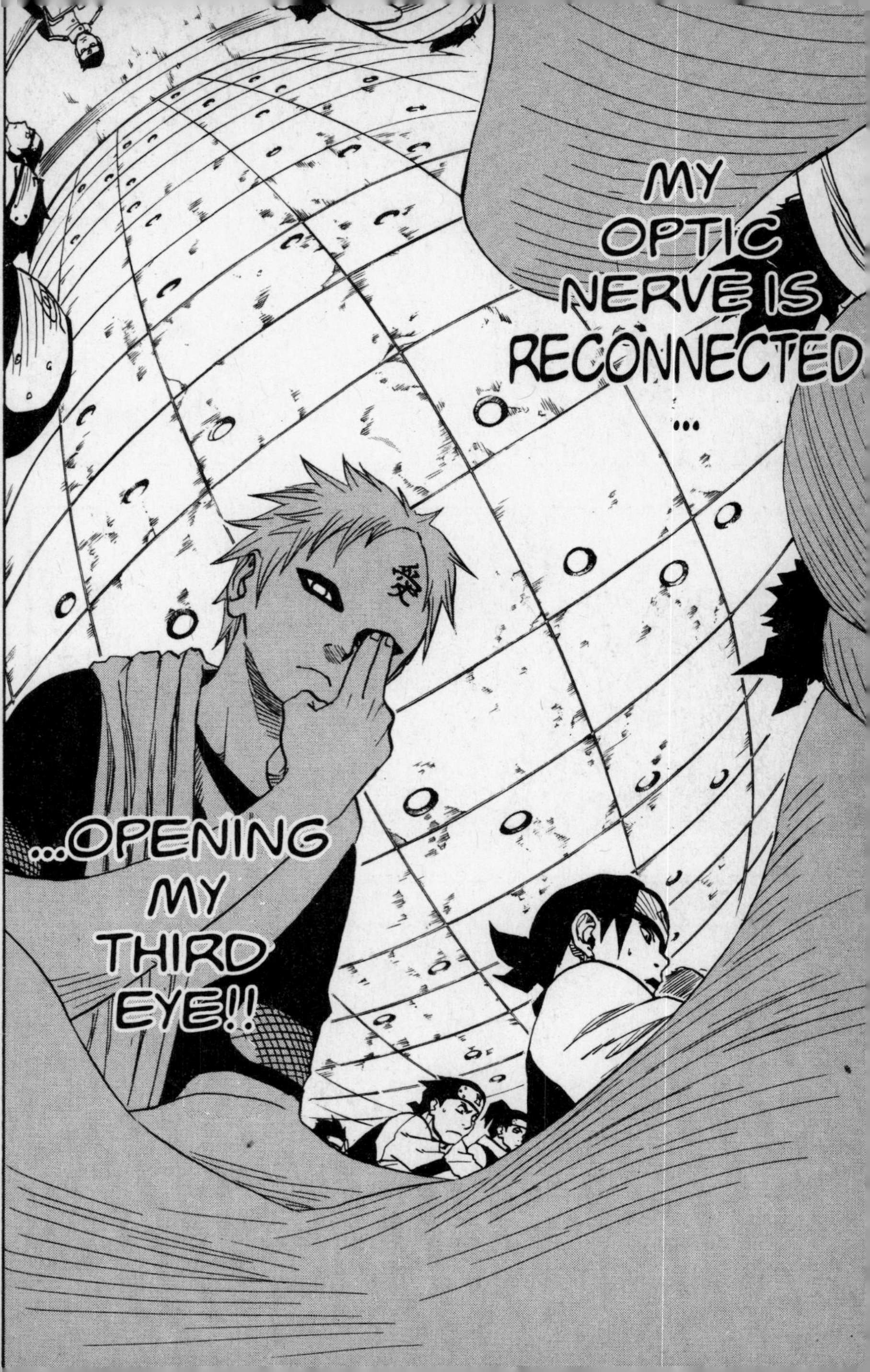
MY OPTIC NERVE IS RECONNECTED ...
...OPENING MY THIRD EYE!!

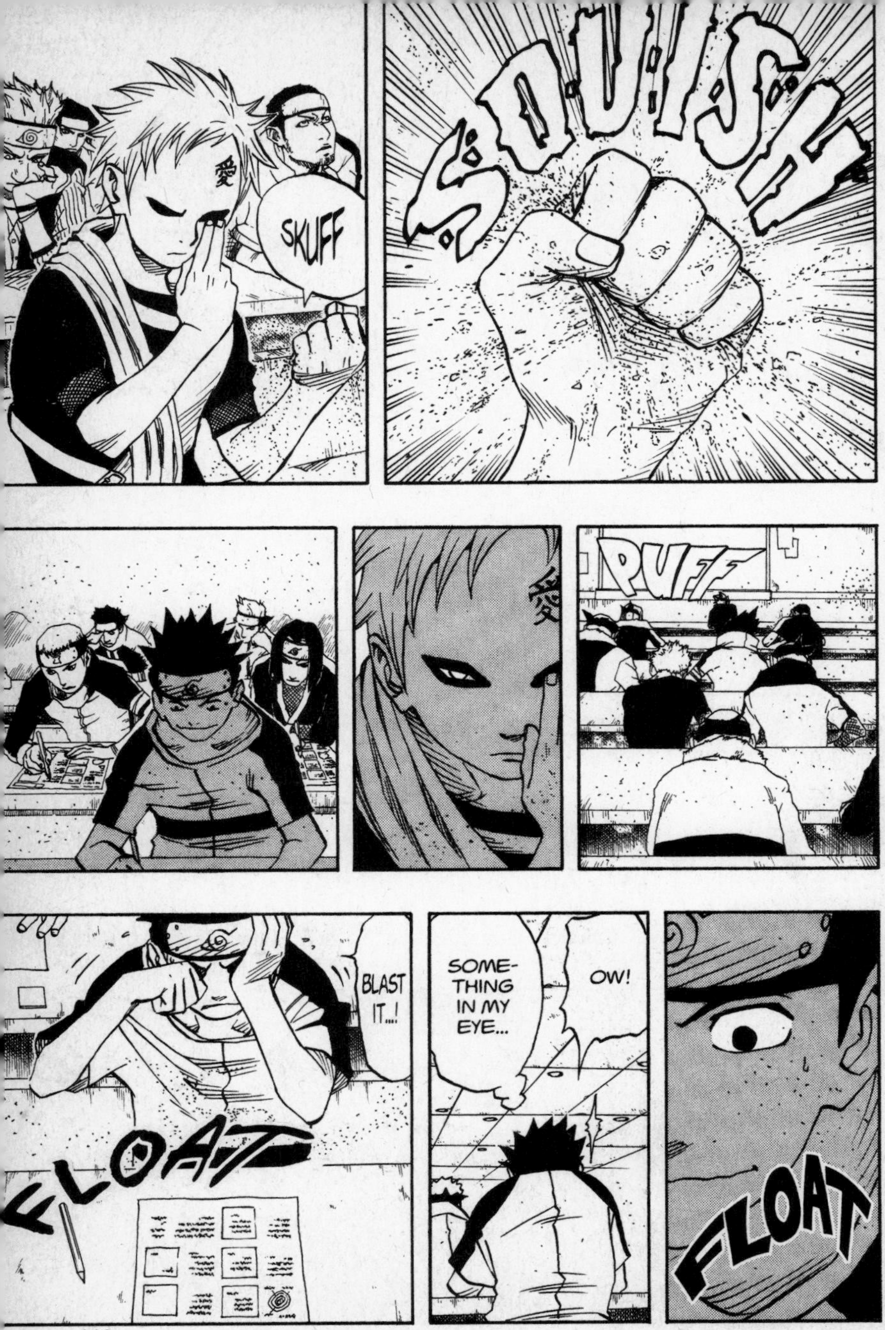
SQUISH
SKUFF
PUFF
FLOAT
OW!
SOME-THING IN MY EYE...
BLAST IT...!
FLOAT

CHUNIN JOURNEYMAN
NINJA SELECTION
EXAMINATION

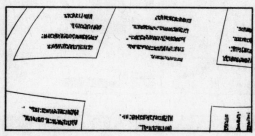

OWW...!

SCRATCH

SCRATCH

SCRATCH

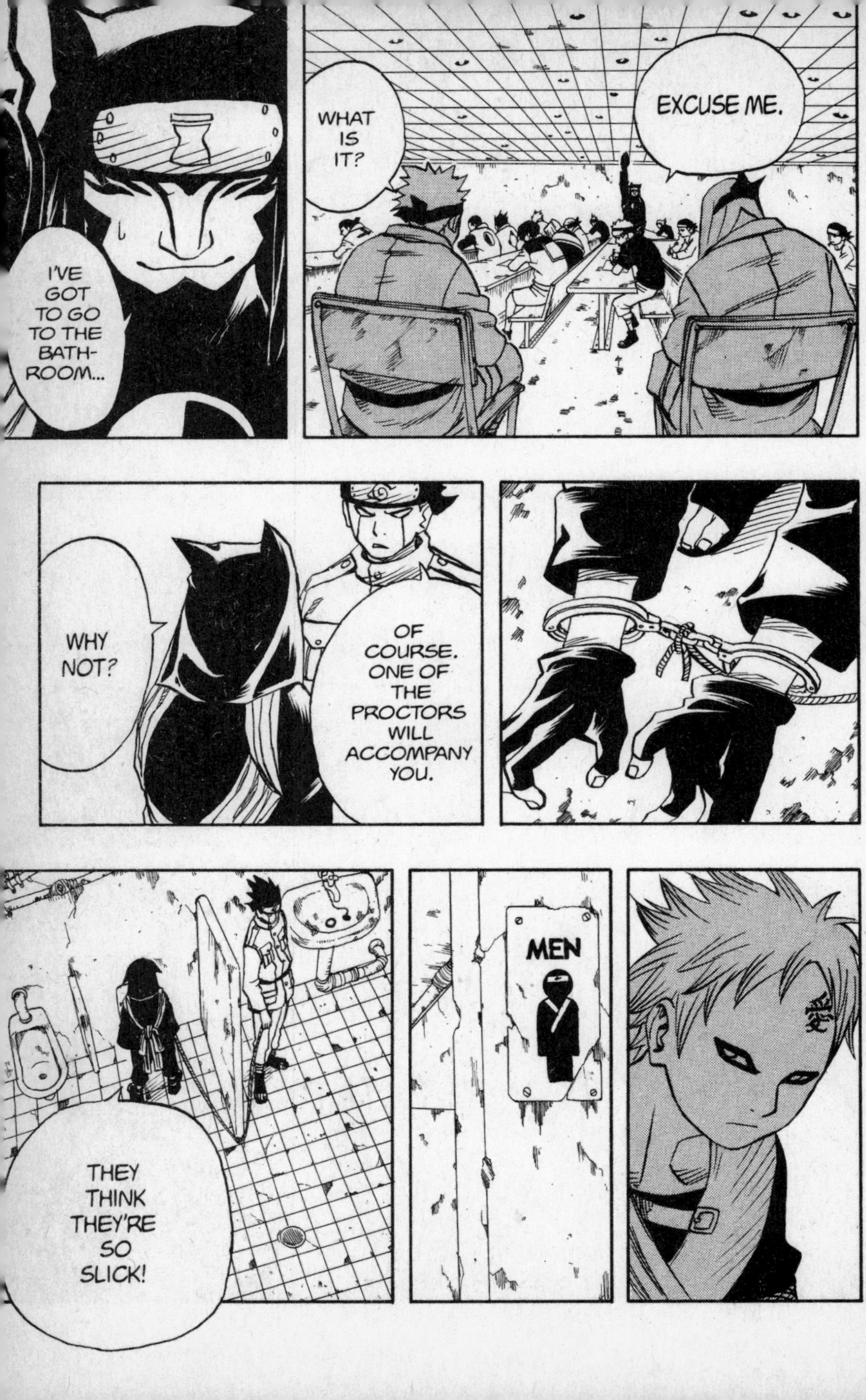
EXCUSE ME.
WHAT IS IT?
I'VE GOT TO GO TO THE BATH-ROOM...
WHY NOT?
OF COURSE. ONE OF THE PROCTORS WILL ACCOMPANY YOU.
MEN
THEY THINK THEY'RE SO SLICK!

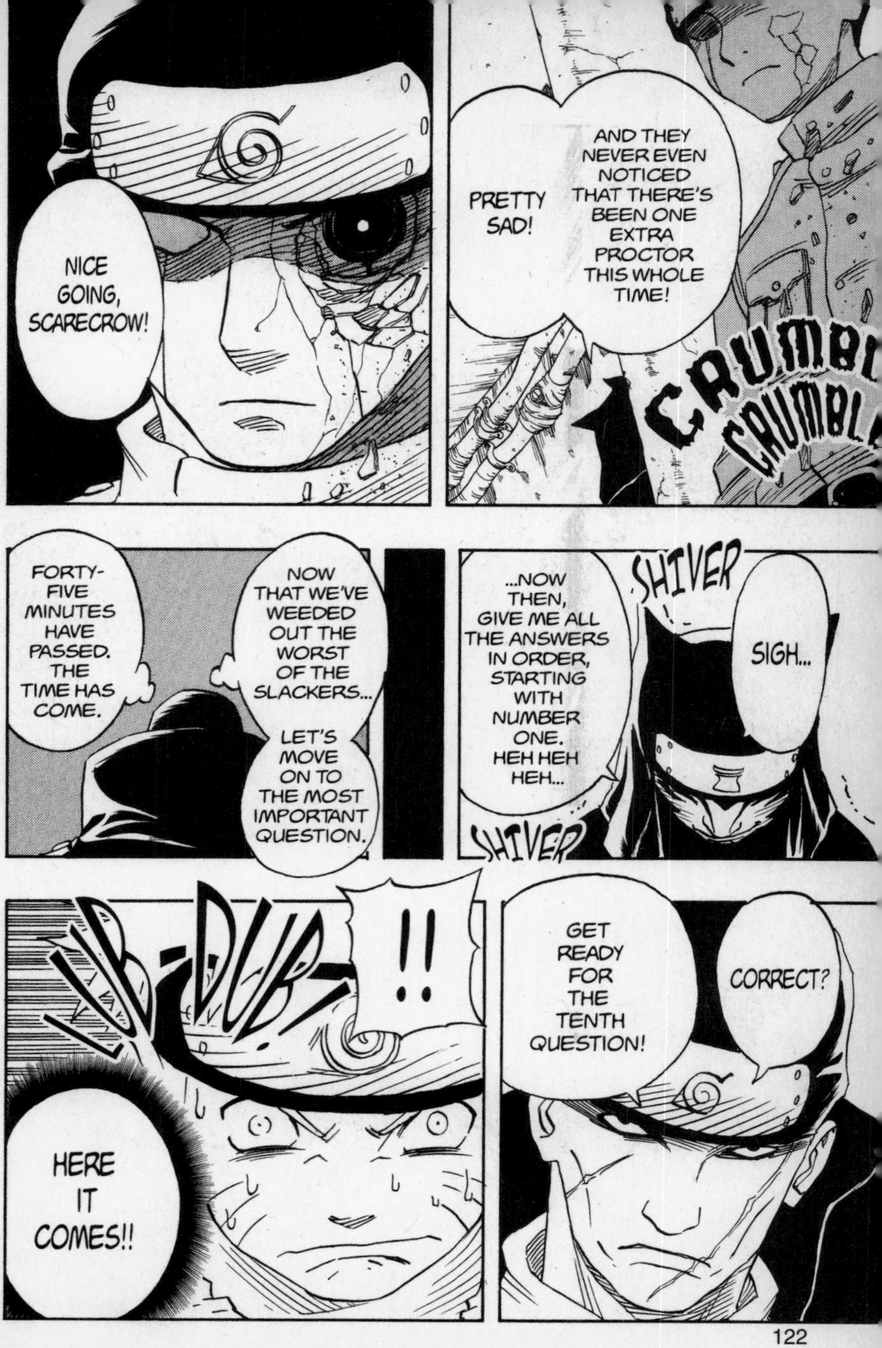
AND THEY NEVER EVEN NOTICED THAT THERE'S BEEN ONE EXTRA PROCTOR THIS WHOLE TIME!
PRETTY SAD!
NICE GOING, SCARECROW!
SIGH...
SHIVER
...NOW THEN, GIVE ME ALL THE ANSWERS IN ORDER, STARTING WITH NUMBER ONE. HEH HEH HEH...
SHIVER
NOW THAT WE'VE WEEDED OUT THE WORST OF THE SLACKERS...
LET'S MOVE ON TO THE MOST IMPORTANT QUESTION.
FORTY-FIVE MINUTES HAVE PASSED. THE TIME HAS COME.
CORRECT?
GET READY FOR THE TENTH QUESTION!
!!
HERE IT COMES!!

ALL RIGHT! HERE IT COMES.
GET READY FOR THE TENTH QUESTION.

Number 43:

The Tenth Question

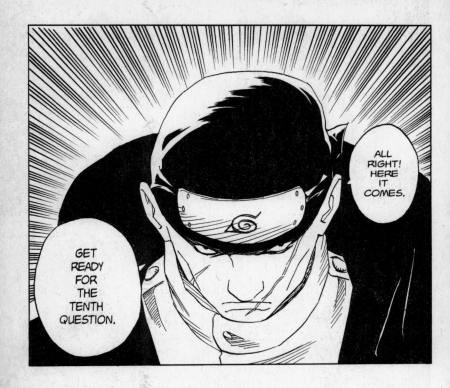

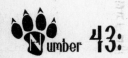

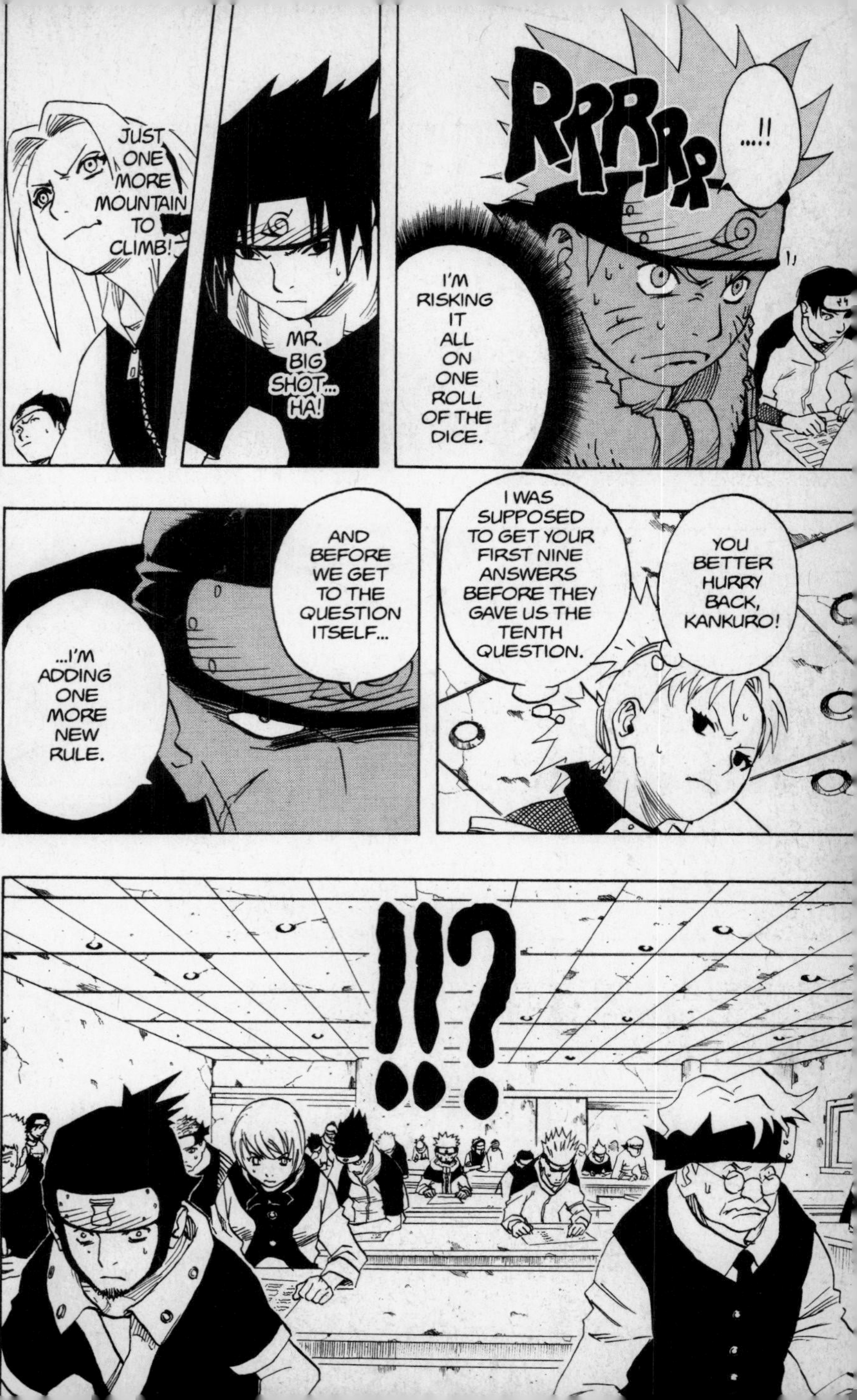
RRRRR
...!!
I'M RISKING IT ALL ON ONE ROLL OF THE DICE.
MR. BIG SHOT... HA!
JUST ONE MORE MOUNTAIN TO CLIMB!
I WAS SUPPOSED TO GET YOUR FIRST NINE ANSWERS BEFORE THEY GAVE US THE TENTH QUESTION.
YOU BETTER HURRY BACK, KANKURO!
AND BEFORE WE GET TO THE QUESTION ITSELF...
...I'M ADDING ONE MORE NEW RULE.
!!?

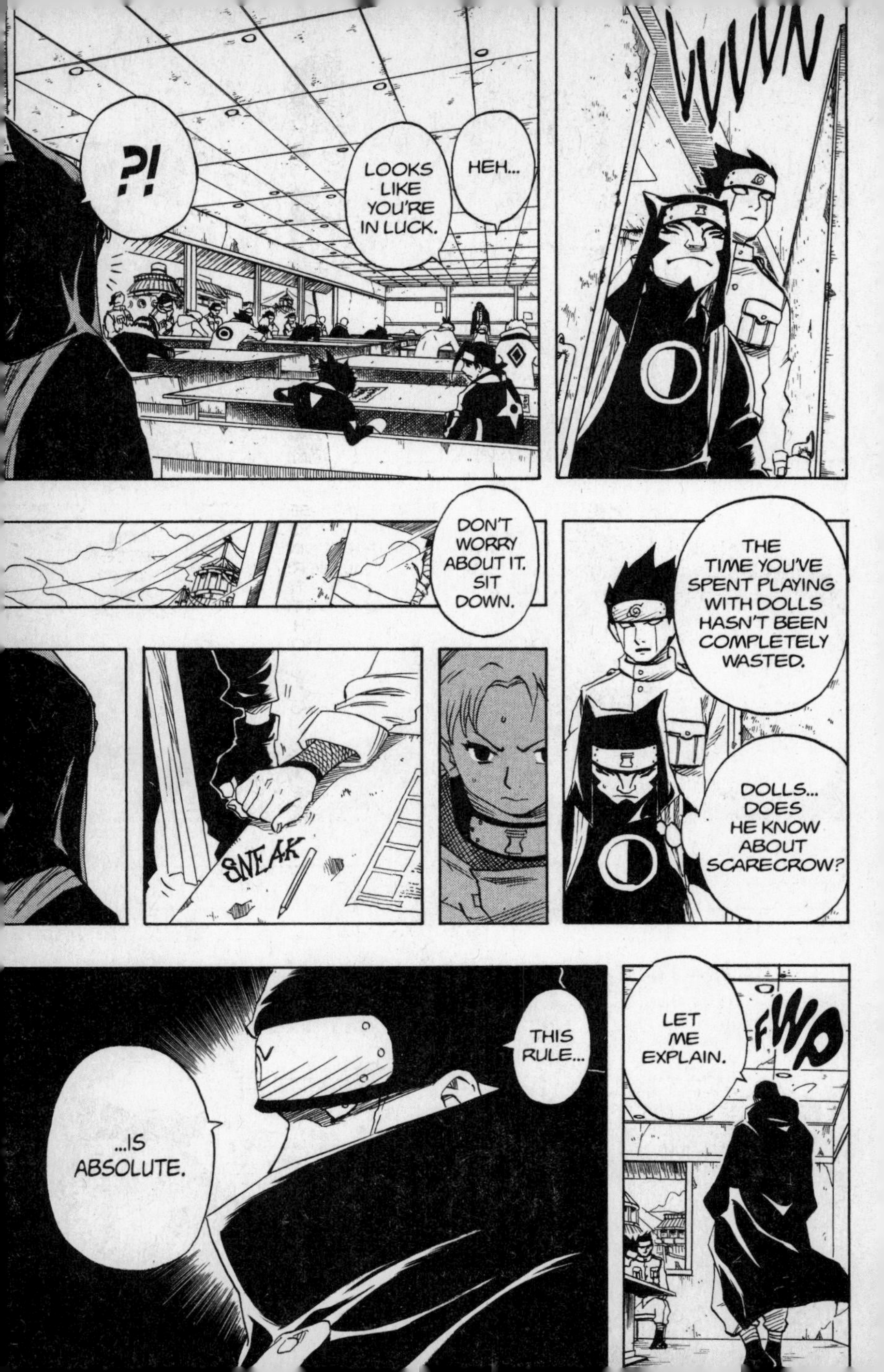
VVVVN
HEH...
LOOKS LIKE YOU'RE IN LUCK.
?!
THE TIME YOU'VE SPENT PLAYING WITH DOLLS HASN'T BEEN COMPLETELY WASTED.
DOLLS... DOES HE KNOW ABOUT SCARECROW?
DON'T WORRY ABOUT IT. SIT DOWN.
SNEAK
LET ME EXPLAIN.
FWP
THIS RULE...
...IS ABSOLUTE.

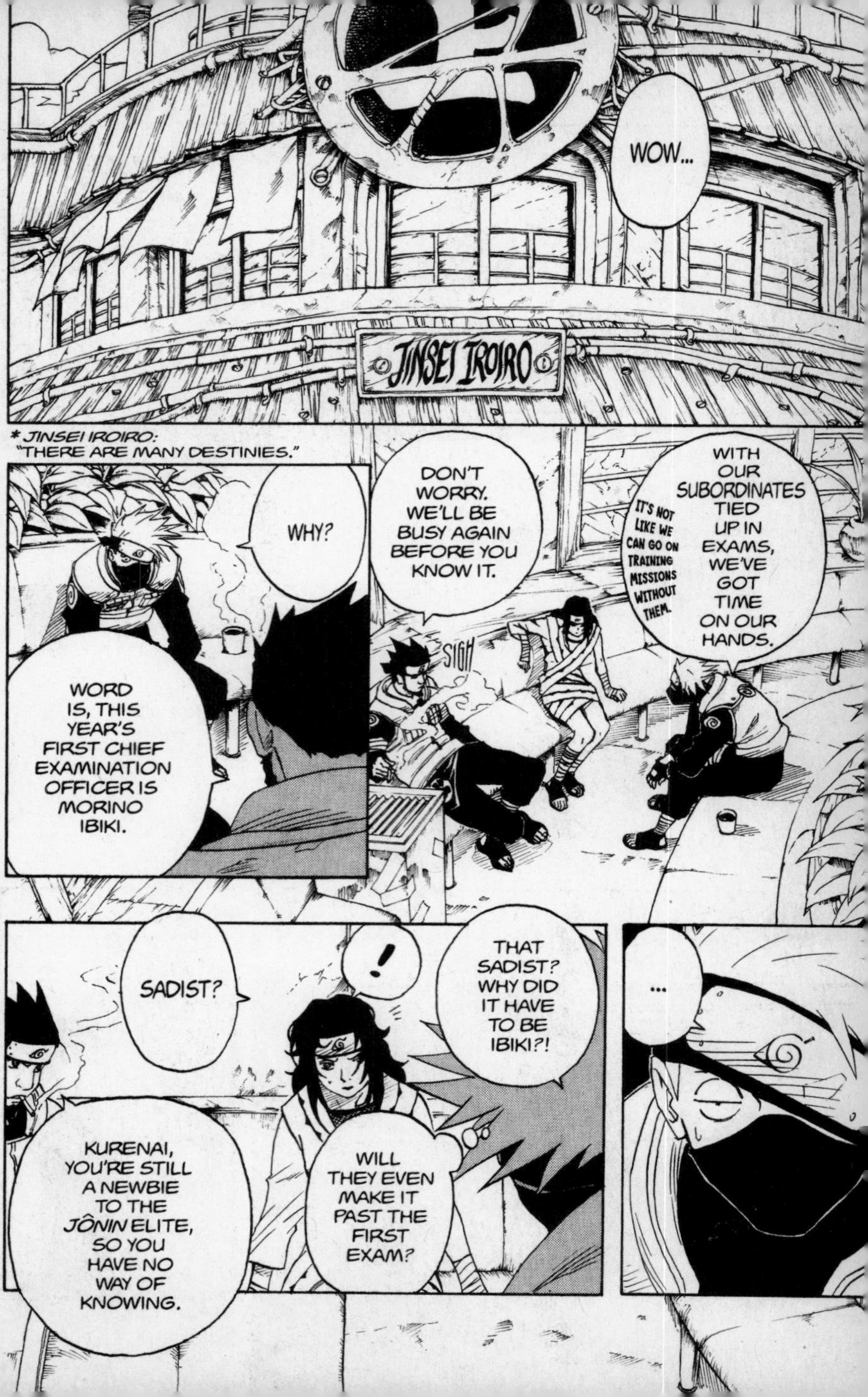
WOW...
JINSEI IROIRO
WITH OUR SUBORDINATES TIED UP IN EXAMS, WE'VE GOT TIME ON OUR HANDS.
IT'S NOT LIKE WE CAN GO ON TRAINING MISSIONS WITHOUT THEM.
DON'T WORRY. WE'LL BE BUSY AGAIN BEFORE YOU KNOW IT.
SIGH
WHY?
WORD IS, THIS YEAR'S FIRST CHIEF EXAMINATION OFFICER IS MORINO IBIKI.
...
THAT SADIST? WHY DID IT HAVE TO BE IBIKI?!
!
SADIST?
WILL THEY EVEN MAKE IT PAST THE FIRST EXAM?
KURENAI, YOU'RE STILL A NEWBIE TO THE JÔNIN ELITE, SO YOU HAVE NO WAY OF KNOWING.

* JINSEI IROIRO: "THERE ARE MANY DESTINIES."

READ THIS WAY

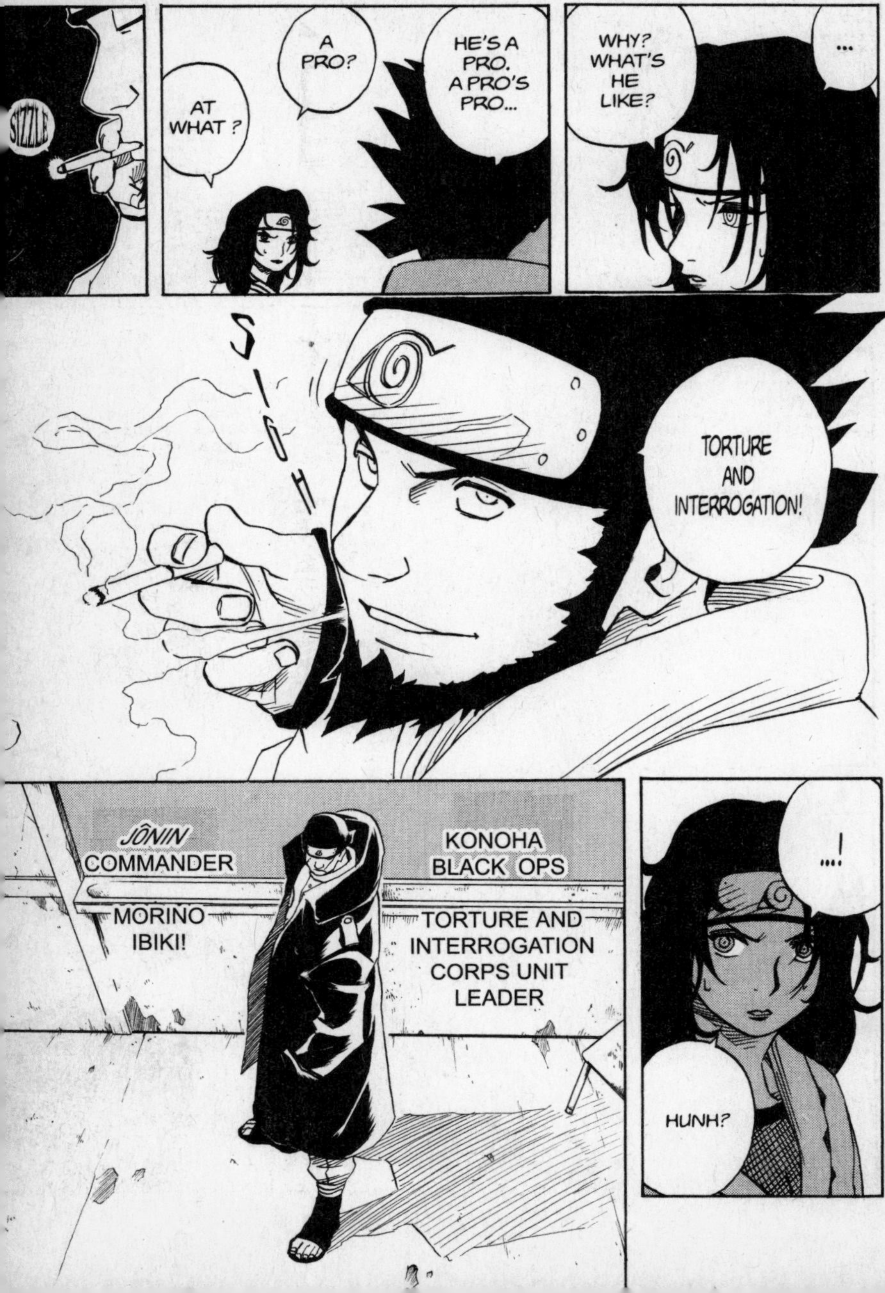
...
WHY? WHAT'S HE LIKE?
HE'S A PRO. A PRO'S PRO...
A PRO?
AT WHAT ?
SIZZLE
TORTURE AND INTERROGATION!
SIGH
...!
HUNH?
KONOHA BLACK OPS
TORTURE AND INTERROGATION CORPS UNIT LEADER
JÔNIN COMMANDER
MORINO IBIKI!

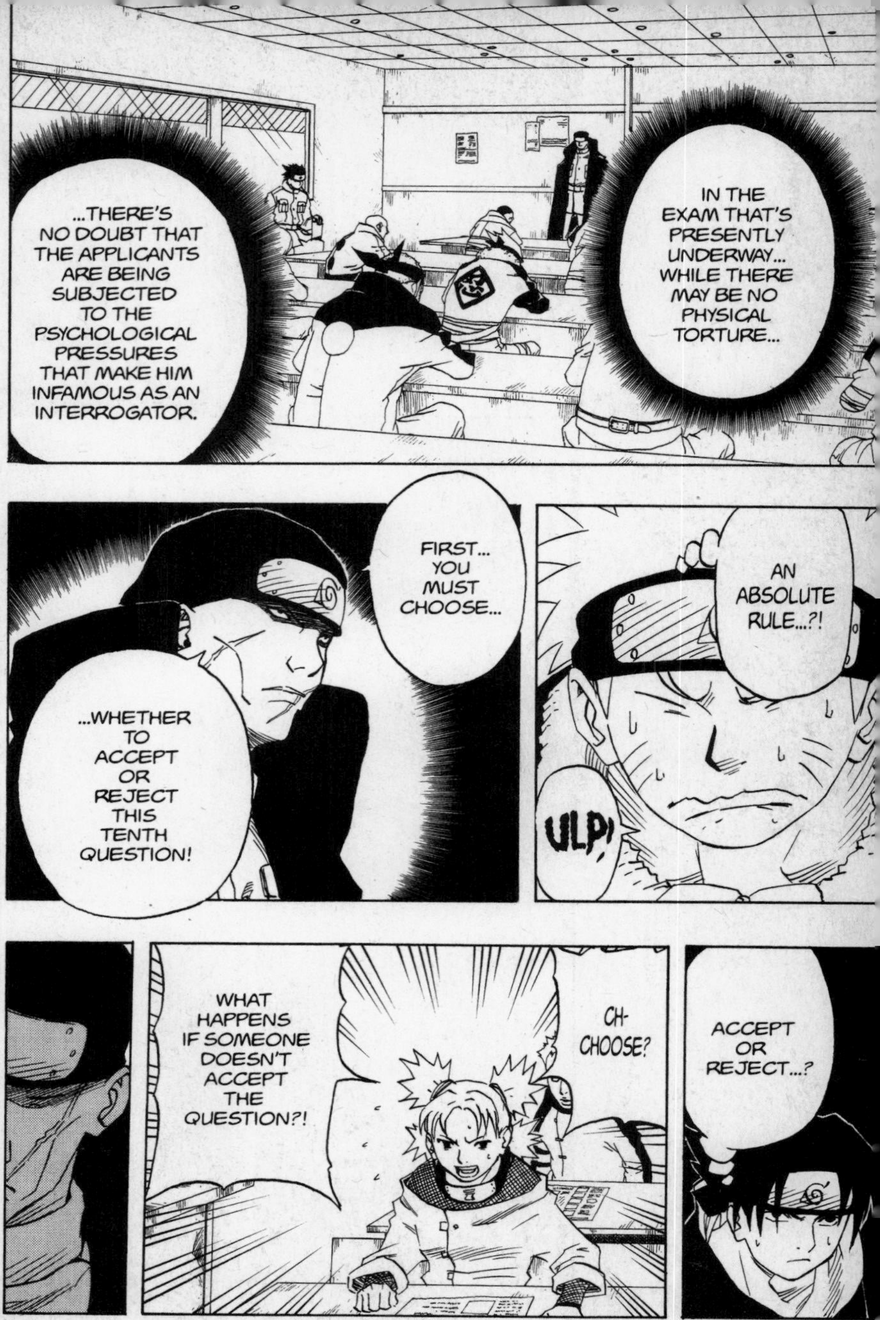
IN THE EXAM THAT'S PRESENTLY UNDERWAY... WHILE THERE MAY BE NO PHYSICAL TORTURE...
...THERE'S NO DOUBT THAT THE APPLICANTS ARE BEING SUBJECTED TO THE PSYCHOLOGICAL PRESSURES THAT MAKE HIM INFAMOUS AS AN INTERROGATOR.
AN ABSOLUTE RULE...?!
ULP!
FIRST... YOU MUST CHOOSE...
...WHETHER TO ACCEPT OR REJECT THIS TENTH QUESTION!
ACCEPT OR REJECT...?
CH- CHOOSE?
WHAT HAPPENS IF SOMEONE DOESN'T ACCEPT THE QUESTION?!

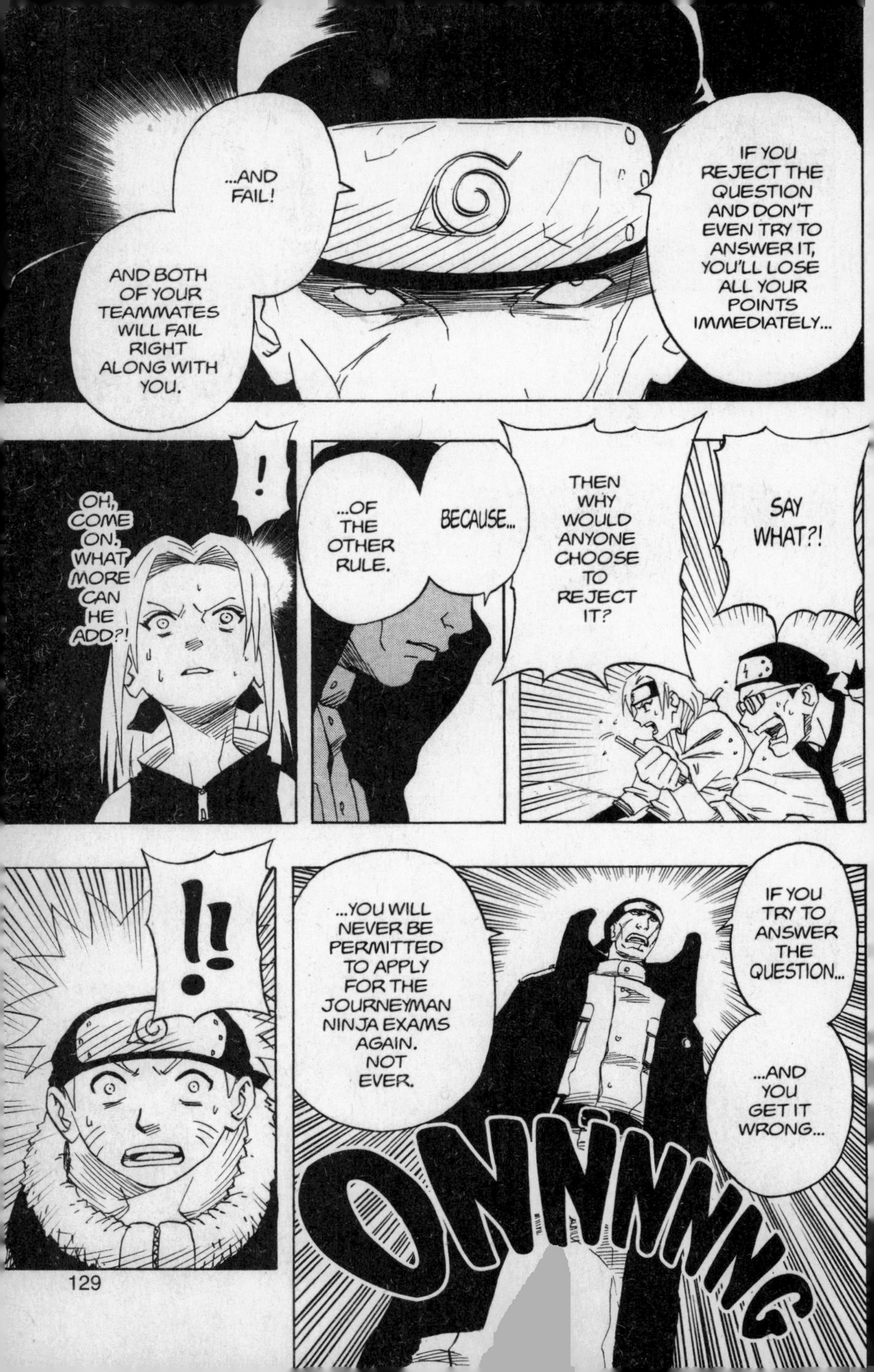
IF YOU REJECT THE QUESTION AND DON'T EVEN TRY TO ANSWER IT, YOU'LL LOSE ALL YOUR POINTS IMMEDIATELY...
...AND FAIL!
AND BOTH OF YOUR TEAMMATES WILL FAIL RIGHT ALONG WITH YOU.
SAY WHAT?!
THEN WHY WOULD ANYONE CHOOSE TO REJECT IT?
BECAUSE...
...OF THE OTHER RULE.
!
OH, COME ON. WHAT MORE CAN HE ADD?!
IF YOU TRY TO ANSWER THE QUESTION...
...AND YOU GET IT WRONG...
...YOU WILL NEVER BE PERMITTED TO APPLY FOR THE JOURNEYMAN NINJA EXAMS AGAIN. NOT EVER.
ONNNNNG
!!

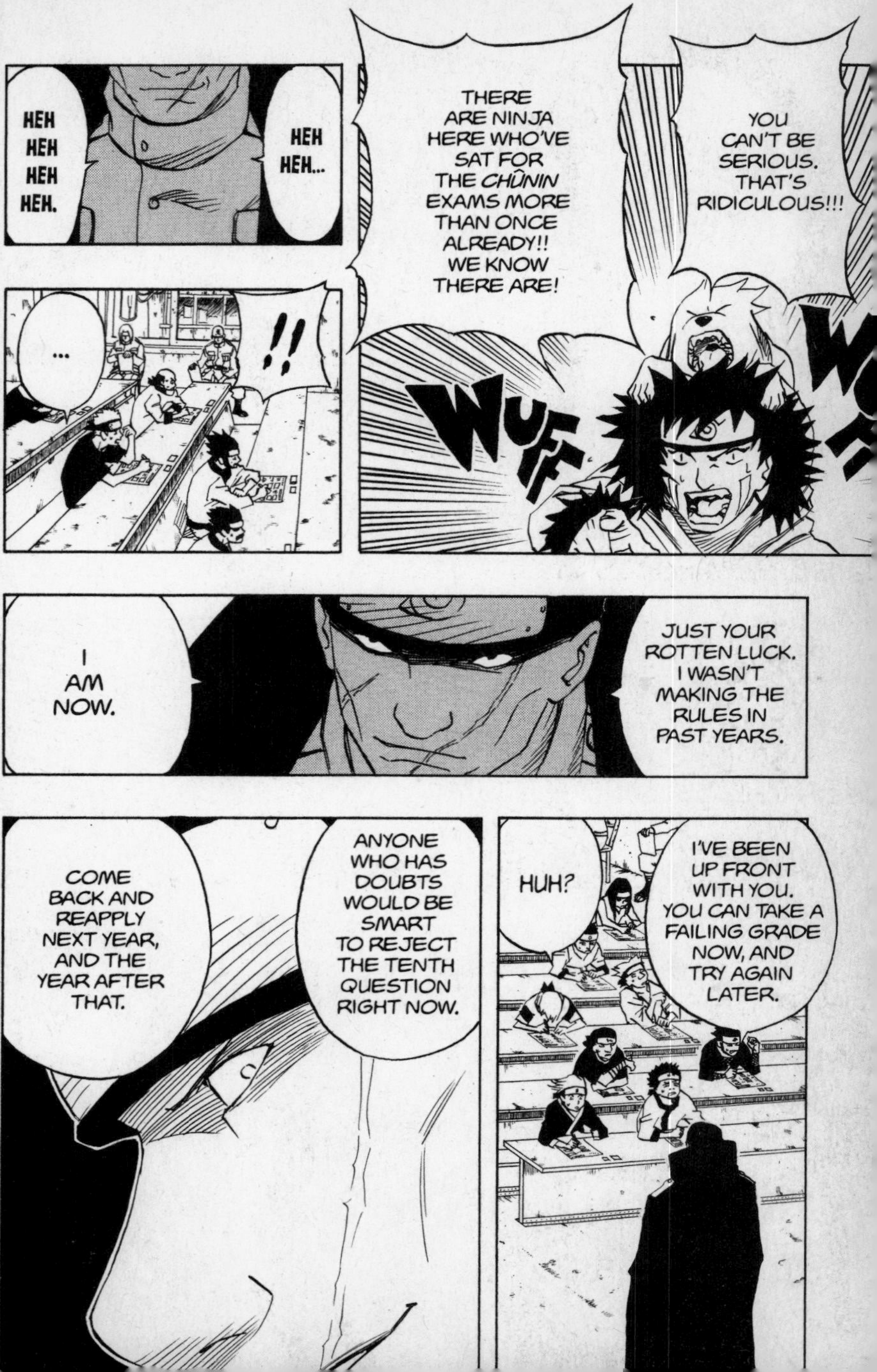

YOU CAN'T BE SERIOUS. THAT'S RIDICULOUS!!!
THERE ARE NINJA HERE WHO'VE SAT FOR THE *CHÛNIN* EXAMS MORE THAN ONCE ALREADY!! WE KNOW THERE ARE!
WUFF
HEH HEH...
HEH HEH HEH HEH.
!!
...
JUST YOUR ROTTEN LUCK. I WASN'T MAKING THE RULES IN PAST YEARS.
I AM NOW.
I'VE BEEN UP FRONT WITH YOU. YOU CAN TAKE A FAILING GRADE NOW, AND TRY AGAIN LATER.
HUH?
ANYONE WHO HAS DOUBTS WOULD BE SMART TO REJECT THE TENTH QUESTION RIGHT NOW.
COME BACK AND REAPPLY NEXT YEAR, AND THE YEAR AFTER THAT.

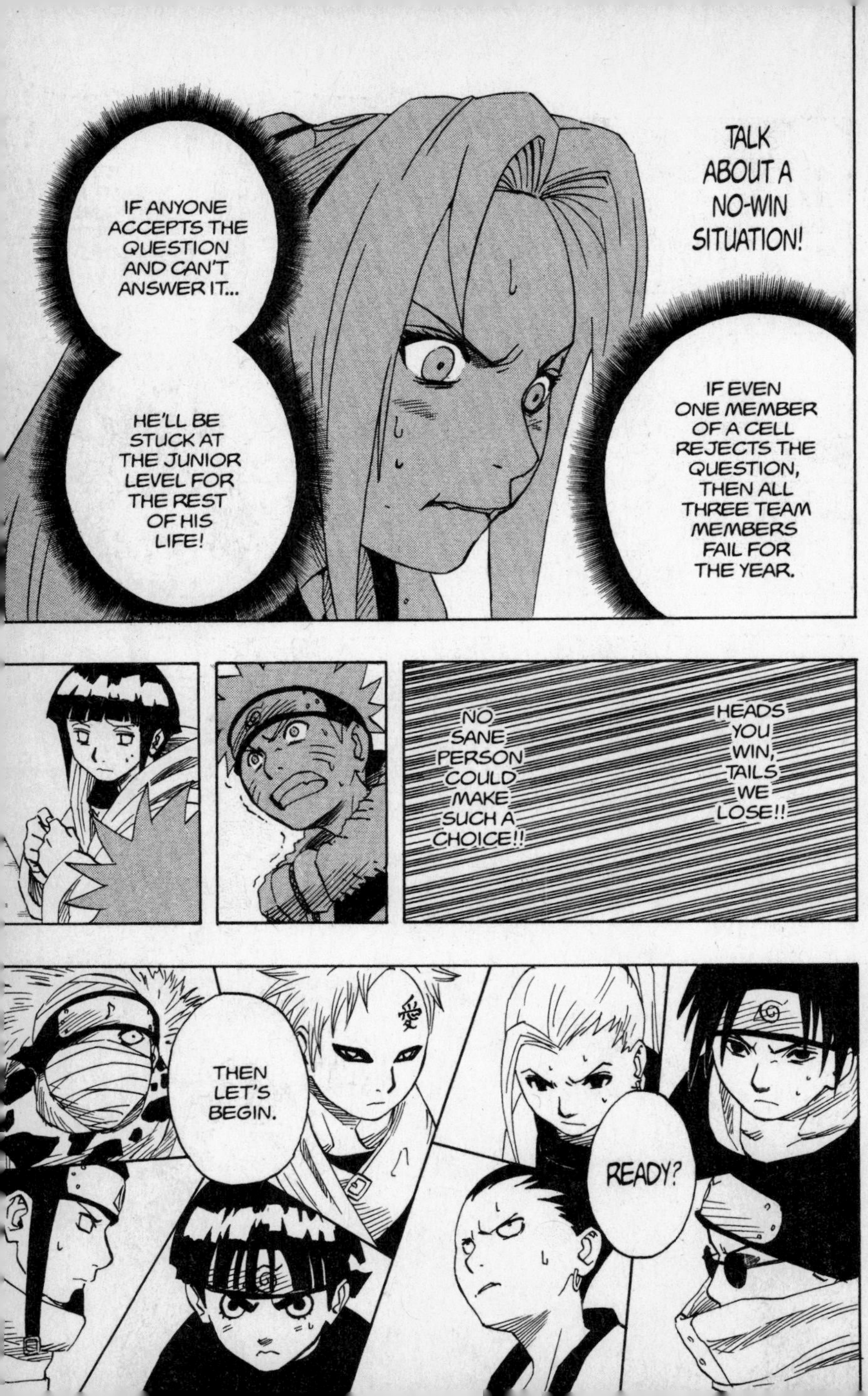
TALK ABOUT A NO-WIN SITUATION!
IF ANYONE ACCEPTS THE QUESTION AND CAN'T ANSWER IT...
HE'LL BE STUCK AT THE JUNIOR LEVEL FOR THE REST OF HIS LIFE!
IF EVEN ONE MEMBER OF A CELL REJECTS THE QUESTION, THEN ALL THREE TEAM MEMBERS FAIL FOR THE YEAR.
HEADS YOU WIN, TAILS WE LOSE!!
NO SANE PERSON COULD MAKE SUCH A CHOICE!!
READY?
THEN LET'S BEGIN.

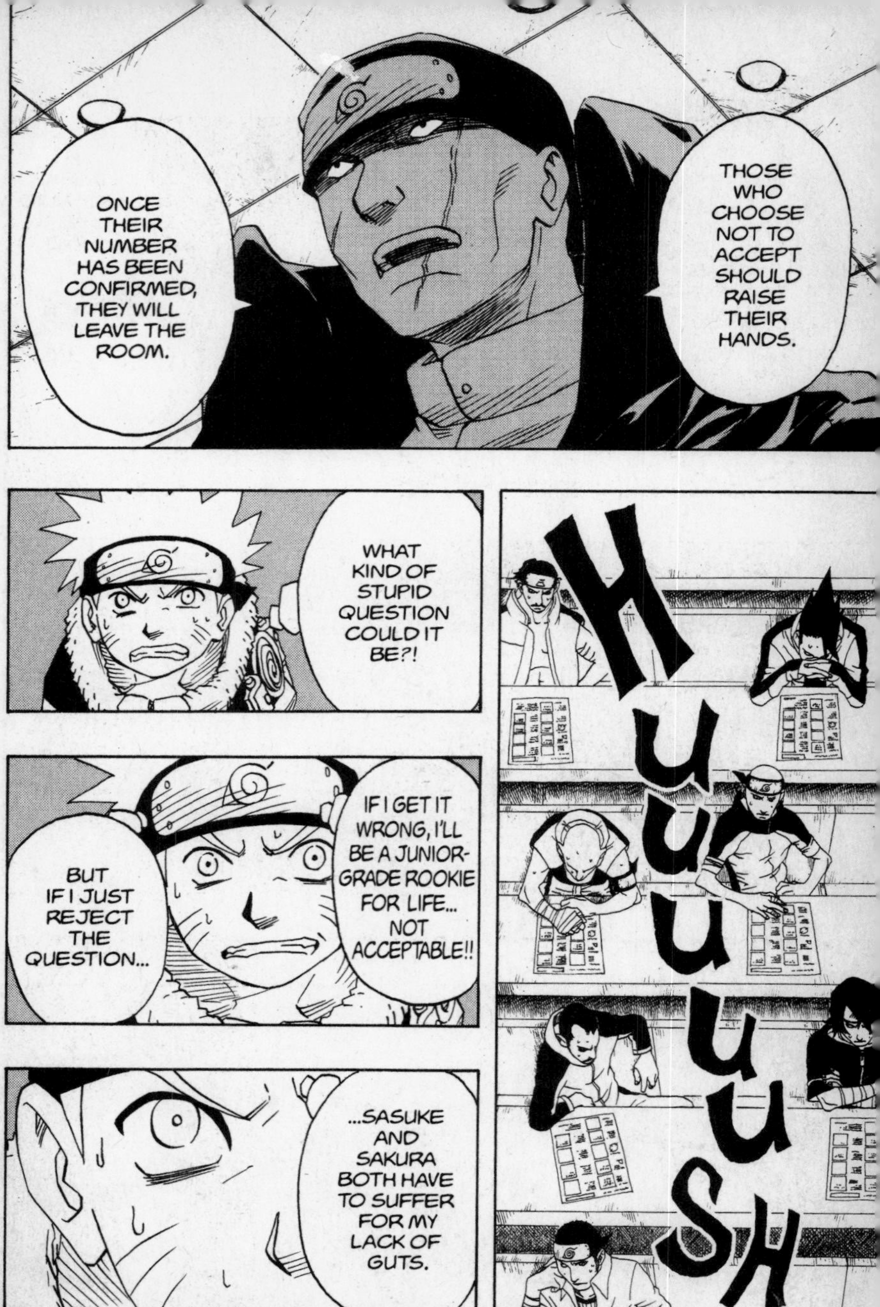
THOSE WHO CHOOSE NOT TO ACCEPT SHOULD RAISE THEIR HANDS.
ONCE THEIR NUMBER HAS BEEN CONFIRMED, THEY WILL LEAVE THE ROOM.
HUUUUUUSH
WHAT KIND OF STUPID QUESTION COULD IT BE?!
IF I GET IT WRONG, I'LL BE A JUNIOR-GRADE ROOKIE FOR LIFE... NOT ACCEPTABLE!!
BUT IF I JUST REJECT THE QUESTION...
...SASUKE AND SAKURA BOTH HAVE TO SUFFER FOR MY LACK OF GUTS.

READ THIS WAY

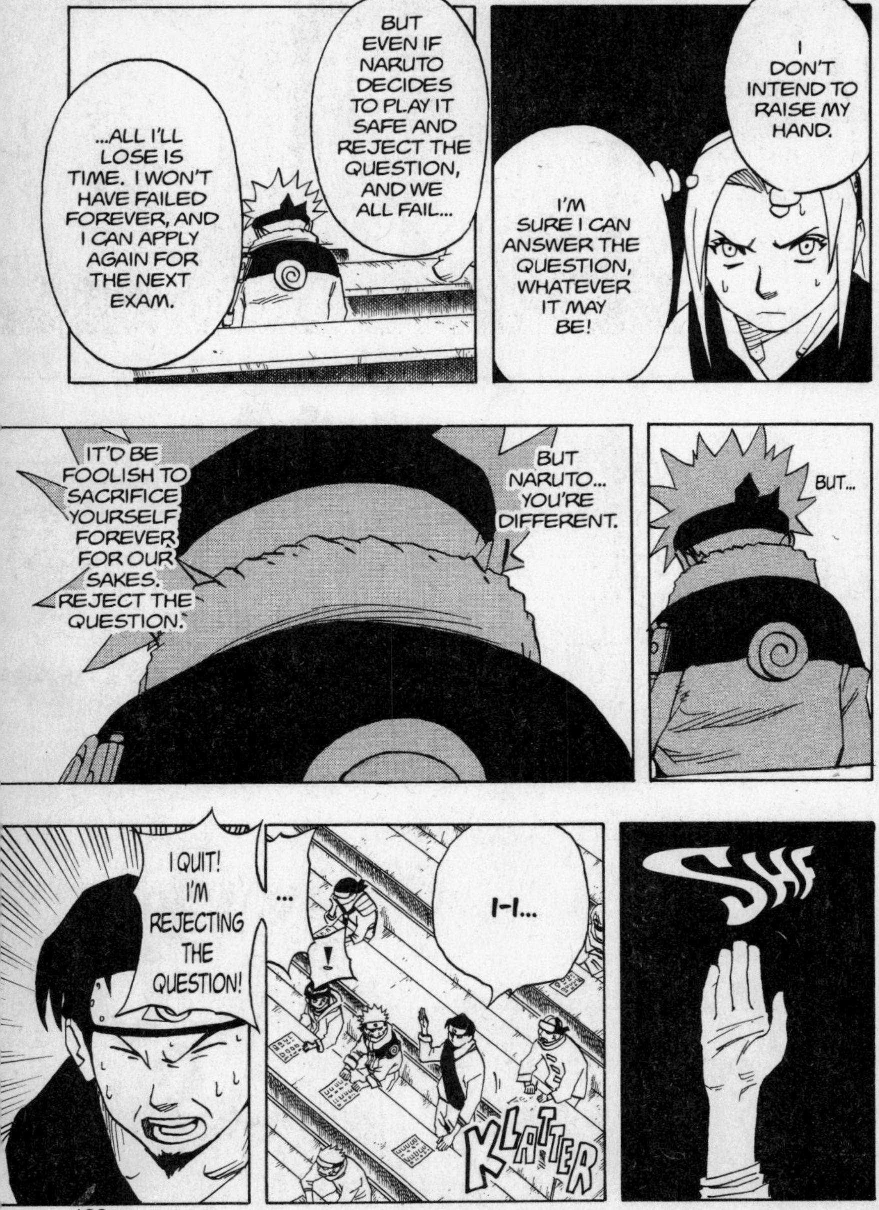
I DON'T INTEND TO RAISE MY HAND.
I'M SURE I CAN ANSWER THE QUESTION, WHATEVER IT MAY BE!
BUT EVEN IF NARUTO DECIDES TO PLAY IT SAFE AND REJECT THE QUESTION, AND WE ALL FAIL...
...ALL I'LL LOSE IS TIME. I WON'T HAVE FAILED FOREVER, AND I CAN APPLY AGAIN FOR THE NEXT EXAM.
BUT...
BUT NARUTO... YOU'RE DIFFERENT.
IT'D BE FOOLISH TO SACRIFICE YOURSELF FOREVER FOR OUR SAKES. REJECT THE QUESTION.
SHF
I-I...
...
!
KLATTER
I QUIT! I'M REJECTING THE QUESTION!

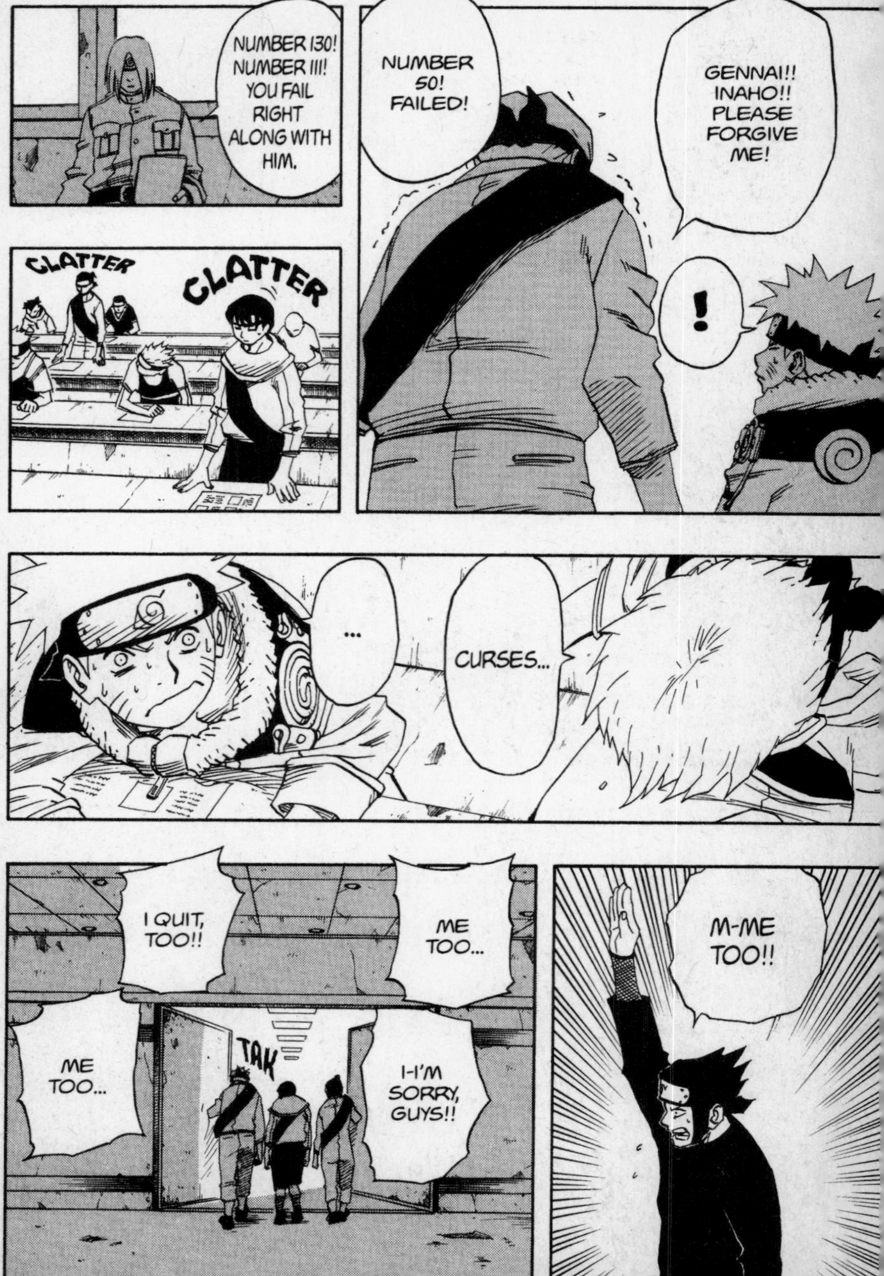
GENNAI!! INAHO!! PLEASE FORGIVE ME!
NUMBER 50! FAILED!
!
NUMBER 130! NUMBER 111! YOU FAIL RIGHT ALONG WITH HIM.
CLATTER
CLATTER
CURSES...
...
M-ME TOO!!
ME TOO...
I QUIT, TOO!!
I-I'M SORRY, GUYS!!
TAK
ME TOO...

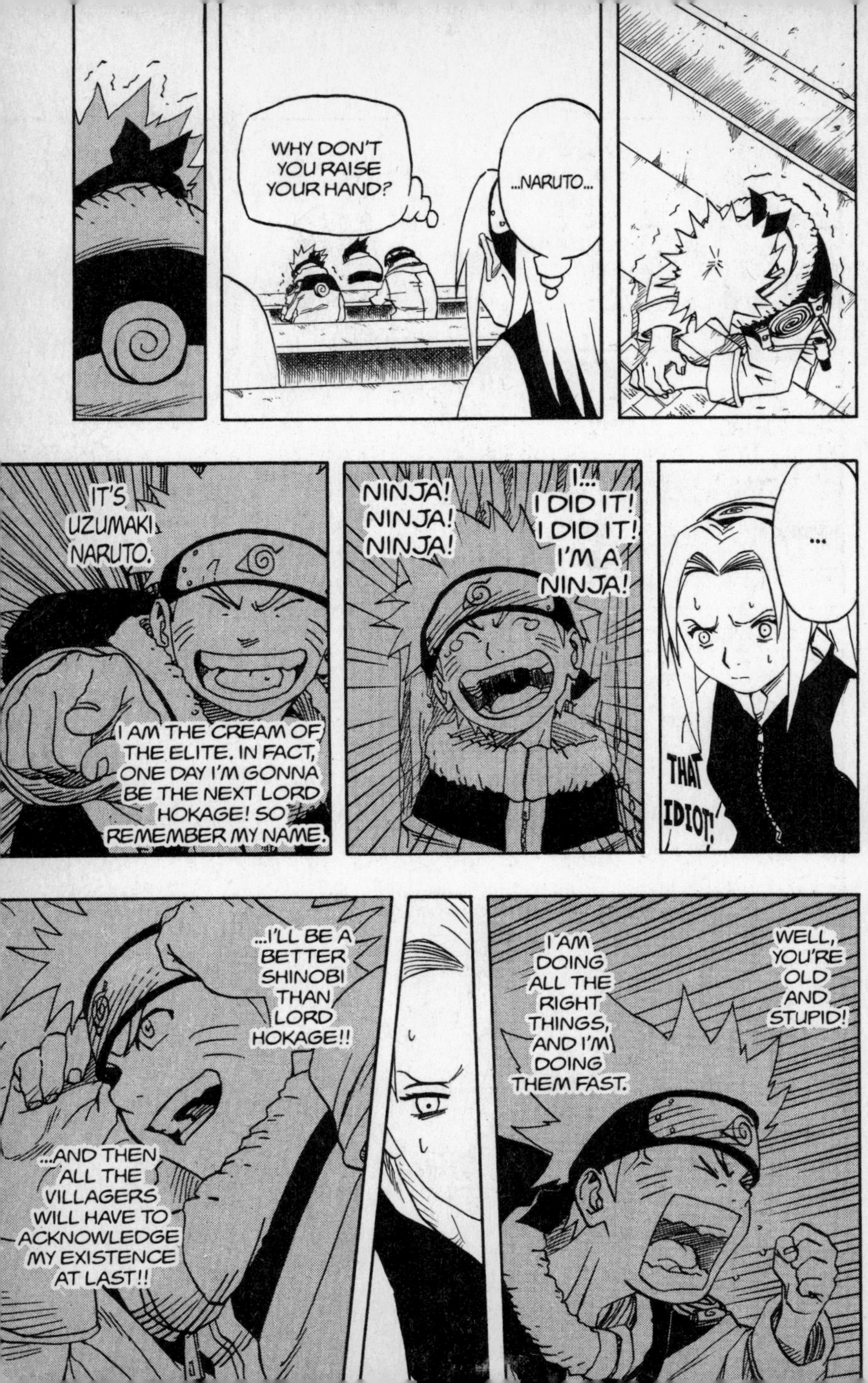
...NARUTO...
WHY DON'T YOU RAISE YOUR HAND?
...
THAT IDIOT!
I... I DID IT! I DID IT! I'M A NINJA!
NINJA! NINJA! NINJA!
IT'S UZUMAKI NARUTO.
I AM THE CREAM OF THE ELITE. IN FACT, ONE DAY I'M GONNA BE THE NEXT LORD HOKAGE! SO REMEMBER MY NAME.
WELL, YOU'RE OLD AND STUPID!
I AM DOING ALL THE RIGHT THINGS, AND I'M DOING THEM FAST.
...I'LL BE A BETTER SHINOBI THAN LORD HOKAGE!!
...AND THEN ALL THE VILLAGERS WILL HAVE TO ACKNOWLEDGE MY EXISTENCE AT LAST!!

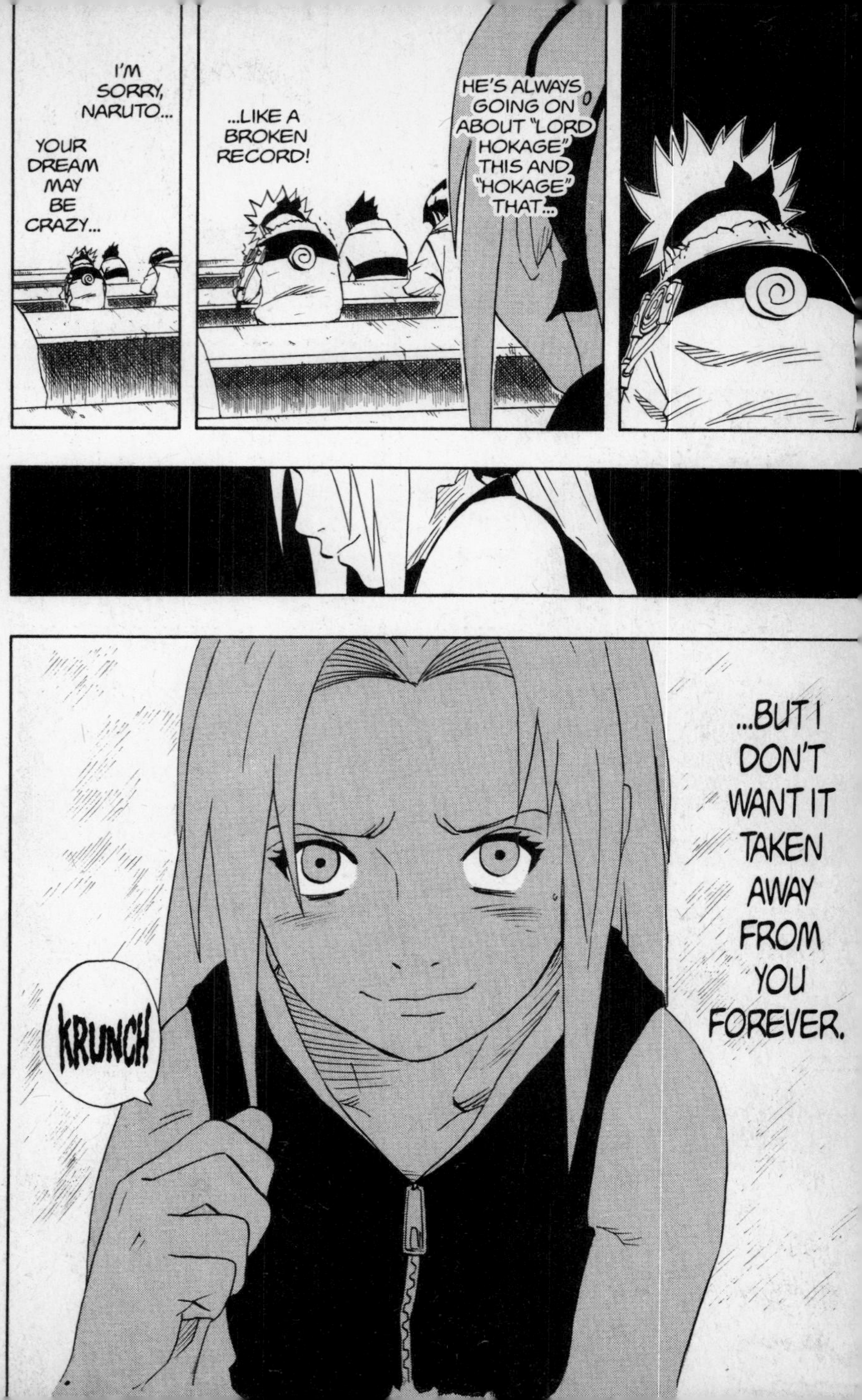
HE'S ALWAYS GOING ON ABOUT "LORD HOKAGE" THIS AND "HOKAGE" THAT...
...LIKE A BROKEN RECORD!
I'M SORRY, NARUTO...
YOUR DREAM MAY BE CRAZY...
...BUT I DON'T WANT IT TAKEN AWAY FROM YOU FOREVER.
KRUNCH

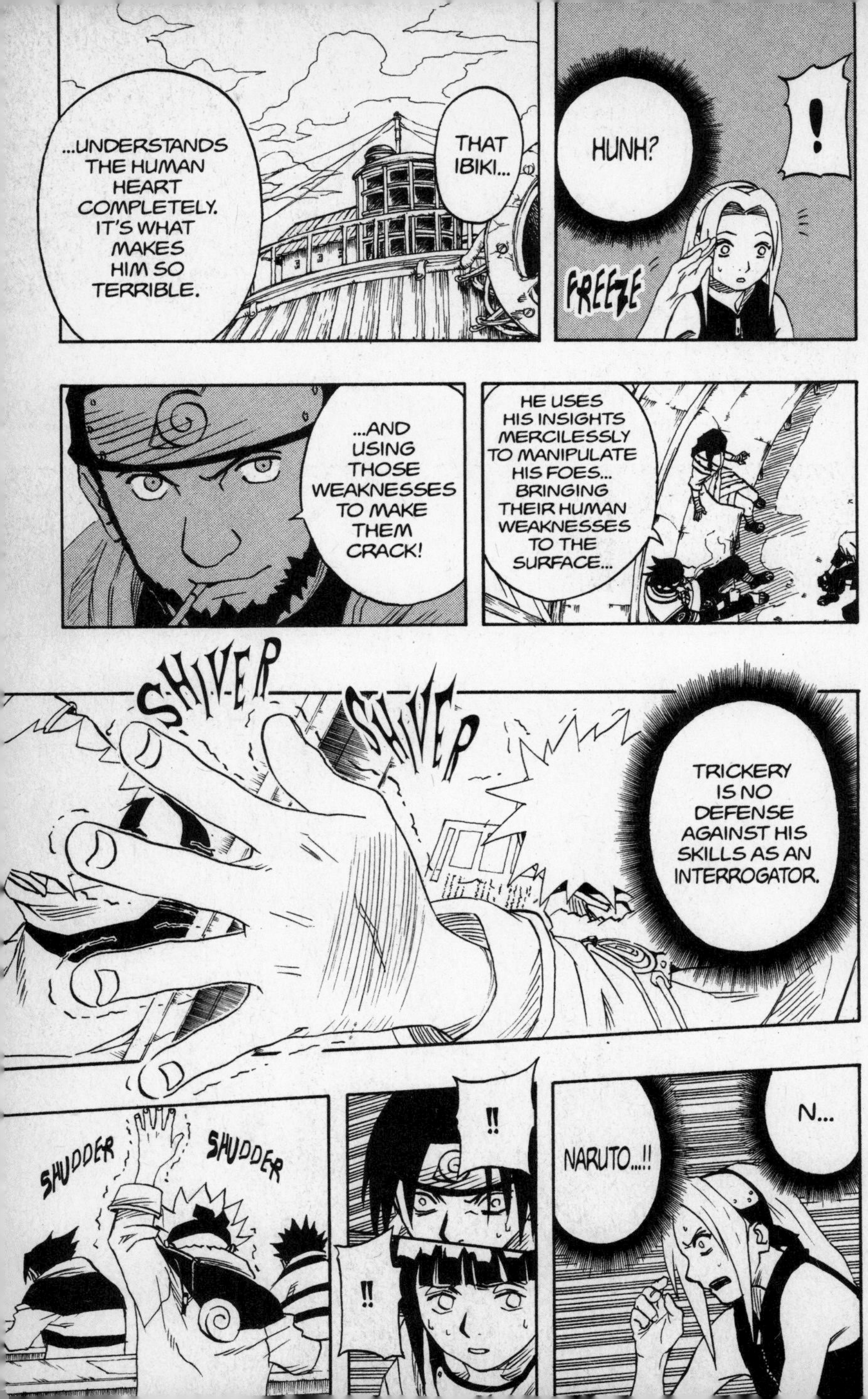
!
HUNH?
FREEZE
THAT IBIKI...
...UNDERSTANDS THE HUMAN HEART COMPLETELY. IT'S WHAT MAKES HIM SO TERRIBLE.
HE USES HIS INSIGHTS MERCILESSLY TO MANIPULATE HIS FOES... BRINGING THEIR HUMAN WEAKNESSES TO THE SURFACE...
...AND USING THOSE WEAKNESSES TO MAKE THEM CRACK!
TRICKERY IS NO DEFENSE AGAINST HIS SKILLS AS AN INTERROGATOR.
SHIVER
SHIVER
N...
NARUTO...!!
!!
!!
SHUDDER
SHUDDER

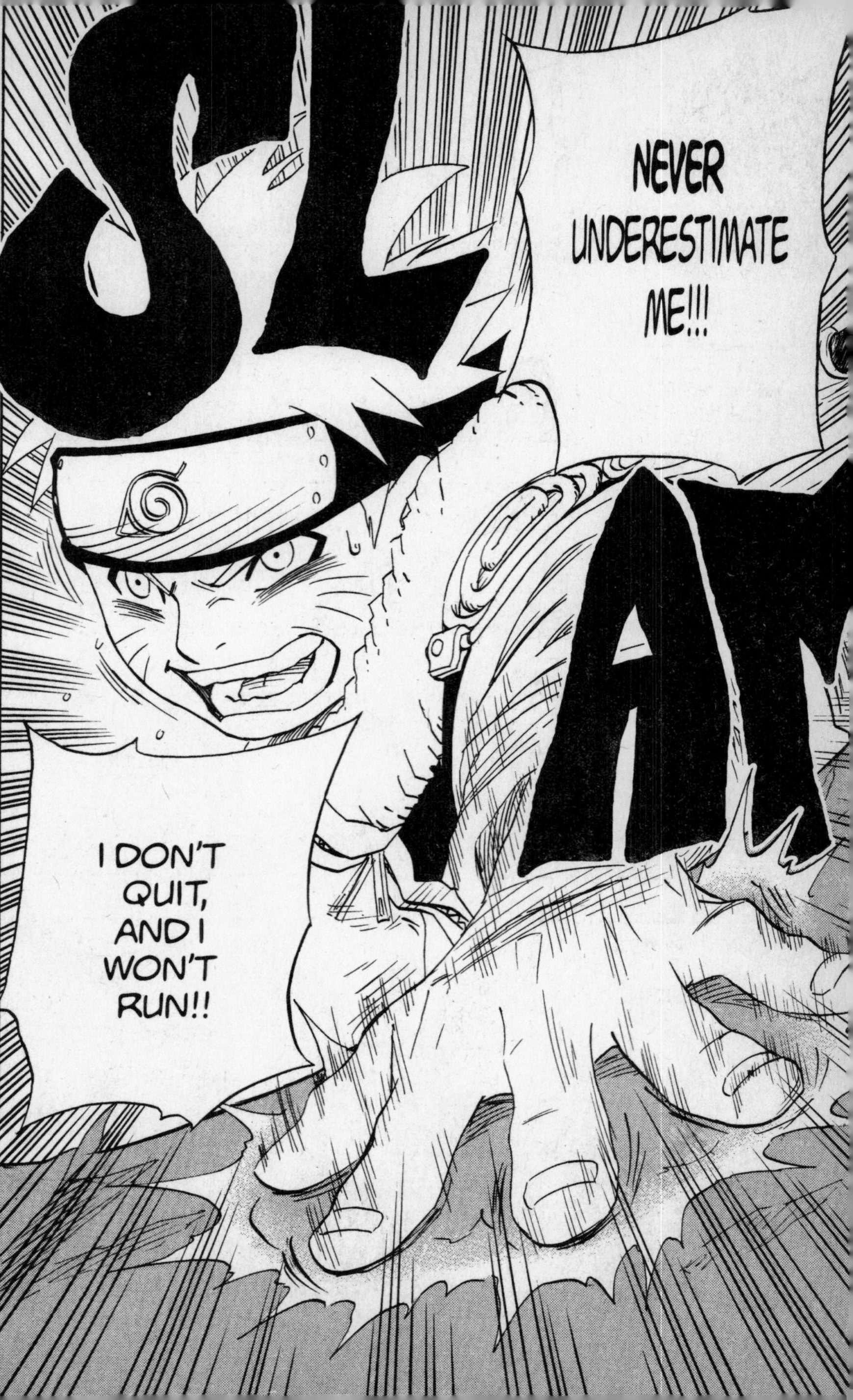
NEVER UNDERESTIMATE ME!!!
SLAM
I DON'T QUIT, AND I WON'T RUN!!

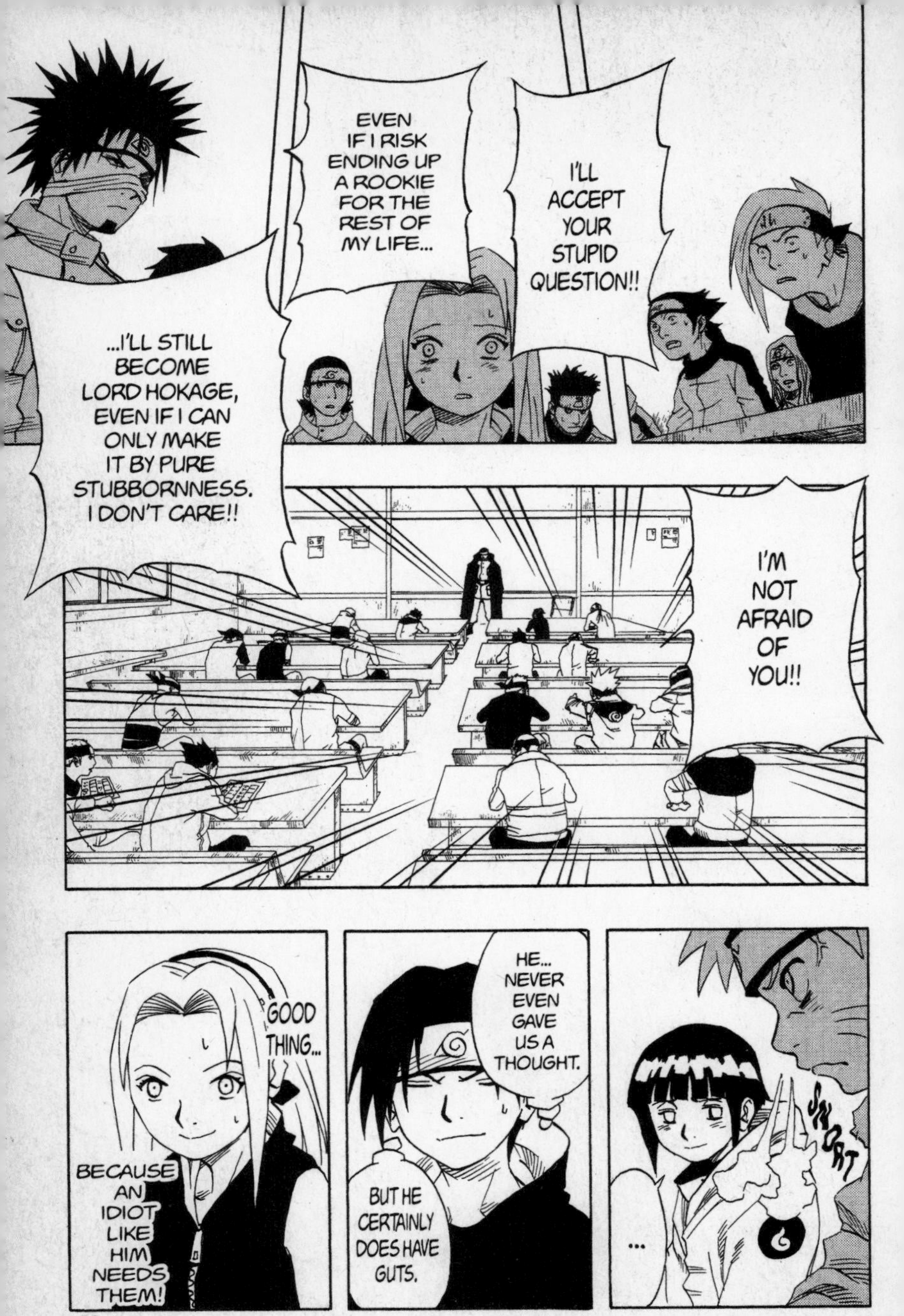
I'LL ACCEPT YOUR STUPID QUESTION!!
EVEN IF I RISK ENDING UP A ROOKIE FOR THE REST OF MY LIFE...
...I'LL STILL BECOME LORD HOKAGE, EVEN IF I CAN ONLY MAKE IT BY PURE STUBBORNNESS. I DON'T CARE!!
I'M NOT AFRAID OF YOU!!
SNORT
...
HE... NEVER EVEN GAVE US A THOUGHT.
BUT HE CERTAINLY DOES HAVE GUTS.
GOOD THING...
BECAUSE AN IDIOT LIKE HIM NEEDS THEM!

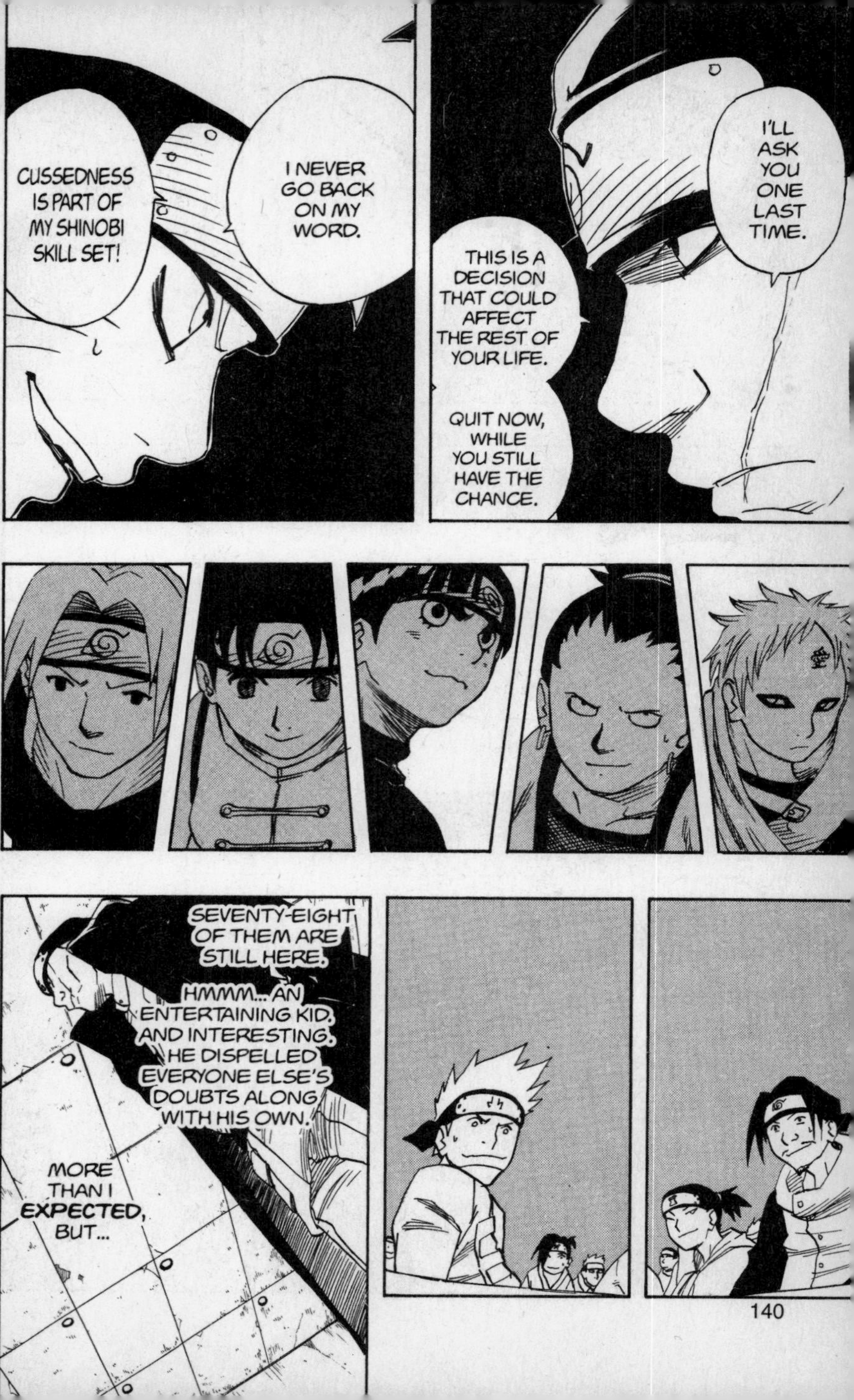
I'LL ASK YOU ONE LAST TIME.
THIS IS A DECISION THAT COULD AFFECT THE REST OF YOUR LIFE.
QUIT NOW, WHILE YOU STILL HAVE THE CHANCE.
I NEVER GO BACK ON MY WORD.
CUSSEDNESS IS PART OF MY SHINOBI SKILL SET!
SEVENTY-EIGHT OF THEM ARE STILL HERE.
HMMM... AN ENTERTAINING KID. AND INTERESTING. HE DISPELLED EVERYONE ELSE'S DOUBTS ALONG WITH HIS OWN.
MORE THAN I **EXPECTED**, BUT...

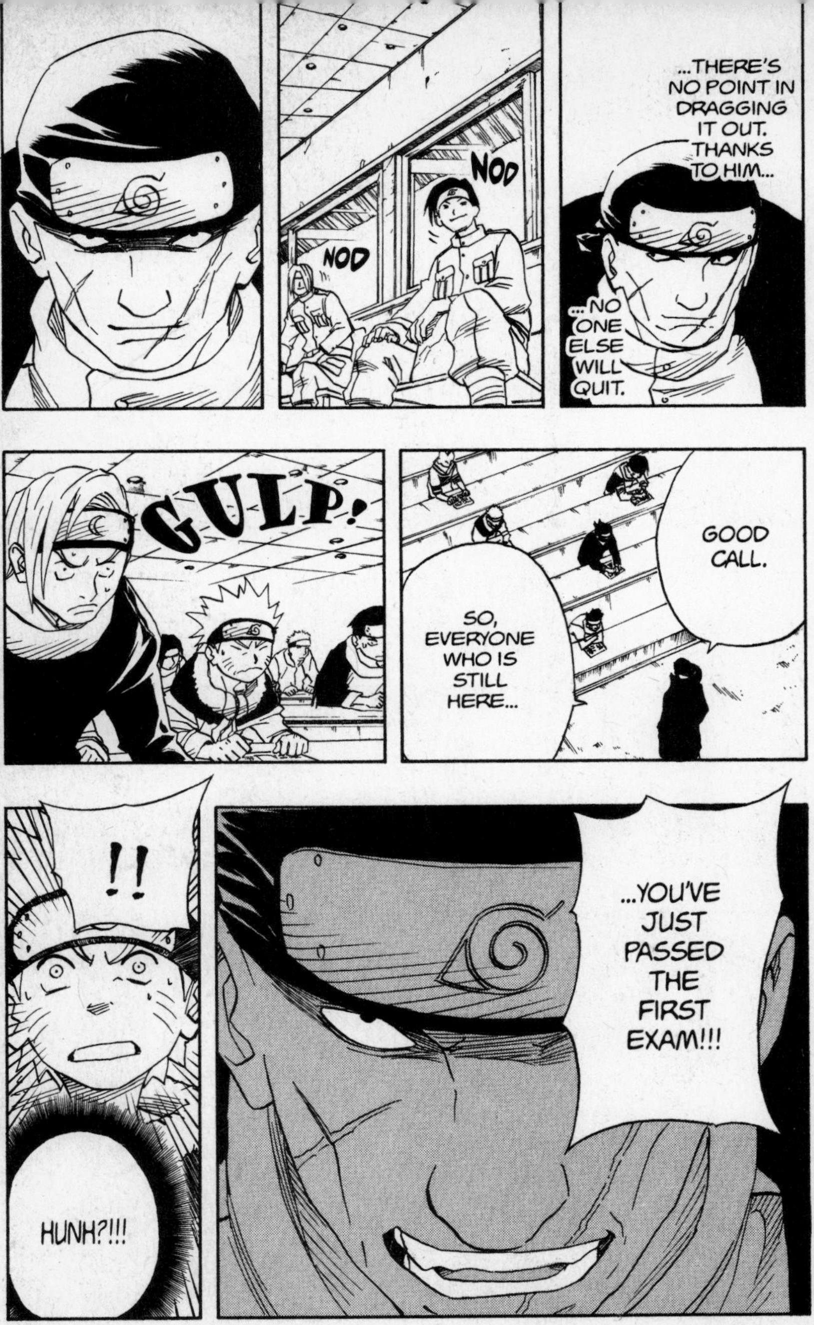
...THERE'S NO POINT IN DRAGGING IT OUT. THANKS TO HIM...
...NO ONE ELSE WILL QUIT.
NOD
NOD
GOOD CALL.
SO, EVERYONE WHO IS STILL HERE...
GULP!
...YOU'VE JUST PASSED THE FIRST EXAM!!!
!!
HUNH?!!!

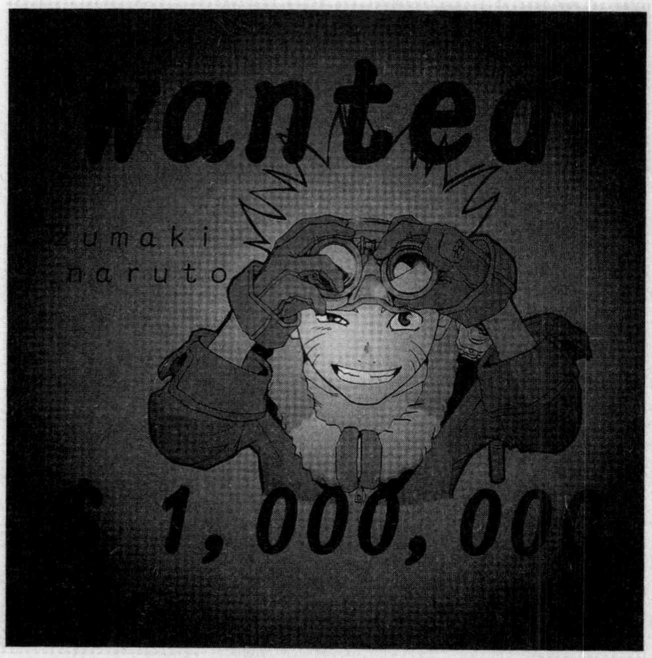
wanted
zumaki
naruto
1,000,00

A FRIEND OF MINE DREW THIS PICTURE OF NARUTO FOR ME.

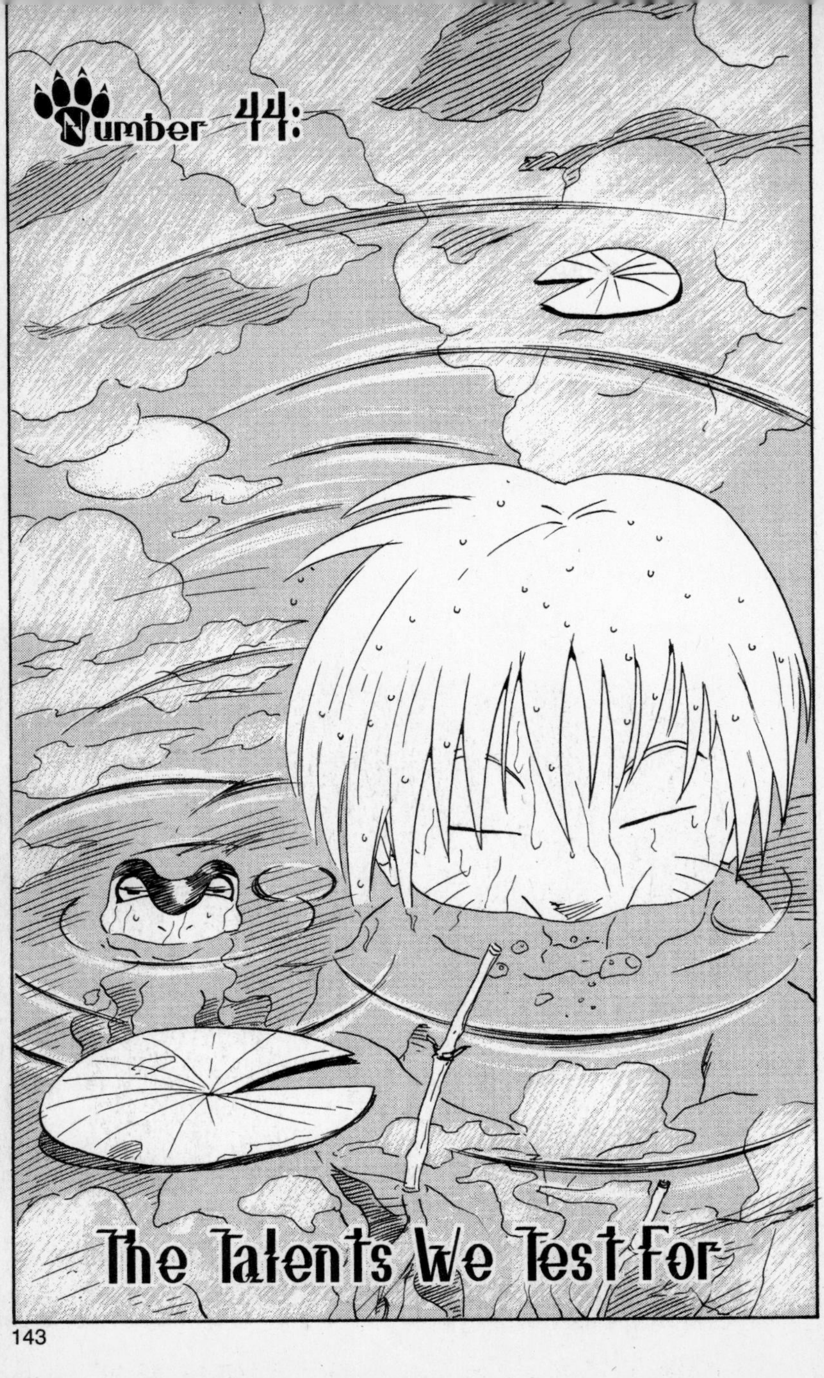
Number 44:
The Talents We Test For

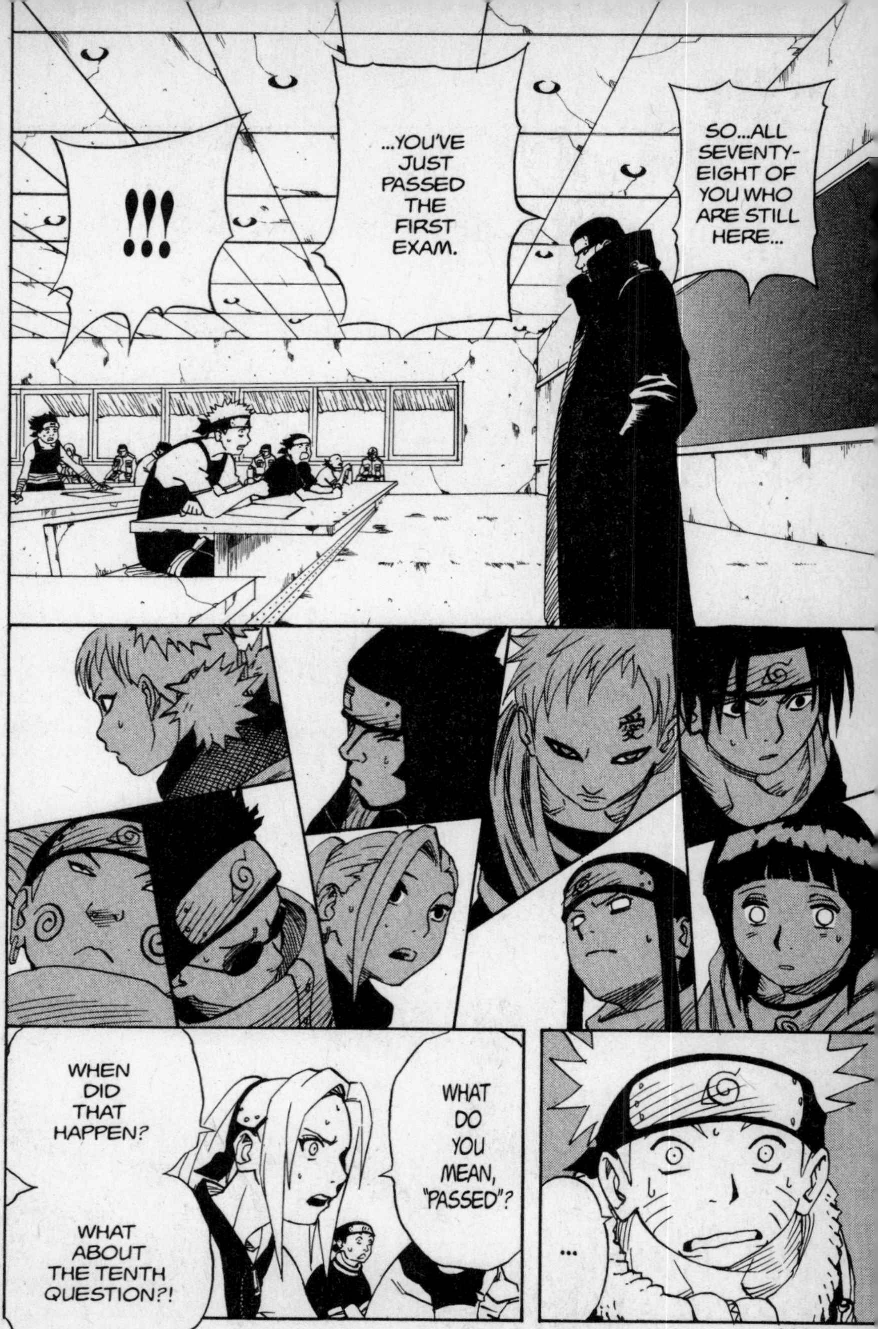
SO...ALL SEVENTY-EIGHT OF YOU WHO ARE STILL HERE...
...YOU'VE JUST PASSED THE FIRST EXAM.
!!!
...
WHAT DO YOU MEAN, "PASSED"?
WHEN DID THAT HAPPEN?
WHAT ABOUT THE TENTH QUESTION?!

READ THIS WAY

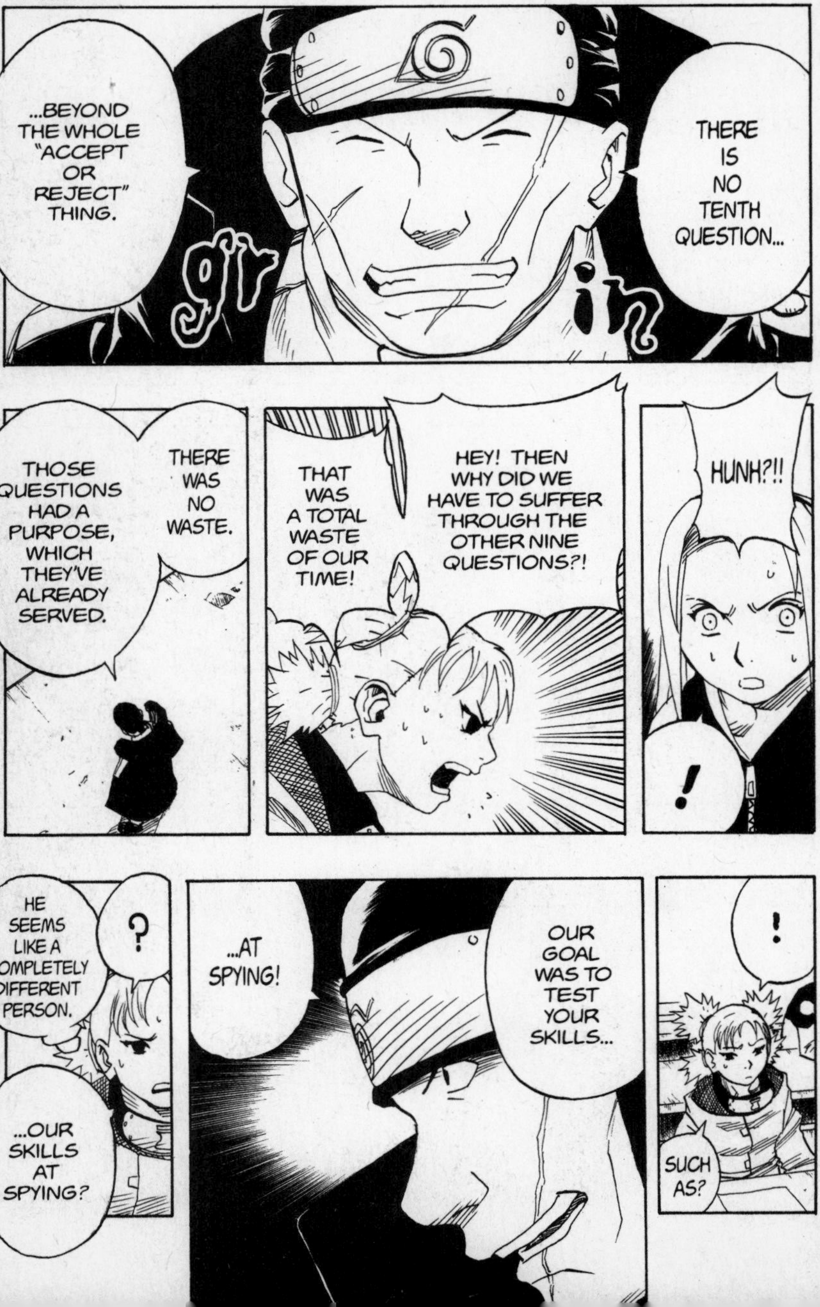
THERE IS NO TENTH QUESTION...
grin
...BEYOND THE WHOLE "ACCEPT OR REJECT" THING.
HUNH?!!
!
HEY! THEN WHY DID WE HAVE TO SUFFER THROUGH THE OTHER NINE QUESTIONS?!
THAT WAS A TOTAL WASTE OF OUR TIME!
THERE WAS NO WASTE.
THOSE QUESTIONS HAD A PURPOSE, WHICH THEY'VE ALREADY SERVED.
!
SUCH AS?
OUR GOAL WAS TO TEST YOUR SKILLS...
...AT SPYING!
?
HE SEEMS LIKE A COMPLETELY DIFFERENT PERSON.
...OUR SKILLS AT SPYING?

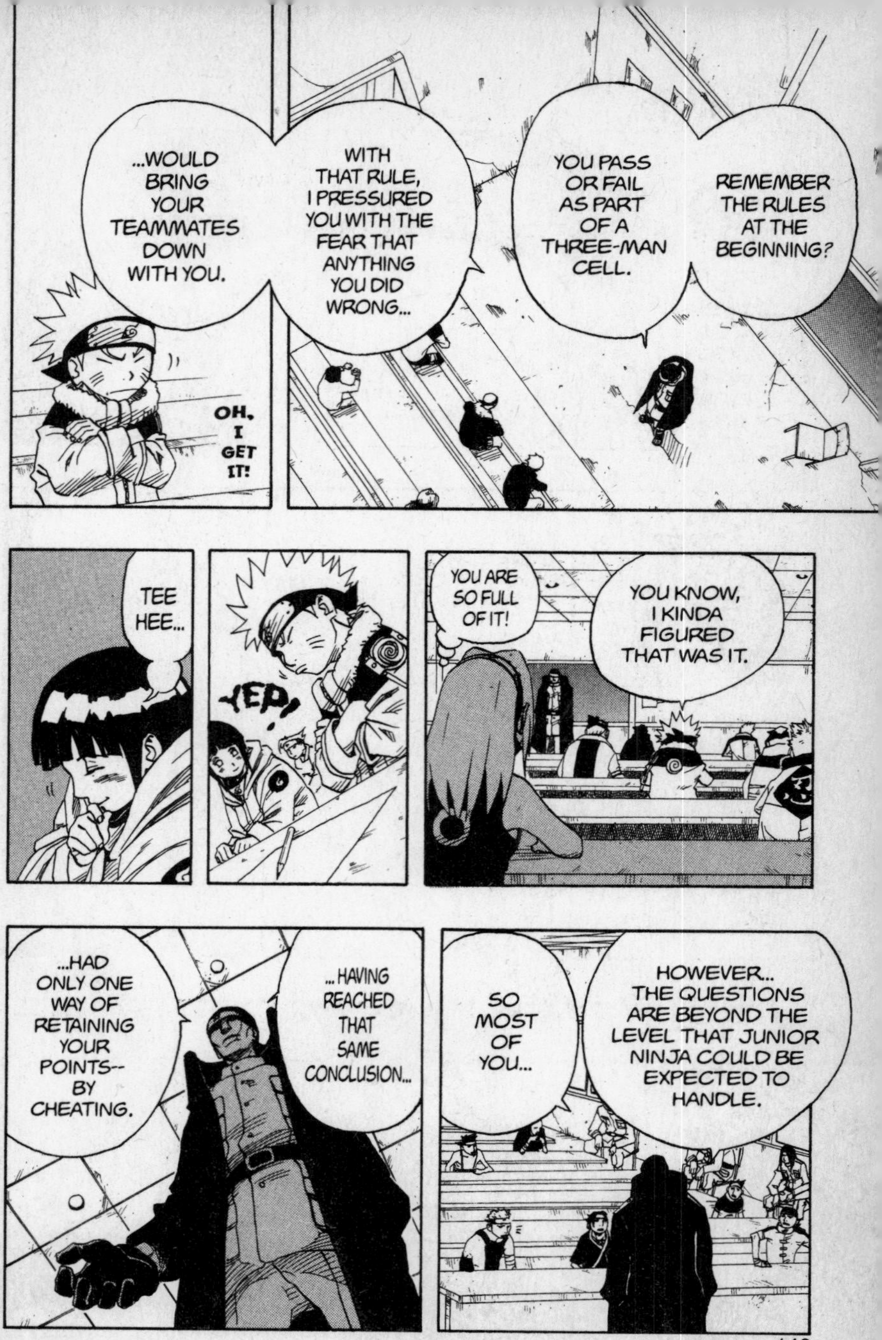
REMEMBER THE RULES AT THE BEGINNING?
YOU PASS OR FAIL AS PART OF A THREE-MAN CELL.
WITH THAT RULE, I PRESSURED YOU WITH THE FEAR THAT ANYTHING YOU DID WRONG...
...WOULD BRING YOUR TEAMMATES DOWN WITH YOU.
OH, I GET IT!
YOU KNOW, I KINDA FIGURED THAT WAS IT.
YOU ARE SO FULL OF IT!
YEP!
TEE HEE...
HOWEVER... THE QUESTIONS ARE BEYOND THE LEVEL THAT JUNIOR NINJA COULD BE EXPECTED TO HANDLE.
SO MOST OF YOU...
...HAVING REACHED THAT SAME CONCLUSION...
...HAD ONLY ONE WAY OF RETAINING YOUR POINTS--BY CHEATING.

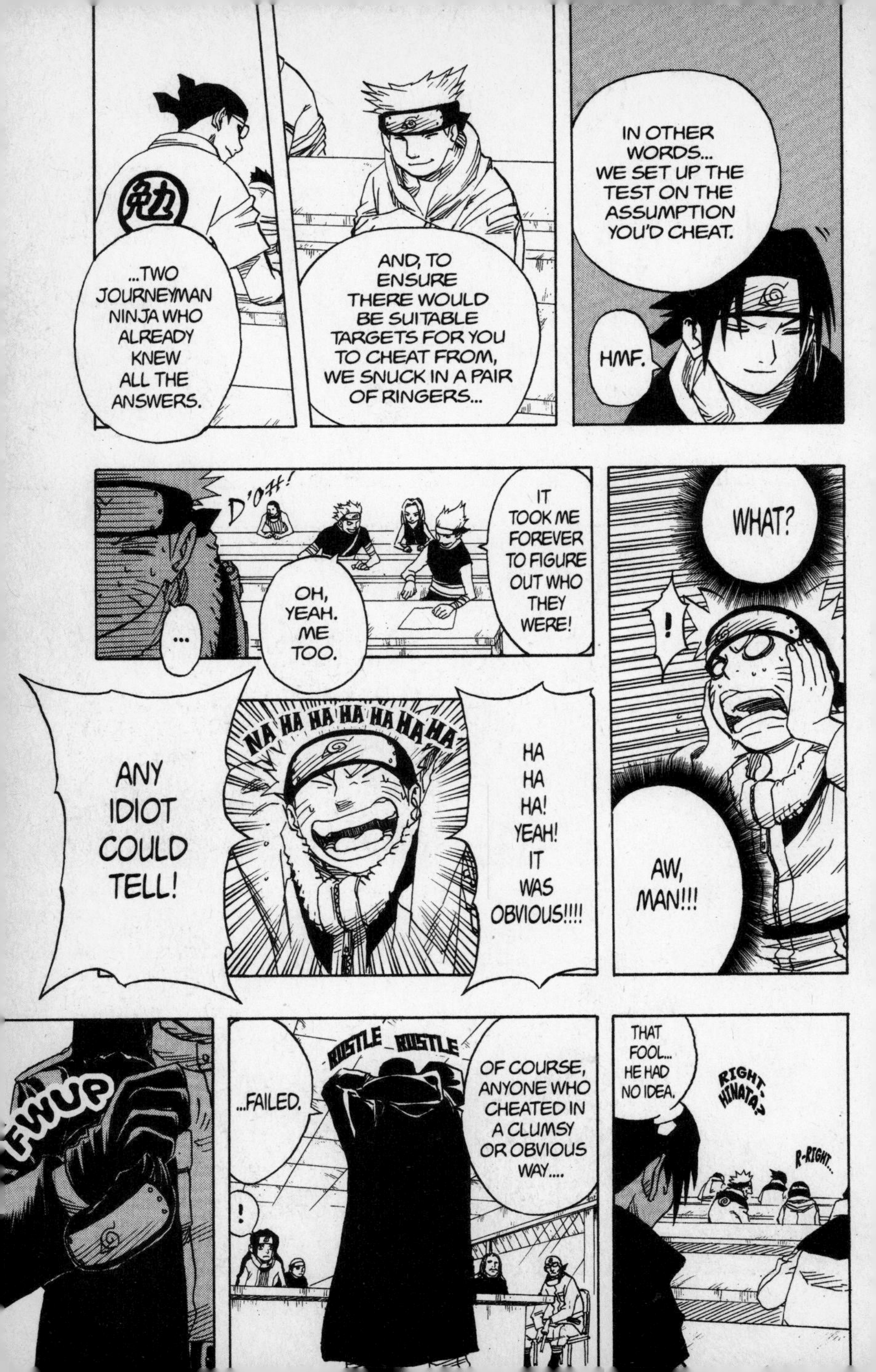
IN OTHER WORDS... WE SET UP THE TEST ON THE ASSUMPTION YOU'D CHEAT.
HMF.
AND, TO ENSURE THERE WOULD BE SUITABLE TARGETS FOR YOU TO CHEAT FROM, WE SNUCK IN A PAIR OF RINGERS...
...TWO JOURNEYMAN NINJA WHO ALREADY KNEW ALL THE ANSWERS.
WHAT?
!
AW, MAN!!!
IT TOOK ME FOREVER TO FIGURE OUT WHO THEY WERE!
D'OH!
OH, YEAH. ME TOO.
...
NA HA HA HA HA HA HA HA
HA HA HA! YEAH! IT WAS OBVIOUS!!!!
ANY IDIOT COULD TELL!
THAT FOOL... HE HAD NO IDEA.
RIGHT, HINATA?
R-RIGHT...
OF COURSE, ANYONE WHO CHEATED IN A CLUMSY OR OBVIOUS WAY....
RUSTLE RUSTLE
...FAILED.
!
FWUP

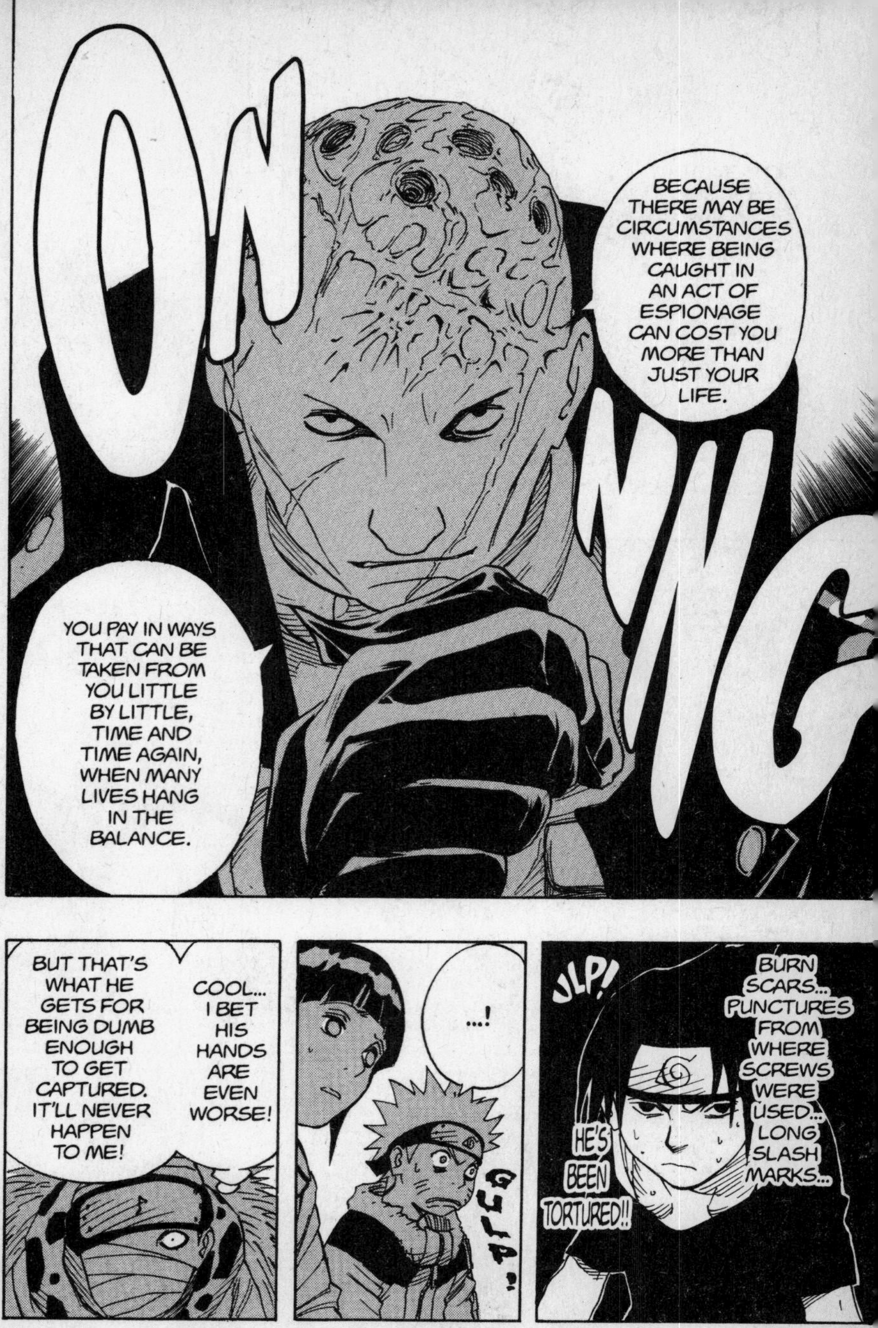
ON
NNG
BECAUSE THERE MAY BE CIRCUMSTANCES WHERE BEING CAUGHT IN AN ACT OF ESPIONAGE CAN COST YOU MORE THAN JUST YOUR LIFE.
YOU PAY IN WAYS THAT CAN BE TAKEN FROM YOU LITTLE BY LITTLE, TIME AND TIME AGAIN, WHEN MANY LIVES HANG IN THE BALANCE.
BURN SCARS... PUNCTURES FROM WHERE SCREWS WERE USED... LONG SLASH MARKS...
ULP!
HE'S BEEN TORTURED!!
...!
GULP
COOL... I BET HIS HANDS ARE EVEN WORSE!
BUT THAT'S WHAT HE GETS FOR BEING DUMB ENOUGH TO GET CAPTURED. IT'LL NEVER HAPPEN TO ME!

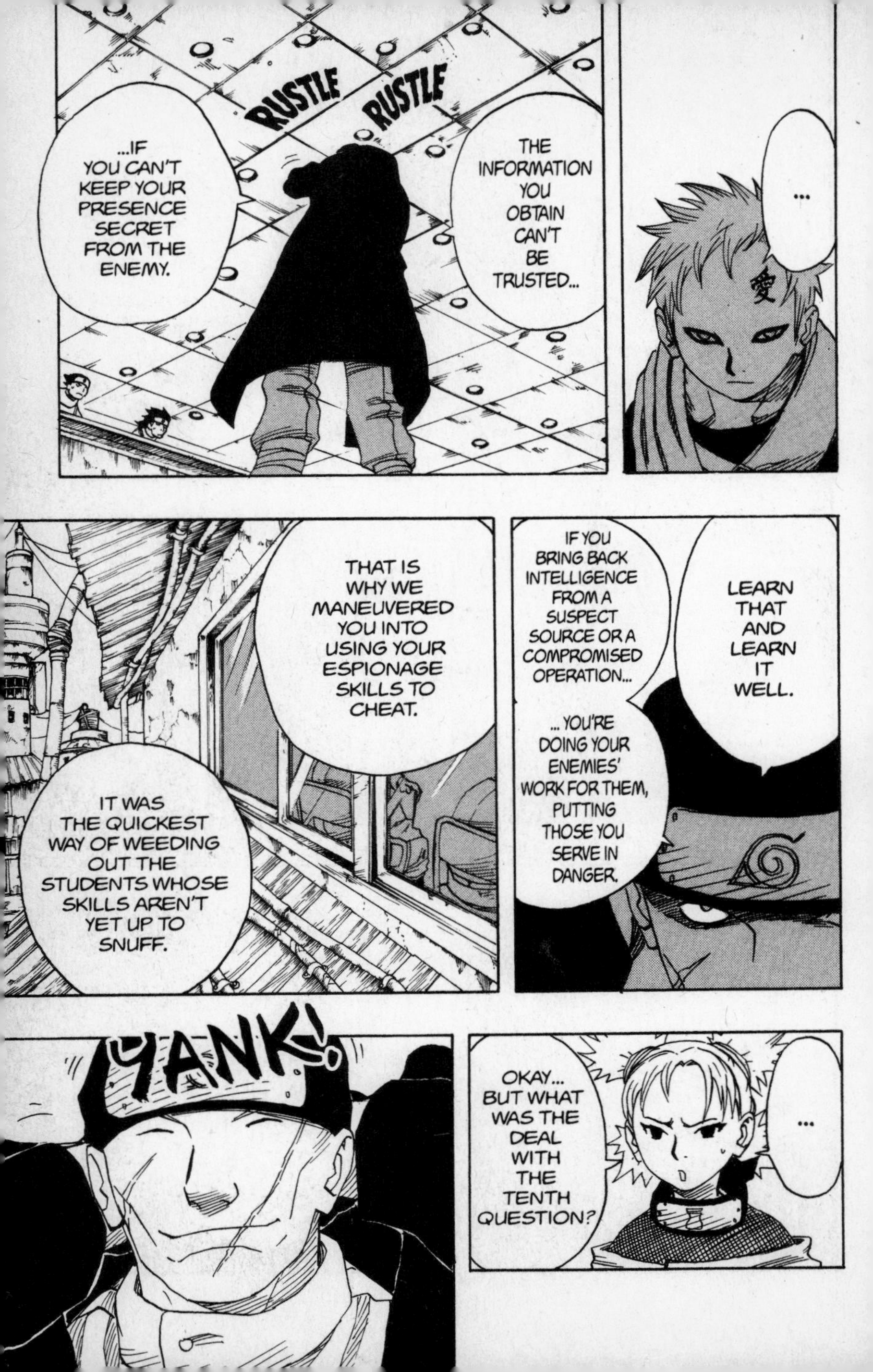
...
THE INFORMATION YOU OBTAIN CAN'T BE TRUSTED...
RUSTLE
RUSTLE
...IF YOU CAN'T KEEP YOUR PRESENCE SECRET FROM THE ENEMY.
LEARN THAT AND LEARN IT WELL.
IF YOU BRING BACK INTELLIGENCE FROM A SUSPECT SOURCE OR A COMPROMISED OPERATION...
... YOU'RE DOING YOUR ENEMIES' WORK FOR THEM, PUTTING THOSE YOU SERVE IN DANGER.
THAT IS WHY WE MANEUVERED YOU INTO USING YOUR ESPIONAGE SKILLS TO CHEAT.
IT WAS THE QUICKEST WAY OF WEEDING OUT THE STUDENTS WHOSE SKILLS AREN'T YET UP TO SNUFF.
...
OKAY... BUT WHAT WAS THE DEAL WITH THE TENTH QUESTION?
YANK!

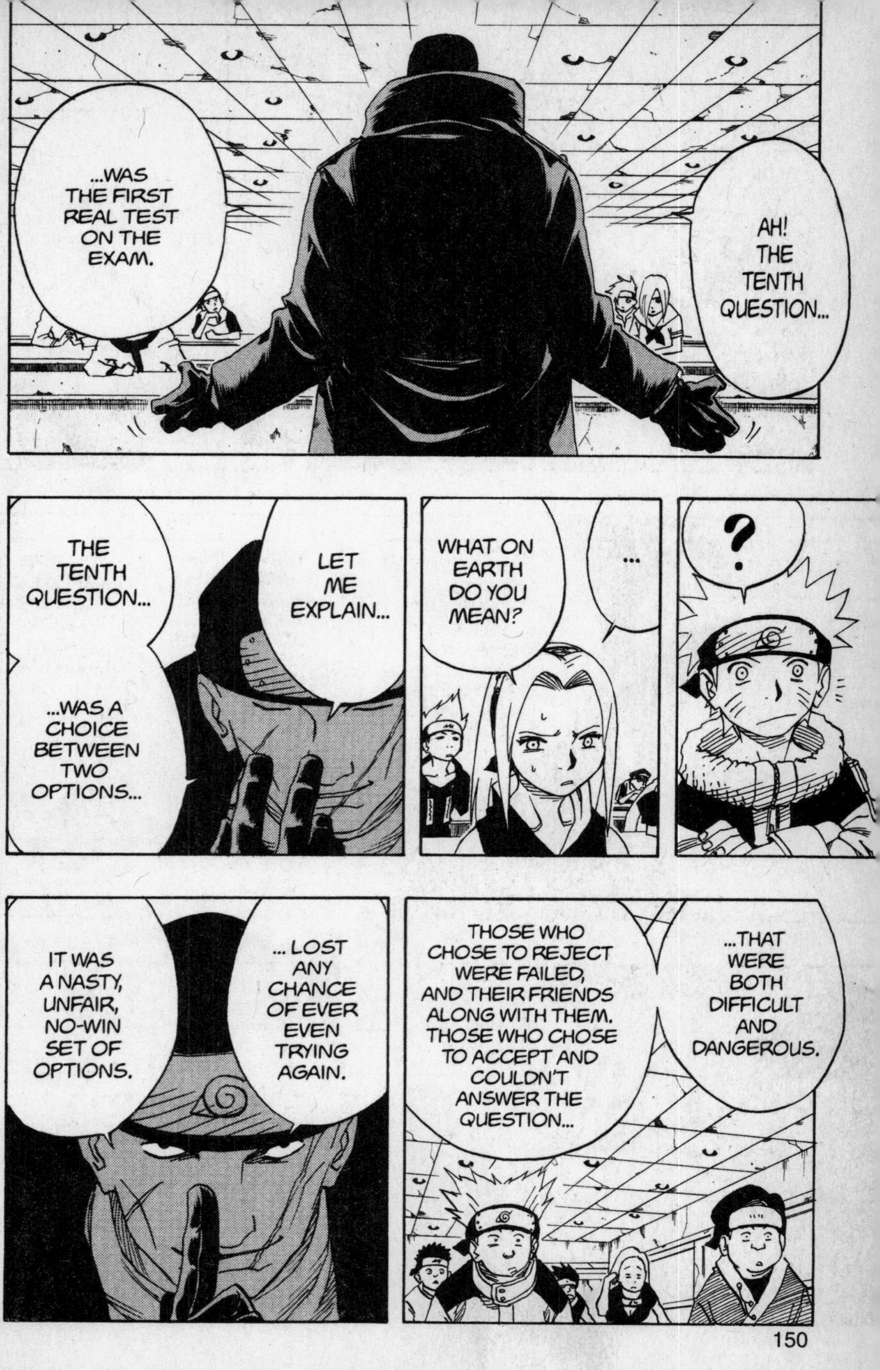
AH! THE TENTH QUESTION...
...WAS THE FIRST REAL TEST ON THE EXAM.
?
...
WHAT ON EARTH DO YOU MEAN?
LET ME EXPLAIN...
THE TENTH QUESTION...
...WAS A CHOICE BETWEEN TWO OPTIONS...
...THAT WERE BOTH DIFFICULT AND DANGEROUS.
THOSE WHO CHOSE TO REJECT WERE FAILED, AND THEIR FRIENDS ALONG WITH THEM. THOSE WHO CHOSE TO ACCEPT AND COULDN'T ANSWER THE QUESTION...
... LOST ANY CHANCE OF EVER EVEN TRYING AGAIN.
IT WAS A NASTY, UNFAIR, NO-WIN SET OF OPTIONS.

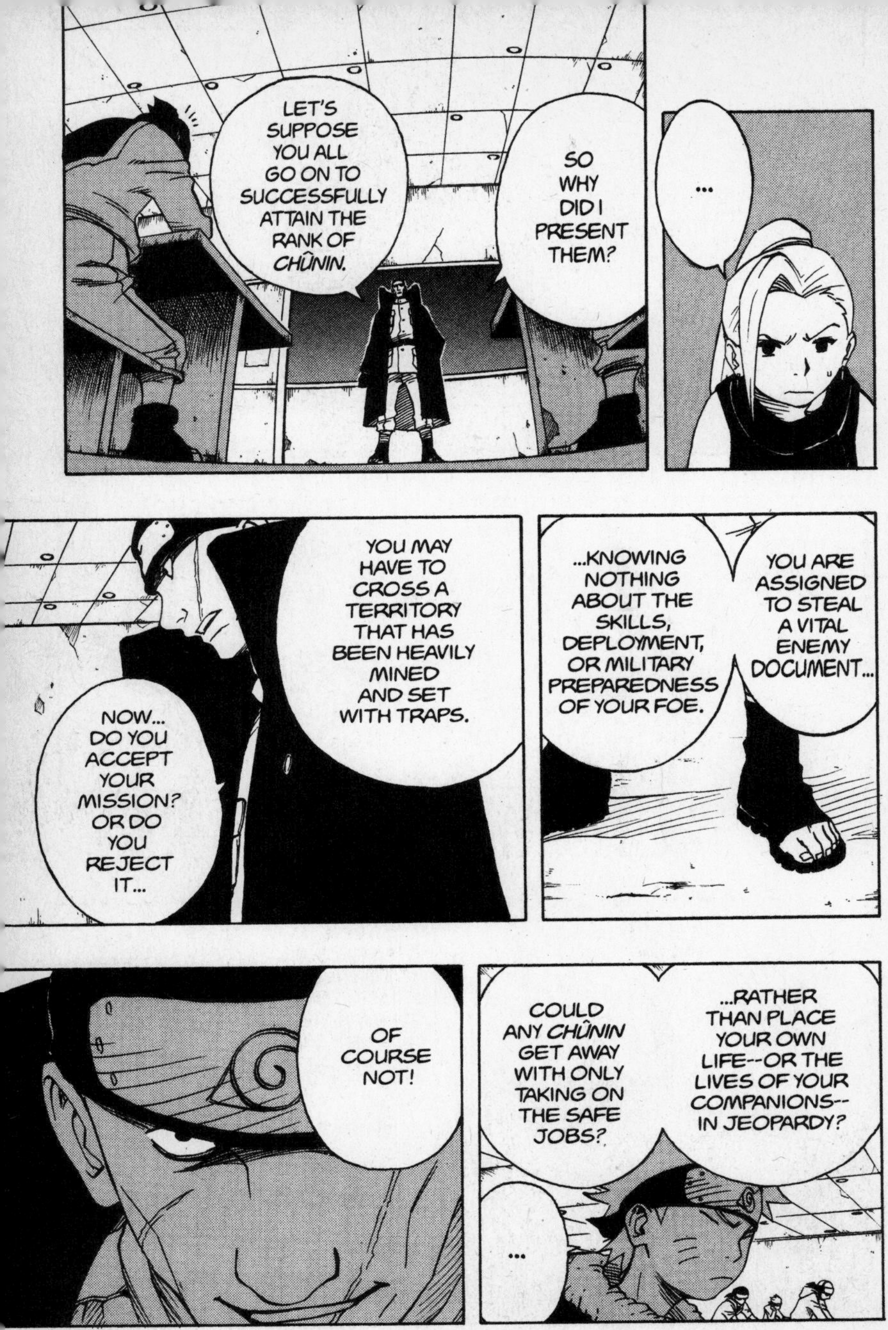
...
SO WHY DID I PRESENT THEM?
LET'S SUPPOSE YOU ALL GO ON TO SUCCESSFULLY ATTAIN THE RANK OF *CHŪNIN.*
YOU ARE ASSIGNED TO STEAL A VITAL ENEMY DOCUMENT...
...KNOWING NOTHING ABOUT THE SKILLS, DEPLOYMENT, OR MILITARY PREPAREDNESS OF YOUR FOE.
YOU MAY HAVE TO CROSS A TERRITORY THAT HAS BEEN HEAVILY MINED AND SET WITH TRAPS.
NOW... DO YOU ACCEPT YOUR MISSION? OR DO YOU REJECT IT...
...RATHER THAN PLACE YOUR OWN LIFE--OR THE LIVES OF YOUR COMPANIONS--IN JEOPARDY?
COULD ANY *CHŪNIN* GET AWAY WITH ONLY TAKING ON THE SAFE JOBS?
...
OF COURSE NOT!

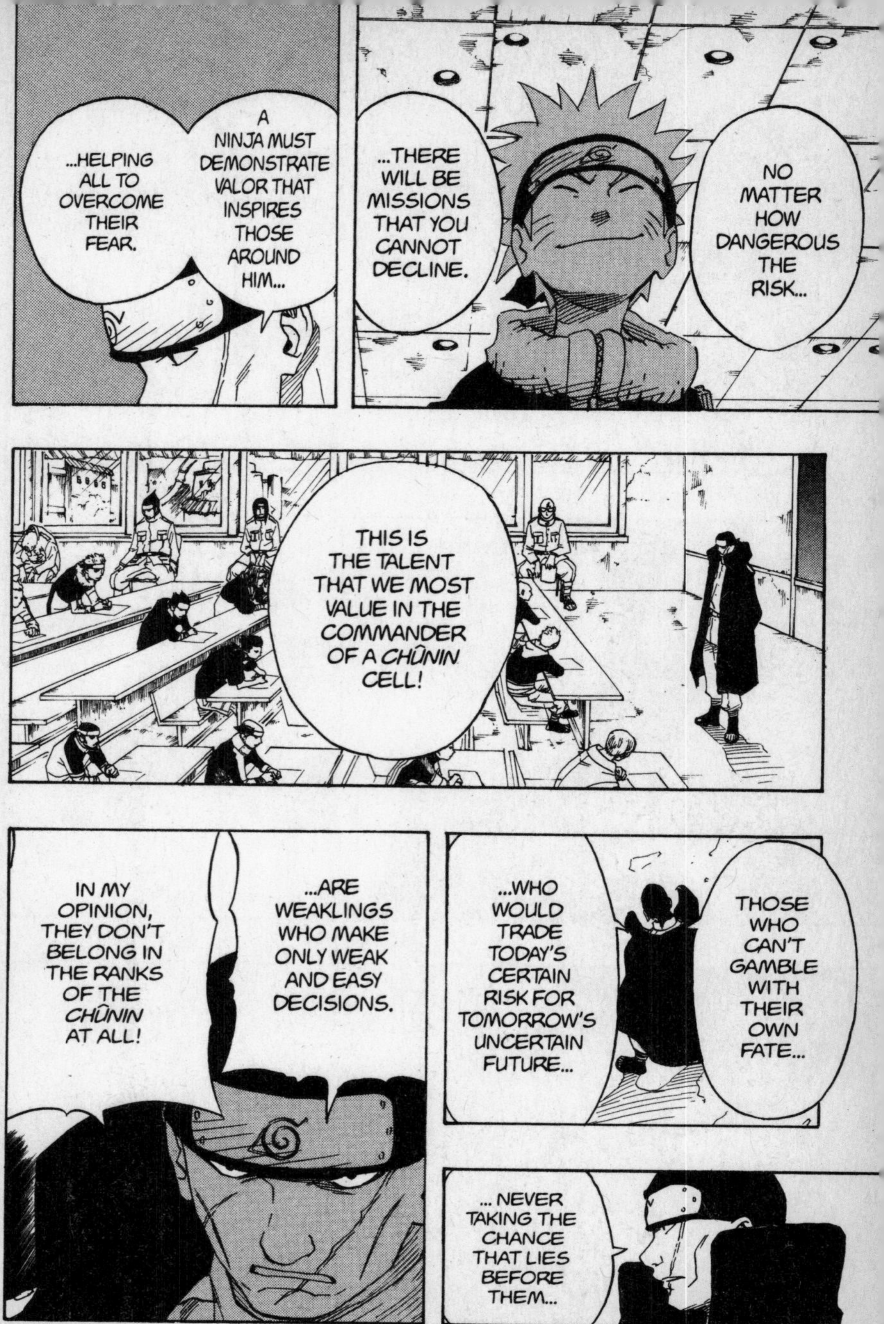
NO MATTER HOW DANGEROUS THE RISK...
...THERE WILL BE MISSIONS THAT YOU CANNOT DECLINE.
A NINJA MUST DEMONSTRATE VALOR THAT INSPIRES THOSE AROUND HIM...
...HELPING ALL TO OVERCOME THEIR FEAR.
THIS IS THE TALENT THAT WE MOST VALUE IN THE COMMANDER OF A *CHÛNIN* CELL!
THOSE WHO CAN'T GAMBLE WITH THEIR OWN FATE...
...WHO WOULD TRADE TODAY'S CERTAIN RISK FOR TOMORROW'S UNCERTAIN FUTURE...
... NEVER TAKING THE CHANCE THAT LIES BEFORE THEM...
...ARE WEAKLINGS WHO MAKE ONLY WEAK AND EASY DECISIONS.
IN MY OPINION, THEY DON'T BELONG IN THE RANKS OF THE *CHÛNIN* AT ALL!

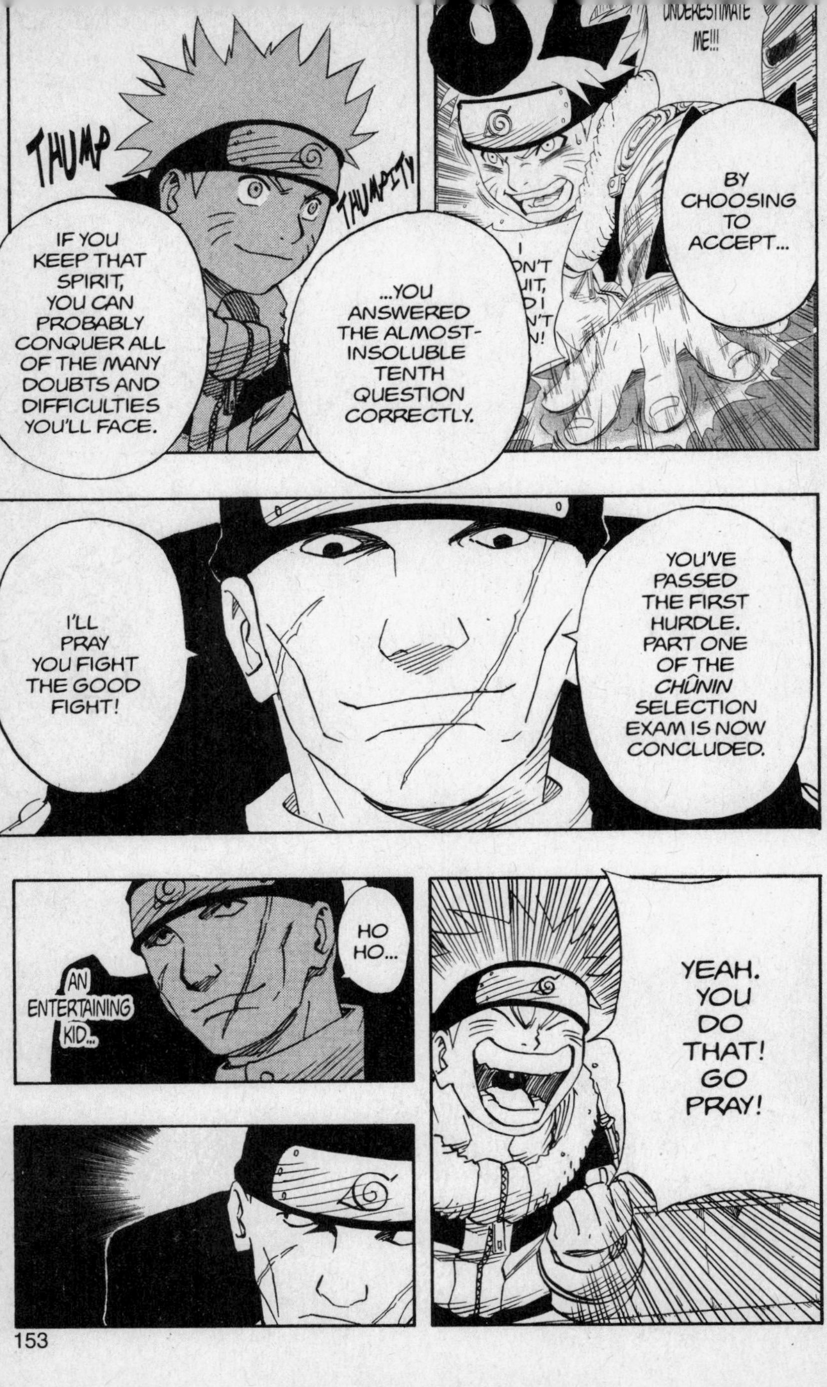
UNDERESTIMATE ME!!!
BY CHOOSING TO ACCEPT...
...YOU ANSWERED THE ALMOST-INSOLUBLE TENTH QUESTION CORRECTLY.
THUMPITY
THUMP
IF YOU KEEP THAT SPIRIT, YOU CAN PROBABLY CONQUER ALL OF THE MANY DOUBTS AND DIFFICULTIES YOU'LL FACE.
YOU'VE PASSED THE FIRST HURDLE. PART ONE OF THE *CHÛNIN* SELECTION EXAM IS NOW CONCLUDED.
I'LL PRAY YOU FIGHT THE GOOD FIGHT!
YEAH. YOU DO THAT! GO PRAY!
HO HO...
AN ENTERTAINING KID...

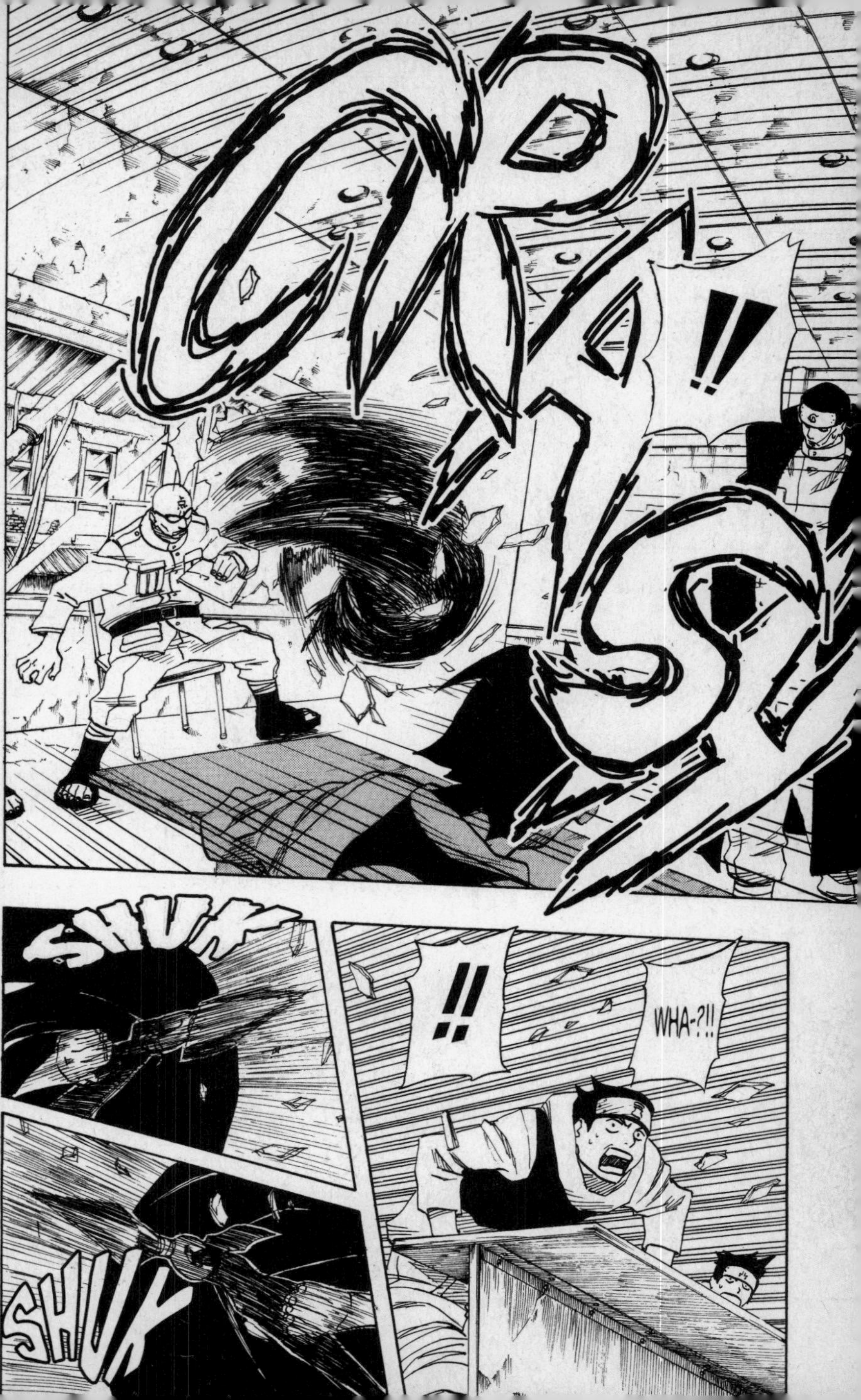
CRASH!!
WHA-?!!
!!
SHUK
SHUK

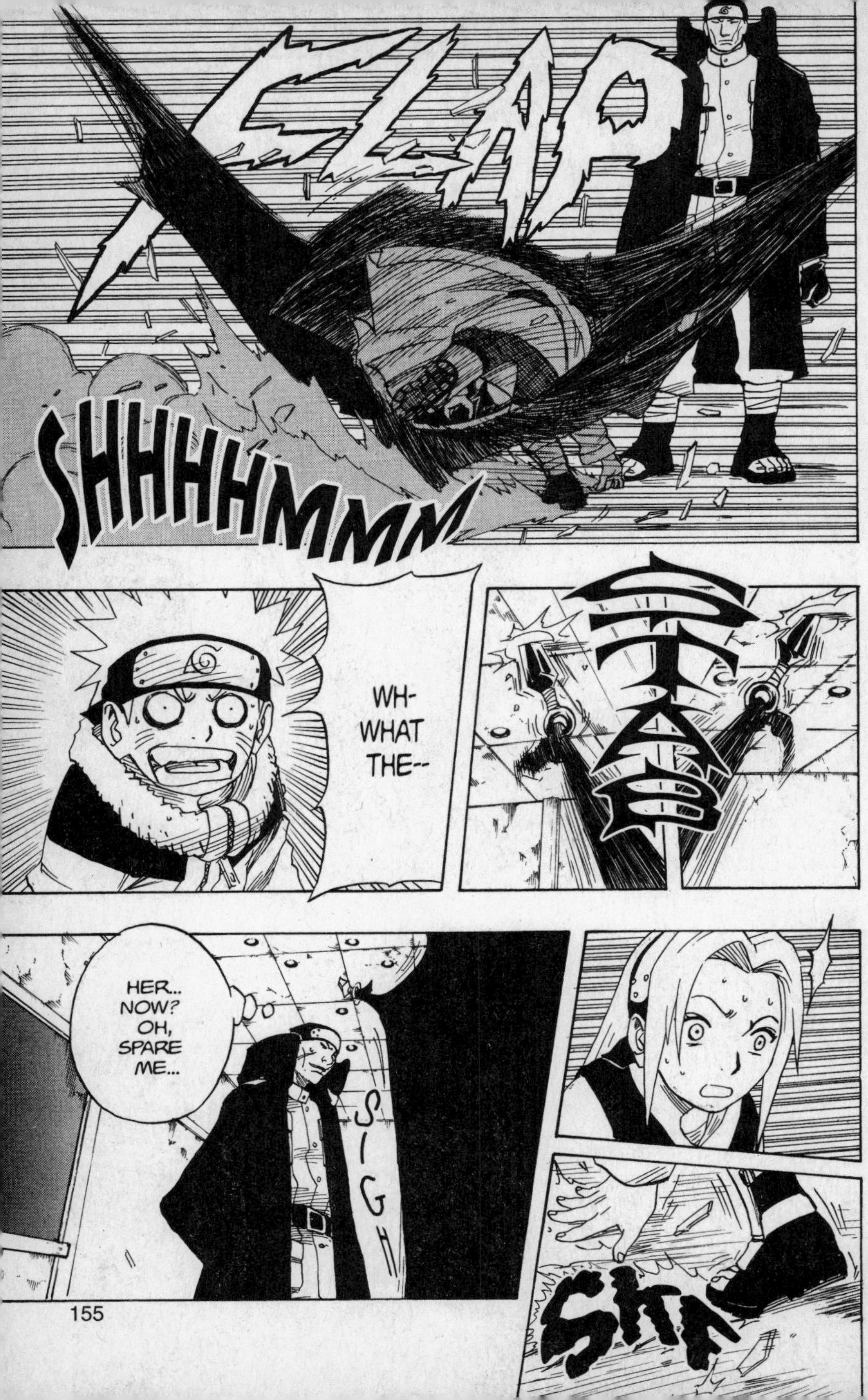
SLAP
SHHHHMMMM
WH- WHAT THE--
HER... NOW? OH, SPARE ME...
SIGH

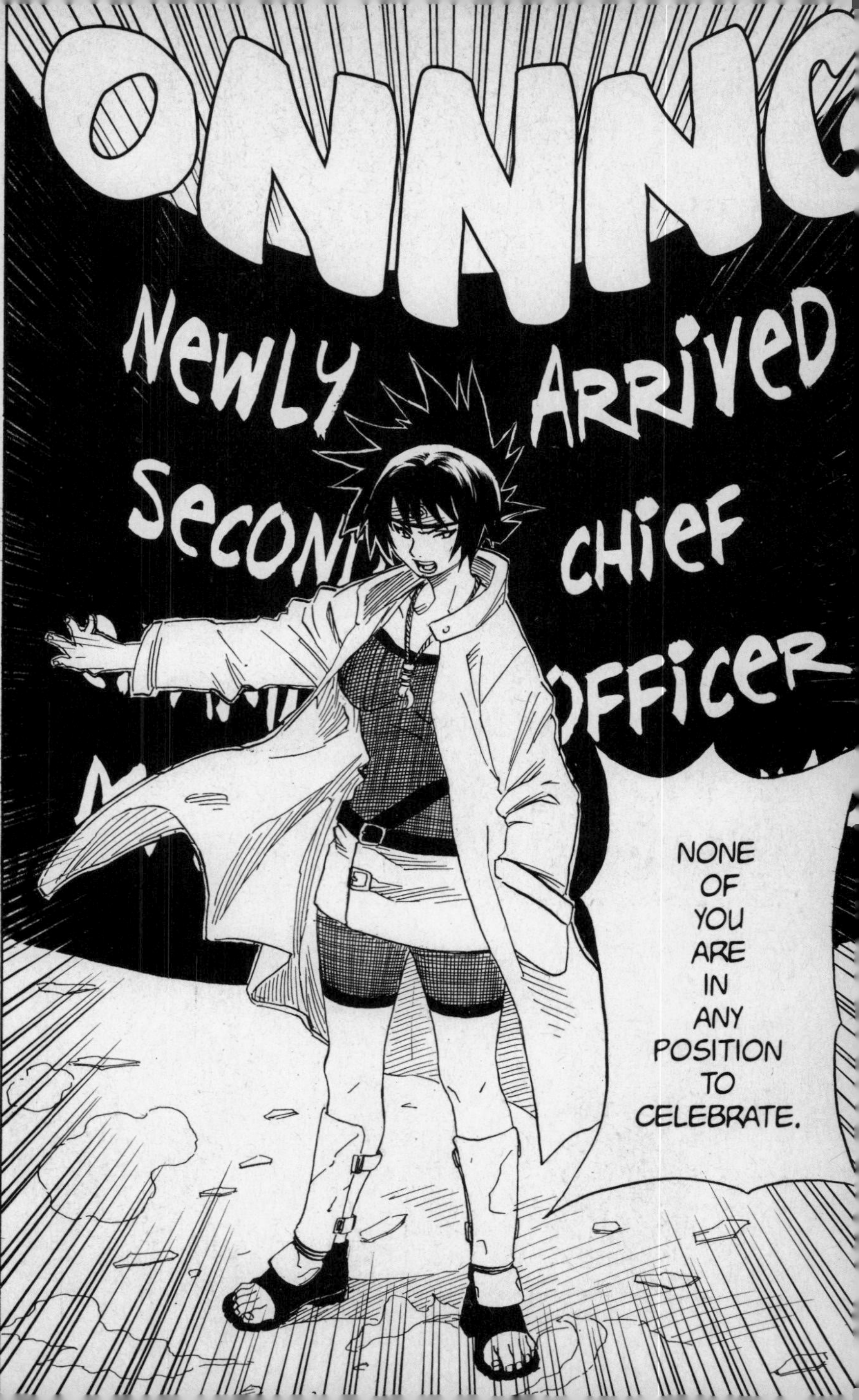
ONNN
Newly Arrived
Secon chief
fficer
NONE OF YOU ARE IN ANY POSITION TO CELEBRATE.

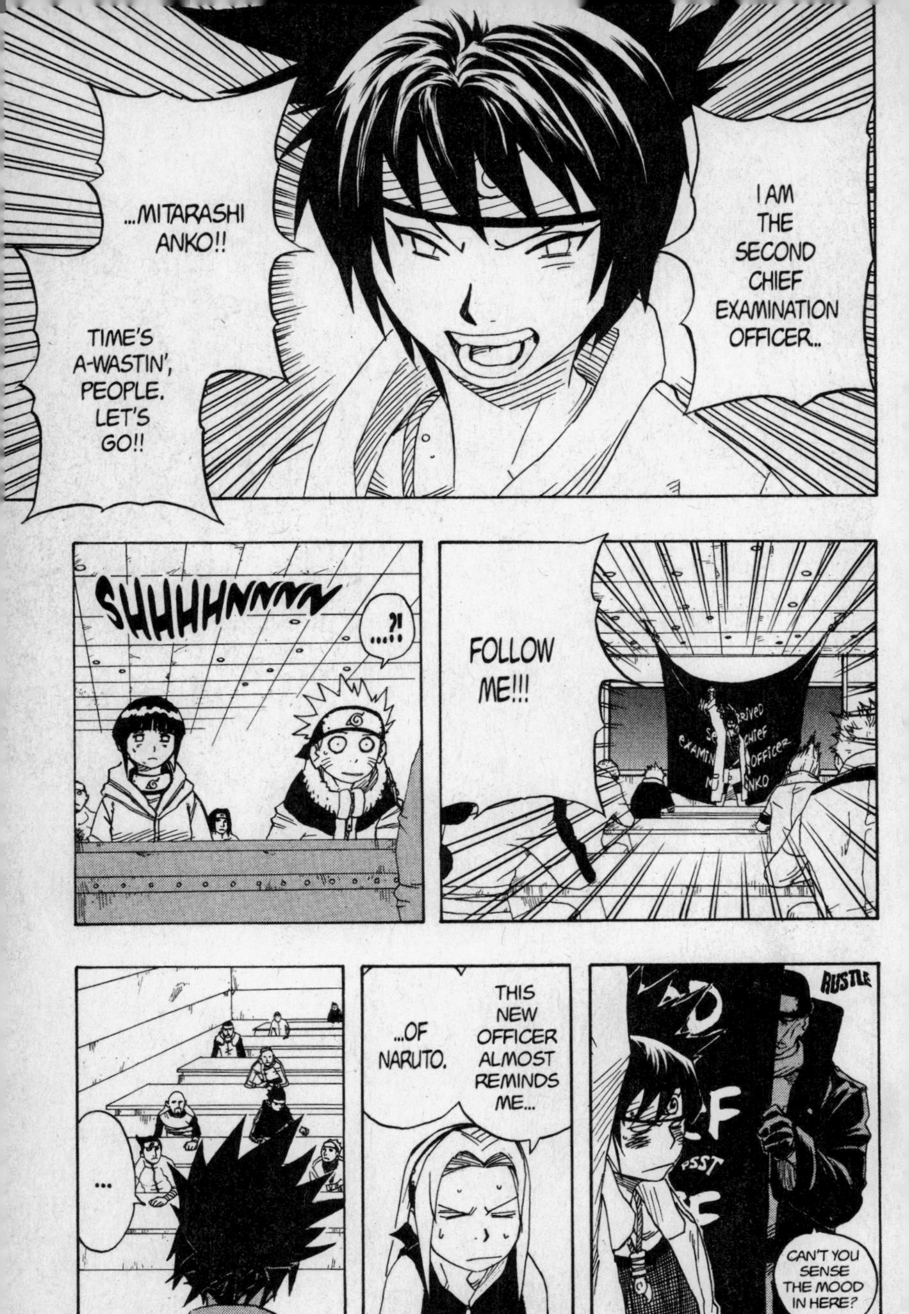
I AM THE SECOND CHIEF EXAMINATION OFFICER..
...MITARASHI ANKO!!
TIME'S A-WASTIN', PEOPLE. LET'S GO!!
FOLLOW ME!!!
SHHHHNNNN
...?!
RUSTLE
PSST
CAN'T YOU SENSE THE MOOD IN HERE?
THIS NEW OFFICER ALMOST REMINDS ME...
...OF NARUTO.
...

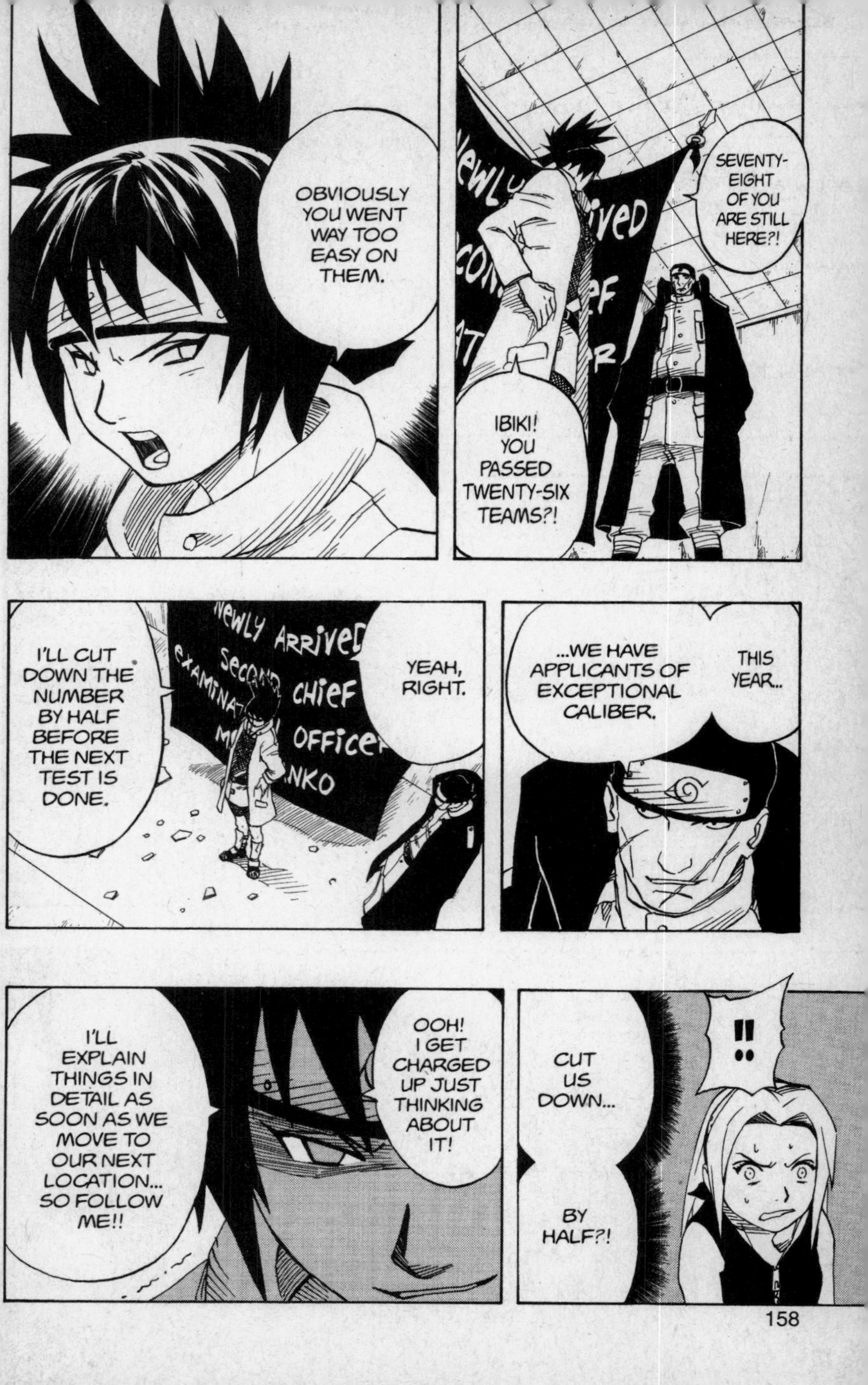
SEVENTY-EIGHT OF YOU ARE STILL HERE?!
IBIKI! YOU PASSED TWENTY-SIX TEAMS?!
OBVIOUSLY YOU WENT WAY TOO EASY ON THEM.
THIS YEAR...
...WE HAVE APPLICANTS OF EXCEPTIONAL CALIBER.
YEAH, RIGHT.
I'LL CUT DOWN THE NUMBER BY HALF BEFORE THE NEXT TEST IS DONE.
!!
CUT US DOWN...
BY HALF?!
OOH! I GET CHARGED UP JUST THINKING ABOUT IT!
I'LL EXPLAIN THINGS IN DETAIL AS SOON AS WE MOVE TO OUR NEXT LOCATION... SO FOLLOW ME!!

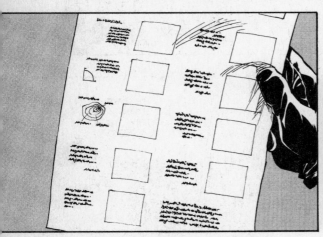

UZUMAKI NARUTO... ...IS A VERY INTRIGUING YOUNG MAN.

HE'S THE KIND OF PERSON WHO THINKS HE CAN PASS THE EXAM... WITH A COMPLETELY BLANK ANSWER SHEET.

HUH.

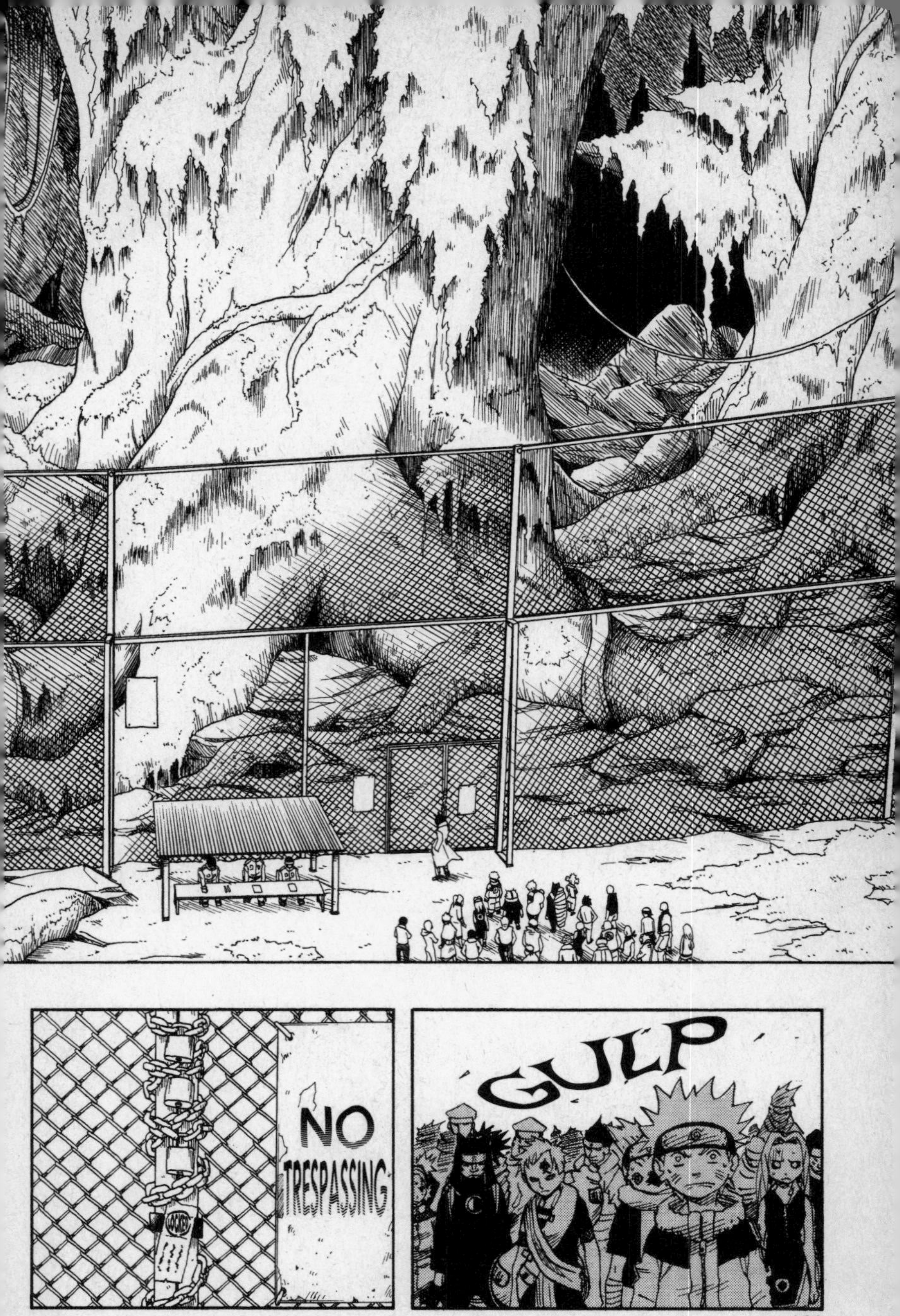
GULP
NO
TRESPASSING

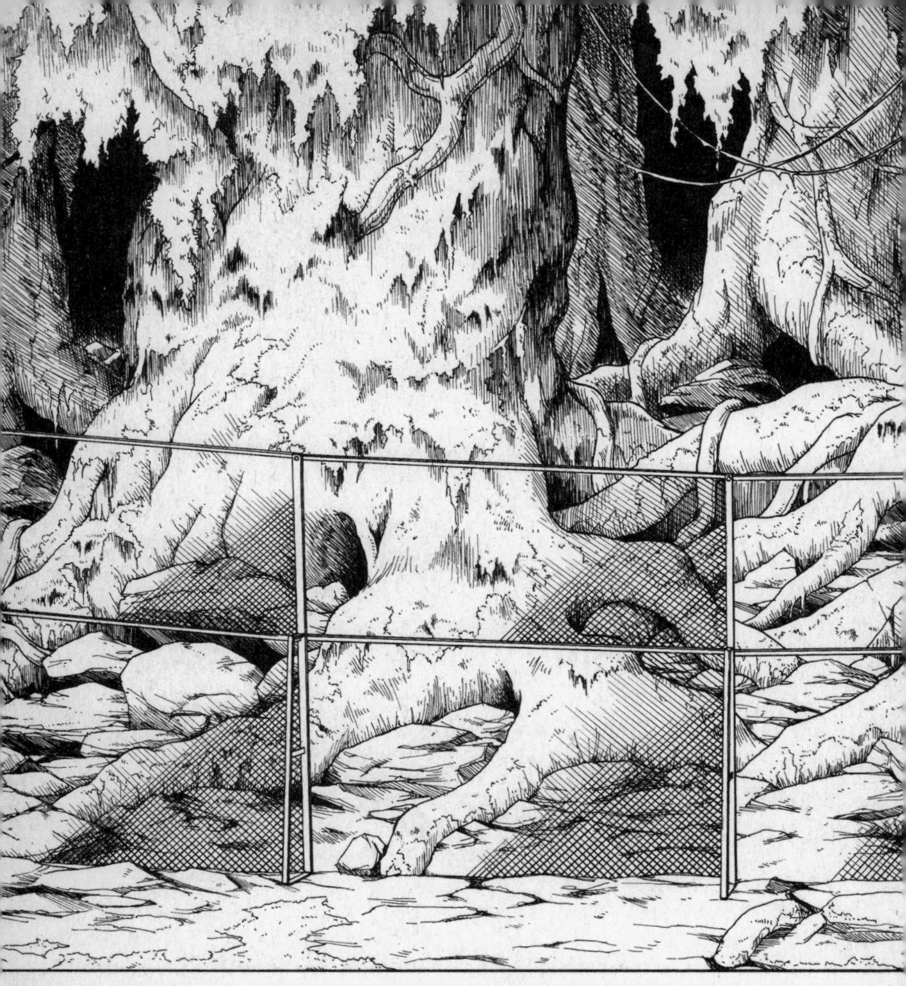

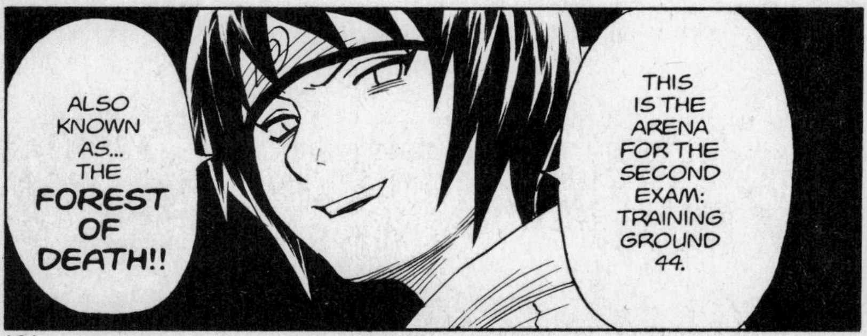
THIS IS THE ARENA FOR THE SECOND EXAM: TRAINING GROUND 44.
ALSO KNOWN AS... THE **FOREST OF DEATH!!**

KISHIMOTO MASASHI'S "I ONLY SHOW YOU THESE THINGS SO YOU'LL UNDERSTAND HOW MUCH I LOVE MANGA" REJECTS CORNER...

THE ROUGH SKETCHES ABOVE SHOW HOW I LAY OUT THE VISUAL FLOW OF AN ACTION SEQUENCE. I TRY TO BE VERY CONSCIOUS OF THE FLOW OF SCENES IN NARUTO, SO AS SOON AS I COME UP WITH AN IDEA FOR AN ACTION SEQUENCE, I CHOREOGRAPH IT IN A SET OF THUMBNAIL DRAWINGS, LIKE STORYBOARDS. I TRY TO KEEP THE OVERALL PAGE COUNT FOR THE CHAPTER IN MIND, BUT THINGS USUALLY KEEP EXPANDING AND OPENING OUT, TAKING UP MORE AND MORE PAGES, WHILE I WORK OUT THE BEST CAMERA ANGLES, WITHOUT EVEN A THOUGHT TO WHERE THE DIALOGUE WILL FALL. NEXT I NUMBER THE SKETCHES, FIGURE OUT WHICH SCENES ARE THE MOST CRUCIAL, MAKE SURE THE TWO-PAGE SPREADS WILL ACTUALLY LAND ON PAGES THAT FACE EACH OTHER... AND THEN I NUMBER THE PAGES AND BREAK THEM DOWN INTO PANELS. THEN I DISCOVER I'VE USED UP MORE PAGES THAN I'M SUPPOSED TO HAVE IN THE ENTIRE CHAPTER... WHICH MEANS I HAVE TO GO BACK AND CUT SEQUENCES AND ERASE THINGS... CRYING LIKE A BABY ALL THE WHILE. YOU KNOW...
IT JUST OCCURRED TO ME...
THIS MAY BE WHY MY SCRIPTS ARE ALWAYS SO LATE!

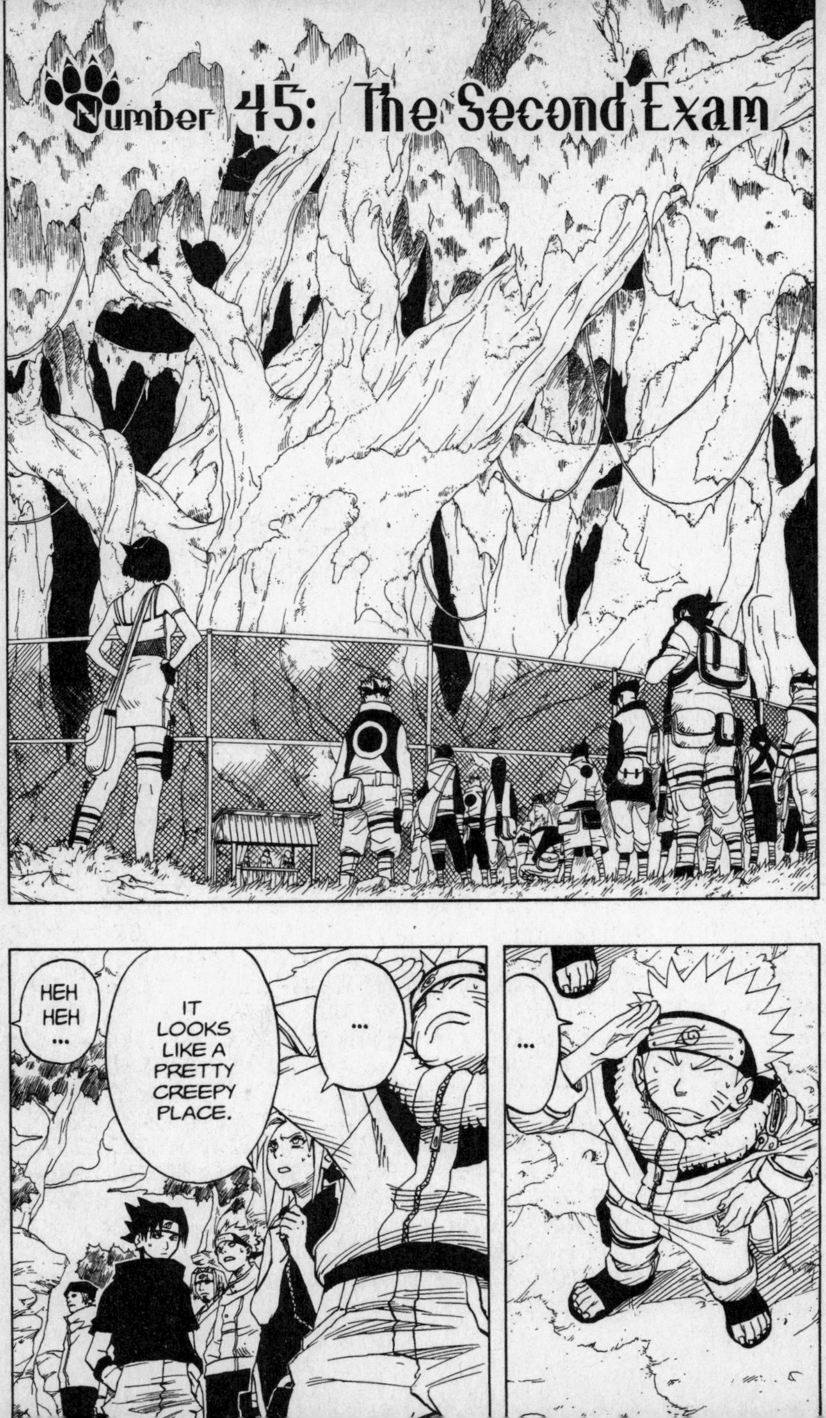
Number 45: The Second Exam
...
...
IT LOOKS LIKE A PRETTY CREEPY PLACE.
HEH HEH ...

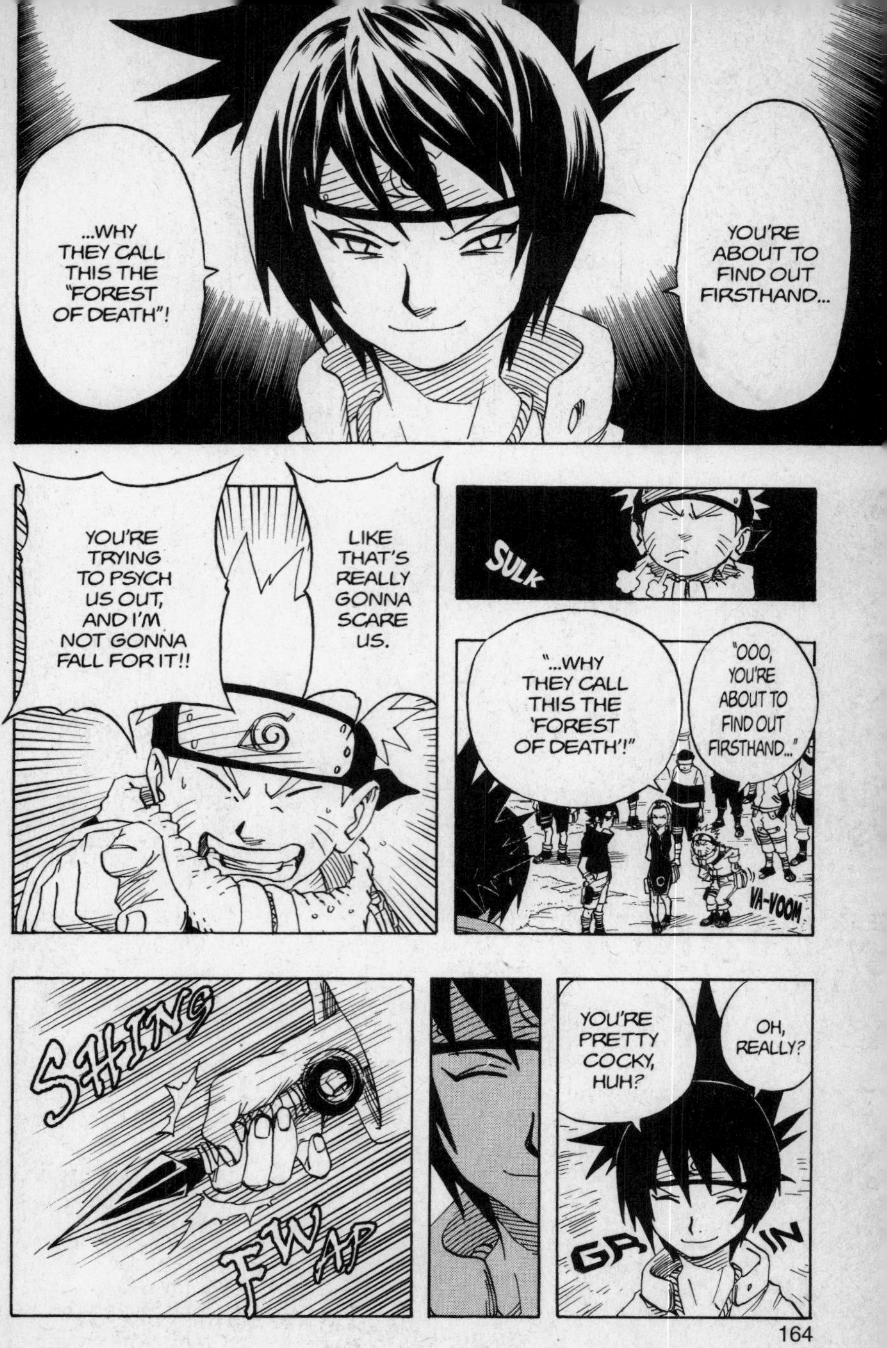
YOU'RE ABOUT TO FIND OUT FIRSTHAND...
...WHY THEY CALL THIS THE "FOREST OF DEATH"!
SULK
"OOO, YOU'RE ABOUT TO FIND OUT FIRSTHAND..."
"...WHY THEY CALL THIS THE 'FOREST OF DEATH'!"
VA-VOOM
LIKE THAT'S REALLY GONNA SCARE US.
YOU'RE TRYING TO PSYCH US OUT, AND I'M NOT GONNA FALL FOR IT!!
OH, REALLY?
YOU'RE PRETTY COCKY, HUH?
GRIN
SHING
FWAP

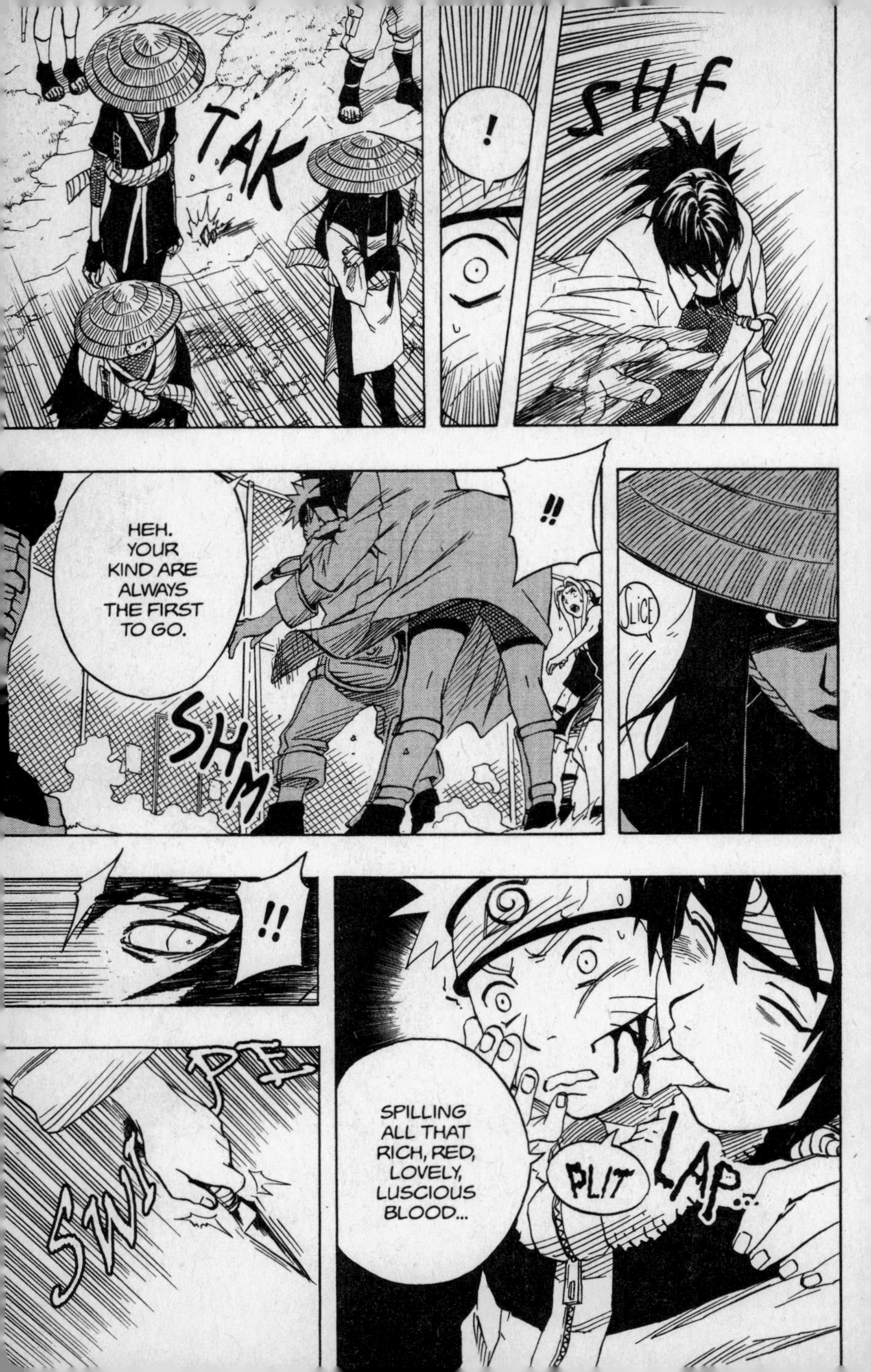
SHF
!
TAK
SLICE
!!
HEH. YOUR KIND ARE ALWAYS THE FIRST TO GO.
SHM
SPILLING ALL THAT RICH, RED, LOVELY, LUSCIOUS BLOOD...
PLIT
LAP...
!!
SWIPE

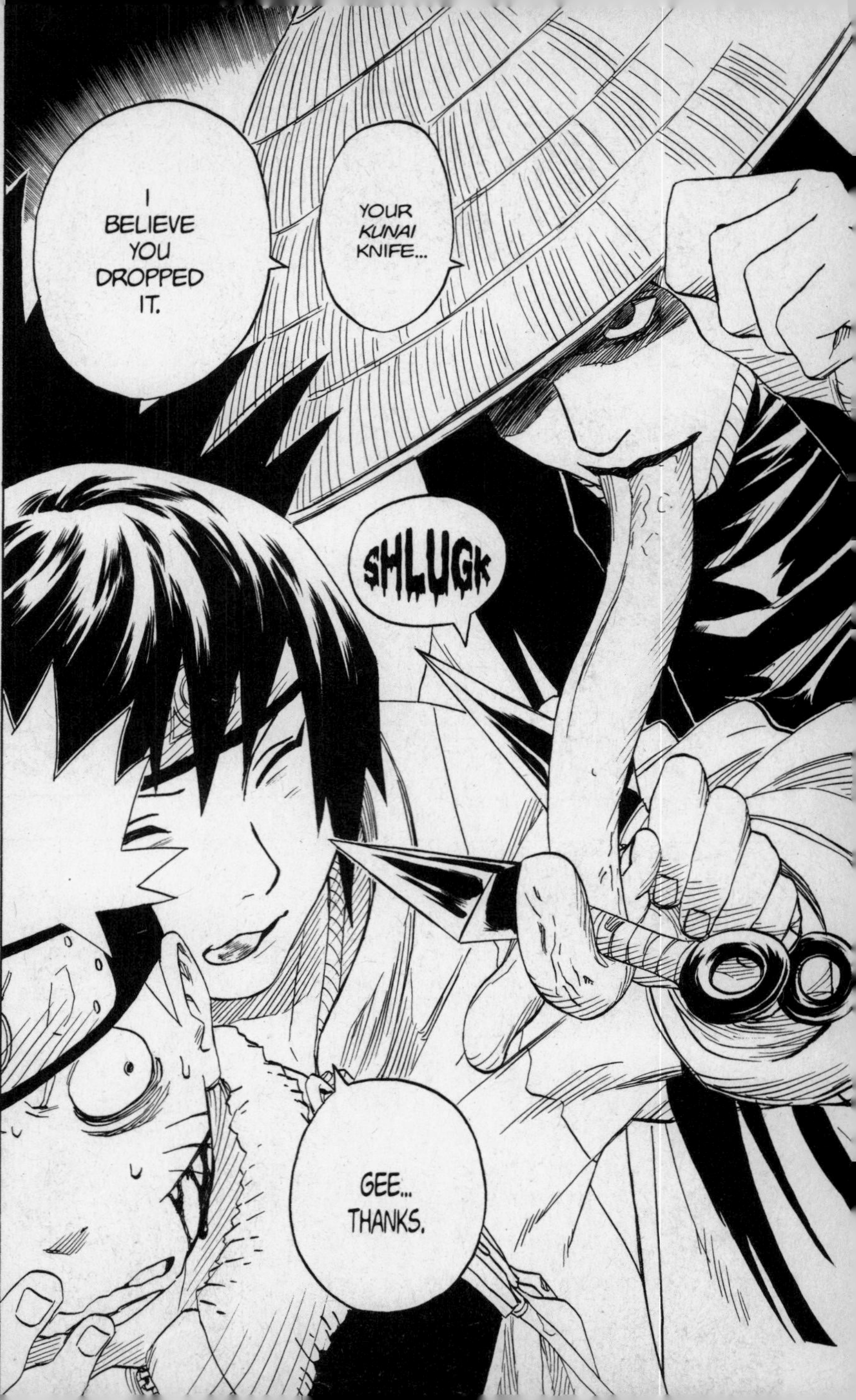
YOUR KUNAI KNIFE...
I BELIEVE YOU DROPPED IT.
SHLUGK
GEE... THANKS.

READ THIS WAY

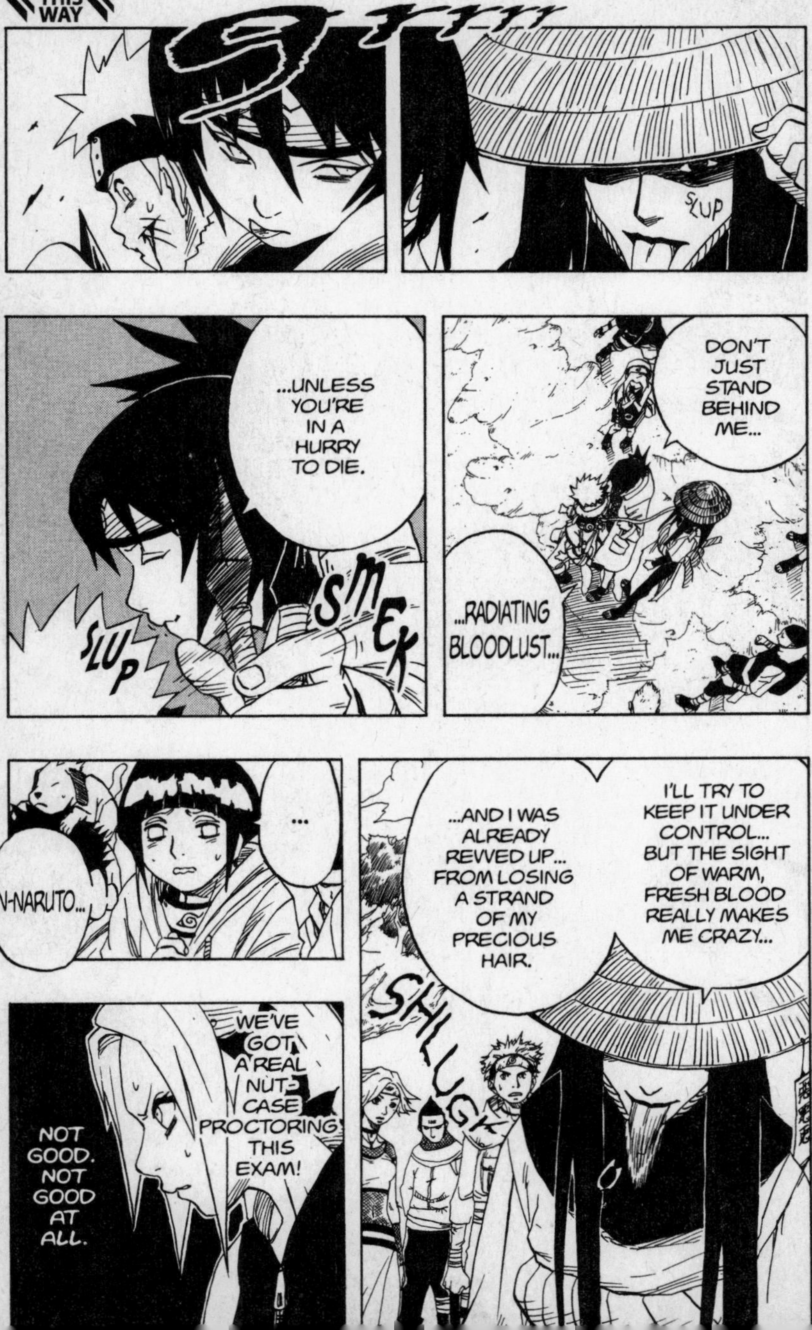

SLUP
DON'T JUST STAND BEHIND ME...
...RADIATING BLOODLUST...
...UNLESS YOU'RE IN A HURRY TO DIE.
SMEK
SLUP
I'LL TRY TO KEEP IT UNDER CONTROL... BUT THE SIGHT OF WARM, FRESH BLOOD REALLY MAKES ME CRAZY...
...AND I WAS ALREADY REVVED UP... FROM LOSING A STRAND OF MY PRECIOUS HAIR.
SHLUGK
...
N-NARUTO...
WE'VE GOT A REAL NUT-CASE PROCTORING THIS EXAM!
NOT GOOD. NOT GOOD AT ALL.

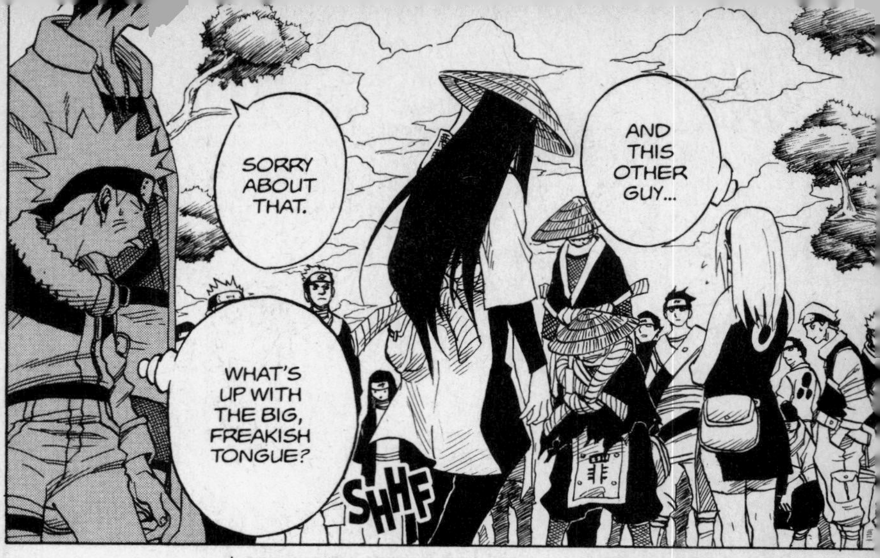
AND THIS OTHER GUY...
SORRY ABOUT THAT.
WHAT'S UP WITH THE BIG, FREAKISH TONGUE?
SHHF

* THE CHARACTER ON THE LOINCLOTH READS "CRIME."

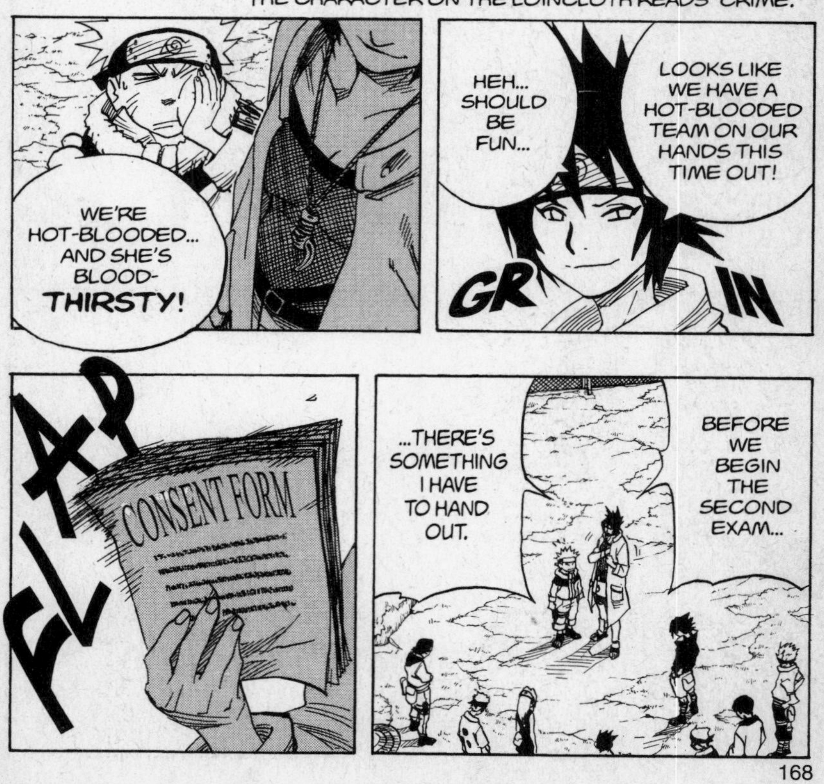
LOOKS LIKE WE HAVE A HOT-BLOODED TEAM ON OUR HANDS THIS TIME OUT!
HEH... SHOULD BE FUN...
GRIN
WE'RE HOT-BLOODED... AND SHE'S BLOOD-THIRSTY!
BEFORE WE BEGIN THE SECOND EXAM...
...THERE'S SOMETHING I HAVE TO HAND OUT.
FLAP
CONSENT FORM

READ THIS WAY

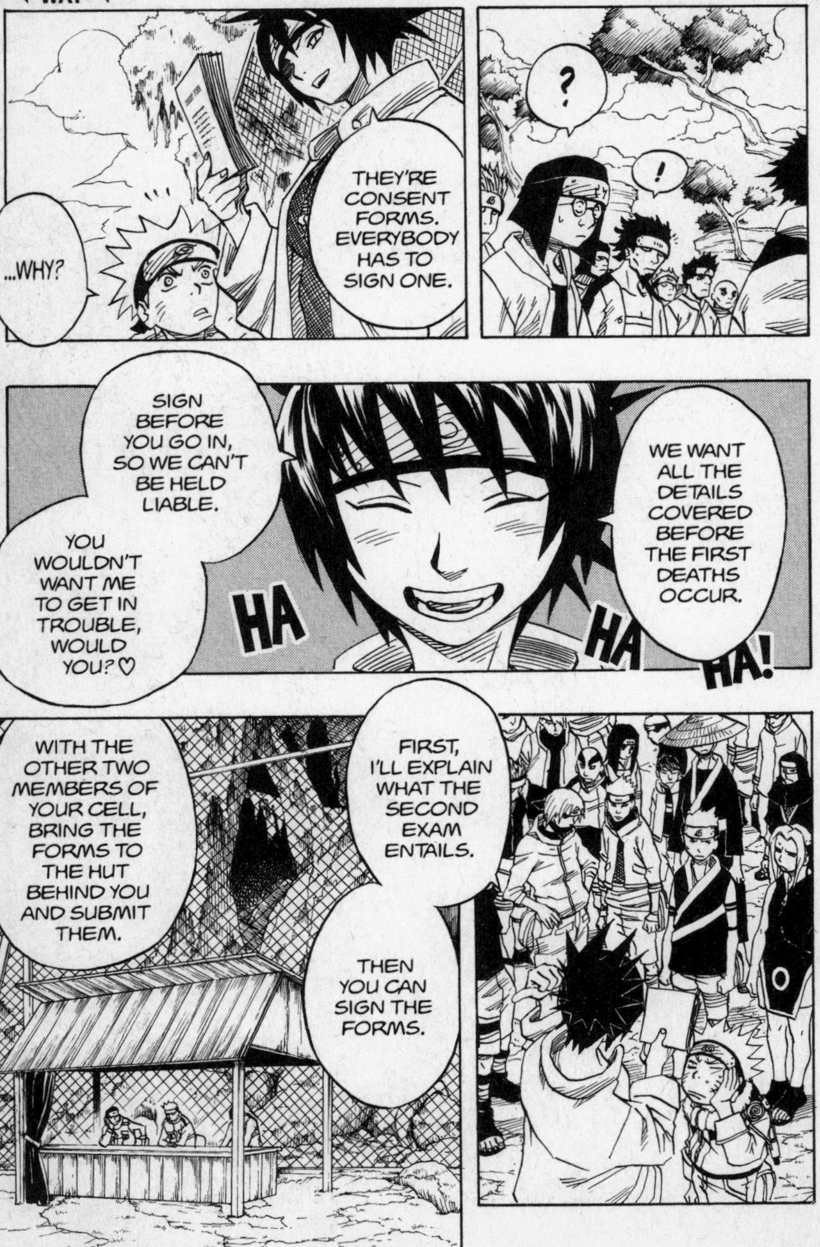
?
!
THEY'RE CONSENT FORMS. EVERYBODY HAS TO SIGN ONE.
...WHY?
WE WANT ALL THE DETAILS COVERED BEFORE THE FIRST DEATHS OCCUR.
HA HA HA!
SIGN BEFORE YOU GO IN, SO WE CAN'T BE HELD LIABLE.
YOU WOULDN'T WANT ME TO GET IN TROUBLE, WOULD YOU?♡
FIRST, I'LL EXPLAIN WHAT THE SECOND EXAM ENTAILS.
THEN YOU CAN SIGN THE FORMS.
WITH THE OTHER TWO MEMBERS OF YOUR CELL, BRING THE FORMS TO THE HUT BEHIND YOU AND SUBMIT THEM.

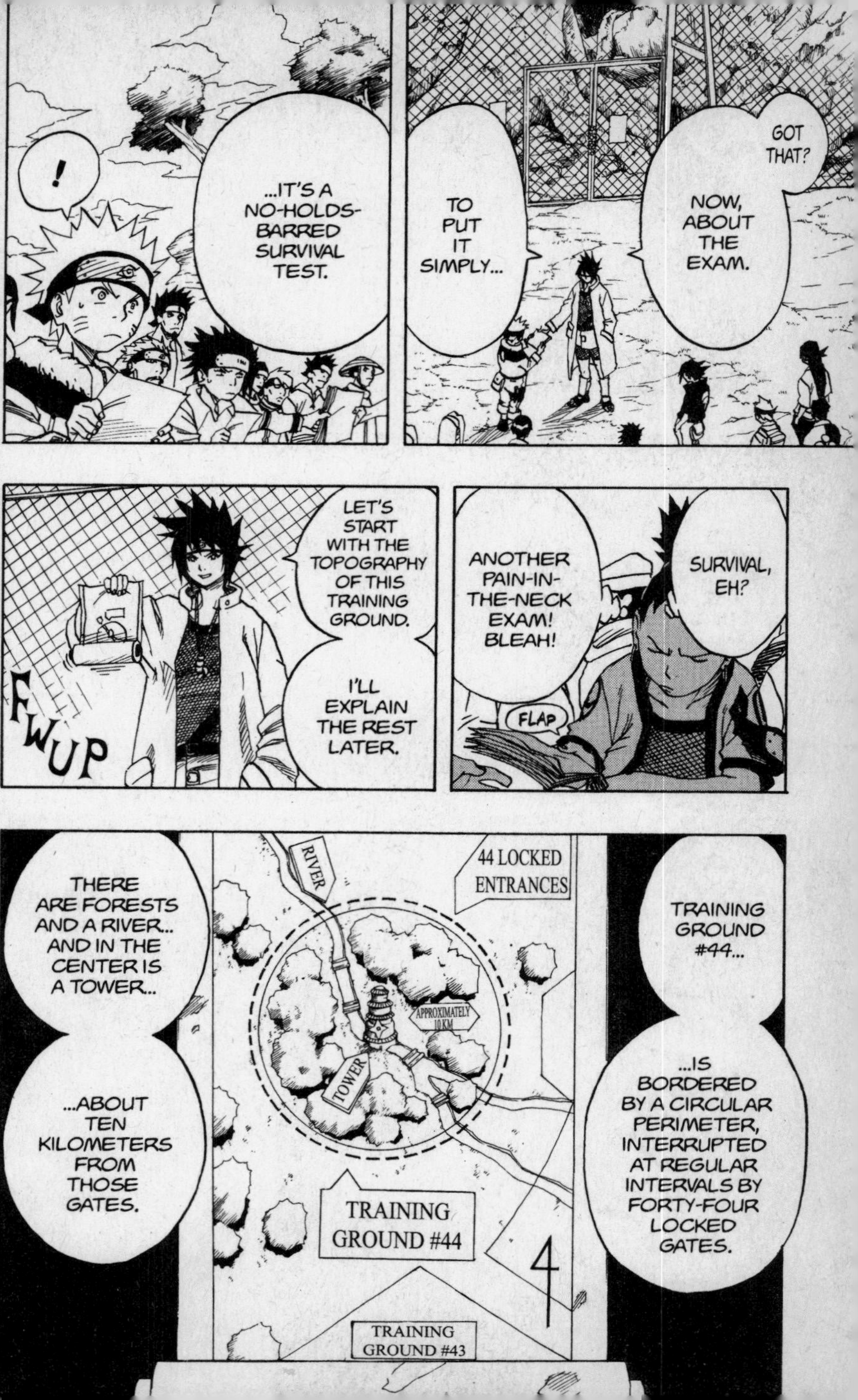
GOT THAT?
NOW, ABOUT THE EXAM.
TO PUT IT SIMPLY...
...IT'S A NO-HOLDS-BARRED SURVIVAL TEST.
!
SURVIVAL, EH?
ANOTHER PAIN-IN-THE-NECK EXAM! BLEAH!
FLAP
LET'S START WITH THE TOPOGRAPHY OF THIS TRAINING GROUND.
I'LL EXPLAIN THE REST LATER.
FWUP
TRAINING GROUND #44...
...IS BORDERED BY A CIRCULAR PERIMETER, INTERRUPTED AT REGULAR INTERVALS BY FORTY-FOUR LOCKED GATES.
44 LOCKED ENTRANCES
RIVER
APPROXIMATELY 10 KM
TOWER
TRAINING GROUND #44
TRAINING GROUND #43
THERE ARE FORESTS AND A RIVER... AND IN THE CENTER IS A TOWER...
...ABOUT TEN KILOMETERS FROM THOSE GATES.

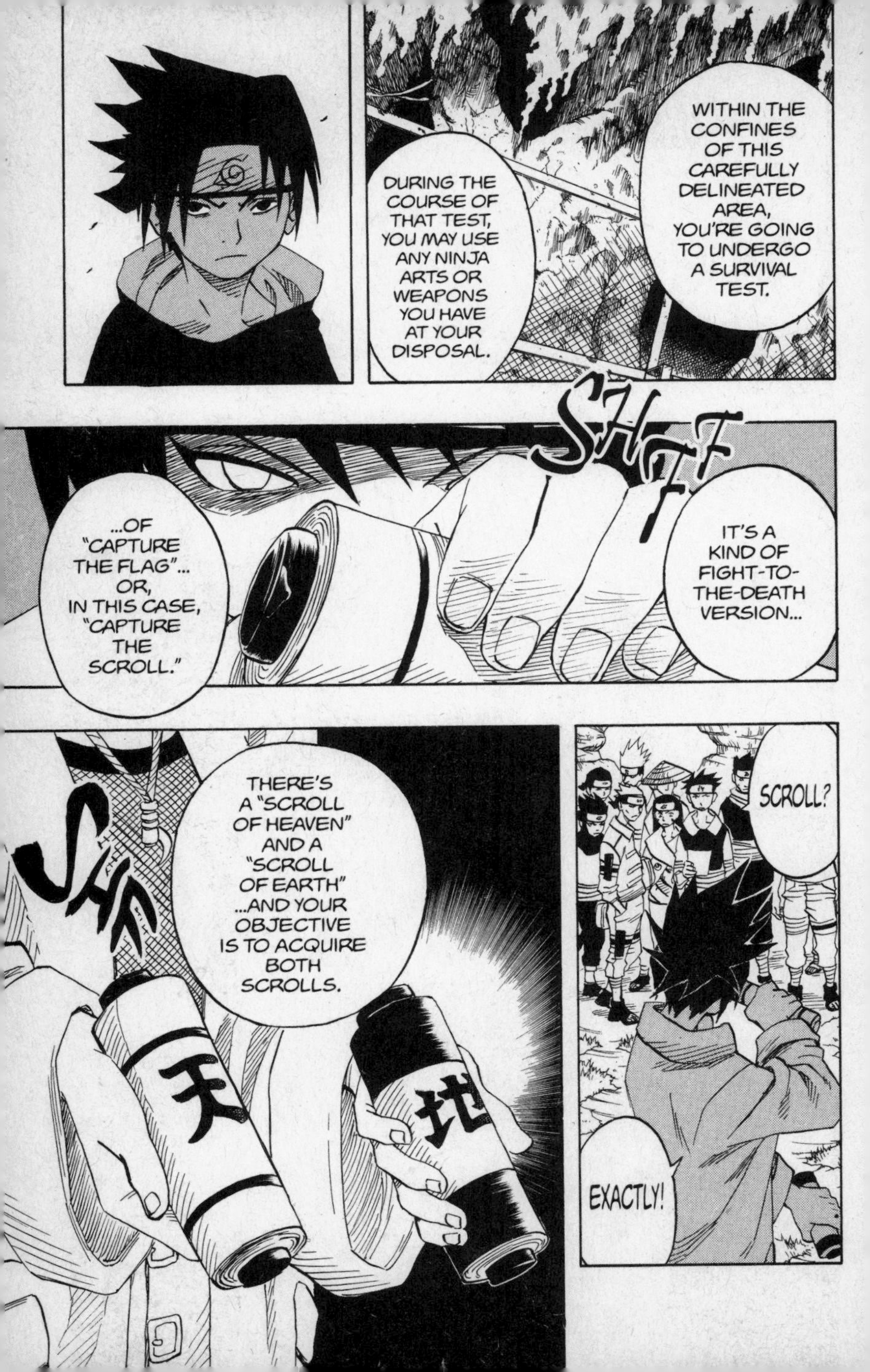
WITHIN THE CONFINES OF THIS CAREFULLY DELINEATED AREA, YOU'RE GOING TO UNDERGO A SURVIVAL TEST.
DURING THE COURSE OF THAT TEST, YOU MAY USE ANY NINJA ARTS OR WEAPONS YOU HAVE AT YOUR DISPOSAL.
SHF
IT'S A KIND OF FIGHT-TO-THE-DEATH VERSION...
...OF "CAPTURE THE FLAG"... OR, IN THIS CASE, "CAPTURE THE SCROLL."
SCROLL?
EXACTLY!
SHF
THERE'S A "SCROLL OF HEAVEN" AND A "SCROLL OF EARTH" ...AND YOUR OBJECTIVE IS TO ACQUIRE BOTH SCROLLS.
天
地

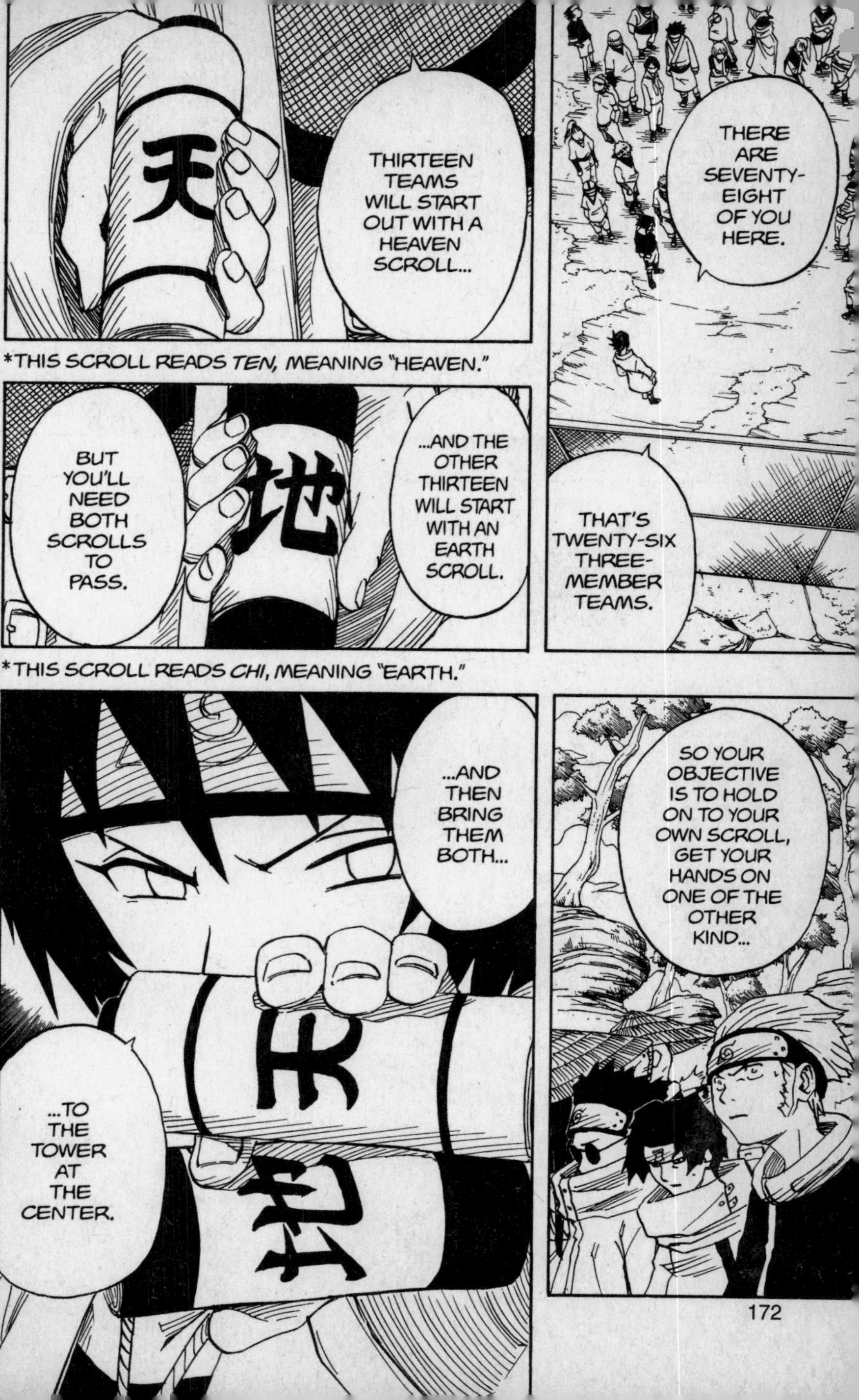
THERE ARE SEVENTY-EIGHT OF YOU HERE.
THAT'S TWENTY-SIX THREE-MEMBER TEAMS.
THIRTEEN TEAMS WILL START OUT WITH A HEAVEN SCROLL...
天
...AND THE OTHER THIRTEEN WILL START WITH AN EARTH SCROLL.
BUT YOU'LL NEED BOTH SCROLLS TO PASS.
地
SO YOUR OBJECTIVE IS TO HOLD ON TO YOUR OWN SCROLL, GET YOUR HANDS ON ONE OF THE OTHER KIND...
...AND THEN BRING THEM BOTH...
...TO THE TOWER AT THE CENTER.

*THIS SCROLL READS *TEN*, MEANING "HEAVEN."

*THIS SCROLL READS *CHI*, MEANING "EARTH."

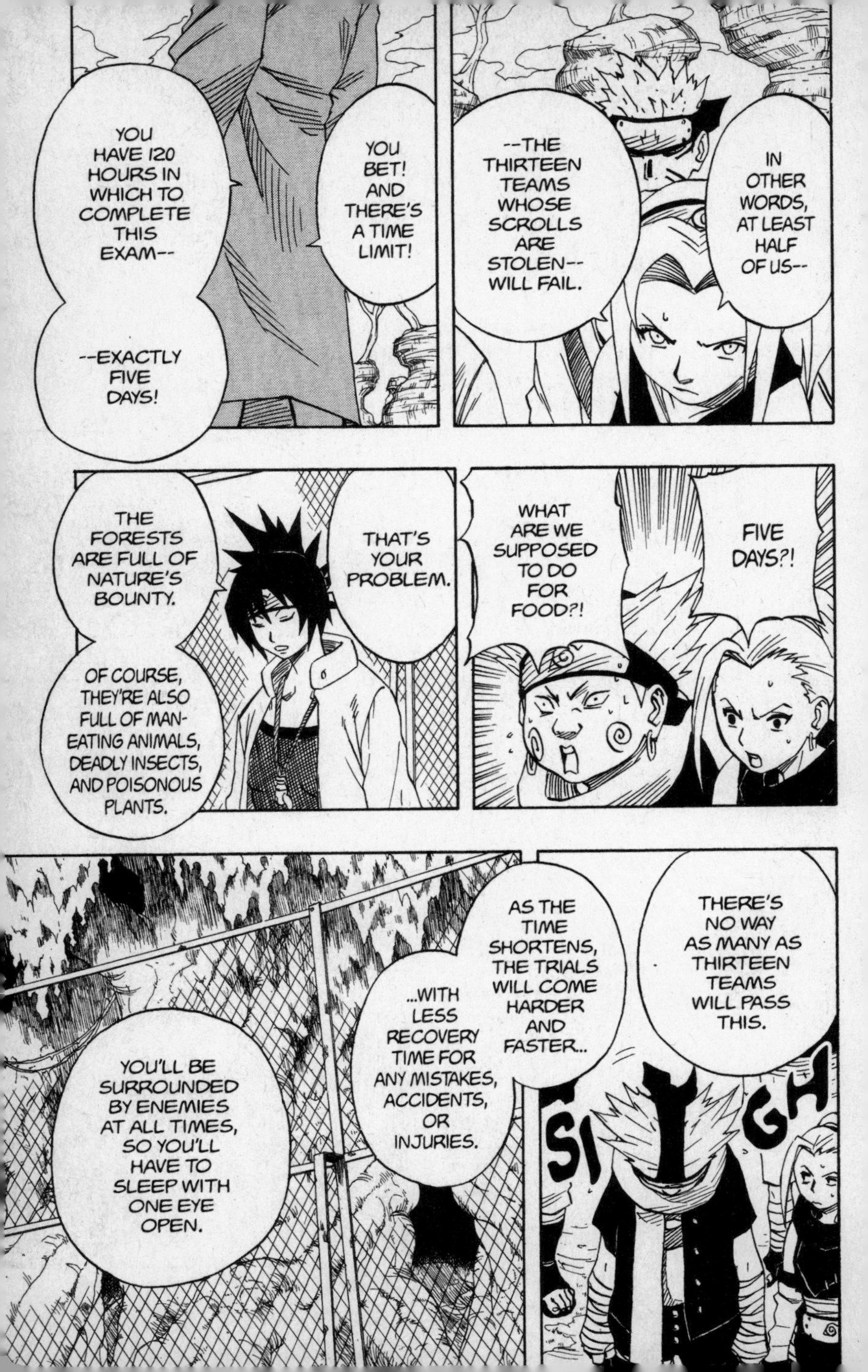
IN OTHER WORDS, AT LEAST HALF OF US--
--THE THIRTEEN TEAMS WHOSE SCROLLS ARE STOLEN-- WILL FAIL.
YOU BET! AND THERE'S A TIME LIMIT!
YOU HAVE 120 HOURS IN WHICH TO COMPLETE THIS EXAM--
--EXACTLY FIVE DAYS!
FIVE DAYS?!
WHAT ARE WE SUPPOSED TO DO FOR FOOD?!
THAT'S YOUR PROBLEM.
THE FORESTS ARE FULL OF NATURE'S BOUNTY.
OF COURSE, THEY'RE ALSO FULL OF MAN-EATING ANIMALS, DEADLY INSECTS, AND POISONOUS PLANTS.
THERE'S NO WAY AS MANY AS THIRTEEN TEAMS WILL PASS THIS.
SIGH
AS THE TIME SHORTENS, THE TRIALS WILL COME HARDER AND FASTER...
...WITH LESS RECOVERY TIME FOR ANY MISTAKES, ACCIDENTS, OR INJURIES.
YOU'LL BE SURROUNDED BY ENEMIES AT ALL TIMES, SO YOU'LL HAVE TO SLEEP WITH ONE EYE OPEN.

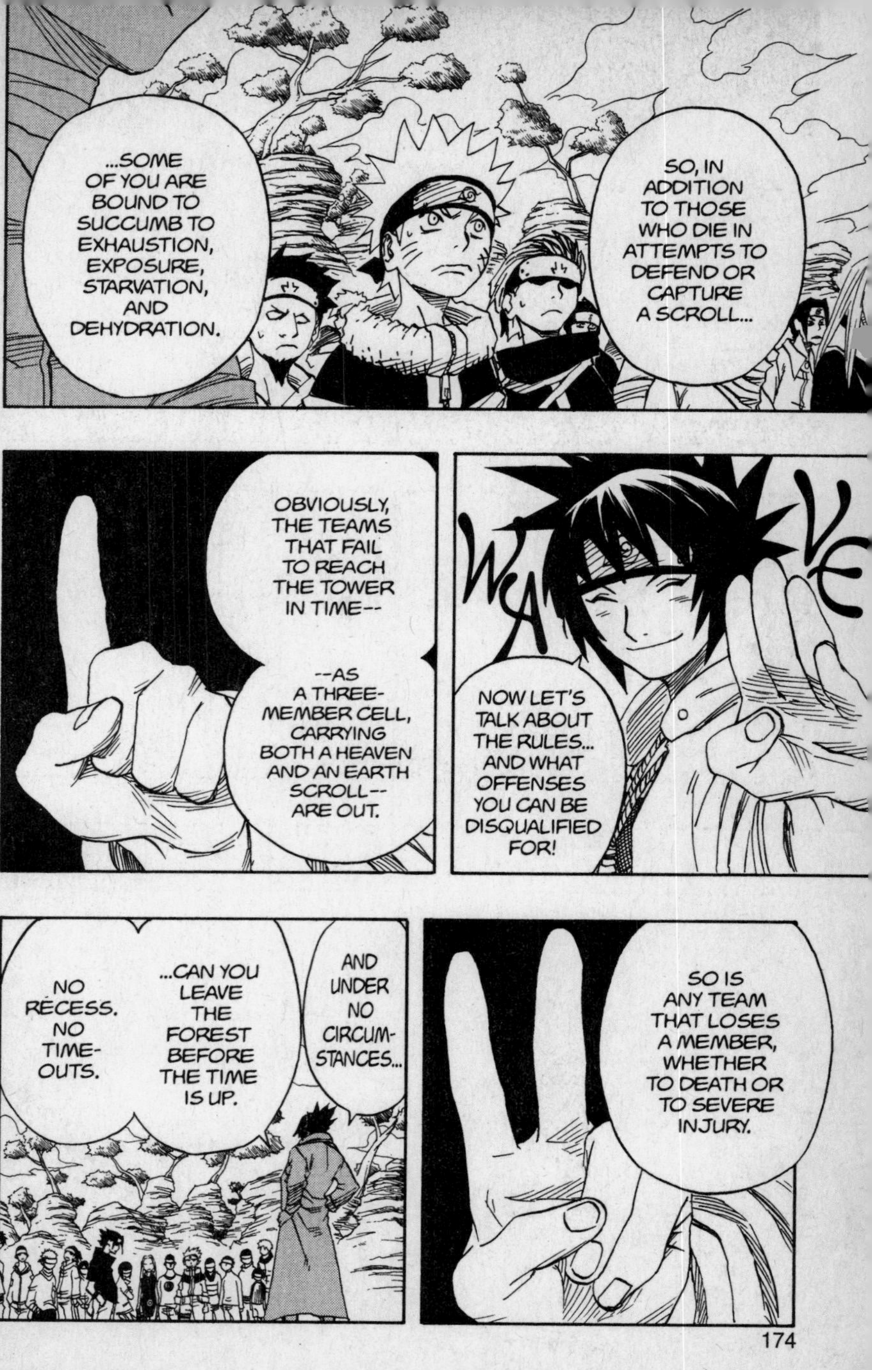
SO, IN ADDITION TO THOSE WHO DIE IN ATTEMPTS TO DEFEND OR CAPTURE A SCROLL...
...SOME OF YOU ARE BOUND TO SUCCUMB TO EXHAUSTION, EXPOSURE, STARVATION, AND DEHYDRATION.
WAVE
NOW LET'S TALK ABOUT THE RULES... AND WHAT OFFENSES YOU CAN BE DISQUALIFIED FOR!
OBVIOUSLY, THE TEAMS THAT FAIL TO REACH THE TOWER IN TIME--
--AS A THREE-MEMBER CELL, CARRYING BOTH A HEAVEN AND AN EARTH SCROLL-- ARE OUT.
SO IS ANY TEAM THAT LOSES A MEMBER, WHETHER TO DEATH OR TO SEVERE INJURY.
AND UNDER NO CIRCUMSTANCES...
...CAN YOU LEAVE THE FOREST BEFORE THE TIME IS UP.
NO RECESS. NO TIME-OUTS.

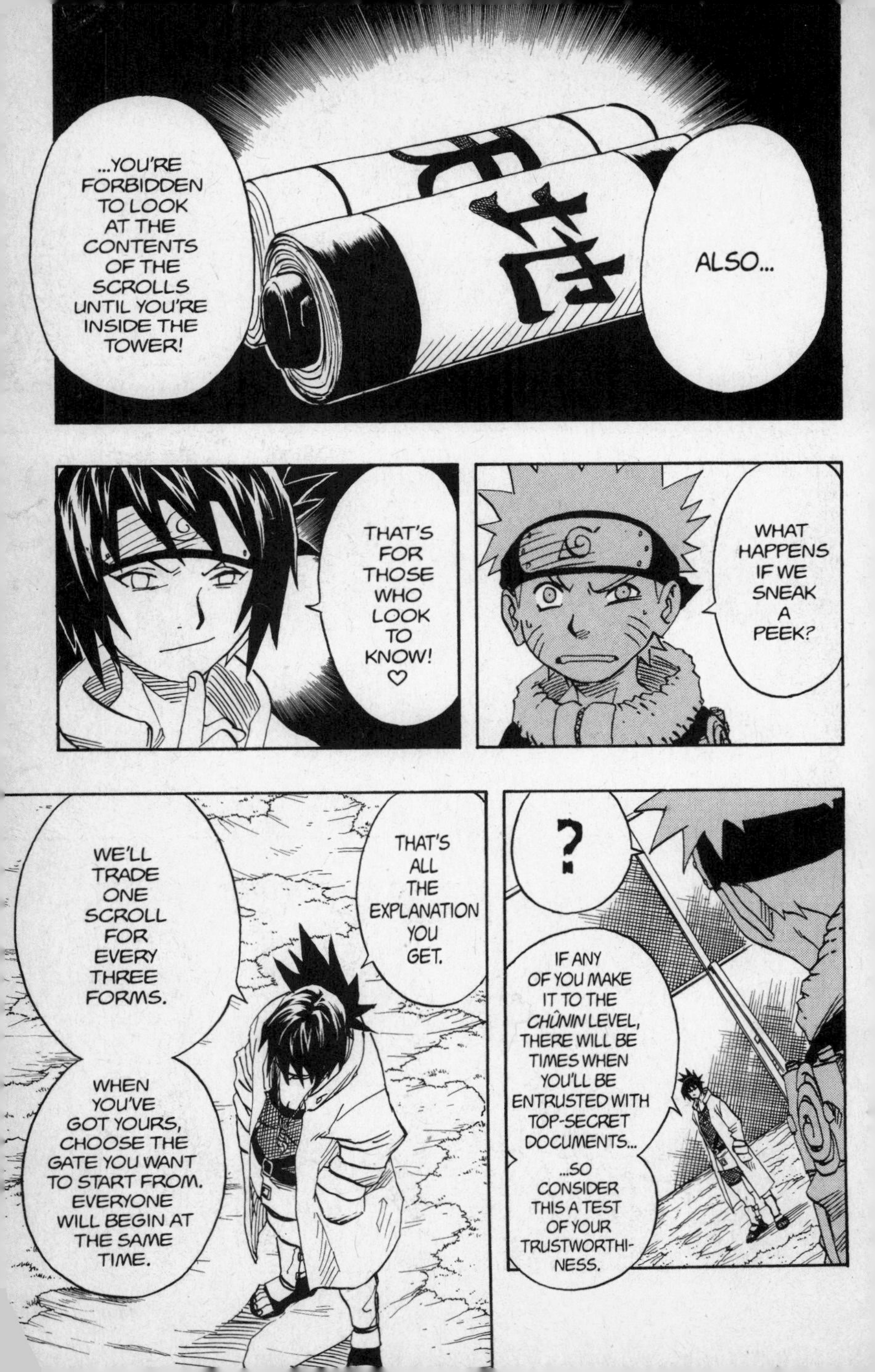
ALSO...
...YOU'RE FORBIDDEN TO LOOK AT THE CONTENTS OF THE SCROLLS UNTIL YOU'RE INSIDE THE TOWER!
WHAT HAPPENS IF WE SNEAK A PEEK?
THAT'S FOR THOSE WHO LOOK TO KNOW! ♡
?
IF ANY OF YOU MAKE IT TO THE *CHÛNIN* LEVEL, THERE WILL BE TIMES WHEN YOU'LL BE ENTRUSTED WITH TOP-SECRET DOCUMENTS...
...SO CONSIDER THIS A TEST OF YOUR TRUSTWORTHI-NESS.
WE'LL TRADE ONE SCROLL FOR EVERY THREE FORMS.
WHEN YOU'VE GOT YOURS, CHOOSE THE GATE YOU WANT TO START FROM. EVERYONE WILL BEGIN AT THE SAME TIME.
THAT'S ALL THE EXPLANATION YOU GET.

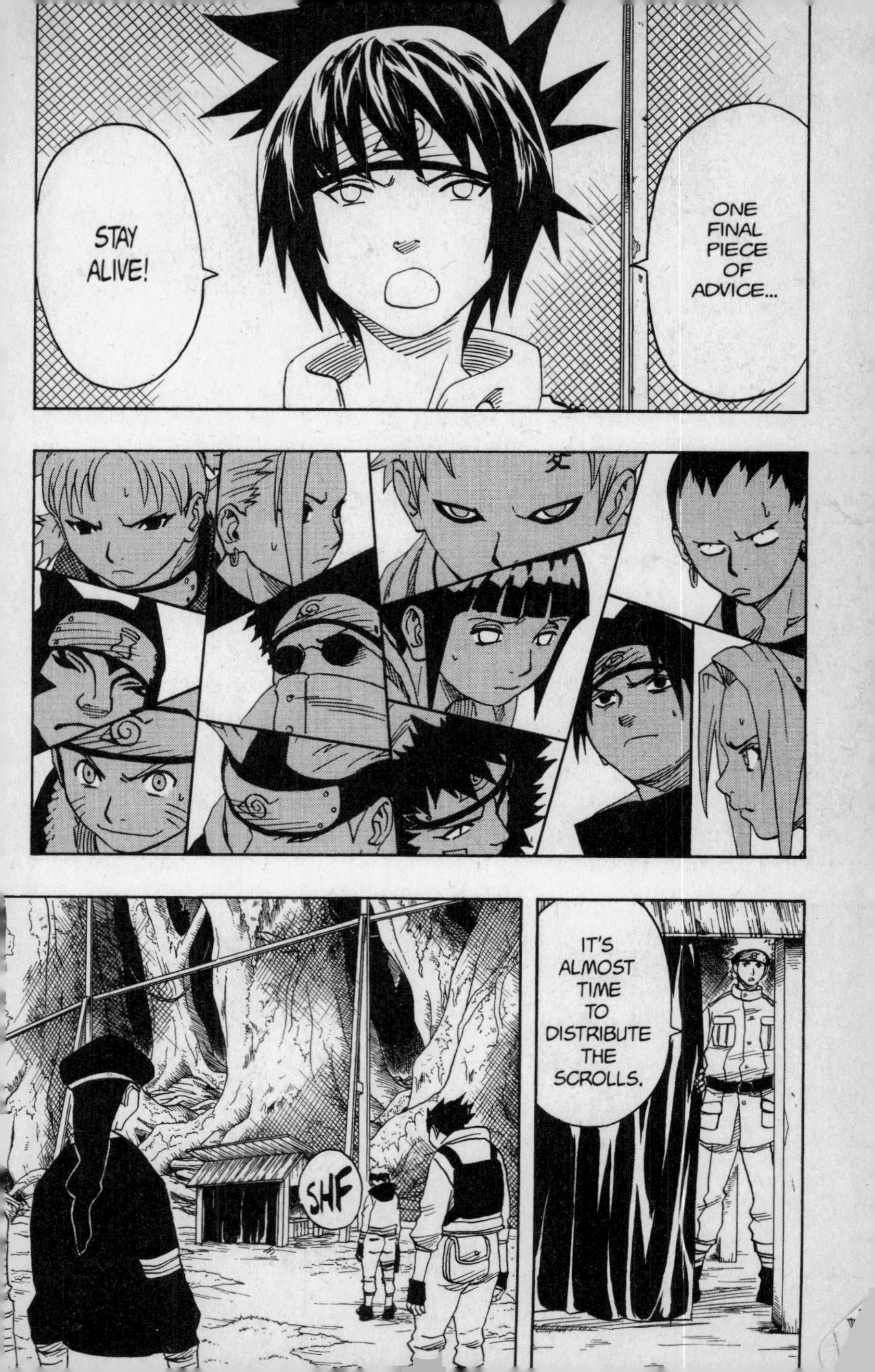
ONE FINAL PIECE OF ADVICE...
STAY ALIVE!
IT'S ALMOST TIME TO DISTRIBUTE THE SCROLLS.
SHF

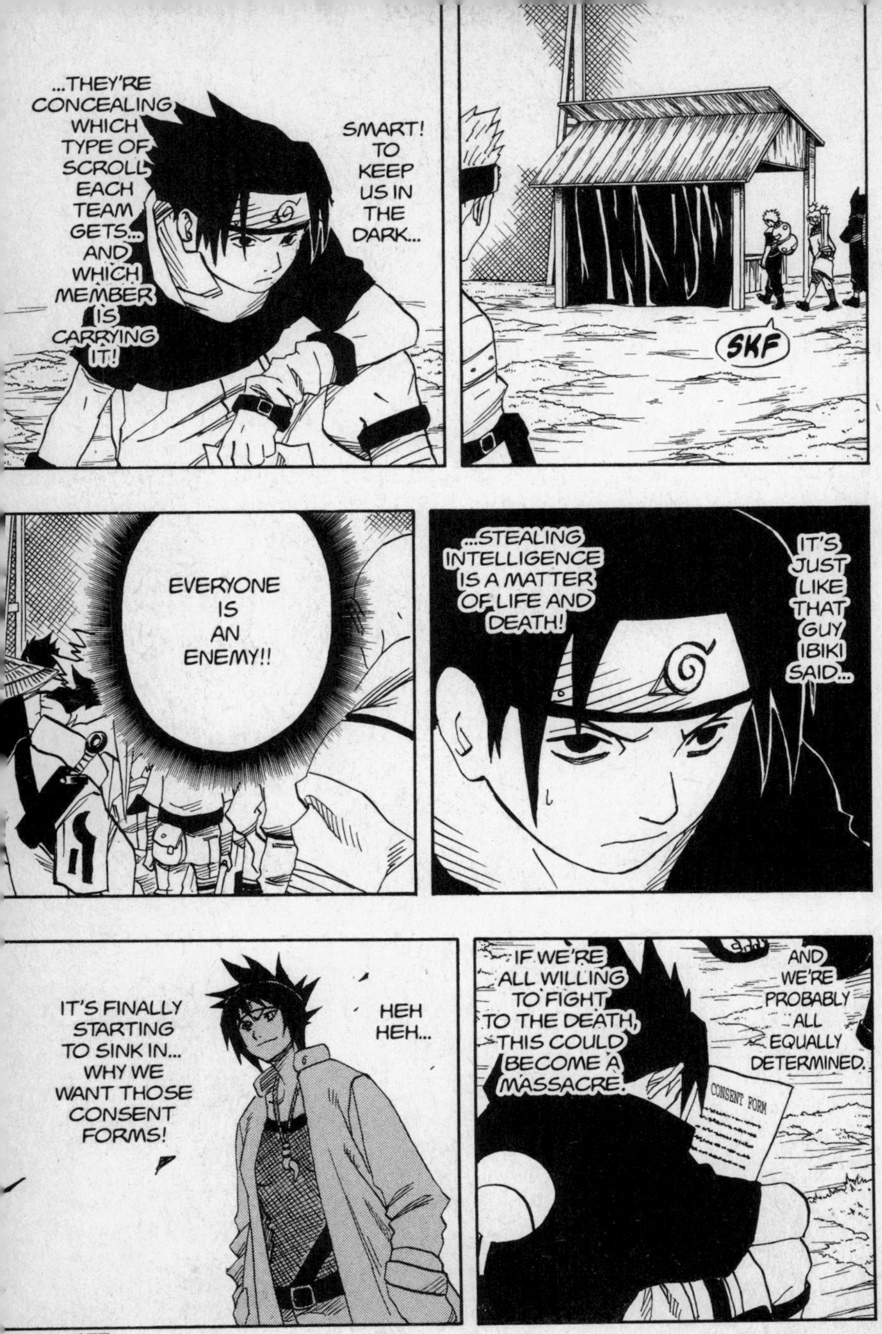
SKF
SMART! TO KEEP US IN THE DARK...
...THEY'RE CONCEALING WHICH TYPE OF SCROLL EACH TEAM GETS... AND WHICH MEMBER IS CARRYING IT!
IT'S JUST LIKE THAT GUY IBIKI SAID...
...STEALING INTELLIGENCE IS A MATTER OF LIFE AND DEATH!
EVERYONE IS AN ENEMY!!
AND WE'RE PROBABLY ALL EQUALLY DETERMINED.
IF WE'RE ALL WILLING TO FIGHT TO THE DEATH, THIS COULD BECOME A MASSACRE.
CONSENT FORM
HEH HEH...
IT'S FINALLY STARTING TO SINK IN... WHY WE WANT THOSE CONSENT FORMS!

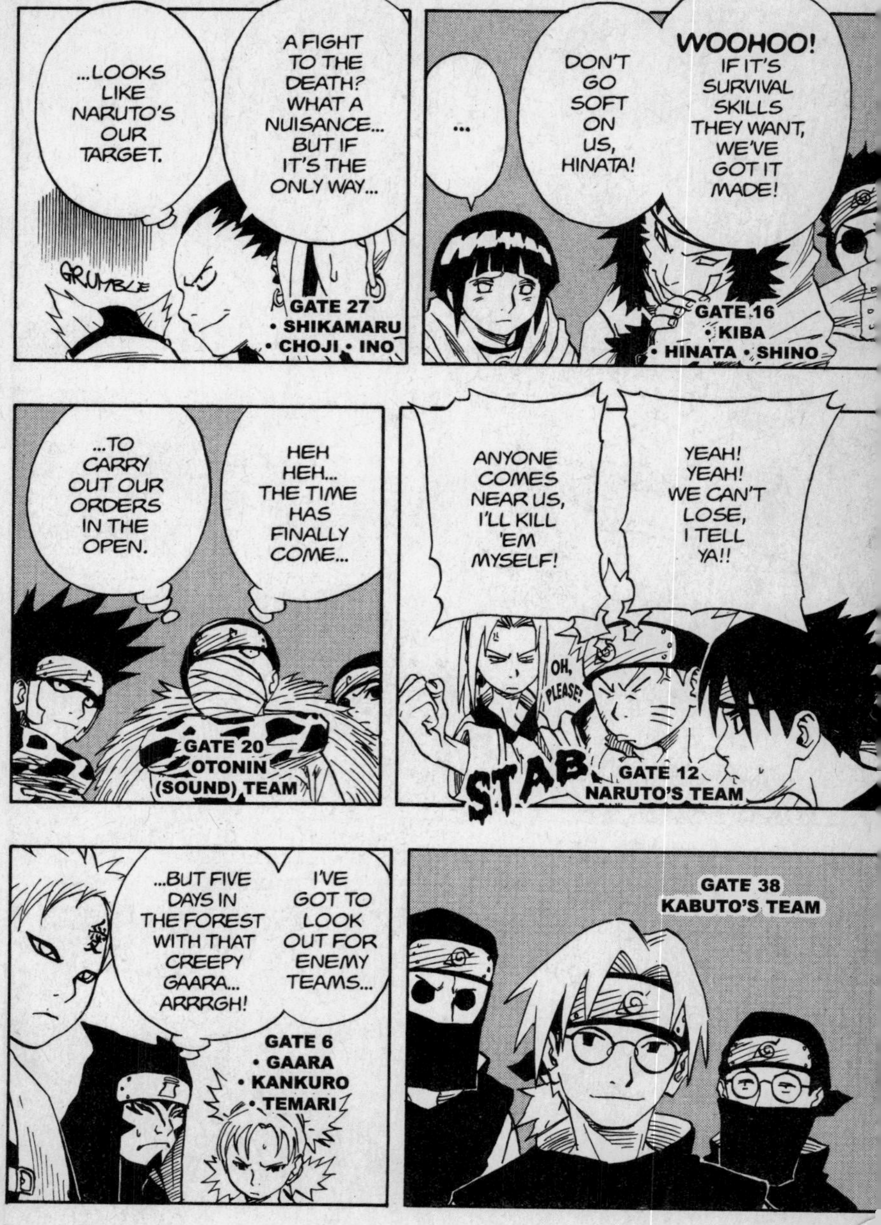
WOOHOO! IF IT'S SURVIVAL SKILLS THEY WANT, WE'VE GOT IT MADE!
DON'T GO SOFT ON US, HINATA!
...
GATE 16 • KIBA • HINATA • SHINO
A FIGHT TO THE DEATH? WHAT A NUISANCE... BUT IF IT'S THE ONLY WAY...
...LOOKS LIKE NARUTO'S OUR TARGET.
GRUMBLE
GATE 27 • SHIKAMARU • CHOJI • INO
YEAH! YEAH! WE CAN'T LOSE, I TELL YA!!
ANYONE COMES NEAR US, I'LL KILL 'EM MYSELF!
OH, PLEASE!
STAB
GATE 12 NARUTO'S TEAM
HEH HEH... THE TIME HAS FINALLY COME...
...TO CARRY OUT OUR ORDERS IN THE OPEN.
GATE 20 OTONIN (SOUND) TEAM
GATE 38 KABUTO'S TEAM
I'VE GOT TO LOOK OUT FOR ENEMY TEAMS...
...BUT FIVE DAYS IN THE FOREST WITH THAT CREEPY GAARA... ARRRGH!
GATE 6 • GAARA • KANKURO • TEMARI

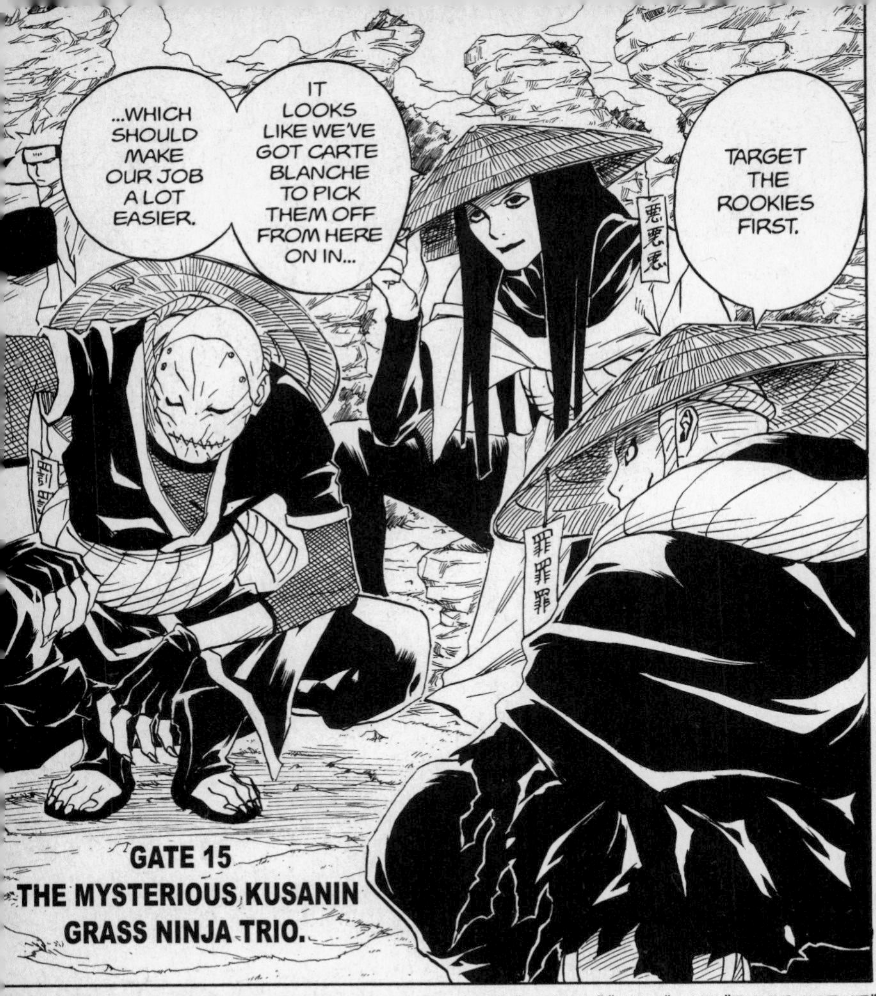
TARGET THE ROOKIES FIRST.
悪悪悪
IT LOOKS LIKE WE'VE GOT CARTE BLANCHE TO PICK THEM OFF FROM HERE ON IN...
...WHICH SHOULD MAKE OUR JOB A LOT EASIER.
罪罪罪

GATE 15 THE MYSTERIOUS KUSANIN GRASS NINJA TRIO.

*THE TAGS ON THE HATS READ (RIGHT TO LEFT) "CRIME," "EVIL," AND "PUNISHMENT."

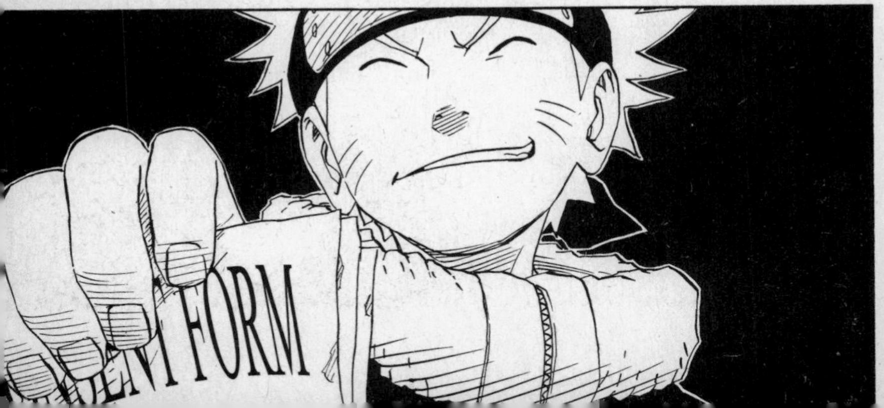
FORM

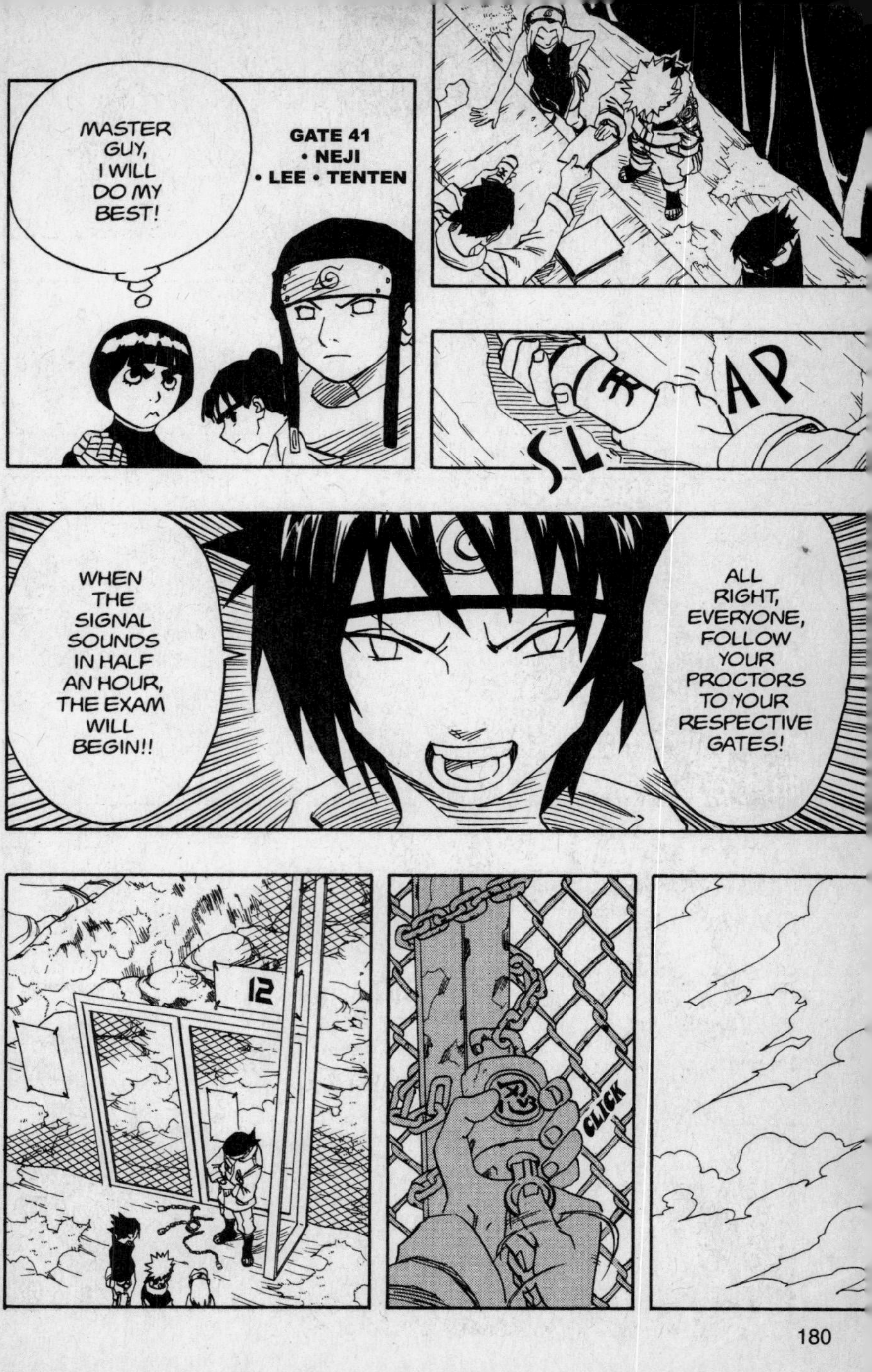
SLAP
GATE 41 • NEJI • LEE • TENTEN
MASTER GUY, I WILL DO MY BEST!
ALL RIGHT, EVERYONE, FOLLOW YOUR PROCTORS TO YOUR RESPECTIVE GATES!
WHEN THE SIGNAL SOUNDS IN HALF AN HOUR, THE EXAM WILL BEGIN!!
12
CLICK

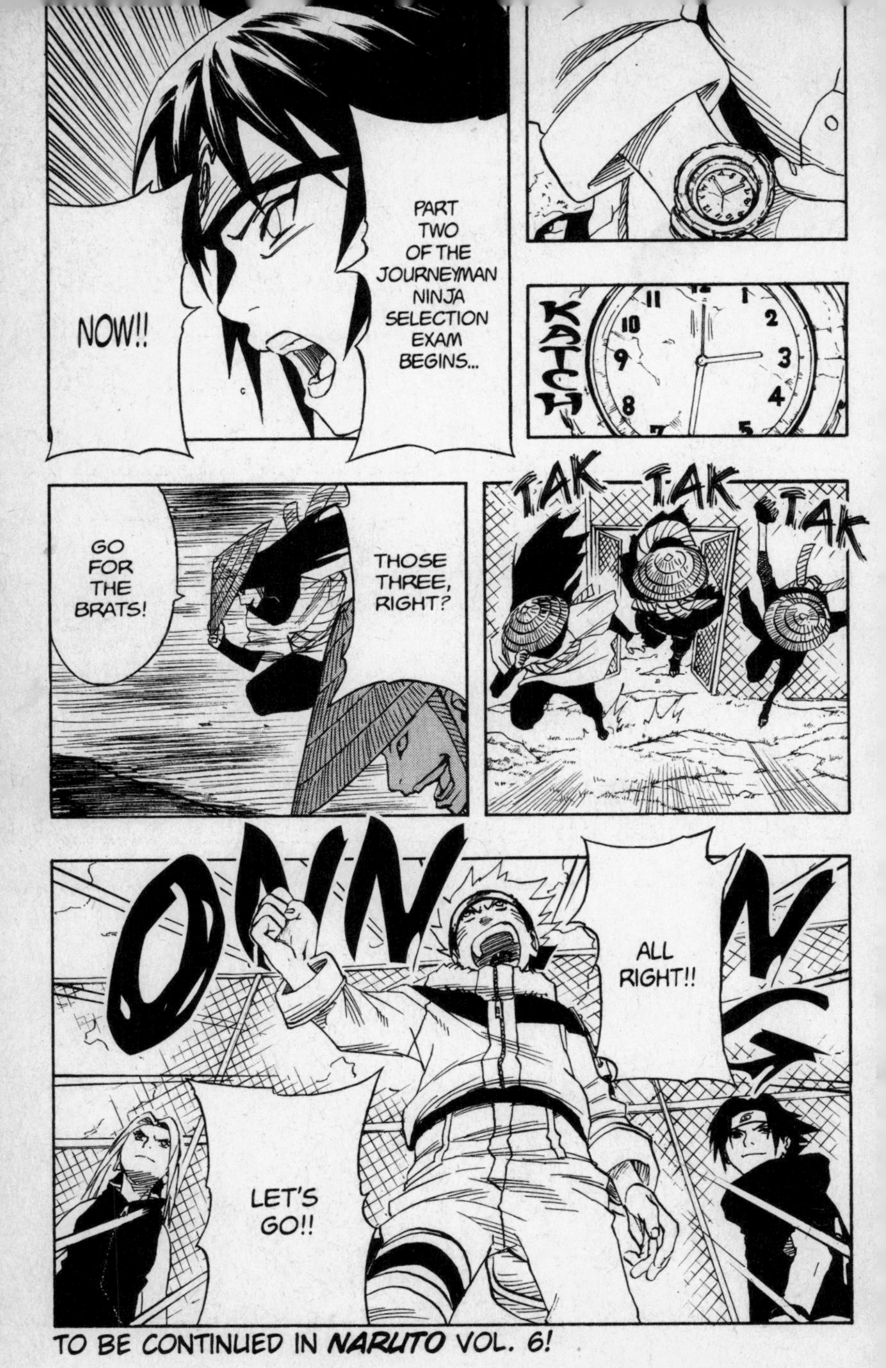
KATCH
PART TWO OF THE JOURNEYMAN NINJA SELECTION EXAM BEGINS...
NOW!!
TAK TAK TAK
THOSE THREE, RIGHT?
GO FOR THE BRATS!
ALL RIGHT!!
ONNN
LET'S GO!!

TO BE CONTINUED IN ***NARUTO*** VOL. 6!

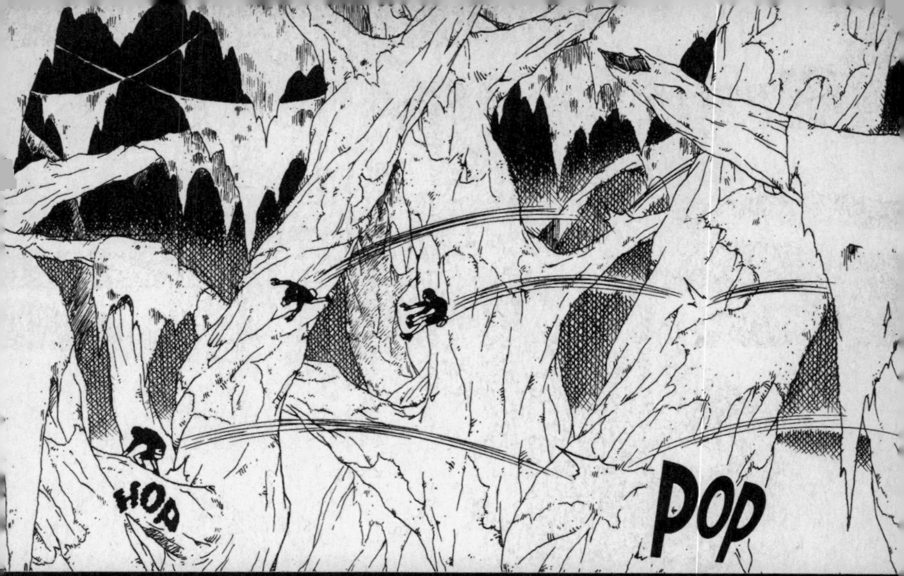
POP
HOP

IN THE NEXT VOLUME...

The students are now in the thick of the Journeyman Ninja Selection Exams' second portion, held in the aptly named Forest of Death. Each team is turned against the others, using stealth and cunning to purloin the scrolls that they need to pass the test while trying to survive the many perils that lurk in the forest. Naruto, Sasuke and Sakura quickly learn that they can trust no one...not even each other. If that's not enough to deal with, there's a mysterious imposter who has it in for Sasuke...and a giant snake on the loose!

AVAILABLE NOW!

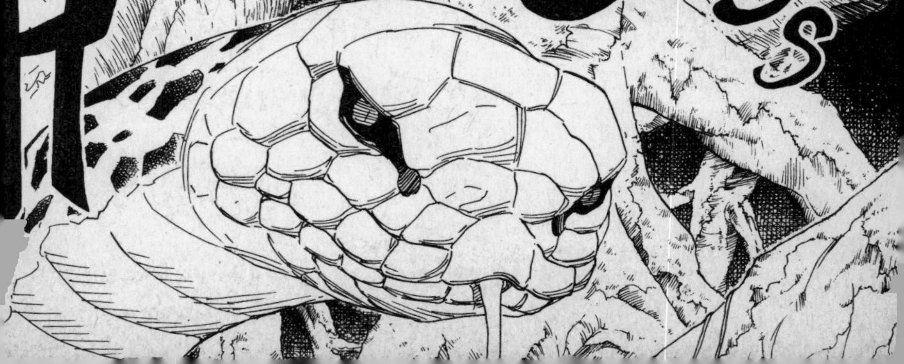
SSSS

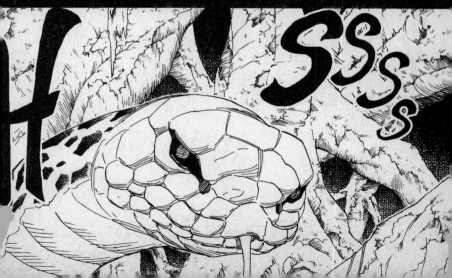

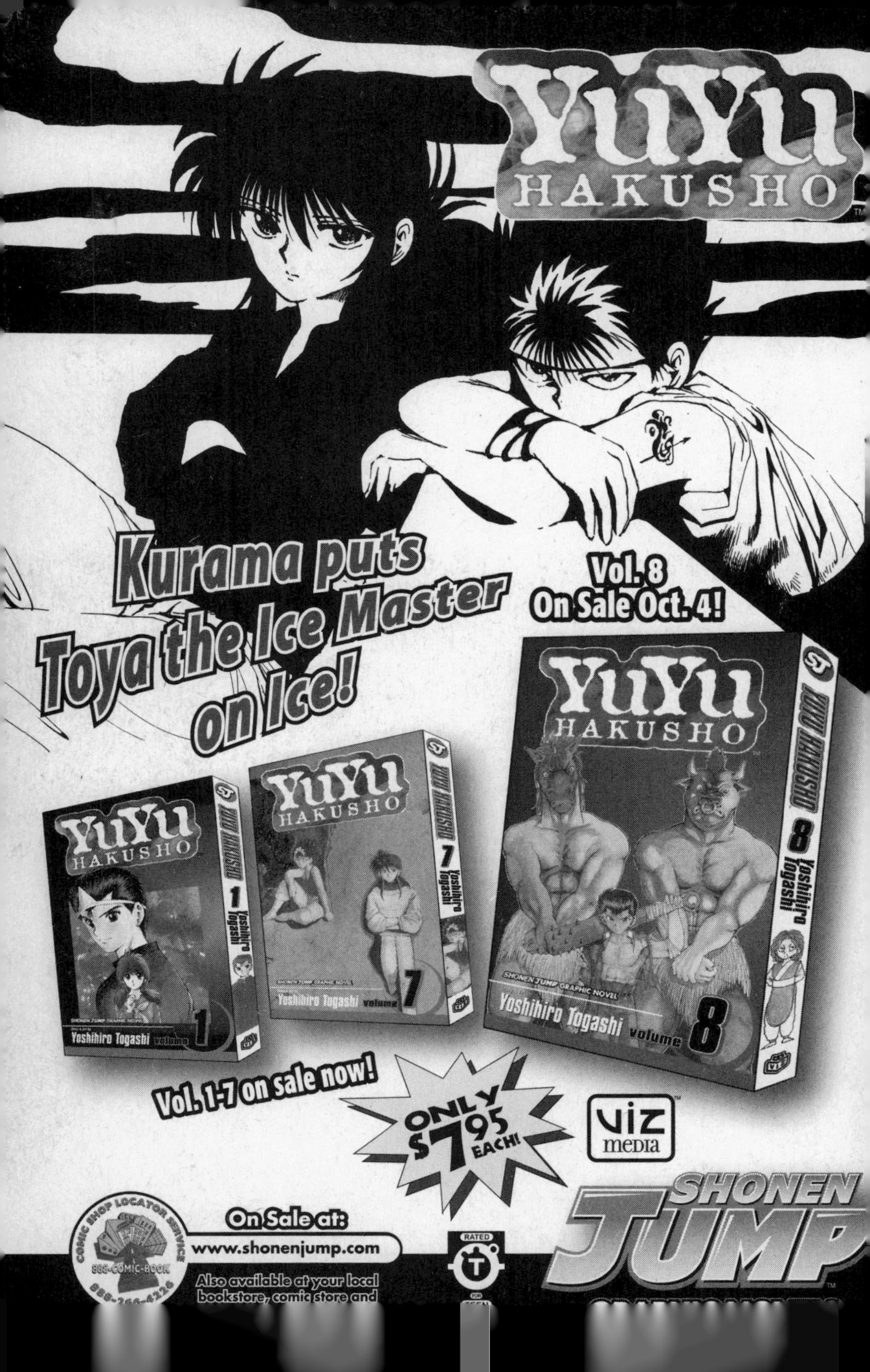
YuYu HAKUSHO
Kurama puts Toya the Ice Master on Ice!
Vol. 8 On Sale Oct. 4!
YuYu HAKUSHO
Yoshihiro Togashi volume 1
YuYu HAKUSHO
Yoshihiro Togashi volume 7
YuYu HAKUSHO
SHONEN JUMP GRAPHIC NOVEL
Yoshihiro Togashi volume 8
Vol. 1-7 on sale now!
ONLY $7.95 EACH!
viz media
COMIC SHOP LOCATOR SERVICE
888-COMIC-BOOK
On Sale at:
www.shonenjump.com
Also available at your local bookstore, comic store and
RATED T
SHONEN JUMP

SHONEN JUMP
THE WORLD'S MOST POPULAR MANGA

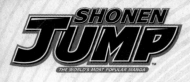

COMPLETE OUR SURVEY AND LET US KNOW WHAT YOU THINK!

☐ Please do NOT send me information about VIZ and SHONEN JUMP products, news and events, special offers, or other information.

☐ Please do NOT send me information from VIZ's trusted business partners.

Name: ______________________________

Address: ______________________________

City: ____________ **State:** ________ **Zip:** ____________

E-mail: ______________________________

☐ **Male** ☐ **Female** **Date of Birth (mm/dd/yyyy):** ___/___/______ (**Under 13? Parental consent required**)

1 Do you purchase SHONEN JUMP Magazine?

☐ Yes ☐ No **(if no, skip the next two questions)**

I like Dragon Balls

If **YES**, do you subscribe?

☐ Yes ☐ No

If **NO**, how often do you purchase SHONEN JUMP Magazine?

☐ 1-3 issues a year

☐ 4-6 issues a year

☐ more than 7 issues a year

and Dragon Ball

2 Which SHONEN JUMP Graphic Novel did you purchase? (please check one)

☐ Beet the Vandel Buster	☐ Bleach	☐ Dragon Ball
☐ Dragon Ball Z	☐ Dr. Slump	☐ Eyeshield 21
☐ Hikaru no Go	☐ Hunter x Hunter	☐ I"s
☐ Knights of the Zodiac	☐ Legendz	☐ Naruto
☐ One Piece	☐ Rurouni Kenshin	☐ Shaman King
☐ The Prince of Tennis	☐ Ultimate Muscle	☐ Whistle!
☐ Yu-Gi-Oh!	☐ Yu-Gi-Oh!: Duelist	☐ YuYu Hakusho

☐ Other ______________________________

Will you purchase subsequent volumes?

☐ Yes ☐ No

3 How did you learn about this title? (check all that apply)

☐ Favorite title	☐ Advertisement	☐ Article
☐ Gift	☐ Read excerpt in SHONEN JUMP Magazine	
☐ Recommendation	☐ Special offer	☐ Through TV animation
☐ Website	☐ Other ____________	

4 Of the titles that are serialized in SHONEN JUMP Magazine, have you purchased the Graphic Novels?

☐ Yes ☐ No

If **YES**, which ones have you purchased? (check all that apply)

☐ Dragon Ball Z ☐ Hikaru no Go ☐ Naruto ☑ One Piece

☐ Shaman King ☐ Yu-Gi-Oh! ☐ YuYu Hakusho

If **YES**, what were your reasons for purchasing? (please pick up to 3)

☐ A favorite title ☐ A favorite creator/artist ☐ I want to read it in one go

☐ I want to read it over and over again ☐ There are extras that aren't in the magazine

☐ The quality of printing is better than the magazine ☐ Recommendation

☐ Special offer ☐ Other

If **NO**, why did/would you not purchase it?

☐ I'm happy just reading it in the magazine ☐ It's not worth buying the graphic novel

☐ All the manga pages are in black and white unlike the magazine

☐ There are other graphic novels that I prefer ☐ There are too many to collect for each title

☐ It's too small ☐ Other ____________

5 Of the titles NOT serialized in the Magazine, which ones have you purchased? (check all that apply)

☐ Beet the Vandel Buster ☐ Bleach ☐ Dragon Ball ☐ Dr. Slump

☐ Eyeshield 21 ☐ Hunter x Hunter ☐ I"s ☐ Knights of the Zodiac

☐ Legendz ☐ The Prince of Tennis ☐ Rurouni Kenshin ☐ Whistle!

☐ Yu-Gi-Oh!: Duelist ☐ None ☐ Other ____________

If you did purchase any of the above, what were your reasons for purchase?

☐ A favorite title ☐ A favorite creator/artist

☐ Read a preview in SHONEN JUMP Magazine and wanted to read the rest of the story

☐ Recommendation ☐ Other

Will you purchase subsequent volumes?

☐ Yes ☐ No

6 What race/ethnicity do you consider yourself? (please check one)

☐ Asian/Pacific Islander ☐ Black/African American ☐ Hispanic/Latino

☐ Native American/Alaskan Native ☐ White/Caucasian ☐ Other

THANK YOU! Please send the completed form to: VIZ Survey
42 Catharine St.
Poughkeepsie, NY 12601

All information provided will be used for internal purposes only. We promise not to sell or otherwise divulge your information.